Early Modern Philosophy

AF072706

ALSO AVAILABLE FROM BLOOMSBURY

The Philosophy of Anne Conway, by Jonathan Head
Portraits of Kant, edited by Steve Naragon
Portraits of Wollstonecraft, edited by Eileen M. Hunt

Early Modern Philosophy

An Inclusive Introduction with Readings

**Written and Edited by
John Grey and Jonathan Head**

BLOOMSBURY ACADEMIC
LONDON • NEW YORK • OXFORD • NEW DELHI • SYDNEY

BLOOMSBURY ACADEMIC
Bloomsbury Publishing Plc
50 Bedford Square, London, WC1B 3DP, UK
1385 Broadway, New York, NY 10018, USA
29 Earlsfort Terrace, Dublin 2, Ireland

BLOOMSBURY, BLOOMSBURY ACADEMIC and the Diana logo are trademarks of
Bloomsbury Publishing Plc

First published in Great Britain 2024

Copyright © John Grey and Jonathan Head

John Grey and Jonathan Head have asserted their right under the Copyright, Designs and
Patents Act, 1988, to be identified as Author of this work.

For legal purposes the Acknowledgements on p. x constitute an extension of this
copyright page.

Cover design by Louise Dugdale
Cover image: Louis de la Forge, *L'Homme et un Traitté de la Formation du Foetus*
(Paris: Charles Angot, 1664)

All rights reserved. No part of this publication may be reproduced or transmitted in any
form or by any means, electronic or mechanical, including photocopying, recording, or
any information storage or retrieval system, without prior permission in writing from the
publishers.

Bloomsbury Publishing Plc does not have any control over, or responsibility for, any third-
party websites referred to or in this book. All internet addresses given in this book were
correct at the time of going to press. The author and publisher regret any inconvenience
caused if addresses have changed or sites have ceased to exist, but can accept no
responsibility for any such changes.

A catalogue record for this book is available from the British Library.

A catalog record for this book is available from the Library of Congress.

ISBN: HB: 978-1-3502-6955-2
PB: 978-1-3502-6954-5
ePDF: 978-1-3502-6956-9
eBook: 978-1-3502-6957-6

Typeset by Deanta Global Publishing Services, Chennai, India
Printed and bound in Great Britain

To find out more about our authors and books visit www.bloomsbury.com and
sign up for our newsletters.

To Violet and Frieda

Contents

Preface ix
Acknowledgments x

Introduction 1

Part I Understanding Human Nature

1 **Early Modern Dualism: René Descartes, Henry More, and Anton Wilhelm Amo** 9

2 **The Mind-Body Problem: René Descartes and Elisabeth of Bohemia** 43

3 **Idealist Responses: Anne Conway and Gottfried Leibniz** 63

4 **Materialist Responses: Thomas Hobbes and Margaret Cavendish** 87

Part II Sociability and Education

5 **The Nature of Love: John Norris, Mary Astell, and Damaris Masham** 115

6 **The Nature of Morality: John Locke and Catharine Trotter Cockburn** 139

7   **The Nature of Education: Anna van Schurman and Mary Astell** 167

8   **Sympathy and Morality: Sophie de Grouchy and David Hume** 191

9   **The Debate about Slavery: Jacobus Capitein and Ottobah Cugoano** 217

Part III Mind and Reality

10 **God and World: Baruch Spinoza and George Berkeley** 245

11 **The Nature of Space: Samuel Clarke and Émilie du Châtelet** 273

12 **The Nature of Causation: David Hume and Thomas Reid** 303

13 **A Transcendental Approach: Mary Shepherd and Immanuel Kant** 329

Conclusion 357

Notes 363
Glossary 375
Index 380

Preface

Most textbooks of early modern philosophy (roughly, Western European philosophy between the years 1600 and 1800 CE) include selections from various primary texts of the period, but little in the way of explanation or exposition. While that is a fine format for many students, many also find it alienating: if you have not studied philosophy or read 400-year-old books before, a textbook that simply presents selections from primary texts (even good primary texts, even carefully selected and arranged!) will not be much help to you. This was the guiding thought behind the current textbook. It is written with our own actual audience in mind: undergraduate students who have little background in philosophy or its history, but an interest in both. If that describes you, our hope is that this textbook will provide an engaging and accessible introduction to one of the most exciting periods in the history of human thought.

Because our goal has been to help new students appreciate the philosophical interest and power of these texts, we have in some cases modernized archaic turns of phrase and punctuation in order to make them more readable. We have also included a glossary of technical terms such as "substance," which early modern authors use with a much different meaning than the term has today. Such terms are indicated with bold font and a dagger symbol (e.g., substance†) when they are first used in each chapter.

Acknowledgments

Extracts 2.1 and 2.2 are used with permission of University of Chicago Press, from *The Correspondence between Princess Elisabeth of Bohemia and René Descartes*, edited and translated by Lisa Shapiro, 2007; permission conveyed through Copyright Clearance Center, Inc.

Extract 8.1 is used with permission of Oxford University Press, from *Sophie de Grouchy's Letters on Sympathy*, translated by Sandrine Bergès, with an introduction, glossary, and commentary by Sandrine Bergès and Eric Schliesser. All rights reserved. No part of this publication may be reproduced, stored in a retrieval system, or transmitted, in any form or by any means, without the prior permission in writing of Oxford University Press, or as expressly permitted by law, by license, or under terms agreed with the appropriate reproduction rights organization. Inquiries concerning reproduction outside the scope of the above should be sent to the Rights Department, Oxford University Press, at 198 Madison Avenue, New York, NY 10016, United States of America. Reproduced with permission of the Licensor through PLSclear.

Excerpt 9.1 is Reprinted by permission of Markus Wiener Publishers, Princeton from *The Agony of Asar: A Thesis on Slavery by the Former Slave—Jacobus Elisa Johannes Capitein, 1717-1747 Capitein, Jacobus* translated from Latin by Grant Parker (Princeton, N.J. 1999).

The authors would like to thank Prof. Katherine Brading for permission to use an extract from the complete translation of Du Châtelet's *Foundations of Physics*, trans. Katherine Brading et al., 2018, available at www.kbrading.org.

Introduction

This book seeks to provide an accessible and inclusive introduction to early modern philosophy. Going beyond the standard list of canonical figures traditionally considered in undergraduate courses on early modern philosophy, we wish to take a more inclusive approach that incorporates a broader spectrum of contributions to the philosophical conversations and debates that took place during this period. Taking this inclusive approach offers both a deeper and a wider view of the early modern period, as we see how both canonical and non-canonical philosophers made substantive and important interventions in disputes that covered a broad range of issues, beyond just those of epistemology (the theory of knowledge) and metaphysics (the theory of reality).

The content of this book is structured around three key debates that formed part of the ongoing conversation between philosophers during this period: (1) the status of human nature (particularly with regard to the distinction between body and soul), (2) the nature of our social relations (including the importance of love, education, and morality), and (3) the relation between the mind and reality. The chapters are written with the aim of offering a glimpse into how these philosophical debates played out between thinkers who were consciously taking part in an ongoing conversation, not only through published works, but also sometimes through letters and face-to-face conversations. Each chapter covers two or three philosophers who offered interesting and significant arguments about the issues covered, and formed part of an ongoing debate that was taking place at the time. We will see that philosophers often offered objections and counterpoints that explicitly challenged the ideas of their contemporaries, with the expectation that their arguments would be responded to in turn. These conversations were often pursued vigorously and passionately, often with a hint of ego sprinkled in, but always with an underlying commitment to the value of truth and the power of argument and rationality.

Each chapter provides explanatory and clarificatory material written by the authors, alongside extended extracts from relevant primary texts. These extracts are intended to provide the reader with the chance to hear these philosophers in their own voice and to gain confidence in reading philosophical texts from this period for themselves. Each philosopher is also introduced with key biographical and other historical details, in order to allow the student to consider the importance of contemporary context in approaching philosophical arguments and theories. To further aid understanding, each section concludes with a short list of key points, as well as questions for further reflection. The authors also offer suggestions for further reading on the philosophers and topics covered. A glossary of key terms is provided at the end of the book too to aid learning of specialist terminology.

Following this introduction, we begin with the debate of Part 1, which concerns theories of human nature from a metaphysical perspective. Chapter 1 considers some dualistic theories that view human beings as a unity of mind and body. The representatives of this view we have chosen are René Descartes, Anton Wilhelm Amo and Henry More, all of whom offer arguments that the mind must be ontologically distinct from the body. However, we see in Chapter 2 that this dualist viewpoint quickly ran into difficulties, including the seeming impossibility of explaining how two ontologically distinct substances could interact in the manner that the mind and body seem to in our everyday lives, as pointed out in correspondence to Descartes by Princess Elizabeth of Bohemia. These problems with the dualist view led to some philosophers adopting a form of monism: either by proposing an ontology formed entirely of spirits or monads (as proposed by Anne Conway and Gottfried Leibniz, discussed in Chapter 3) or one that has exclusively material things (as suggested by Margaret Cavendish and Thomas Hobbes, discussed in Chapter 4).

Part 2 of this book moves on to connected debates on social matters, with the themes of love, morality, sympathy, education, and religion. We begin in Chapter 5 with a discussion of the possible role of love in our lives: in response to John Norris's claim that only God is the proper object of our love, both Mary Astell and Damaris Masham provide arguments that instead seek to leave space for legitimate love of others in this world. In this way, love is vindicated as properly informing our actions and directly shaping our social relationships. Chapter 6 continues the debate regarding the impact of the existence of God on our actions. As we shall see, John Locke's attempt to explain how we acquire knowledge of morality by means of experience led to accusations of atheism. In response to such charges, Catherine Cockburn sought to defend Locke's approach, arguing that an account that grounds our moral knowledge in experience does not necessarily conflict with a commitment to the existence of God as the ground of our moral obligations. Chapter 7 turns to the question of education, which became of importance as some women slowly became freer to engage in current intellectual debates. Education was denied to the vast majority of women at the time, and even those who were educated would have received their teaching at home and were denied access to formal educational institutions. This chapter considers Anna van Schurman's and Mary Astell's arguments concerning the relation between education and reason and the education that should be offered to women, and how these debates concerning women's education links to other debates that are covered in the book, such as Cartesian arguments regarding the relation between mind and body. Chapter 8 turns to questions about the origins of morality. Sophie de Grouchy posits sympathy as the basis of our motivation to act morally and offers a naturalist account of how individuals come to have feelings of sympathy, which can then be developed with the aid of reason. In a similar vein, David Hume follows a naturalist approach and gives a prominent place to sympathy in the nexus of our moral feelings. However, unlike Grouchy, Hume argues that reason plays little to no role in the development of our morality. Finally, Chapter 9 examines the early modern debates about the morality of slavery. It presents selections from the writings of two eighteenth-century ex-slaves, Jacobus Elisa Johannes Capitein and Quobna Ottobah Cugoano. Capitein defends the view that slavery is in fact compatible with the Christian religion, so that a Christian nation can (and perhaps should) retain the institution of slavery. Cugoano rejects this, and argues that there is no possible moral, theological, or natural justification of slavery. This survey of the philosophical discourse about slavery in the 1700s concludes the second part of the book.

The final part of the book moves to questions related to the foundations of science, ranging over debates regarding the fundamental nature of reality and the human mind that seeks to understand it. Baruch Spinoza and George Berkeley, considered in Chapter 10, both provide a significant challenge to our supposedly common sense understanding of the relation between mind and world through the question of the latter's dependence on God. Both philosophers seem to undermine a significant distinction between God and world: Spinoza denies that God has any personal characteristics and describes God as in some sense identical with nature; and Berkeley construes objects in the world as ideas generated by the divine will, rather than as mind-independent material things. Chapter 11, on the other hand, seeks to show how philosophers were reacting to new discoveries in physics in the early eighteenth century. In the first section, we see how Newtonian physics led to philosophical debates concerning the nature of space, as found in the Leibniz–Clarke correspondence, which centered on the question of whether space is absolute or relative. We then look at the metaphysics of Émilie du Châtelet, who sought to offer a philosophical refinement of Newtonian physics in her work, *The Foundations of Physics*. Following Leibniz's lead, she applies two foundational principles (the principle of contradiction and the principle of sufficient reason) to establish apparently necessary metaphysical truths, such as the existence of simple, irreducible monads. The focus on physics continues in Chapter 12, where we consider Hume's famous account of causation, based on a new science of human nature that produces a more nuanced empiricist approach than had been attempted to date. Hume found that his empiricism could easily lead to skeptical conclusions, including with regard to our knowledge of causal relations. We will then see how Thomas Reid sought to overcome the potential skeptical implications of Hume's approach, including by undermining the latter's representationalist theory of mind. The final chapter covers two figures who were inspired by their reservations with Hume's philosophy to explore new approaches to metaphysics and overcome the divide between rationalist and empiricist thought. Both Immanuel Kant and Mary Shepherd sought to provide a rational justification for our causal beliefs, against Hume's view that they are ultimately unjustifiable. However, whether either of them can truly overcome the specter of Humean skepticism is open for debate.

In following these debates, we will be covering a period of just under two centuries: from René Descartes's groundbreaking text, *Meditations* (first published in 1641), that offers famous arguments regarding knowledge, God, and the self, to Mary Shepherd's works from the 1820s that seek to respond to the problems posed by David Hume's skepticism. Though some would question our extension of the "early modern period" into the nineteenth century, nevertheless we think that Shepherd's philosophical contributions mark a natural and appropriate finishing point to the ongoing intellectual discussions we consider in this work. Also, it should be emphasized that though we are seeking to provide a more inclusive approach to studying philosophy in the early modern period, we are also aware that inclusivity is a goal that we will have failed to fully attain. The selection of material covered here no doubt to some extent reflects the interests and biases of the authors, and there are doubtless many other perspectives and traditions we could have covered instead that probed even further away from the canon. However, we hope that this book will be accepted as our first attempt at providing a more inclusive approach, one which will doubtless need revising as scholars continue to investigate traditionally overlooked philosophers and philosophical traditions, and as our intellectual biases continue to be challenged. It is our hope that students will be inspired by this book to go further than we have done in broadening our viewpoint upon early modern philosophy and challenging the traditional canon that has been taught in our educational institutions until very recently.

Finally, the writing of this book has also been guided by our conviction of the importance of studying the history of philosophy, whether it be of the early modern period or not. Philosophy is ultimately a conversation, carried out across generations and centuries, about some of the most important issues that face us as human beings. Without an understanding of the history of philosophy, reading philosophy written today is akin to overhearing only the very end of a long conversation: you might understand something of what is being said, but it wouldn't be possible to grasp fully its significance and meaning. Philosophers are always creatures of their own time, responding to what has come before and engaging in conversations with their contemporaries. In order to comprehend their theories and arguments, it is therefore necessary to understand what they are responding to. While we must not overlook just how different the world inhabited by early modern philosophers was to ours, philosophy deals with the perennial concerns about the nature of life and the world that continue to haunt us today. We should therefore not be afraid to look at these pioneering and interesting people of the past, not necessarily for answers, but perhaps for inspiration and guidance. Using their viewpoints, approaches, and arguments, we might find that they help shake us from our own entrenched contemporary perspectives, even if we are considering issues that may not have even occurred to them at the time. In this way, the history of philosophy becomes something we can all play a part in, by looking at the world, humanity, and our future with a secure foundation in a sense of the past.

Part I

Understanding Human Nature

1

Early Modern Dualism: René Descartes, Henry More, and Anton Wilhelm Amo

Chapter Outline

1a.	Dualism in Descartes	12
1b.	Henry More's Dualism	22
1c.	Dualism in Anton Wilhelm Amo	31
Questions for Reflection		42

Humans appear to have two distinct facets or aspects to their existence. On the one hand, humans are *physical*—or, as the early modern authors typically preferred to say, "corporeal." You can see and touch a human, trace their shape, and weigh them on a scale. Each of these (being visible and tangible, having shape and weight) is a state of the body. On the other hand, humans also have interior *mental* lives, a stream of conscious experiences peculiar to each person. A human can imagine an elephant, form beliefs about what would happen if the elephants went extinct, fear that elephants will go extinct, intend to work toward their preservation, and so on. Each of these (imagining, believing, fearing, intending) is a state of the mind.

Once we have identified these two aspects of human existence, we face important philosophical questions. Do the mind and body depend on one another in some way? Could one exist without the other? Most generally, *what is the relationship between the human body and the human mind?* This question animated many of the most famous debates among early modern philosophers. As we shall see, authors in this period constructed a dizzying array of answers to it. This chapter, however, focuses on the answer that was undoubtedly the most influential in the period: **substance dualism**†.

To understand the philosophical position known as substance dualism, we first need to understand the meaning that authors in this period accord to the term **substance**†. Today, we tend to use the word to refer to a particular kind of matter—as in, "The table was coated in a powdery substance." This is not what most philosophers in the early modern period mean when they use the term "substance," however. For these authors, following medieval and even ancient philosophers before them, to call something a substance is to say that it could exist independently of any other thing (besides, perhaps, God).

With this definition in hand, it looks as though we can differentiate substances from non-substances in the following way: something is a substance if and only if there is no other object that must exist in order for it to exist. A horse, for instance, seems to satisfy this independence criterion. (Not all of the philosophers in this volume would agree, but we'll stick with common sense for now.) That is, there doesn't seem to be anything else besides the horse such that, if that thing ceased to exist, then so would the horse. The horse's shape, size, and organic parts could be altered or replaced without destroying the horse itself—as frequently occurs in the life of an ordinary horse. And although the horse was brought into existence by its parents, it wouldn't cease to exist just because its parents did. Of course, you might object, doesn't the horse need air, food, and water to continue to exist? Yes, but not any *specific* air, food, or water is required. However, not everything satisfies the independence criterion. For example, the horse's shape couldn't exist without the horse. If the horse ceased to exist, so would its particular shape. So, according to the independence criterion—at least on the face of it—even though the horse itself is a substance, its shape is *not* a substance.

Now we are in a position to state the philosophical theory known as substance dualism. According to this theory, *the human body and the human mind are distinct substances*. That is, your body could in principle exist even if your mind did not, and your mind could in principle exist even if your body did not. This is a controversial position. Today, it is common enough to conflate your mind with your brain, and to assume that we will (eventually) be able to explain the mental aspect of human existence entirely in terms of the human brain and body. Substance dualism denies this. Dualists typically hold that your mind *interacts* with your brain and body—that is, your thoughts can causally influence your brain and body, and your brain and body can causally influence your thoughts. Yet they deny that your mind depends for its existence on your brain or body.

Each of the philosophers in the following sections endorses substance dualism. However, each of them has a different picture of what the mind is, what the mind's powers are, and what the mind's relationship with the body consists in.

René Descartes: Brief Chronology

- 1596: Born in Touraine, France.
- 1597: Descartes's mother dies when he is one year old.
- 1607-1615: Attends the prominent Jesuit college of La Flèche.
- 1616-1618: Travels throughout Europe working as a mercenary soldier.
- 1618: Begins his earliest works on mathematics and physics.
- 1628: Moves to Holland.
- 1629: Descartes begins work on *The World*, with a heliocentric model of the cosmos.
- 1633: After the Church's condemnation of Galileo, Descartes abandons *The World*.
- 1637: Publishes *Discourse on Method* along with his *Optics, Geometry,* and *Meteorology*.
- 1639–40: Drafts the *Meditations on First Philosophy* and shares it with Mersenne, asking him to solicit objections from leading intellectuals of the day.
- 1641: Publishes *Meditations on First Philosophy*, along with the accompanying Objections and his Replies.
- 1643: Begins correspondence with Princess Elisabeth of Bohemia.
- 1644: Publishes a comprehensive presentation of his philosophical system, entitled *Principles of Philosophy*. The work is dedicated to Elisabeth.
- 1649: Publishes *Passions of the Soul*, a treatise on the psychology of emotions. Descartes then moves to Stockholm at the invitation of Queen Christina of Sweden.
- 1650: Dies in Stockholm.
- 1663: Descartes's works are placed on the Church's *Index of Prohibited Books*.

1A. DUALISM IN DESCARTES

Descartes's arguments for substance dualism have been so influential in the history of modern philosophy that, even today, the view is frequently called "Cartesian dualism." The following selections from his *Meditations on First Philosophy* (1641) focus on those arguments. The text presents Descartes's line of reasoning as though he were simply recording each step as it occurred to him over the course of six nights, each corresponding to one of the six Meditations.

In the First Meditation, he sets out a series of skeptical scenarios—imaginary situations in which your ordinary beliefs about yourself and about the world, while seeming to you to be true, turn out to be false. By the end of the First Meditation, it is apparent that it is possible we are mistaken about almost all of our beliefs. However, Descartes's purpose is not to argue that we can't know anything. Quite the opposite: he wants to show us that there are some things it is not even *possible* to doubt. A famous passage in the Second Meditation identifies such a truth: "I am, I exist." This is true whenever you think it. Finally, in the Sixth Meditation, he argues that, since we can clearly and distinctly conceive of our mind apart from our body, our mind can in principle exist without our body.

Extract 1.1: Descartes's *Meditations on First Philosophy*

Meditation One.

. . . All that I have, up to this moment, accepted as possessed of the highest truth and certainty, I received either from or through the senses. I observed, however, that these sometimes misled us; and it is the part of prudence not to place absolute confidence in that by which we have even once been deceived.

But it may be said, perhaps, that, although the senses occasionally mislead us respecting minute objects, and such as are so far removed from us as to be beyond the reach of close observation, there are yet many . . . [sensations] it is manifestly impossible to doubt; as for example, that I am in this place, seated by the fire, clothed in a winter dressing gown, that I hold in my hands this piece of paper, with other intimations of the same nature. But how could I deny that I possess these hands and this body, and withal escape being classed with persons in a state of insanity . . . ?

Though this be true, I must nevertheless here consider that I am a man, and that, consequently, I am in the habit of sleeping, and representing to myself in dreams those same things, or even sometimes others less probable, which the insane think are presented to them in their waking moments. How often have I dreamt that I was in these familiar circumstances, that I was dressed, and occupied this place by the fire, when I was lying undressed in bed? At the present moment, however, I certainly look upon this paper with eyes wide awake; the head which I now move is not asleep; I extend this hand consciously and with express purpose, and I perceive it; the occurrences in sleep are not so distinct as all this. But I cannot forget that, at other times I have been deceived in sleep by similar illusions; and, attentively considering those cases, I perceive so clearly that there exist no certain marks by which the state of waking can ever be distinguished from sleep . . .

Let us suppose, then, that we are dreaming, and that all these particulars . . . are merely illusions; and even that we really possess neither an entire body nor hands such as we see. Nevertheless, it must be admitted at least that the objects which appear to us in sleep are, as it were, painted representations which could not have been formed unless in the likeness of realities; and, therefore, that those general objects, at all events, namely, eyes, a head, hands, and an entire body, are not simply imaginary, but really existent. . . .

Nevertheless, the belief that there is a God who is all powerful, and who created me, such as I am, has, for a long time, obtained steady possession of my mind. How, then, do I know that he has not arranged that there should be neither earth, nor sky, nor any extended thing, nor figure, nor magnitude, nor place . . . ? And further, as I sometimes think that others are in error respecting matters of which they believe themselves to possess a perfect knowledge, how do I know that I am not also deceived each time I add together two and three, or number the sides of a square, or form some judgment still more simple, if more simple indeed can be imagined? . . .

I will suppose, then, . . . that some malignant demon, who is at once exceedingly potent and deceitful, has employed all his artifice to deceive me; I will suppose that the sky, the air, the earth, colors, figures, sounds, and all external things, are nothing better than the illusions of dreams, by means of which this being has laid snares for my credulity; I will consider myself as without hands, eyes, flesh, blood, or any of the senses, and as falsely believing that I am possessed of these . . .

Meditation Two.

. . . But how do I know that there is not something . . . of which it is impossible to entertain the slightest doubt? Is there not a God, or some being, by whatever name I may designate him, who causes these thoughts to arise in my mind? But why suppose such a being, for it may be I myself am capable of producing them? Am I, then, at least not something? But I before denied that I possessed senses or a body; I hesitate, however, for what follows from that? Am I so dependent on the body and the senses that without these I cannot exist? But I had the persuasion that there was absolutely nothing in the world, that there was no sky and no earth, neither minds nor bodies; was I not, therefore, at the same time, persuaded that I did not exist? Far from it: I assuredly existed, since I was persuaded. But there is I know not what being, who is possessed at once of the highest power and the deepest cunning, who is constantly employing all his ingenuity in deceiving me. Doubtless, then, I exist, since I am deceived; and, let him deceive me as he may, he can never bring it about that I am nothing, so long as I shall be conscious that I am something. So that it must, in fine, be maintained, all things being maturely and carefully considered, that this proposition, "I am, I exist," is necessarily true each time it is expressed by me or conceived in my mind. . . .

But what can I now say that I am, since I suppose there exists an extremely powerful, and, if I may so speak, malignant being, whose whole endeavors are directed toward deceiving me? Can I affirm that I possess any one of all those attributes of which I have lately spoken as belonging to the nature of body? After attentively considering them in my own mind, I find none of them that can properly be said to belong to myself. . . . Let us pass, then, to the attributes of the soul. The first mentioned were the powers of nutrition and walking; but, if it be true that I have no body, it is true likewise that I am capable neither of walking nor of being nourished. Perception is another attribute of the soul; but perception too is impossible without the body; besides, I have frequently, during sleep, believed that I perceived objects which I afterward observed I did not in reality perceive. Thinking is another attribute of the soul; and here I discover what properly belongs to myself. This alone is inseparable from me. I am—I exist: this is certain; but how often? As often as I think; for perhaps it would even happen, if I should wholly cease to think, that I should at the same time altogether cease to be. I now admit nothing that is not necessarily true. I am therefore, precisely speaking, only a thinking thing, that is, a mind, understanding, or reason, terms whose signification was before unknown to me. . . .

But what, then, am I? A thinking thing, it has been said. But what is a thinking thing? It is a thing that doubts, understands, [conceives], affirms, denies, wills, refuses; that imagines also, and perceives. . . .

Meditation Six.

. . . [B]ecause I know that all which I clearly and distinctly conceive can be produced by God exactly as I conceive it, it is sufficient that I am able clearly and distinctly to conceive one thing apart from another, in order to be certain that the one is different from the other, seeing they may at least be made to exist separately, by the omnipotence of God; and it matters not by what power this separation is made, in order to be compelled to judge them different; and, therefore, merely because I know with certitude that I exist, and because, in the meantime, I do not observe that aught necessarily belongs to my nature or essence beyond my being a thinking thing, I rightly conclude that my essence consists only in my being a thinking thing [or a substance whose whole essence or nature is merely thinking]. And although I may, or rather, as I will shortly say, although I certainly do possess a body with which I am very closely conjoined; nevertheless, because, on the one hand, I have a clear and distinct idea of myself, in as far as I am only a thinking and unextended thing, and as, on the other hand, I possess a distinct idea of body, in as far as it is only an extended and unthinking thing, it is certain that I [am] entirely and truly distinct from my body, and may exist without it.

[From René Descartes, *The Method, Meditations and Philosophy of Descartes*, translated by J. Veitch, with an introduction by F. Sewall (Washington: M. Walter Dunne, 1901). Some language has been modernized.]

In the First Meditation, Descartes hopes to find a class of beliefs that is immune to doubt. To identify this class of beliefs, he sets out a series of increasingly severe skeptical scenarios, then he examines which kinds of belief are undermined by the skeptical scenario in question.

First, he observes that beliefs based on our senses are not immune to doubt, since our senses have deceived us in the past. We have all seen optical illusions, for instance, in which the way things look does not accurately represent the way things are. This concern does not seem very serious, though. As Descartes goes on to say, the fact that our senses deceive us in some special cases does not imply that we cannot trust our senses in normal cases.

After this optimistic note, however, Descartes moves to another skeptical scenario: *the dreaming doubt*. Many of us have had the experience of dreaming something so vividly that, upon waking, it seems as though the events we dreamed really occurred. Such experiences can obviously be emotionally distressing. A very realistic dream of a fight with a loved one, or trouble at work, can color one's mood even after recognizing that it was only a dream. What Descartes points out, however, is that such experiences also lead to a skeptical puzzle. If you have in the past had a dream that was so vivid you thought it was real, how do you know you're not dreaming presently? Descartes claims that "there exist no certain marks by which the state of waking can ever be distinguished from sleep," and thus it does not seem to be possible to tell whether you are really awake or merely dreaming at any given moment. You might be dreaming right now.

It is tempting to respond to this skeptical argument by drawing on scientific studies of dreams. In dreams, text—the page of a book, the writing on a chalkboard, the numbers on a clock—is supposed to appear blurry or otherwise difficult to discern. You might object to the dream argument on this basis: you're reading these words right now, after all, and they don't appear blurry or indecipherable to you. If you were dreaming, however, these words would appear blurry or indecipherable. So, you're not dreaming right now.

The problem with this objection, though, is that it relies on beliefs that are called into question by the dreaming doubt itself. Your belief that written text appears blurry in dreams *could simply be part of your dream*, not something that has any basis in reality. For this reason, it is not an effective objection to the dreaming doubt.

Descartes concludes that, for all we know, all of the details we observe around us right now, and all of the observational and experimental data used in the sciences, "are merely illusions." Our scientific beliefs, then, are not immune to doubt. Moreover, since our dreams sometimes represent our bodies as being very different than they actually are, it's possible "that we really possess neither an entire body nor hands such as we see." This is a striking and disturbing consequence. All of the characteristics of your body—even those you take to be most essential to who you are—might merely be figments of your dream. Your beliefs about those characteristics are not immune to doubt.

Now, many of our beliefs about logic or mathematics *would* still be true even if it turns out we are presently dreaming. Whether you are awake right now or not, a square will still have four sides and the sum of 2 and 3 will still be 5. However, Descartes closes the First Meditation with a skeptical scenario that calls even these logical and mathematical beliefs into doubt.

In this scenario, you are to imagine that a powerful but malicious entity is controlling all of your experiences and thoughts. This entity—whatever it is—wants to deceive you into believing what is false. Any experiences you have, and any lines of reasoning you undertake, are carefully calculated by the deceiver to lead you to draw false conclusions. For instance, whereas ordinarily you take your appearance in the mirror as evidence of what you look like, in this skeptical scenario, your appearance in the mirror is designed by the deceiver to mislead you. (Because this scenario is so outlandish and dramatic, scholars sometimes call it *the hyperbolic doubt*.)

Indeed, you could even be mistaken about the number of sides of a square or the sum of 2 and 3. Both of these beliefs depend on experiences or lines of reasoning that the deceiver could manipulate. This is so even if your belief is founded on rigorous mathematical proof. The deceiver can make you believe that your premises logically entail your conclusion even when they do not. The same holds true of all logical and mathematical beliefs: although they survive the dreaming doubt, they are not *entirely* immune to doubt.

To reiterate, Descartes does not believe that there really is an evil deceiver controlling our thoughts and experiences. This is merely a thought experiment. It is intended to show that it is possible that we are mistaken even about those beliefs that we commonly take to be most certain. Moreover, though Descartes frames this scenario with a reference to his "belief that there is a God who is all powerful," and though he sometimes refers to the deceiver as an "evil demon," this thought experiment does not really depend upon a belief in the supernatural. Philosophers and scientists today sometimes consider the possibility that we are living in a computer simulation. On this "simulation hypothesis," although it *feels* like you are a human being, made of flesh and bone, living in the twenty-first century on the planet Earth, *in fact* you are merely an instance of a program that perfectly simulates a human living in the twenty-first century on Earth. If that's possible, it also seems possible that our programmers are actively interfering with our experiences and reasoning to make us form false beliefs. (Perhaps they are studying our ability to reach the truth in adverse conditions.) The simulation hypothesis thus raises precisely the same doubts as the possibility of Descartes's demon.

In the Second Meditation, Descartes proposes a belief that he takes to be immune to all doubt. He writes, "'I am, I exist,' is necessarily true each time it is expressed by me or conceived in my mind." This belief is frequently called the *cogito*, a name drawn from Descartes's more famous statement in another work: "I think, therefore I am [*Cogito ergo sum*]." Even the possibility that you are being intentionally misled by an all-powerful and malicious deceiver cannot raise any doubts here. After all, if the deceiver is tricking you, then you are being tricked. And if you are being tricked, then you *are*—that is, you exist. Here, at last, we have a belief that survives even the most hyperbolic doubt.

Still, it is not so obvious what is left of you after this thought experiment. Apparently you are not to be identified with any of your physical qualities whatsoever, not even your having a brain. What remains of the self, in that case? Since the only thing that you can be absolutely certain about is that you really are thinking right now, Descartes infers that your power of thinking is the *only* essential feature that you have. Descartes is clear on this score: "I am therefore, precisely speaking, only a thinking thing," a substance capable of thinking—that is, a mind or soul. (When referring to this thinking substance, Descartes sometimes uses the Latin *mens*, which means mind, and sometimes uses *anima*, which means soul.)

Again, although Descartes was a devout Catholic, it is important to recognize that he does not rely on any specifically religious beliefs or doctrines in his argument for this claim about the self. The argument so far is remarkably simple. You can doubt all of your physical qualities, but you cannot doubt your own existence. So it is conceivable that you exist even if you lack all of your physical qualities. Thus, strictly speaking, your "self" does not consist in your body, or your brain, or any physical process, but in thought alone.

After the Second Meditation Descartes moves to a number of different topics, including the existence of God and the powers of the soul (powers such as understanding, willing, and sensing), before eventually returning to the question of how the mind is related to the body. Although the Second Meditation establishes that the self is properly identified with mind rather than body, the argument up to that point leaves open a possibility that substance dualism excludes. Recall that, according to substance dualism, your mind does not depend on any physical qualities or processes. Yet the argument so far seems to leave open the possibility that the mind depends upon the body. However, Descartes's most famous argument for substance dualism, presented in the Sixth and final Meditation, closes this gap.

The Sixth Meditation argument for substance dualism starts by establishing a connection between what is *conceivable* and what is *possible*. Specifically, Descartes argues that if two things can be **clearly and distinctly**[†] conceived apart from one another, then it is possible for them to exist apart from one another. For example, if you are wearing trousers right now, the left and right legs of the trousers are actually connected together. However, you can form a clear conception of each leg apart from the other—you can form an idea of the shape, size, and texture of the left leg without thinking of the right leg at all, and vice versa. So, although the legs are *actually* connected together, they *could* exist apart, independently of one another. And the same holds true, Descartes believes, of any two things that can be conceived apart from one another: if we can clearly conceive of each without the other, then they are independent of one another. Why should we accept this? Here, Descartes appeals to his belief in God: whatever you can clearly and distinctly conceive, God has the power to make real. Thus, *anything you can clearly and distinctly conceive is possible.*

Why include the restriction to clear and distinct ideas, though? The point of this restriction is to allow that we sometimes have obscure and confused ideas that are not genuinely possible. For instance, suppose Sam has not studied geometry, and he finds it conceivable that a right triangle has a base that is longer than its hypotenuse. It would be a serious problem for Descartes if Sam's confused conception of geometry entailed that it is possible for such a triangle to exist. But when we think about the connection between what we can conceive and what is genuinely possible, ideally we have ruled out confusions of the sort that Sam is laboring under. Hence the restriction on Descartes's principle: if you can *clearly and distinctly* conceive of something, then that thing is possible; however, we often fail to form clear and distinct concepts, relying on obscure or confused ones instead. In such cases, our concepts might not correspond to any genuine possibility.

Next, Descartes claims to have a clear and distinct idea of mind without body, and also of body without mind. Bodies are substances that have length, breadth, and width, and that occupy some position in space. (This is what Descartes means when he says that bodies are "extended": they have extension in the three spatial dimensions.) Since we can represent these geometrical features of a body without attributing any thoughts or perceptions to it, we can clearly and distinctly conceive of a body existing without any mind. That part of the argument is perhaps unsurprising, since few of us would be tempted to attribute thoughts or perceptions to most of the physical objects around us, though these objects surely count as bodies in Descartes's sense.

More surprising is Descartes's claim to have a clear and distinct concept of mind absent any body. Yet this is what he believes the First and Second Meditations allowed us to do. During those Meditations, we were invited to conceive of ourselves as existing in a scenario where all physical appearances are mere illusions. This is just to conceive of ourselves as conscious, thinking beings that are incorporeal ("unextended," in Descartes's terminology). So, just as we have a clear and distinct concept of a body existing without any mind, likewise we have a clear and distinct concept of a mental substance—our own mind—existing without any body.

With these premises in place, it is easy to see how Descartes's argument for substance dualism is intended to proceed. If two things can be clearly and distinctly conceived without one another, then those things can exist apart from one another. And, as we have just seen, the mind and the body can be clearly and distinctly conceived without one another. So, Descartes concludes, the mind and the body can exist apart from one another. For this reason, although they *interact* with one another, your mind is not *produced* by your body or brain: your mind could exist without either of them, so it does not depend on them for its existence.

The position Descartes has developed in these passages is one particularly influential form of substance dualism, but it is not the only version of that position that was on offer in the early modern period. In the second half of the seventeenth century, another influential form of substance dualism was developed by the philosopher Henry More. In the next section, we turn to More's distinctive version of this idea.

Key Points

- Substance dualism is the thesis that the human mind and the human body are distinct substances that could exist independently of one another.
- In the *Meditations*, Descartes defends a version of substance dualism.
- The main argument he offers is based on the premise that if we can clearly and distinctly conceive of two things apart from one another, then it is possible for them to exist independently of one another.
- For Descartes, the mind is a thinking, unextended substance, while the body is an extended, unthinking substance.

Suggested Further Reading

Carriero, John. "Chapter 6: The Sixth Meditation." In *Between Two Worlds: A Reading of Descartes's Meditations*, 359–425. Princeton: Princeton University Press, 2009.

Hoffman, Paul. "The Union and Interaction of Mind and Body (Part 1)." In *Essays on Descartes*, 77–87. New York: Oxford University Press, 2009.

Rodriguez-Pereyra, Gonzalo. "Descartes's Substance Dualism and His Independence Conception of Substance." *Journal of the History of Philosophy* 46, no. 1 (2008): 69–89.

Rozemond, Marleen. *Descartes's Dualism*. Cambridge, MA: Harvard University Press, 1998.

Simmons, Alison. "Cartesian Consciousness Reconsidered." *Philosophers' Imprint* 12, no. 2 (2012): 1–21.

Wilson, Margaret Dauler. "Chapter VI: Mind, Body, and Things Outside Us." In *Descartes*, 177–220. New York: Routledge, 1978.

1B. HENRY MORE'S DUALISM

Henry More, a British philosopher and theologian, was one of the leading figures in the movement known as Cambridge Platonism. Although the names of intellectual movements can at times be misleading, in More's case the name is entirely accurate: he lived and worked in Cambridge for his entire adult life, and much of his work draws explicitly upon the ideas and arguments of Plato and his followers. The overarching idea that animates almost all of More's philosophical works is that it is possible to defend the central doctrines of Christianity *on purely rational grounds*. For instance, in his 1653 book, *An Antidote against Atheism*, he developed several purely philosophical arguments for the existence of God. And the full title of his subsequent 1659 book on the soul makes his mission clear: *The Immortality of the Soul, So farre forth as it is demonstrable from the Knowledge of Nature and the Light of Reason*. So, although More was an extremely well-read scholar of theology, his main contributions to philosophy are his arguments for traditional religious beliefs on the basis of premises that (he hopes) will be rationally acceptable even to atheist and agnostic readers.

Henry More: Brief Chronology

- 1614: Born in Grantham, Lincolnshire.
- 1631: Begins attending Christ's College at Cambridge University as a student.
- 1636: After completing his degree, he continues his studies at Cambridge.
- 1639: Elected as a Fellow of Christ's College, remaining for the rest of his life.
- 1642: Publishes his first book, *Psychodia Platonica*, a collection of poems about Platonist philosophy. Over twenty more books follow in subsequent years.
- 1646: Reads Descartes's *Principles of Philosophy*, becoming profoundly interested in the Cartesian philosophy.
- 1648: Begins a brief correspondence with Descartes, expressing both a deep admiration for, and serious objections to, Descartes's philosophy.
- 1650: Begins an ongoing correspondence with Anne Conway (then Anne Finch).

Early Modern Dualism: René Descartes, Henry More, and Anton Wilhelm Amo

- 1659: Publishes *The Immortality of the Soul*, in which he presents his own version of substance dualism (extracted below).
- 1664: Elected as a Fellow of the Royal Society of London, indicating his interest in and involvement with developments in experimental science.
- 1687: Dies in Cambridge.

The following extract, drawn from *The Immortality of the Soul*, focuses on More's account of the nature of the human soul and its union with the human body. The selection from Book I, Chapter III, sets out the general definitions of the terms "spirit" and "body," highlighting the conceptual differences between these two kinds of substance. The selection from Book I, Chapter VIII, describes a further subdivision within the category of spirits: plants, nonhuman animals, and human beings each have different kinds of spirit. Finally, the selection from Book II, Chapter XIV, discusses More's striking account of the union between soul and body.

Extract 1.2: More's The Immortality of the Soul

Book I. Chap. III.

1. The greatest and grossest Obstacle to the belief of *the immortality of the Soul*, is that confident opinion some have that the very notion of *a Spirit* is a piece of Non-sense and perfect Incongruity in the conception thereof. Wherefore to proceed by degrees to our main design, and to lay our foundation low and sure, we will in the first place expose to view the genuine notion of *a Spirit*, in the *general* [sense]; and afterwards of Several kinds of Spirits: that it may appear to all, how unjust that cavil is against *Incorporeal Substances*, as if they were mere Impossibilities and contradictory Inconsistencies. I will define therefore *a Spirit* in general thus, *A Substance penetrable and indiscerpible*. The fitness of this definition will be the better understood, if we divide *Substance* in general into these first kinds, namely *Body* and *Spirit*, and then define *Body* to be *A Substance impenetrable and discerpible*. Whence [the] contrary kind to this is fitly defined, *A substance penetrable and indiscerpible*. . . .

Book II. Chap. VIII.

. . .

2. Now this *General notion* [of spirit] can be contracted into *Kinds*, by no other *Differences* than such as may be called peculiar Powers or

Properties belonging to one *Spirit* and excluded from another... From which it will follow, that if we describe these *several kinds of Spirits* by *immediate* and *intrinsic* Properties, we have given as good Definitions of them as any one can give of any thing in the world.

3. We will begin with what is most simple, *the Seminal Forms* of things... *A Seminal Form is a created Spirit organizing duly-prepared Matter into life and vegetation proper to this or the other kind of Plant.* It is beyond my imagination what can be excepted against this Description, it containing nothing but what is very coherent and intelligible. For in that it is a spirit, it can *move Matter* intrinsically, or at least *direct the motion* thereof. But in that it is not an *Omnipotent* Spirit, but *Finite* and Created, its power may well be restrained to *duly-prepared Matter* both for vital union and motion, [since] He that has made *these Particular Spirits* has varied their Faculties of Vital union according to the diversity of the preparation of *Matter*, and so limited the whole comprehension of them all, that none of them may be able to be vitally joined with any *Matter* whatever. And the same first Cause of all things that gives them a power of uniting with & moving of *matter duly-prepared*, may also set such laws to this motion, that when it lights on matter fit for it, it will produce such and such a Plant, that is to say, it will shape the matter into such Figure, Colour and other properties, as we discover in them by our Senses.

4. This is the First degree of *Particular Life* in the world, if there be any purely of this degree Particular. But now, as *Aristotle* has somewhere noted, the Essences of things are like Numbers, whose *Species* are changed by adding or taking away a unit: add therefore another *intrinsic power* to this of *Vegetation*, viz. *Sensation*, and it becomes *the Soul of a Beast....A Subject therefore which includes both Vegetation and Sensation is the general notion of the Soul of a Brute.* Which is distributed into a number of kinds, the effect of every *intrinsic power* being discernible in the constant shape and properties of every distinct kind of Brute Creatures.

5. If we add to *Vegetation* and *Sensation Reason* properly so called, we have then a settled notion of the *Soul of Man*; which we may more completely describe thus: *A created Spirit with Sense and Reason, and a power of organizing terrestrial Matter into human shape by vital union with [that matter]* . . .

8. The *Platonists* write of other Orders of *Spirits* or *Immaterial Substances* . . . But there being more Subtlety then either usefulness or assurance in such like Speculations, I shall pass them over at this time; having already, I think, irrefutably made good, That there is no incongruity

nor incompossibility comprised in the Notion of *Spirit* or *Incorporeal Substance*. . . .

Book II. Ch. XIV.

. . .

8. [The foregoing analysis of the concept of souls] makes little to the clearing of the *manner of their descent* . . ., which cannot be better understood then by considering their *Union* with the Body generated, or indeed with any kind of Body whatever, where the Soul is held captive, and cannot quit herself thereof by the free *imperium* [power] of her own Imagination and Will. For what can be the cause of this cohesion, the very Essence of the Soul being so easily penetrative of *Matter*, and the dimensions of all *Matter* being alike penetrable everywhere? . . . And therefore it is inconceivable how her *Union* should be so with any of it, as that she should not be able at any time to glide freely from one part thereof to another as she pleases.

It is plain therefore, that this *Union of the Soul with Matter* does not arise from any such gross *Mechanical* way, as when two Bodies stick one in another by reason of any toughness and viscosity . . .; but from a *congruity* of another nature, which I know not how better to term than *Vital*: which *Vital Congruity* is chiefly in the *Soul* itself, it being the noblest Principle of Life; but is also in the *Matter*, and is there nothing but such modification thereof as fits the *Plastick* part of the Soul, and tempts out that Faculty into act.

9. Not that there is any *Life* in the *Matter* with which this in the *Soul* should sympathize and unite; but it is termed *Vital* because it makes the *Matter* a *congruous* Subject for the Soul to reside in, and exercise the functions of *life*. For that which has no *life* itself, may tie to it that which has. As some men are said to be tied by the teeth, or tied by the ear, when they are detained by the pleasure they are struck with from good Music or delicious Viands. But neither is that which they eat *alive*, nor that which makes the Music . . . For there is nothing in all this but mere Matter and corporeal motion, and yet our *vital* functions are affected thereby. . . .

10. . . . And therefore that which ties the Soul and this or that Matter together, is an irresistible and imperceptible pleasure, if I may so call it, arising from the *congruity* of *Matter* to the *Plastic* faculty of the Soul: which *Congruity in the Matter* not failing, nor that in the Soul, the *Union* is at least as necessary as the continuation of eating and drinking, so long as Hunger and Thirst continues, and the Meat and Drink proves good. But

either satiety in the Stomach or some ill taste in the Meat may break the *congruity* on either side, and then the action will cease with the pleasure thereof. . . .

11. What are the *strings* or *cords* that tie the Soul to the Body, or to what Vehicle else soever, I have declared as clearly as I can. From which it will be easy to understand the *manner of [the soul's] descent*. For assuredly, the same *cords* or *strings* that tie her there, may draw her thither: Where the carcass is, there will the Eagles be gathered.

[From Henry More, A Collection of Several Philosophical Writings of Dr. Henry More (Cambridge: James Flesher, 1662). Some language has been modernized.]

In the selection from Descartes, we saw that he viewed the mind or soul as an "unextended" substance, in the sense that it entirely lacks spatial dimensions and location in space. The sole attribute of the mind is that it is a thing that thinks, and (for Descartes) the capacity for thought need not be moored to any bodily organ or physical process. The picture that More develops in the preceding passages is also a form of substance dualism; like Descartes, he holds that the human body and mind are distinct substances bound together in a kind of causal union. However, More disagrees with Descartes about the essential characteristics of the human mind. While Descartes holds that the human mind entirely lacks extension in the spatial dimensions, More believes this would make the union of a person's mind and body impossible to explain. How could your mind's decisions cause your body's actions if it does not make physical contact with your body? (This issue, known as the *mind-body problem*, is one we return to in the next chapter.)

Instead, More takes souls or spirits in general to be extended, just as bodies are. What then is the difference between spirits and bodies? More's answer is that these two kinds of substance differ in two ways, namely, (1) in whether they can be penetrated by other substances, and (2) in whether their parts can be actually divided or separated from one another. Bodies, he writes, are impenetrable—that is, bodies cannot move through one another without resistance. By contrast, spirits are penetrable: they can freely move through bodies. The second difference is that bodies are "discerpible," while spirits are "indiscerpible." Elsewhere in this book, More explains that when he says a substance is discerpible, he means that its parts can be actually divided from one another. Bodies clearly have this property: a tree's parts can be chopped up and used to make separate pieces of furniture. By contrast, More thinks that although spirits have parts, those parts cannot be actually divided from one another. Note that the term "actually divisible" is intended to allow that some parts of a spirit are *conceptually* divisible: we can mark the difference, conceptually, between a spirit's capacity for sensation and its capacity for reason, but we cannot chop up the spirit's sense and reason in the way we chop up the trunk and limbs of a tree.

Notably, More's definition of a spirit as a substance that is penetrable and indiscerpible does *not* require that spirits are all capable of thought. This marks a striking departure from the Cartesian picture. Indeed, Descartes seems to have believed that among the entire animal kingdom, only humans have minds (or souls, or spirits—all the same concept, for Descartes). Other species of animals, he believed, act not on the basis of understanding or reason, but solely on the basis of unthinking biological mechanism. Near the very end of Descartes's life, Henry More engaged in a brief but lively correspondence with him, in which More was strongly critical of this part of Descartes's philosophical system. The preceding extract nicely illustrates More's alternative position: every living being has a spirit, though different kinds of living being have different kinds of spirit. Plants have a soul with a power of "vegetation" (roughly, a capacity for homeostasis and growth); nonhuman animals have this power, but also the power to sense their environment; and humans have both of these powers as well as the power of reason. Humans, then, are distinctive not in virtue of the fact that they have a soul at all—even *plants* have souls, on More's view. Rather, what is distinctive about the human soul is its capacity for reason or understanding.

In this regard, More's concept of the human soul has affinities to a much older position than the one we saw in Descartes's *Meditations*. Aristotle's work *On the Soul* (or *De Anima*) had a great deal of sway during the medieval and renaissance periods, and More is consciously drawing upon it here. According to Aristotle, *the soul is the form of life*, such that different living organisms have different kinds of soul.

What does this mean? The basic idea can be illustrated using any living thing you like—say a houseplant, such as a fern. The fern is made of a bunch of particles, which we'll call its *matter*. The fern's matter isn't inert. It is constantly moving and interacting with other things. And, in fact, if the fern's matter stopped doing this, the fern would cease to be. So, what's keeping the fern alive? On Aristotle's view, the answer is that the fern has a certain *form* that serves to structure the motions and interactions of its matter. When the fern takes in water from the soil, or grows in the direction of the sun, Aristotle's explanation is that the fern's soul is structuring its activities in that way.

If this is your view of the soul, then lots of things have souls—any living thing, in fact. But Aristotle thought we could usefully distinguish three kinds or levels of soul. Some souls, like those of plants, are only capable of basic life processes, such as those involved in nutrition and growth. Some souls, like those of dogs, are additionally capable of having sensations, perceptions that represent their environment. And some souls, like those of human beings, are even better yet: they are capable of reason, which allows humans to unify and understand the general principles that explain their particular sensory experiences. Hence we have the following hierarchy of souls:

- Nutritive Soul
- Sensitive Soul
- Rational Soul

These are each *aspects* of the human soul. Your nutritive soul is responsible for your digesting your breakfast. Your sensitive soul is responsible for your seeing these words right now, and your rational soul is responsible for your interpreting their meaning.

It is easy to see More's discussion of the soul as building upon the Aristotelian picture just outlined. However, *unlike* Aristotle, More here treats the soul as a substance unto itself, distinct from and independent of the body. On this point, More's notion of the soul is intended to be compatible with certain traditional Christian beliefs: it is something that could exist without the body, and therefore the soul can survive the death of the body. (This point is central to More's philosophical project, motivating the title of the entire book: *The Immortality of the Soul*.)

Given that the soul is a substance distinct from the body, More faces the problem of explaining the union between the mind or soul and the body. After all—as More himself observes—if spirits are by definition entirely penetrable and able to move freely through other things, it is hard to see why your soul "should not be able at any time to glide freely" wherever in the material world that you desire. More thus owes an explanation of how the human soul comes to be bound to one particular body.

The solution, More thinks, cannot be a mechanistic explanation of the sort we might give to account for how two bodies come to be bound together. For example, suppose we wanted to explain why an insect becomes stuck after alighting upon a droplet of tree sap. A typical explanation of this event—drawing on the adhesive quality of the sap—simply *presupposes* that the insect does not have the power to move freely through matter. (If the insect did have such a power, the adhesion of the sap would be entirely irrelevant.) Some other mode of explanation is required.

More's preferred explanation is that there is what he calls a "vital congruity" between the soul and the particular body to which it is bound. The body is not like a prison in which the soul is caged—we have seen that, for More, the soul cannot be bound by matter in *that* way. Rather, the soul is *drawn* to the body by "an irresistible and imperceptible pleasure" that accompanies their union. He provides several analogies to make clearer this initially obscure claim. The soul is bound to the body in the same way that a person gets caught up in the sound of a beautiful piece of music or a delicious meal. A person isn't literally "bound" by a piece of music, but they may become *absorbed* by it, focusing their attention entirely on the music for a time. Notice, too, that when a person is so absorbed, they are focused on the music itself rather than on the pleasure that the music is bringing them. This, presumably, is why More describes the pleasure caused in the soul by its vital congruity with the body to be "imperceptible." Finally—and this is a crucial element of More's explanation—one and the same piece of music might be appealing to one person and entirely unappealing to another. Likewise, a particular soul might get caught up in a particular body without being similarly drawn to another body.

The analogy also sheds light on how the soul's union with the body ultimately ends. The problem is a difficult one for Descartes: on the Cartesian view, there is no substantial difference between a living human body and a corpse. Both are extended substances, and they share very similar qualities. The human mind is bound up in intimate union with the living human body; why would it flee the scene when that body becomes a corpse? More's solution to the problem once again draws on his notion of vital congruity. Alterations of the body—such as, for instance, severe clogging of the arteries around the heart—can break its congruity with the soul in much the same way that alterations to a piece of music can cause a rapt audience's interest to wane. Indeed, the audience's absorption is inevitably temporary: when the music stops, becomes dissonant, or simply goes on too long, even someone who was previously absorbed in the music will relax their focus on it and turn to other things. On More's view, the same sorts of explanations account for the eventual separation of the soul from the body.

Key Points

- Against Descartes, More holds that the soul (and any substance) is extended.
- Though the soul is extended and therefore has parts, More also holds that it is *indiscerpible*: its parts are not actually divisible from one another.
- For More (following long tradition that traces back to Aristotle), there is a hierarchy of types of soul: *vegetative* souls, *sensitive* souls, and *rational* souls.
- The union of soul and body is the result of a *vital congruity* between the two.

Suggested Further Reading

Cohen, Leonora. "Descartes and Henry More on the Beast-Machine: A Translation of their Correspondence Pertaining to Animal Autonomism." *Annals of Science* 1 (1936): 48–61.

Gabbey, Alan. "Henry More and the Limits of Mechanism." In *Henry More (1614–1687): Tercentenary Studies*, edited by S. Hutton, 55–76. Dordrecht: Kluwer Academic, 1982.

Henry, John. "A Cambridge Platonist's Materialism: Henry More and the Concept of Soul." *Journal of the Warburg and Courtauld Institutes* 49 (1986): 172–95.

Reid, Jasper. *The Metaphysics of Henry More*. Dordrecht: Springer, 2012.

1C. DUALISM IN ANTON WILHELM AMO

Anton Wilhelm Amo, originally born somewhere in West Africa around the turn of the seventeenth century, is one of very few black philosophers of the early modern period that is known about today. It appears that he was originally taken to Europe by missionaries in order to receive religious training as a pastor or missionary. When the cost of this education proved to be higher than planned, they sent him to work as a court servant for a German duke instead. (The Holy Roman Empire did not officially recognize "slave" as a legal status, yet Amo likely had nowhere else to call home. He therefore entered adulthood in something of a legal no-man's land and would have had to acquiesce to the duke's wishes in most things.) He seems to have worked in the duke's court until, roughly at the age of twenty-seven, he was able to enroll as a university student. Initially, he focused his studies on the law, with a particular interest in the legal rights of those who, like him, had been taken from Africa and brought to—stranded in—Germany. After defending a thesis on this topic, though, he returned to university and took up the study of philosophy. In 1734, Amo published a dissertation (selections of which are included below) that defends a very extreme form of substance dualism. Five years later, he took a post teaching philosophy at the University of Jena, and he appears to have been the first person born in Africa to teach at a European university.

Anton Wilhelm Amo: Brief Chronology

- *c.* 1700: Born in West Africa.
- 1707: Taken to Amsterdam as a young child.
- 1708: Sent to Germany to be a servant in a ducal court, where he was baptized.
- 1727: Enrolls as a student at the University of Halle.
- 1729: Defends a law thesis entitled *On the Right of Moors in Europe*.
- 1730: Enrolls as a student at the University of Wittenburg.
- 1734: Publishes a philosophical dissertation, *On the Impassivity of the Human Mind*, on the question of whether the power of sensation is properly attributed to the mind or the body.

> - 1738: Publishes a short work entitled *Treatise on the art of philosophizing soberly and accurately.*
> - 1739: Begins teaching classes at the University of Jena.
> - 1748: Returns to West Africa, for reasons that are not known.
> - 1752: A Swiss traveler reports meeting with Amo in the town of Axim, in what is now Ghana. (The date of Amo's death is currently unknown.)

In the following extract from Amo's dissertation, he sets out the surprising position that the mind is not properly said to be the subject of sensation. The mind does not have sensations or a faculty of sensing; instead, the body is the subject of sensations, and the mind acts on the body to form ideas that represent its sensations. The dissertation contains two chapters, each of which is broken up into several sections ("Members") and numbered subsections. In the first chapter, Amo sets out the definitions of many of the technical terms he will use in his argument, including "spirit," "human mind," and "perception." The second chapter then presents the main argument for his thesis, namely, that sensation and the faculty of sensing lie in the body rather than the mind.

Extract 1.3: Amo's On the Impassivity of the Human Mind

Chapter I

Of the impassivity of the human mind, we understand: the absence of perception and the ability to perceive in the human mind. . . .

Member I

. . .

Section I

What kind of thing is spirit?

That the human mind is a spirit, is a revelation that is truly certain, thus we need to understand what we mean when we call something a "spirit." To us a spirit is, a substance of pure activity, immaterial, has understanding within itself, and acts voluntarily out of its intentions, on the basis of its conscious aims or ends.

Note I. To understand and to become conscious of anybody or any thing is synonymous.

Note II. By intention, we understand; that operation of the spirit, by which we can become conscious of something that can be used to achieve an aim.

Note III. The aim is that which the soul is quietened and is free of its preceding work when it has been presently attained.

Exposition of the preceding description of the spirit

Exposition I. I say that the substantial essence of a spirit is pure activity, insofar as you may also say this: the spirit itself does not admit of any passions.

On the proof of this statement

If the spirit perceives, or admits any passions into itself, then it may be asserted such activities must take place through the spirit being communicable with, or penetrable, or in fact touched.

Note I. By *communication*, I understand: when its parts, distinctive properties or effects, by means of a certain action, can become present in an appropriate or proportional way in another being.

Example. In the way a fire can pass its heat onto a glowing iron, though we do not see the communication of itself.

Note II. By penetration, I understand: The passage through the parts of one being by another by means of a certain action.

Note III. By being touched, our immediate perception teaches us [what that means]; but lest we may be seen to speak words without ideas, by *touch*, I understand: when two surfaces touch each other mutually at some physical or perceptible point.

Applications

Assertion I. All spirits exist apart from all passions.

Reason I. With regard to another being's parts, properties and effects, none of them are able to become present in another particular spirit by a mediating action; otherwise, the other spirit may be contained by this spirit in its essence and substance, something which it ought not to contain. Besides, it is a material concept to contain and to be contained, thus we are not able to truthfully assert this of a spirit. Therefore, a spirit cannot perceive through such communication, i.e. the material parts, properties, and effects of a being would become present there by means of some action.

Reason II. No spirit, either through itself or through its accidents, receives material and perceptible parts, properties and effects, as it is in fact contrary or opposite to perceptible being; but between contrary opposites, nothing can be given or communicated. . .

I have said that a spirit cannot perceive or undergo passions through communication; to continue.

Assertion II. No spirit perceives or undergoes passions through the manner of penetration, because penetration is: the passage of a being between the parts of another being; but no spirit enjoys the use of constituent parts; Therefore; [a spirit] is outside all passions, to the extent that a passion can happen through the manner of penetration, or through the passage between the parts of another being.

Assertion III. Nor does a spirit perceive or undergo passions through contact; for whatever touches and is touched by a body is a body. . . Likewise contact is when two surfaces mutually touch at some physical point; we are not able to predicate either a perceptible point, nor a surface, of a spirit, therefore it can have no passion, insofar as such could come about through contact . . .

Note. Although I may not know the manner with which God and other non-material spirits understand themselves, their own operations, or other things, yet it seems probable to me that they do not understand things through ideas; as an idea is: a momentary operation of our mind, which itself represents or poses as present a thing that had previous been taken hold of by perception and the sense organs. Indeed, they are not in God and other posited non-material spirits, which do not have sensations, nor sense-organs, nor a living, organic body. Likewise, there is no representation in God, for otherwise a representation of the future, the past or absent things might be granted to God; and yet in God there cannot be granted knowledge of the past and future, nor of absent things; but all things are present within his cognition, therefore it is not granted to him through representation; because a representation presupposes an absent thing that requires to be represented. It follows consequently that for God and other spirits, themselves, their own operations and other things are understood without any ideas or remembered perceptions, but our minds understand and work through ideas, on account of our close link and relationship with our body . . .

Statement III. All spirits act with their own free will, i.e. internally, its own actions are determined towards particular ends, and not forced from elsewhere to act.

Reason. If a spirit may be forced from elsewhere, it might be so either of by a forcing spirit or by matter. If by another spirit, the spontaneity, or ability to freely act and react, remains safe in both. If forced by matter, this is unable to happen to a spirit, because it is always active, whereas matter is always passive, and undertakes all actions in itself from an agent.

Statement IV. A spirit acts out of intentions, i.e. from previous knowledge of things which ought to be done, related to a goal that can follow from its own actions.

Reason. Indeed, in this consists the nature of an action, by something that acts from rationality and understanding . . .

Section III

A description of the human mind as a type

The human mind is a purely active and immaterial substance, which is involved with a closely-related living and organic body, [and is thereby able] to understand and act on account of intentions which determines it to conscious ends.

Note I. The relation between body and mind consists in these: 1) the spirit may use the body as a subject on its behalf, 2) and as a mediating instrument for its own actions.

Note II. Instrument and medium differ in this; the instrument is applied practically for the sake of the end, and the medium is used theoretically to pursue the end. . . .

Member II

. . .

Section I

Explanation of what perception is

Generally speaking, perception is: being really affected by immediately present and material things, with regard to their sensible properties, through our sense-organs . . .

Section II

What our faculty of perception is

With these easily-described premises regarding the faculty of perception, it is certainly the case that: our living and organic body is of such an arrangement that the animal may be affected by immediately-present material and sensible things.

Note. This perceptual faculty was called by the ancients the sensitive soul, by which it was explained as distinct from the rational and vegetable soul. . . .

Chapter II

Containing applications of those things deduced extensively in the preceding

The state of the debate.

A man does not perceive material things by the mind, but by the living and organic body. This is said and defended against that opinion of Descartes' in: the *Letters*, Part I, Letter 29, where he has it that: "For two things are in the human soul, on which the whole cognition depends, insofar as it is possible for it to have [cognition] of its own nature, either as that one [thing] which thinks, or alternatively as that thing which is able to be unified with a body, with which it can *act* and *suffer*."

To which words, we therefore teach and dissent: that the mind acts with the body by means of a mutual union, we concede; but we deny that it suffers with the body. . . .

Thesis I. Negative.

The human mind is not affected by perceptible things.

Statement. The proposition means the same as if it were said: the human mind is not affected by perceptible things, even though it may be things presently proximate to its own body in which it is contained; but the perceptions that arise in the body, are [first] discerned, and then understood by being brought into its own operations . . .

Demonstration I of Thesis. Whatever perceives, that thing lives; whatever lives, is nourished; whatever lives and is nourished, grows; whatever exists in this manner, in the end lays open its own first principles; whatever lays open its own first principles, is from first principles; all things that are from first principles have their own constituent parts; whatever exists in this manner, is a divisible body; consequently if a human mind itself perceives in this way, it follows that it is a divisible body.

Demonstration II of Thesis. No spirit perceives material things; and yet the human mind is a spirit, therefore it does not perceive material things.

The greater demonstration [is from] Chapter I, Member I, Section I, Explanation I, with notes and applications underneath. The minor [demonstration] admits of no contradiction.

Note I. To live and to sense are two inseparable predicates, for this reason, by transposition: all that lives necessarily senses, and all that senses necessarily lives; thus, the presence of the one will necessarily imply the presence of the other. . . .

Section II.

Thesis II. Nor is the faculty of perception contained within the mind.

Demonstration. That which is capable of the circulation of blood, is that which is capable of the principle of life; that which is capable of this, also has the faculty of perception. But the body is capable of the circulation of blood and the principle of life . . . [It] follows, that the principle of life and the faculty of perception are not in the mind; but coincide in the body. . . .

Section III.

Thesis III. Therefore, perception and the faculty of perception coincide in the body.

Demonstration. Perception and faculty of perception either coincides with the mind or the body. But not the mind, which has been extensively deduced, and so the body; see the demonstrations of theses I and II.

Final note. The goal of composing this discourse were [answering] opposing opinions . . . lest we may not confound those things which, respectively, come together within, and diverge into, the body and the mind. For indeed whatever consists unmixed in the operations of the mind, is solely in the mind; but truly whatever presupposes perception and the faculty of perception, involving material concepts, is granted entirely to the body. *END.*

[Anton Wilhelm Amo, Inaugural Philosophical Dissertation on the Impassivity of the Human Mind (Wittenberg: Schlomach, 1734). Translation by Jonathan Head.]

The opening chapter makes it clear that Amo embraces substance dualism: the human mind is a spirit, and a spirit is a "purely active and immaterial substance"; its activity consists in the fact that it is constantly thinking and acting for the sake of some intended end or goal. The body, however, is a purely passive, material substance. While bodies do communicate motion to one another, they are not strictly *acting* on one another when they do this. When a tree branch breaks a window during a storm, it is tempting to see the tree branch as acting on the window. Yet, for Amo (and many authors following Descartes's lead), the tree branch is itself merely passively transmitting motion that was previously transmitted to it. The tree branch—and indeed any material substance whatsoever—never initiates any action.

By contrast, the mind is purely active. Like all spirits, the mind is a substance engaged in "understanding and operating spontaneously and intentionally." It is a thinking substance, as Descartes has it, but Amo wants to emphasize the point that all thought involves both spontaneity and intentionality. To say that the mind operates *spontaneously* means that it is wholly self-determined. As Amo puts it, the mind "is not compelled by anything else at all to operate"; that is, no external substance determines the mind to form the ideas or conscious states that unfold within it. And to say that the mind operates *intentionally* means that the mind's activities are guided by some conscious goal or end state—a state that, as Amo writes, "it intends to attain through its operation."

The requirement that all the operations of the mind must be spontaneous and intentional is shockingly strict. Among other things, it implies that the mind cannot have any unconscious thoughts, since the operations of the mind are supposed to be guided by an end that is conscious. There may, of course, be extremely obscure and confused ideas that the mind is only dimly aware of. For instance, in reading this paragraph, you become conscious of the number of sentences it contains. However, since that knowledge is peripheral to your goals, it remains obscure in your mind. Such thoughts might sometimes be so obscure that they seem unconscious. However, truly unconscious thought is, on this picture, impossible.

Still, in attributing these properties to the mind's operations, Amo is largely in alignment with then-common Cartesian views about the mind. The position that all thought is conscious may strike us as odd today, but it seems to have been accepted by Descartes as well as many of his followers. In fact, the possibility of unconscious thought was even rejected by a number of historical figures who have traditionally been portrayed as bitter enemies of Cartesian philosophy: John Locke, for instance, holds that if a thought is not conscious to you, then it cannot properly be *your* thought.

Yet the general lesson that Amo wishes to draw from this picture of the mind goes far beyond the standard Cartesian position. For Amo, "All spirits exist apart from all passions." To understand his meaning here, it is important to note that **passion**† is a technical term. It is used by philosophers in the early modern period to refer to a state that is brought about in one thing by the action of another. A passion, in this sense, is literally a *passive state*. This notion is thus much broader than the meaning that the term has today. Emotions *are* passions, in this sense, since they typically arise without spontaneity in response to external factors. However, not all passions are emotions. Indeed, the kind of passion in which Amo is most keenly interested is not emotion, but *sense perception*.

Why does Amo take sensations to qualify as passions? Consider an example such as the visual sensation of a penguin that you have when you see one at a zoo. Amo has it that this sensation is produced when your eyes are "affected . . . by the sensible properties" of the penguin—the texture of its feathers, the shape of its body, the color of its beak, and the like. Obviously these things don't *immediately* affect your eyes, but they initiate the relevant part of the causal chain that eventually leads to your visual sensation. Now, given that your sensation is produced by the properties of the penguin affecting your sense organs, your sensation of the penguin is neither spontaneous (since it is determined externally) nor intentional (since its appearance does not depend on your purpose). And, of course, there's nothing special about the example of the penguin; Amo takes similar reasoning to apply to all sensations. Sensation requires one's sense organs to be affected by the sensible properties of an external body. For this reason, sensations are inevitably passive states, or passions.

With all of this in the background, we can now turn to Amo's main argument, which is set out in Chapter 2 of his dissertation. In outline, the argument is straightforward:

(1) The mind is not affected by sensible things.
(2) The faculty (or power) of sense perception is not in the mind.
(3) So, sensation and the faculty of sense perception belong to the body.

The conclusion, line (3), follows by logic from lines (1) and (2) when these premises are supplemented with Amo's claim that sense perception inheres either "with the mind or the body." This supplementary premise is based, presumably, on Amo's belief that the concepts of *spirit* and *body* are logical contraries. If something is not immaterial, he argues, then it is material; and if it is not material, then it is immaterial. Thus, once it is established that no immaterial being, or spirit, is the subject of sensation, it follows that the subjects of sensation must instead be material beings, or bodies.

This still leaves us with the remaining question—and it is a serious one—of why Amo endorses premises (1) and (2) in the first place. Most of his efforts to justify his reasoning are directed at establishing premise (1). He provides three related proofs of the claim that the mind is not affected by sensible things (two of which are included in this extract). The first proof is based on the key assumption that having sensations and being alive are "inseparable predicates": if something has sensations, then it is alive; and if something is alive, then it has sensations. Perhaps the more interesting of the two is the first proof. There, Amo observes that *being alive* involves biological processes of nourishment and growth, and anything that can undergo these processes must be composed of parts. After all, nourishment consists in replacing or supplementing the parts of an organism, and growth requires adding new parts to an organism. Yet spirits, including the human mind, are not composed of parts. So they are not alive—and so, finally, they do not have sensations.

This proof passes a bit too quickly over the question of *why* we ought to accept the assumption that anything that has sensations must be alive. One possible explanation comes from Amo's definition of sense perception, according to which sensations are generated when an individual is "really affected, through our sense organs" by the sensible properties of a body that is present. Amo might have assumed, reasonably enough, that only living things can have sensory organs. If so, then it would indeed follow that only living things can have sensations. (Or perhaps this is too quick. What is the principled difference between the sensory organs of the human body and the robotic sensors of the Mars rover?)

It is also worth summarizing Amo's second proof that the mind is not affected by sensible things. This proof, unlike the first and third, does *not* draw on the inseparability of living and sensing. Although the proof itself is brief, this is because it draws on much of the groundwork laid earlier in the dissertation (and discussed earlier in this section). It has already been established that the human mind is a spirit, and, like all spirits, not subject to any passions. We have also seen that sensation is a type of passion. Drawing on these points, Amo observes, it follows that the human mind cannot have sensations.

All of this reasoning is provided in service to what Amo calls his "negative" thesis, that the human mind is not affected by sensible things. As we have seen, his arguments rely crucially on two central assumptions: that the human mind is not composed of parts and that it is not subject to any passions. Yet even after tracing the reasoning from these assumptions to Amo's conclusion, it remains somewhat unclear how Amo understands the process of sensation. Return to our earlier example of the penguin at the zoo. If your visual sensation of the penguin is a state (or "affection") of your body only, but is *not* present in your mind, how is it that you come to be conscious of it? Fortunately, several passages from the dissertation shed light on how Amo thinks the human mind relates to bodily sensations.

One important passage along these lines occurs during Amo's concise discussion of the union of the mind and body in §3 of Chapter 1, Member 1. There he writes, "The relation between body and mind consists in these: (1) the spirit may use the body as a subject on its behalf, (2) and as a mediating instrument for its own actions." Neither of these essential features of the mind-body union has the body acting on the mind. This confirms that, on Amo's view, the mind's connection with the body can *only* be an active one. The mind's influence on the body is a one-way street, and the body simply has no power to affect the mind. So, our conscious experience of sensation must be the result of the mind acting on the body.

A second, even more illuminating passage appears in a note appended to Chapter 1, Assertion 3. In this note, Amo compares human and divine cognition: he speculates that divine cognition, as opposed to human cognition, does not rely on ideas. While explaining his reasons for this view, he observes that an idea is "a momentary operation of our mind, which itself represents or poses as present a thing that had previous been taken hold of by perception and the sense organs." The mind doesn't passively receive sensations. Rather, the body passively receives sensations, and then the mind actively forms mental representations or ideas of the content of those sensations.

Taken together, these passages suggest that the process Amo believes is involved in sensory cognition looks like this:

(i) The sensible qualities of a present material object affect your sense organs.
(ii) A corresponding sensation is (passively) produced in your body.
(iii) Your mind (actively) produces an idea that represents the sensed object.

Let's return one final time to our penguin—what happens when you look at it? On Amo's account, the story goes like this. The penguin's sensible qualities affect your eyes, which causes your body to have a sensation. Up to this point in the story, the sensation is not strictly speaking a sensation "of" the penguin. It is *caused* by the penguin, but it is also caused by many other things—the light source in the room, the paint on the walls, the shape of your eye, and so on. Thus, the fact that the penguin is one of these many causes wouldn't be enough to make the sensation a representation of the penguin in particular. However, your mind then *uses* this sensation to produce, spontaneously and intentionally, an idea that represents the penguin in particular.

Though Amo's position that the mind is never subject to passions is a serious constraint on his account of sensation, it also leads him to a fascinating and creative account of sense perception. The mind does not passively receive the data of sensation, but plays an active role in constructing its own conscious awareness of sensible objects. The mind is both artist and canvas; raw sensation is merely its medium.

Suggested Further Reading

Menn, Stephen. "The Argument of the *Impassivity* and the *Distinct Idea*." In *Anton Wilhelm Amo's Philosophical Dissertations on Mind and Body*, edited and translated by S. Menn and J. E. H. Smith, 101–47. New York: Oxford University Press, 2020.

Meyns, Chris. "Anton Wilhelm Amo's Philosophy of Mind." *Philosophy Compass* 14, no. 3 (2019): 1–13.

Sephocle, Marilyn. "Anton Wilhelm Amo." *Journal of Black Studies* 23, no. 2 (1992): 182–7.

Walsh, Julie. "Amo on the Heterogeneity Problem." *Philosophers' Imprint* 19, no. 41 (2019): 1–18.

Key Points

- Amo takes the mind to be a wholly active, immaterial substance, and he takes the body to be a wholly passive, material substance.
- The mind is active in the sense that its operations are *spontaneous* (or self-determined) and *intentional* (guided by some end or goal).
- Amo's central thesis is that, contrary to the way we commonly speak, the human mind does not have sensations.
- On Amo's alternative account of sensory cognition, the body first passively receives a sensation, which the mind then uses to actively construct the idea of a sensible object.

Questions for Reflection

- Do you agree with Descartes that you could conceivably exist without a body or brain? What would that existence be like?
- Descartes and Amo believe the mind is not composed of parts, while More holds that it does. Do you think the mind is composed of parts? If it has parts, what would they consist of?
- Amo argues that our experience of sensed objects requires the mind to actively construct representations of those objects. Can you think of any specific cases in which our sensory knowledge seems to go beyond our sensations themselves?

2

The Mind-Body Problem: René Descartes and Elisabeth of Bohemia

Chapter Outline

2a. Elisabeth's Mind-Body Problem 45
2b. Descartes on the "Primitive Notion" of Mind-Body Union 52
Questions for Reflection 62

Each of the authors discussed in the previous chapter—Descartes, More, and Amo—denies that the mind is a material or physical entity. As we have now seen, although these authors disagree with one another about various details regarding precisely how your mind is related to your brain and body, they all agree that a proper understanding of a human being requires us to treat the mind and brain as two distinct things. Your mind is not your brain, nor is it any part or process within your brain.

To say that the mind and brain are two distinct things is in part to say that they have different properties. On the picture developed by Descartes, one of the most influential views in the early modern period, the mind is essentially an immaterial, thinking substance, while the brain and body are essentially material, unthinking substances. The human brain is spatially extended, with a particular weight (about three pounds), texture (soft and squishy), and shape (something like a large walnut). The mind, by contrast, is not spatially extended at all, according to Descartes. It has no particular weight, texture, or shape.

Typically, the physical properties that a material object has—its shape, mass, density, and so on—are a crucial factor for predicting and explaining its causal interaction with other things. That is, to understand the effects that one material object will produce in another, we need to know something about the physical properties of both objects. For example, to explain what happens when we strike a human brain with a tennis racket, we need to appeal to the physical characteristics of the racket and of the brain. Not *every* physical property would be salient in the explanation of the (messy) result. The color of the racket won't matter, for instance. But if we were entirely ignorant of the physical properties either of the brain or of the racket, we would have no possible avenue to either predict or explain their interaction.

These observations suggest a problem for **substance dualism**†. For Descartes, the mind and body are distinct entities that causally interact with one another: the mind receives sensations and images from the body, and the body is moved by acts of will (or **volitions**†) in the mind. Now, as we've just seen, when two objects are supposed to interact, any suitable explanation of the result must draw on the physical properties of both interacting objects. Yet, on this view, the mind *has* no physical properties. Thus, it appears, there is no possible explanation of the interaction between the mind and the brain or body. This is the **mind-body problem**†.

Contemporary philosophers sometimes frame the mind-body problem as a paradox, a set of independently plausible premises that is mutually unacceptable or contradictory:

(1) The mind has no physical properties.
(2) The mind interacts with material objects (the brain/body).
(3) Interacting with material objects requires physical properties.[1]

This is a logically inconsistent set of claims; if any two are true, the other must be false. However, in its earliest historical incarnations in the early modern period, the problem is posed as an *explanatory demand*, and that is the formulation of the problem we will primarily focus on here. While it's not impossible that an immaterial substance interacts with a material one, it's also just not clear how the interaction is supposed to work. By what mechanism does a volition of the mind push the springs of the body? What explains the fact that your body and brain respond appropriately when you decide (i.e., your mind wills) to stand up and stretch?

In this chapter, we examine one of the earliest recorded discussions of the mind-body problem, raised by Princess Elisabeth of Bohemia in her correspondence with Descartes. As we shall see, even Descartes's best account of mind-body interaction still leaves many questions unanswered. Chapters 3 and 4 discuss prominent alternatives to the Cartesian approach that were developed in the late sixteenth and early seventeenth centuries.

2A. ELISABETH'S MIND-BODY PROBLEM

> ### Princess Elisabeth of Bohemia: Brief chronology
>
> - 1618: Born in Heidelberg.
> - 1619: Elisabeth's father, Frederick V, is crowned king of Bohemia.
> - 1620: After military defeat, Frederick and his family flees to Brandenburg.
> - 1621: Frederick and his wife move to The Hague. (Elisabeth and several siblings remain at Brandenburg until the late 1620s, when they rejoin their parents.)
> - 1633: King Wladislaw of Poland (a Catholic) proposes marriage. Negotiations ensue.
> - 1635: Elisabeth refuses to convert to Catholicism, so the marriage does not proceed.
> - 1643: Reads Descartes's *Meditations* and initiates correspondence with him.
> - 1644: Descartes dedicates his *Principles of Philosophy* to Elisabeth.
> - 1649: At Elisabeth's bidding, Descartes composes the *Passions of the Soul*, an examination of the psychology of emotions.
> - 1650: Descartes dies in Stockholm.
> - 1660: Enters the Lutheran convent at Herford. Her cousin, Elizabeth Louise, is the abbess.
> - 1667: Her cousin dies, and Elisabeth becomes abbess of the convent.
> - 1676-77: Quakers including Robert Barclay and William Penn visit the convent, trying unsuccessfully to persuade Elisabeth to convert.
> - 1680: Dies at the Herford convent.

Princess Elisabeth of Bohemia (Elisabeth Simmern van Pallandt) was the daughter of Frederick V and Elizabeth Stuart, prince-elector and electress of the Palatinate in the Holy Roman Empire. When Elisabeth was still a child, her family's critical role in the events leading to the Thirty Years' War led to their exile from their homeland. She spent most of her youth in Brandenburg and, later, The Hague. In spite of her exile, she became acquainted with a number of prominent mathematicians, philosophers, scientists, and political figures, some of whom she corresponded with at length. Her correspondents included Constantijn Huygens, Robert Barclay, William Penn, Nicolas Malebranche, and—most significantly—René Descartes.

In 1643, after what appears to have been a careful study of Descartes's *Meditations on First Philosophy*, Elisabeth wrote to him to ask "how the soul of a human being (it being only a thinking substance) can determine the bodily spirits, in order to bring about voluntary actions." This initiated a correspondence that went on, in fits and starts, until Descartes's death roughly seven years later.

The provenance of the surviving copies of Elisabeth's side of the correspondence is odd enough to warrant some discussion.[2] Elisabeth intended her letters to Descartes to remain private. Even in her very first letter to him, she requested that he not share her letters with anyone else. Nevertheless, after Descartes died in 1650, his friend Pierre Chanut hoped to publish a volume that included the correspondence with Elisabeth. Chanut at that point already had Elisabeth's letters, which had remained among Descartes's possessions even after his move to Sweden. He wrote her to ask for permission to publish them. In reply, Elisabeth not only refused to have the letters published, but ordered that her side of the correspondence should be returned to her immediately. Chanut complied. The earliest published collections of Descartes's correspondence did not include Elisabeth's side of their exchanges.

Elisabeth's letters were then lost for the following two centuries. Around 1875, an antiquarian bookseller discovered copies of the letters in the library of a castle associated with Elisabeth's family. Who made these copies? This remains a mystery. It is likely that Chanut secretly made copies of her letters before returning the originals, and that the copies we have today were based on these. (The copies we have today cannot be from Chanut directly: they are drafted on paper that dates to the eighteenth century, well after he could have made his initial copies.) However, much of this is speculative and little more can be said about the surviving documents with any certainty.

We include this information about the mysterious provenance of Elisabeth's letters to emphasize some important differences between these letters and the philosophical texts we examined in the previous chapter. Those texts were all intended for publication and a (relatively) broad audience. Accordingly, the arguments are typically easy to identify, the line of reasoning typically easy to follow. When we examine the letters exchanged by Descartes and Elisabeth, by contrast, the philosophical arguments are interspersed among discussions of more personal, and occasionally political, matters. At times, both authors draw on shared, but unstated, assumptions, which we must make explicit in order to understand their disagreement. To that end, in this chapter we will frequently go beyond mere summary of the letters themselves, drawing also upon other texts that shed additional light on the positions advanced by Descartes and Elisabeth.

Only the first five letters exchanged between the two deal directly with the interaction of mind and body. The excerpts presented here are drawn from those initial letters. We have grouped the letters into two separate extracts: (1) Elisabeth's initial presentation of the mind-body problem and Descartes's proposed solution to it, followed by (2) Elisabeth's restatement of the problem and Descartes's second attempt at addressing it. The second exchange closes with Elisabeth's last word on the mind-body problem, which Descartes never resolves to her satisfaction.

Extract 2.1: Elisabeth's Initial Exchange with Descartes

Elisabeth to Descartes, 6 May 1643

M. Descartes,

I learned, with much joy and regret, of the plan you had to see me a few days ago; I was touched equally by your charity in willing to share yourself with an ignorant and intractable person and by the bad luck that robbed me of such a profitable conversation. . . .

But today M. Palotti has given me such assurance of your goodwill toward everyone, and in particular toward me, that I chased from my mind all considerations other than that of availing myself of it. So I ask you please to tell me how the soul of a human being (it being only a thinking substance) can determine the bodily spirits, in order to bring about voluntary actions. For it seems that all determination of movement happens through the impulsion of the thing moved, by the manner in which it is pushed by that which moves it, or else by the particular qualities and shape of the surface of the latter. Physical contact is required for the first two conditions, extension for the third. You entirely exclude the one [extension] from the notion you have of the soul, and the other [physical contact] appears to me incompatible with an immaterial being. This is why I ask you for a more precise definition of the soul than the one you give in your *Metaphysics*, that is to say, of its substance separate from its action, that is, from thought. For even if we were to suppose them inseparable (which is however difficult to prove in the mother's womb and in great fainting spells) as are the attributes of God, we could, in considering them apart, acquire a more perfect idea of them. . . .

Your affectionate friend at your service,

Elisabeth.

Descartes to Elisabeth, 21 May 1643

Madame,

... I can say in truth that the question your Highness proposes seems to me that which, in view of my published writings, one can most rightly ask me.... I will try here to explain the manner in which I conceive of the union of the soul with the body and how the soul has the power [*force*] to move it.

First, I consider that there are in us certain primitive notions that are like originals on the pattern of which we form all our other knowledge. There are only very few of these notions; for, after the most general—those of being, number, and duration, etc.—which apply to all that we can conceive, we have, for the body in particular, only the notion of extension ...; and for the soul alone, we have only that of thought ...; and finally, for the soul and body together, we have only that of their union, on which depends that of the power the soul has to move the body and the body to act on the soul, in causing its sensations and passions.

... I believe that we have heretofore confused the notion of the power with which the soul acts on the body with the power with which one body acts on another ... For example, in supposing that heaviness is a real quality, of which we have no other knowledge but that it has the power to move a body in which it is toward the center of the earth, we have no difficulty in conceiving how it moves the body, nor how it is joined to it; and we do not think that this happens through a real contact of one surface against another, for we experience in ourselves that we have a specific notion for conceiving that; and I think that we use this notion badly, in applying it to heaviness, which, as I hope to demonstrate in my Physics, is nothing really distinct from body. But I do think that it was given to us for conceiving the way in which the soul moves the body....

Your Highness's very humble and obedient servant,

Descartes.

[From L. Shapiro (ed.), The Correspondence between Princess Elisabeth of Bohemia and René Descartes (Chicago: University of Chicago Press, 2007)].

Mind-body interaction presents philosophical difficulties in both directions: the difficulty arises whether we ask how the mind is able to affect the body or how the body is able to affect the mind. In her first letter to Descartes,

Elisabeth specifically focuses on the mind-to-body version of the problem. How is it that, by an act of will, an immaterial substance (your mind) is able to cause a material substance (your body) to move?

Elisabeth considers three factors that might figure in a suitable causal explanation of a body's motion, then dismisses each as inapplicable in the case of mind-body interaction. When one object, A, causes another, B, to move, the three factors that determine *how* object B moves are (1) the "impulsion" of B by A, (2) "the manner in which [B] is pushed" by A, and (3) "the particular qualities and shape of the surface" of A. Presumably the shape of B would also be relevant, but Elisabeth is more concerned here with the shape of the mov<u>er</u> than with the mov<u>ed</u> object. Her point, at any rate, is that at least *one* of these three factors must be available to us if we wish to explain the motion that A produces in B. Indeed, it seems in ordinary cases we appeal to all three factors. For instance—to use a slightly more conventional example than a human brain—imagine that a tennis ball, flying at great speed across the court, is struck by a racket. The ball then returns across the court, still flying at great speed. Why did it do that? The following observations all seem relevant: (1) the racket struck the ball, (2) the angle of the racket was perpendicular to the ball's path when they collided, and (3) the racket's surface was relatively flat (rather than curved) and elastic (rather than hard, fragile, liquid, and so on). These correspond to the three factors that Elisabeth lists.

The problem is that none of these three factors are present in the case of mind-body interaction. Suppose you (your mind) will yourself to stand up, and this causes you (your body) to stand. In this interaction, your mind does not literally *collide* with your body or brain. In consequence, neither of the first two factors is applicable: they both require that the interacting objects come into physical contact with one another. What about the third factor, the "particular qualities and shape of the surface" of the mover? Here, too, Descartes's position rules out the possibility of appealing to such things to explain mind-body interaction. The mind simply has none of the relevant qualities—shape, size, and so on.

The challenge is a serious one. Though Elisabeth's letter was penned almost 400 years ago, her concerns about substance dualism still resonate today. However, it is important to recognize several philosophical and scientific assumptions that are involved in this specific framing of the problem.

First, this presupposes that causal explanations of physical effects must be mechanical. That is, such explanations must appeal solely to

- mechanical <u>properties</u>, such as *shape, size, quantity,* and *motion,* and
- mechanical <u>relations</u>, such as *parthood* and *collision*.

Call this the *mechanical view of causation*. This was a popular idea early in the seventeenth century, and it was advanced by a number of influential early modern scientists (or, as they preferred to call themselves, "natural philosophers"), such as Galileo Galilei (1564–1642). However, this view is not generally shared by philosophers or scientists today. For example, the moon's orbit around the earth is explained in terms of the force of gravity, but this force is non-mechanical: it attracts the two bodies to one another, even though they are not in contact. So, not all causal relationships are properly understood on the model of mechanical interaction. Still, though the mechanical view of causation is incorrect in the details, it is based on a goal that we might yet find appealing. Elisabeth takes mechanical causal interaction to be a model of intelligibility. When two bodies with known mechanical properties collide, there is no mystery in what happens next, no questions about how that physical system will evolve over time that are in principle unanswerable. The intelligibility of such interactions is codified in the natural laws that govern them.

Compare this with the case of mind-body interaction on the Cartesian picture. You will yourself to stand up, then you stand up. By analogy with the case of the collision of two bodies, we might hope that the resulting state of your body is intelligible and predictable on the basis of features of (i) the previous state of your body, and (ii) the volition or act of will that initiated the motion. Indeed, we might hope to spell out a collection of laws that governs mind-body interaction. Such hopes are dashed as soon as we start to consider what would be involved in this project. Did you stand lazily, with a weary sigh, or quickly and excitedly? It depends on your volition. Yet this generalization is clearly uninformative, falling far short of the standard set by the laws that govern the interaction of two bodies. And—this is the real problem—it is not at all clear how to fill in the missing details, given the picture of the mind we have from Descartes. Your volition to stand up is a particular thought in your mind, what Descartes calls a "mode" of your mind. Like all modes of your mind, it is spatially unextended; it is not located in space at all. Given this picture, it is not even clear why a volition in *your* mind should not cause *someone else's* body to respond! Thus, although there does seem to be some causal connection between <u>what you will to do</u> and <u>what you do</u>, the connection seems unintelligible if the mind and body are understood in the Cartesian way.

A second assumption Elisabeth makes here is also worth flagging. Since she takes the mechanical view of causation to provide the appropriate model for understanding the mind's interactions with the body, her challenge to Descartes also presupposes that the living human body is to be understood in purely mechanical terms, just like any other physical object. She presupposes, that is, that the living human body considered in itself has no spiritual component or aspect: any suitable explanation of how the human body moves must be given in purely mechanical terms, just as we would account for the motions of a clock. Call this the *mechanical view of life*.

While this view of the human body as nothing more than a sophisticated biological machine might seem like a surprising assumption (and we shall see that later philosophers do not always accept it), it is unsurprising in context. Descartes himself is clear that he accepts the mechanical view of life, and he is generally hostile to the idea that there are any deep differences between the explanations we give for natural bodies, such as a living human body, and artifacts such as clocks. In a telling passage, he writes, "[I]t is no less natural for a clock constructed with this or that set of wheels to tell the time than it is for a tree which grew from this or that seed to produce the appropriate fruit."[3] And in a later work, the *Passions of the Soul*:

> [L]et us recognize that the difference between the body of a living man and that of a dead man is just like the difference between, on the one hand, a watch or other automaton (that is, a self-moving machine) when it is wound up and contains in itself the corporeal principle of the movements for which it is designed, together with everything else required for its operation; and, on the other hand, the same watch or machine when it is broken.[4]

Passages such as these indicate Descartes's mechanical view of life. The difference between a living human body and a sophisticated machine, such as a robot, is not that some special spark of life is imbued in the human body but absent from the robot. If the robot is sophisticated enough, there might *be* no physical difference between the two bodies. The difference is only that the living human body is bound up in union with a mind, or thinking substance, while the robot is not.

We have seen, then, that Descartes endorses both the mechanical view of causation and the mechanical view of life. Thus, when Elisabeth frames the mind-body problem using these views, she is highlighting the way that Descartes's own principles lead to the difficulty at issue. This makes the problem even more serious for Descartes. It is his very own philosophical commitments that generate the problem; so, to solve the problem, he seems to be forced to give up or at least to modify some of his philosophical views.

2B. DESCARTES ON THE "PRIMITIVE NOTION" OF MIND-BODY UNION

Notably, Elisabeth frames the problem in a way that suggests she is genuinely open to possible solutions. It is perhaps because of this that Descartes takes the problem seriously for the first time. Elisabeth was not the first to pose questions in this vein to Descartes. Prior to the publication of his *Meditations*, Descartes tasked his friend, Marin Mersenne, to solicit objections to Descartes's work from a number of prominent intellectuals. He then drafted replies to these objections and published both the objections and his replies as a kind of lengthy appendix to the *Meditations*. And already in these objections, the seeds of the mind-body problem have been planted. Pierre Gassendi, author of the fifth set of objections, writes:

> How can something corporeal take hold of something incorporeal so as to keep it joined to itself? And how can the incorporeal grasp the corporeal to keep it reciprocally bound to itself, if it has nothing at all to enable it to grasp or be grasped?[5]

But Descartes does not yet take the challenge seriously when he pens his reply to Gassendi:

> At no point do you produce objections to my arguments; you merely put forward doubts that you think follow from my conclusions, though in fact they merely arise from your desire to call in the imagination to examine matters which are not within its proper province.[6]

Rather than addressing the problem, he dismisses it.

Other early formulations of the mind-body problem draw on principles that Descartes himself would not have accepted. One noteworthy example of this can be seen in the work of the skeptical philosopher Simon Foucher (1644–96). A number of historians of philosophy have pointed to Foucher's writings as providing an early and influential version of the problem.[7] Foucher's main concern, however, was not the explanation of voluntary motion. Rather, he was concerned with the point that Cartesian principles appear to make it impossible for the mind to represent spatially extended bodies. Foucher writes:

> For . . . all our ideas are only ways of being of our soul. We know immediately and truly only these ideas . . . But it is always our soul, and since [for the

Cartesians] our soul has nothing in it that is *like* matter and extended beings, it is difficult to conceive how it could represent anything other than its own ideas.[8]

This worry is related to the mind-body problem, but Foucher's concern here is in the first instance about *representation*. If an idea is a state of the soul (or mind), and the soul is not spatially extended, how could an idea possibly represent something that *is* spatially extended? (Of course, if the mind cannot even represent the body, it will be that much more difficult to explain mind-body interaction in turn.)

Foucher's assumption here is that, in order for one thing, A, to represent another thing, B, it is necessary that A and B must bear some likeness to one another. Philosophically, this assumption is so general as to be somewhat dubious. The word "blue" doesn't resemble the color it represents. The pieces on a game board may represent the players of the game without bearing any real similarity to them. And it seems possible that paintings may represent concepts or moods without directly depicting them: the most famous paintings of the abstract expressionist Mark Rothko consist of large blocks of color, but they convey a wide range of emotions.

Perhaps more importantly, it is unlikely that Descartes would have assented to this assumption in the first place. One of the features of Cartesian ideas is that they can represent objects without being like those objects. When you think about a tree, you don't need to have anything in your mind that itself has the shape, size, or parts that that tree has. In Cartesian terminology, your idea of the tree contains that tree's properties "objectively" but not "formally": the idea *represents* those properties, but it does not *have* those properties. So, there is in general no need (on Descartes's view) for representations to bear a likeness to their objects. In consequence, Foucher's version of the mind-body problem—which takes aim at the very possibility of minds representing bodies—is premised upon assumptions Descartes does not share.

Elisabeth's version of the mind-body problem does not share the flaws of these other early presentations of the problem by Gassendi and Foucher. And so, perhaps because Elisabeth's presentation of the problem indicates that she is genuinely interested in a solution, or perhaps because her letter is clearly based on Descartes's own principles, his initial reply to Elisabeth (in Extract 2.1) is lengthy and informative. He begins by describing three "primitive notions" that we draw on to understand different kinds of phenomena. The first of these is a primitive notion of spatial extension, which is what we apply when we form knowledge of bodies and their causal relationships with one another. This notion is primitive in the sense that it does not require any other concept. In order to understand what happens when a tennis racket collides with a ball, you need to draw on your primitive notion of spatial extension; the ideas you have of the racket, the ball, and their collision, all depend on that primitive notion. (This conceptual dependence is asymmetrical: you can understand spatial extension without knowing anything about tennis.)

The second primitive notion is of thought, which we apply when we form knowledge of minds, ideas, and their relationships with one another. This, presumably, is the notion that on Descartes's view allows us to recognize the faculties or powers of the mind. It also allows us to discern whether an idea is caused by us. For instance, if you close your eyes and will yourself to calculate the sum of 7 and 5, your volition is clearly a cause of the resulting thought. Your volition explains why you formed that thought. However, this causal relationship is—also clearly—not of the same kind as the mechanical interaction between two colliding bodies. None of the properties that matter in a mechanical explanation are relevant here. So, Descartes thinks, this is the work of a different primitive notion (thinking), and a different kind of causation falling under that primitive notion.

The first two primitive notions, then, concern the two domains that we saw Descartes was keen to carve out in the *Meditations* (discussed in 1.1). There is the domain of the physical, characterized in terms of spatial extension and its modes, subject to mechanical causation. And there is the domain of the mental, characterized in terms of thought and its modes, in which the mind's volitions can (non-mechanically) cause it to form and attend to certain ideas. The third primitive notion, however, is that of the union between the human mind and the human body, a bridge between these two separate domains.

Descartes's claim that we have a *primitive* idea of the union between our mind and our body is surprising. Just as the primitive notions of thought and extension are independent of one another, the implication here is that our notion of the mind-body union is independent of both the idea of mind and the idea of body. That sounds odd: How could I understand the causal relationship between my thoughts and my body's actions without drawing on my understanding of my thoughts and my body?

One way to make sense of Descartes's position here is to reflect on some instances of the causal relationships that, on his view, fall under these three primitive notions. Here are three examples:

(a) The wind blows the branch of a tree, causing the branch to bend.
(b) While solving a math problem, you prove that $x > 0$; this causes you to believe that $x > 0$.
(c) You decide to do push-ups; this causes you to get down on the ground and do push-ups.

Descartes's thought seems to be that each of these three scenarios describes a perfectly intelligible instance of causation, but that each involves a different *kind* of causal relationship. In case (a), Descartes takes the interaction to consist in the communication of a quantity of motion from one body (the wind) to another (the branch). This communication of motion is determined entirely by the laws of nature and does not reflect any genuine activity or agency in bodies themselves.

By contrast, in case (b), the interaction consists in the clarity and distinctness of your thoughts securing the agreement of your will. In general, the fact that your intellect represents something does not (for Descartes) entail that you must believe or affirm it as true. For example, when you think about the plot of a work of fiction, your intellect represents a series of events, but you don't necessarily believe that those events occurred. In this case, though, your intellect represents a mathematical truth ($x > 0$) very clearly and distinctly. (This clarity and distinctness is provided by the proof itself: a proof allows your intellect to move from premises you clearly and distinctly understand, step by step, to a particular conclusion. The clarity and distinctness of your premises comes to be shared by the conclusion at the end of the process.) Because of the clarity and distinctness of this thought, your will assents: you do not merely entertain the thought, you affirm it as *true*.

Notably, the causal connection here cannot be understood to involve the transference of a quantity of motion, nor is it the passive result of the laws of nature. Descartes thinks that you have the power to resist the strong inclination of your will: you *could* still entertain the possibility that this mathematical truth is false. (Of course, it would be weird to do so. You'd probably only do this if you were deeply immersed in the hyperbolic doubts Descartes proposed in the First Meditation. But it is *possible*, at least.) In this sense, the causal relationship between your two thoughts reflects activity and agency on your part.

What then are we to say of case (c), in which your decision to exercise causes you to exercise? It is clearly not like the wind pushing the tree branch, since (for Descartes) it involves genuine activity on your part rather than passive determination by the laws of nature. But neither is it entirely like the case in which you assent to an idea because of its clarity and distinctness in your understanding. One obvious difference is that mind-body causation involves bodily motion, whereas purely mental causation does not. But there are also other interesting differences. For instance, in the case where the intellect secures the agreement of the will, it is a mark of your agency that you might resist this influence. It reflects a power in you to suspend belief despite even the strongest inclinations that you have to believe something. By contrast, in the case where you will your body to act, the fact that your body might resist *this* influence is a mark of the *limits* of your agency. When your body fails to act in accordance with your will, this does not indicate your power, but your weakness or frailty.

As a result, the case of mind-body causation differs from both the case of purely physical causation and the case of purely mental causation. It is not mere passive determination by the laws of nature, but it *does* involve the production of motion in the natural world. So, if we follow Descartes in treating the mind and body as distinct substances with incommensurable natures, we do seem forced to regard their interaction as involving a novel kind of causal relationship. And this is one motivation for Descartes's claim that "the power the soul has to move the body and the body to act on the soul, in causing its sensations and passions" falls under a different primitive notion from either that of body or of soul.

But what is the *content* of this primitive notion, precisely? Here Descartes claims that the primitive notion of mind-body union has previously been misapplied to the purely physical phenomenon of the attraction of bodies toward the Earth. This suggestion requires a bit of background. When early modern scientists wanted to explain why bodies fall when you drop them, they might say: bodies have a *real quality* of heaviness, and this quality has the power to move the body in which it resides toward the Earth's center. When you let go of a rock and it drops to the ground, this motion is due to the rock's real quality of heaviness. Notice that this is not a mechanical explanation. It is not given in terms of the rock's shape, size, or previous state of motion. For this reason, Descartes thinks that explanations based on so-called real qualities are bankrupt when it comes to purely physical phenomena, such as gravity.[9] However, he suggests, this kind of explanation *is* appropriate when we are thinking about the union between the mind and body. The mind has the power to move the body in the same way that people previously (and incorrectly) thought that a rock's real quality of heaviness had the power to move it toward the ground.

This suggestion did not satisfy Elisabeth, as we can see when we turn to their second exchange about this topic in June 1643.

Extract 2.2: Elisabeth's Second Exchange with Descartes

Elisabeth to Descartes, 10 June 1643

M. Descartes,

... [T]he life which I am constrained to lead does not leave enough time at my disposal to acquire a habit of meditation in accordance with your rules. Now the interests of my house, which I must not neglect, now some conversations and social obligations which I cannot avoid, beat down so heavily on this weak mind with annoyance or boredom, that it is rendered useless for anything else at all for a long time afterward: this will serve, I hope, as an excuse for my stupidity in being unable to comprehend, by appeal to the idea you once had of heaviness, the idea through which we must judge how the soul (nonextended and immaterial) can move the body; nor why this power to carry the body toward the center of the earth, which you earlier had falsely attributed to a body as a quality, should sooner persuade us that a body can be pushed by some immaterial thing, than the demonstration of a contrary truth (which you promise us in your physics) should confirm us in the opinion of its impossibility. In particular, since this idea ... can be feigned due to the ignorance of that which truly moves these bodies toward the center, and since no material cause presents itself to the senses, one would then attribute this power to its contrary, an immaterial cause. But I nevertheless have never been able to conceive of such an immaterial thing as anything other than a negation of matter which cannot have any communication with it.

I admit that it would be easier for me to concede matter and extension to the soul than to concede the capacity to move a body and to be moved by it to an immaterial thing. For, if the first is achieved through *information*, it would be necessary that the spirits, which cause the movements, were intelligent, a capacity you accord to nothing corporeal. And even though, in your *Metaphysical Meditations*, you show the possibility of the second, it is altogether very difficult to understand that a soul, as you have described it, after having had the faculty and the custom of reasoning well, can lose all of this by some vapors, and that, being able to subsist without the body, and having nothing in common with it, the soul is still so governed by it. ...

Your very affectionate friend,

Elisabeth

Descartes to Elisabeth, 28 June 1643

Madame,

I have a very great obligation to your Highness in that she, after having borne my explaining myself badly in my previous letter . . . , deigns again to have the patience to listen to me on the same matter, and to give me occasion to note the things which I omitted. Of which the principal ones seem to me to be that, after having distinguished three sorts of ideas or primitive notions which are each known in a particular way and not by a comparison of one with the other—that is, the notion that we have of the soul, that of the body, and the union which is between the soul and the body—I ought to have explained the difference between these three sorts of notions and between the operations of the soul through which we have them, and to have stated how we render each of them familiar and easy to us. . . .

First, then, I notice a great difference between these three sorts of notions. The soul is conceived only by the pure understanding; the body, that is to say, extension, shapes, and motions, can also be known by the understanding alone, but is much better known by the understanding aided by the imagination; and finally, those things which pertain to the union of the soul and the body are known only obscurely by the understanding alone, or even by the understanding aided by the imagination; but they are known very clearly by the senses. From which it follows that those who never philosophize and who use only their senses do not doubt in the least that the soul moves the body and that the body acts on the soul. But they consider the one and the other as one single thing, that is to say, they conceive of their union. For to conceive of the union between two things is to conceive of them as one single thing. Metaphysical thoughts which exercise the pure understanding serve to render the notion of the soul familiar. The study of mathematics, which exercises principally the imagination in its consideration of shapes and movements, accustoms us to form very distinct notions of body. And lastly, it is in using only life and ordinary conversations and in abstaining from meditating and studying those things which exercise the imagination that we learn to conceive the union of the soul and the body. . . . I am, &c.

Elisabeth to Descartes, 1 July 1643

M. Descartes,

. . . What you write [in your previous letter] makes me see clearly the three sorts of notions that we have, their objects, and how we ought to make use of them.

I also find that the senses show me that the soul moves the body, but they teach me nothing (no more than do the understanding and the imagination) of the way in which it does so. For this reason, I think that there are some properties of the soul, which are unknown to us, which could perhaps overturn what your *Metaphysical Meditations* persuaded me of by such good reasoning: the nonextendedness of the soul. This doubt seems to be founded on the rule that you give there, in speaking of the true and the false, that all error comes to us in forming judgments about that which we do not perceive well enough. Though extension is not necessary to thought, neither is it at all repugnant to it, and so it could be suited to some other function of the soul which is no less essential to it. At the very least, it makes one abandon the contradiction of the Scholastics, that it [the soul] is both as a whole in the whole body and as a whole in each of its parts. I do not excuse myself at all for confusing the notion of the soul with that of the body for the same reason as the vulgar; but this doesn't rid me of the first doubt, and I will lose hope of finding certitude in anything in the world if you, who alone have kept me from being a skeptic, do not answer that to which my first reasoning carried me. . . .

Your very affectionate friend at your service,

Elisabeth.

[From L. Shapiro (ed.), The Correspondence between Princess Elisabeth of Bohemia and René Descartes (Chicago: University of Chicago Press, 2007)].

Let's begin with Elisabeth's reply to Descartes's first letter, which sets out her basic objections to Descartes's suggested solution to the mind-body problem. The problem is an explanatory one: how are we to understand the manner in which a person's will causes their body to move? Descartes's proposal, as we have seen, is to explain this phenomenon in the way that scientists of his time mistakenly explained gravity: it is the result of a non-mechanical power to cause a body to move.

Elisabeth finds this suspicious. She agrees with Descartes's verdict about the explanation of gravity in terms of the power that a body's heaviness has to move that body toward the center of the Earth. Such explanations are inadequate. It is entirely uninformative to say that a rock's heaviness moves it toward the center of the Earth by means of its power to do so. This amounts simply to "ignorance of that which truly moves these bodies toward the center." But if that explanation is inadequate in the case of a purely physical phenomenon, such as gravity, why ought we to accept such an explanation in the case of mind-body interaction? Elisabeth's position is that we shouldn't. Nothing has really been explained when we say that the mind moves the body by means of its *power* to move the body. We have gained no insight into the workings of the mind-body union. Notably, the fact that (following Descartes's lead) we are thinking about this interaction using a different "primitive notion" doesn't seem to make a difference. The bankruptcy of the proposed explanation isn't ameliorated by this.

Whereas her focus in her first letter is on the mechanism by which the mind influences the body, the argument of Elisabeth's June 1643 letter expands to consider the troubles facing causal influence in both directions, mind-to-body and body-to-mind. It is unclear how the mind could cause the body to move unless the parts of the brain that control those motions "were intelligent, a capacity [Descartes] accord[s] to nothing corporeal." Moreover, it is unclear how the body could affect the mind's capacity to think and reason to the dramatic extent that it appears to. If reason is a capacity of the mind alone (as Descartes holds), how is it that a person loses their ability to reason well when they drink a few ounces of whisky, or when they have a bad fever? What we would *expect* to see, on the Cartesian picture, is that such altered states of the body may inhibit the body's receptivity to the commands of the mind. We would expect, in other words, that in such cases the body is something like a drone with damaged antennae; communication with the pilot is broken, but the pilot (and the controls) is unaffected. Yet what we observe in practice is that altered states of the body commonly affect the abilities of the mind itself.

It is hard to reconcile facts such as these with Descartes's account of the mind-body union. And Descartes does not answer the challenge well in his second letter on the topic, of June 1643. His position there is that we learn what we know of the mind-body union on the basis of "life and ordinary conversations and in abstaining from meditating and studying," which entails that the mind-body union is not something we can comprehend via philosophical inquiry of the sort Elisabeth has initiated. This is a disappointing reply. Elisabeth notes, in her final letter on this topic, that there is no problem about *whether* the mind and body interact. They clearly do. The problem is to explain *how* they are able to interact, given the constraints imposed by Descartes's substance dualism.

Elisabeth does suggest an alternative picture, though she does not develop it in detail in these letters (nor in her other surviving writings). "[I]t would be easier for me to concede matter and extension to the soul," she writes in her June 1643 letter, "than to concede the capacity to move a body and to be moved by it to an immaterial thing." The mind-body problem arises only because we have supposed, following Descartes, that the mind has no physical properties: it is not a material substance and it has no spatial extension. We might therefore view the mind-body problem as an argument against the claim that the mind has no physical properties. This is Elisabeth's proposal in her final letter of July 1643: that Descartes may be incorrect about "the nonextendedness of the soul."

What might it mean to say that the mind has spatial extension? There are a number of different pictures of the mind that one might adopt. One way forward would be to take up *nonreductive materialism*, the view that material objects—such as brains—can have mental properties, but that these mental properties are not reducible or identical to any physical properties, such as patterns of brain activity. This would dissolve the mind-body problem, since it would allow that (part of) the body is capable of thinking. But it would still involve a form of dualism, since it postulates an unbridgeable divide between mental and physical properties.

Though scholars have sometimes interpreted Elisabeth as a nonreductive materialist, this does not appear to be her considered view.[10] On the nonreductive materialist position, thought is a property of substances that are essentially material and spatially extended. Yet, in her brief sketch of her position in the July 1643 letter, she grants Descartes the point that "extension is not necessary to thought." This implies that on Elisabeth's view, thought *could* exist without any extended substance, contrary to nonreductive materialism.

Unfortunately, in subsequent correspondence, Descartes and Elisabeth turned their attention to other topics and did not return to the subject of the mind-body problem. Nevertheless, it would become one of the major open philosophical problems in Western Europe during the seventeenth and eighteenth centuries. During this period, philosophers devised numerous creative solutions to the problem. Some stayed close to Descartes's views, while others ranged far afield. In the next chapter, we turn to a family of solutions to the mind-body problem that take a surprising approach: denying the Cartesian position that the mind and body are two distinct kinds of substance in the first place.

Key Points

- *The mind-body problem* is the problem of explaining how it is possible for the mind to causally interact with the body.
- Elisabeth of Bohemia's version of the mind-body problem is based on Descartes's commitment to the *mechanical philosophy*, according to which all physical interactions must be understood in terms of mechanical properties and relations.

- Descartes's proposed solution is that we have a "primitive notion" of mind-body union. The union cannot be understood in terms of anything else.
- Elisabeth objects that this explains our knowledge *that* the mind and body are united, but it doesn't seem to give us any knowledge of *how* the union works.

Suggested Further Reading

Garber, Daniel. "Understanding Interaction: What Descartes Should Have Told Elisabeth." *The Southern Journal of Philosophy* 21, no. 5 (1983): 15–32.

Janssen-Lauret, Frederique. "Elisabeth of Bohemia as a Naturalistic Dualist." In *Early Modern Women on Metaphysics*, edited by E. Thomas, 171–87. Cambridge: Cambridge University Press, 2018.

O'Neill, Eileen. "Mind-Body Interaction and Metaphysical Consistency: A Defense of Descartes." *Journal of the History of Philosophy* 25, no. 2 (1987): 227–45.

Shapiro, Lisa. "Volume Editor's Introduction." In *The Correspondence between Princess Elisabeth of Bohemia and René Descartes*, edited by L. Shapiro, 1–51. Chicago: University of Chicago Press, 2007.

Tollefsen, Deborah. "Princess Elisabeth and the Problem of Mind-Body Interaction." *Hypatia* 14, no. 3 (1999): 59–77.

Questions for Reflection

- What exactly is the relationship between your mind and your brain?
- How, if at all, does a living body differ from a sophisticated, self-moving machine?
- Do you think it's possible that there might be no possible explanation for the union of your mind and your body? (Must *everything* have an explanation?)
- Before we consider other philosophers' proposals in subsequent chapters: how would you propose to solve the mind-body problem?

3

Idealist Responses
Anne Conway and Gottfried Leibniz

Chapter Outline

3a.	Conway on Spirits and Matter	64
3b.	Leibniz on the Nature of Substance	75
	Questions for Reflection	86

The **mind-body problem**† arose due to difficulties connected with explaining how two completely different kinds of thing, spirit/mind and matter/body, can interact. Such a problem is potentially avoided if we abandon dualism and instead opt for **substance monism**†, which is the thesis that there is only one fundamental type of thing in the universe. There are different kinds of monism, and we will explore two of them over the next couple of chapters. In this chapter, we are going to consider two versions of idealist monism and the thinkers that argue for it: Anne Conway and Gottfried Leibniz. Both Conway and Leibniz believe that all things are fundamentally thinking, perceiving things, which we can call spirits (in the case of Conway) or **monads**† (in the case of Leibniz). As a result of this metaphysical perspective, spatial and corporeal properties are viewed as secondary phenomena. In different ways, their commitment to a kind of monism allows both Conway and Leibniz to avoid the interactionist problem faced by substance dualism.

3A. CONWAY ON SPIRITS AND MATTER

> ### Anne Conway: Brief Chronology
> - 1631: Born in London
> - 1650: Begins formative philosophical correspondence with Henry More
> - 1651: Marries Edward Conway and moves to Ragley Hall in Warwickshire, which becomes an important center of intellectual activity
> - 1670: Meets close friend and philosophical collaborator, Francis Mercury van Helmont
> - *c.* 1675–6: Converts to Quakerism
> - 1679: Dies at Ragley Hall, leaving behind scattered philosophical notes
> - 1690: Publication of her only philosophical work, *Principles*, in a Latin translation in Amsterdam
> - 1692: First publication of the *Principles* in an English translation

In Anne Conway's only published work, translated as *Principles of the Most Ancient and Modern Philosophy*, she presents us with a metaphysics that seeks to avoid the problems that she saw with both dualism and a **materialist monism**† (according to which all things that exist in the universe are fundamentally material). Conway sought to undermine both dualism and materialist monism in one go by attacking the very idea of matter; rather, she argues, all things are fundamentally spirit.

However, Conway does not seek to dismiss our experience of material (or corporeal) things as ultimately illusory. So, how do we account for the appearance of matter if all things are spirits? Conway attempts to do this by introducing the idea of matter as "condensed spirit," in analogy with how water vapor can condense into liquid water, and then solidify into ice. Spirit comes in both more ethereal and more corporeal forms (just as H_2O can appear as vapor, liquid water, or ice), and those things we know as material objects are spirits that have taken on corporeality. Therefore, while it may appear that there are two fundamental types of things in the universe, there is in fact only one, spirit, which appears to us in different forms.

In the following extract, Conway offers two arguments in support of idealist monism. Before we can begin, though, there are some other elements of her philosophy that we need to consider. Conway believes that her system of spirits at various degrees of ethereality include both God and Christ. God sits at the very top of the metaphysical hierarchy as the most perfect, infinitely ethereal spirit. For Conway, goodness and ontological state are connected: the better you are (from a moral perspective), the more ethereal a form you can take. Hence, the most perfect being, God, must be the most ethereal being, and those spirits who have taken on a more corporeal form must have fallen in some way from a moral perspective. In the extract that follows, Conway uses various assumptions regarding the nature of God, morality, and its link to a corporeal state to establish her key theory of idealist monism:

Extract 3.1 — Conway, *Principles of the Most Ancient and Modern Philosophy* (Chapter VII, pp. 84–97)

> The first reason [in favor of idealist monism] shall be from the aforementioned order of things, which I have already proved to be in three parts; namely, God the Supreme or Highest, Christ the Medium or Middle, and the Creature the lowest in order. This Creature is but one essence or substance with regard to its nature or essence, as is above demonstrated, so that it only differs *secundum modos existendi*; or, according to the manners of existence; among which one is corporeality, of which there are many degrees, so that a thing may more or less approach to, or recede from, the state or condition of a body or spirit. But because a spirit (between these two) is more excellent in the natural order of things, by how much the more a creature is a spirit . . . so much the nearer it approaches to God, who is the highest spirit.
>
> Hence a body may always be more and more spiritual *ad infinitum* [to infinity]; because God who is the first and supreme spirit is infinite, and does not nor cannot partake of the least corporeality. Such is the nature of a creature that, unless it degenerates, it always draws nearer and nearer to God in its likeness. But because there is no being which is every way contrary to God, (viz. there is no being, which is infinitely and unchangeably evil, as God is infinitely and unchangeably good; nothing infinitely dark, as God is infinitely light; nor any thing infinitely a body, having nothing of spirit, as God is infinitely a spirit, having nothing of body), hence it is manifest that no creature can become more and more a body *ad infinitum*, although the same may become more and more a spirit *ad infinitum*; and nothing can become more infinitely dark, though it may become infinitely more light.

By the same reason nothing can be evil *ad infinitum*, although it may become more and more good *ad infinitum*: and so indeed, in the very nature of things, there are limits or bounds to evil, but none to good. And after the same manner, every degree of sin or evil has its punishment, grief, and chastisement connected to it, in the very nature of the thing, by which the evil is again changed into good. This punishment or correction, though it be not presently perceived by the creature when it sins, yet is preserved in those very sins which they commit, and its due time will appear. Then every sin will have its punishment, and so the pain and chastisement will be felt by the creature. In that way, the creature will be again restored to its former state of goodness, in which it was created, and from which it cannot fall or slide anymore. Because by its great chastisement it has acquired a greater strength and perfection; and so is ascended so far above that indifferency of will, which before it had to good or evil, that it wills only that which is good, and neither is it any more capable to will any evil . . .

And hence may be inferred, that all the creatures of God, which heretofore degenerated and fell from their primitive goodness, must after certain periods be converted and restored, not only to as good, but to a better state than that in which they were created. For divine operation cannot cease: and hence it is the nature of every creature to be still in motion, and always to change either from good to good, or from good into evil, or from evil again into good; and because it cannot proceed infinitely to evil, for there is no example of infinite evil, hence it must necessarily return to the good or slide into eternal silence, which is contrary to its nature.

But if it be said that it goes into eternal torments, I answer, if by eternal you mean an infinity of ages, which shall never cease, that is impossible; because every pain and torment excites or stirs up an operating spirit or life in every thing which suffers. As we observe by continued experience, and as reason teaches us, this is necessarily the case because through feeling and enduring pain, every kind of crassness or grossness in spirit or contracted body is reduced. As a result, the spirit captivated or detained in that grossness or crassness is set free, and made more spiritual, and consequently more active and operative, through suffering.

Now seeing as a creature cannot proceed infinitely to evil, nor slide down into inactivity or silence, nor into eternal suffering, it incontestably follows that it must at length return to good; and by how much the greater its sufferings are, so much the sooner shall it return and be restored. And so we see how a thing (while remaining the same substance) may be marvellously changed in respect of the manners of its existence; so that a certain holy and blessed spirit, or angel of light, could by his voluntary action become a wicked and cursed spirit of darkness; which change or metamorphosis certainly is as great as if a spirit were changed into a body.

And if it be here enquired, whether those spirits became more corporeal by their transgression, than they were in their primitive state before they fell, I answer yes; for as I have already shown, a spirit is capable of corporeality, *Secundum majus & minus*, or more or less; although not infinitely, yet in many degrees. Hence it is, they could remain so for many ages, and have nothing of such a corporeal crassness, as things in the visible world have, such as hard stones or metals, or the bodies of men and women. For certainly the bodies of the worst spirits have not such a crassness as any visible body, and yet all that grossness of visible bodies came from the Fall of Spirits from their First State. And so the spirits after long and various periods, could contract this grossness to themselves, although they could not come together, and at one and the same time fall into a universal grossness, so that the whole body of any fallen spirit should be in all its parts equally gross; rather, some parts become grosser and grosser, and the other corporeal parts of this spirit (which are its immediate vehicle, and wherewith it is most intimately united) retain a certain tenuousness or subtlety, without which the spirit could not be so moveable and active as otherwise it would; and with these subtler and more tenuous parts of the body, the principal spirit (together with its ministering spirits, so many of them as it can possibly gather together) departs out of those thicker parts of the body, which leaves it as so many dead bodies that are no longer fit to serve the said spirits in those operations which they exercise in their present state . . .

The second reason that created spirits are convertible into bodies, and bodies into spirits, I shall deduce from a serious and due consideration of the divine attributes; from which, as from a treasury of instructions, may be manifested the truth of all things. For since God is infinitely good, and communicates his goodness in infinite ways to his creatures; so that there is no creature that does not receive something of his goodness, and that very greatly: And since the goodness of God is a living goodness, which has life, power, love, and knowledge in it, which he communicates to his creatures, how can it be that any dead thing should proceed from him, or be created by him, such as mere body or matter, according to their hypothesis, who affirm that the same is wholly inconvertible to any degree of life or knowledge? It is truly said of one that God made not death, and it is as true, that he made no dead thing: For how can a dead thing depend on him, who is life and charity? Or how can any creature receive so vile and diminutive an essence from him (who is so infinitely giving and good) that should partake nothing of life or knowledge, nor ever be able to aspire to it, not in the least degree?

Has not God created all his creatures for this end, that in him they might be blessed, and enjoy his divine goodness in their several states and conditions? But how can this be without life or sense? Or how can anything that lacks life enjoy divine goodness?

Carrying this argument further, the divine attributes are commonly and rightly distinguished into communicable and incommunicable. The incommunicable are that God is a being, subsisting by himself, independent, unchangeable, absolutely infinite, and most perfect: The communicable are, that he is spirit, life, and light, that he is good, holy, just, wise etc. But now there are none of these communicable attributes, which are not living, indeed life itself, and because every creature has a connection with God in some of his attributes, now I demand, in what attribute dead matter has [an attribute shared with the divine], or a body that is incapable of life and sense forever? ...

Moreover, considering that the creatures of God, so far as they are creatures, ought necessarily in some things to resemble their creator, now I demand, in what way is dead matter like God? ...

But as considering the other attributes of matter, viz. impenetrability, taking a shape, and mobility, certainly none of these have any place in God, and so are none of his communicable attributes; but rather essential differences or attributes of diversity, whereby the creature as such is distinguished from God. In addition, mutability is another of those differential attributes, from which it cannot be said that mutability is one of the communicable attributes of God. And in like manner, impenetrability, taking a shape, and mobility do not pertain unto the communicable attributes of God; but to those ways only in which the creatures differ from him. And given dead matter does not partake of any of the communicable attributes of God, we must conclude that it is a mere *non ens*, or nothing, a false fiction or chimera, and so an impossible thing.

If they say, it [dead matter] has a metaphysical goodness and truth, as every being is good and true: Again, I demand, what is that goodness and truth? For it has no connection with any of the communicable attributes of God, it will be neither good nor true, and so a mere fiction, as was said before. Moreover, seeing as it cannot be said how dead matter does in any way partake of divine goodness, much less can it be shown how it may be capable of acquiring a greater perfection *ad infinitum*, which is the nature of all creatures, viz. to increase, and infinitely advance towards a greater perfection, as was demonstrated before. But what further progress in goodness or perfection can dead matter make? Because after it has suffered infinite changes of motion or shape it is constrained to always remain dead as before, and if motion and figure contribute nothing to the receiving of life, then certainly this is never made the better; nay, is not in the least degree promoted in goodness.

[From *The Principles of the Most Ancient and Modern Philosophy* (London: np., 1692). Translation amended].

Let us begin with the first argument that Conway puts forward in favor of her monist theory (though, as we shall see, the two arguments rather blend into each other). It is based on the necessary connection that Conway posits between moral worth and ontological status. The greater a being you are from a moral standpoint, the more ethereal form you will take, and vice versa, the worse moral being you are, the more corporeal form you will take. By this reasoning, any kind of matter that is entirely devoid of spirit and has no semblance of life or perception—**dead matter**†, in Conway's terms— will be something that has committed some kind of absolute evil. Conway argues, though, that such a thing could not exist in a universe created by God (assuming, as she does, that God exists). Any kind of completely dead matter would be so contrary to the being of God (so *unlike* God, in other words), that it could not possibly exist.

In this text, we find Conway presupposing that all of creation must be like God in some fundamental ways, including being a spirit and having some form of life. We see in this passage a reference to Conway's key distinction between the communicable and incommunicable divine attributes, that is, those attributes that can be shared between God and creation, and those that cannot. The distinction is drawn on the basis that some of God's attributes can only be conceived of in an absolute state and others can be understood as occurring in more limited ways. Let's consider God's property of being immutable (i.e., entirely unchanging) and perfectly good. Creation cannot be immutable, as there is no scale of immutability (you are either completely immutable or you are not), but it can be good to some extent, due to the fact that there can be a sliding-scale of goodness. Thus, goodness is a communicable attribute and immutability is an incommunicable divine attribute. Conway's argumentative move following on from this distinction is the claim that all beings within creation must exemplify all the communicable divine attributes (including life and goodness) to at least some extent. This is based on her assumption of an account of creation that implies a principle of substantial similarity between God and the universe.

Conway's theory of creation is outlined in Chapter 2 of her *Principles*. Here, God's creative action is characterized as an inevitable outpouring of his goodness, in the manner of a fountain from which water eternally flows:

"God is infinitely good, loving and bountiful, indeed goodness and charity itself; an infinite fountain and father of goodness, charity and bounty. Now how can it be that this fountain shall not always plentifully flow, and send from itself living waters? And shall not this ocean perpetually abound with its own efflux to the production of creatures, and that with a certain continual stream?"[1] In this quote, creation by God is described as stemming from a desire to spread his goodness, indeed *himself*, as much as he is able. Through creation, God is essentially communicating or expressing himself. A number of significant metaphysical claims follow from this, including the theory that all things in creation (as a communication of God himself) must have a minimal, fundamental likeness to God. It is this underlying assumption by Conway that leads to her claims regarding the impossibility of there being dead matter, which would be so unlike God that it could not have been part of the process of the divine communication of life and goodness that characterizes all of creation. As a result, both Cartesian dualism and materialist monism must be false.

Another strand of Conway's argument is connected to her response to one of the key debates in the philosophy of religion. One of the philosophical challenges Conway has to deal with in her philosophy is something that eventually faces any system that wishes to postulate God, namely, the **problem of evil**[†]. How can there be evil in a world created by an all-good God? If God has created all things, then has he not created all evil too? How could an all-good God create evil, though? Given the fact that there is evil in the world, there seems to be no way in which it could have been created by the kind of God assumed by mainstream theists.

One traditional way of avoiding this problem is to suggest that evil is not something created by God; rather, it is a lack, or privation, of goodness. Evil is a gap in creation where goodness could be, but this potential goodness has been lost due to events in creation that God has reason to allow. Such an approach to answering the problem of evil is often traced back to the early Christian philosopher Augustine (354–430), though how much he actually relies upon this argumentative strategy is a matter of scholarly debate. In his *Confessions*, he writes:

> it was clear to me that those things that are corrupted remain good. If they were supremely good, or if they had no goodness in them, they could not be corrupted; because if supremely good, they were incorruptible, and if not good at all, there were nothing in them to be corrupted . . . But if they are deprived of all good, they will cease to be. For if they be deprived of all good,

and cannot be at all corrupted, they will become better by remaining incorruptible. And what is more monstrous than to assert that those things which have lost all their goodness are made better?[2]

Here, Augustine makes a link between goodness and being. On that basis, if we understand evil as a lack or privation of goodness, then it will also be equivalent to a lack of being. Consequently, if a being were to be wholly morally corrupted, they would cease to be entirely. However, some goodness will always remain in all creatures, due to the supposed absurdity of a creature existing who is so evil that they could not be further corrupted (and could therefore seem to be a morally praiseworthy being by no longer doing corruptible things).

Conway takes a similar approach to answering the problem of evil, though she has to take care that her response allows for her commitment to the **principle of plenitude**[†], according to which God creates as much as he is able and thus there are as many created things as there could be. Creation is necessarily full, as far as Conway is concerned, and thus it may be unclear how there could be any gap or space in which there is a privation of goodness. Conway avoids this potential problem through an aspect of her philosophy that we have already discussed, namely, her link between evil and an increase in corporeality. On this view, evil does not bring about a gap in the universe where goodness could be, strictly speaking, but rather replaces spiritual God-likeness with corporeality. So, in contrast with Augustine, we have more of an idea of a straight swap of evil for good: a more ethereal being is replaced by a more corporeal being. However, this is not all Conway has to say on the matter, and her response to the problem of evil has two further parts: (1) a free will defense and (2) claims regarding the purifying effects of falling into corporeality that ultimately justify God allowing it to occur (which we see mentioned in the extract earlier).

First, the free will defense. Conway argues that as God cannot create another perfect, immutable being, he is necessarily confined to creating imperfect, ever-changing creatures (although he still acts freely). In addition, change is only possible on the basis of a creature having an "indifferent" will (in the sense of a will that has a genuine choice between different options for action): "that indifference of acting, or not acting, can by no means be said to be in God because this would be an imperfection, and would make God like corruptible creatures; for this indifference of will is the foundation of all change and corruptibility in creatures."[3] All things in creation must have an "indifferent" will, and it is this alone which is the basis of evil. If God were to create anything at all, he had to create such beings, and given that it is good overall that there is a creation, he can be excused from having created beings who can do evil things. So, we have a first strand for a defense of God's decision to allow for the existence of evil in the created universe. In allowing for spirits to take on corporeality through their own wrongdoing, and by framing this transformation within a wider narrative of ultimate redemption, Conway is able to use her idealist monism to offer an intriguing solution to the problem of evil. God had no choice but to create beings with free will, which can unfortunately be misused in order to commit wrongdoing.

However, the ontological process this brings about (a fall from ethereality into corporeality) is for the best, as it is ultimately a process of purification that leads to a journey back towards God and goodness. As we saw in the passage earlier, Conway claims that the pain and suffering associated with misuse of free will and thereby falling away from God has a naturally purifying effect, such that the creature in question is made ready to turn back towards the good. Though the specifics of this purification process are not wholly clear from the text, Conway argues that the result is a positive one in the long run, in that the creature will inevitably end up in a state that is even better (i.e., more God-like) than they ever had before, on the basis of having committed evil and thereby gone through great suffering. On this account, the existence of evil is therefore explained by its being contextualized within a wider scheme of fall and redemption for all creatures. While evil should by no means be celebrated, it is nevertheless a necessary part of an overall positive story of the universe, as creatures fall away from God only to return purified and more ready to do good than ever before. As a result, God is justified in allowing the existence of creatures who have a free will that is used to commit evil. Conway states that "nature always works to a greater perfection of subtlety and spirituality, as this is the most natural property of all motion and operation."[4] Though evil will occur in the universe, all things naturally tend back towards the perfection of God, and thus nature as a whole is justified.

We are now led to a second strand of Conway's argument against the possibility of dead matter, as referred to in the extract earlier. All things in creation take part in the overall scheme of fall and redemption that sees creatures ultimately return to a more God-like state. Conway uses this underlying theory of salvation to argue that there could be no such thing as dead matter, insofar as such a thing could have no prospect of any redemption. As we have seen, Conway argues that all creatures naturally progress back towards a more spiritual, God-like state, due to the purifying effect of suffering. However, a being that was merely dead matter could not suffer in any way. Indeed, it would have no sense of a life in which it could act in a more or less God-like manner, and so there could be no prospect of its improvement. Thus, there could be no dead matter, as there can be no such thing as a being in creation that cannot ultimately achieve redemption.

There are a number of aspects of Conway's argument that are rather appealing. For one thing, her philosophy offers a picture of the universe of all involved in a shared effort to achieve salvation. Conway's emphasis upon the unified nature of all beings in the universe integrates human beings into the world and their environment in a manner that Cartesian dualism is arguably unable to achieve. Nothing that is created by God is left languishing in a material condition from which it can never improve; rather, all beings have the same opportunities for renewal and for becoming closer to God. Such a perspective upon humankind's intertwined destiny with the whole of nature could potentially provide inspiration for philosophers who wish to explore new viewpoints upon our relationship to our environment.

However, in critiquing this position, it is by no means clear that Conway offers an argument that follows straightforwardly from a traditional understanding of the nature of God. In her arguments, Conway does not seem to account for potentially quite plausible theist explanations for the creation of dead matter. As an example, we might grant to Conway the importance of creatures having the opportunity to grow (both morally and spiritually) and thus God being justified in granting to us the kind of free will that allows us to do evil. Within this framework, however, dead matter might have an important function in giving us opportunities to use something external to ourselves (which is not another creature) either productively or destructively. In response to this point, Conway might claim that God could not create something that is dead, but such a limitation on divine creative power is certainly something that many theists would not accept and it would require a separate argument that we do not find clearly articulated in the *Principles*. Thus, there are some potentially difficult objections we can put to Conway's attempt to offer an ontology that, among other things, tries to overcome the problem of interaction that beset Cartesian dualism.

Key Points

- Conway seeks to avoid both Cartesian dualism (and its problem of interaction) and materialist monism.
- In the *Principles*, Conway proposes a spirit-based monism, according to which matter is construed as condensed spirit.
- Conway argues that God could not create dead matter, due to his perfect goodness.
- In explaining the possibility of matter, Conway offers a response to the problem of evil that invokes both a free will defense and a claim that a fall into material form has a purifying function that prepares a creature for redemption.

Suggested Further Reading

Borcherding, Julia. "Loving the Body, Loving the Soul: Conway's Vitalist Critique of Cartesian and Morean Dualism." In *Oxford Studies in Early Modern Philosophy: Vol. IX*, edited by Rutherford, 1–35. Oxford: Oxford University Press, 2019.

Grey, John. "Conway's Ontological Objection to Cartesian Dualism." *Philosophers' Imprint* 17, no. 13 (2017): 1–19.

Head, Jonathan. *The Philosophy of Anne Conway*, ch. 2. London: Bloomsbury Academic, 2021.

Lascano, Marcy P. "Anne Conway: Bodies in the Spiritual World." *Philosophy Compass* 8, no. 4 (2013): 327–36.

McRobert, Jennifer. "Anne Conway's Vitalism and Her Critique of Descartes." *International Philosophy Quarterly* 40, no. 1 (2000): 21–35.

3B. LEIBNIZ ON THE NATURE OF SUBSTANCE

Gottfried Leibniz: Brief Chronology

- 1646: Born in Leipzig, son of a professor of moral philosophy
- 1661: Begins studying philosophy at the University of Leipzig
- 1667: Gains doctorate in law and begins academic work in numerous disciplines while working for the Elector of Mainz
- 1672–6: Lives in Paris, one of the most important intellectual centers of the time, becoming familiar with numerous significant thinkers, such as the Cartesian Nicolas Malebranche
- 1676: Joins the service of the House of Brunswick in Hanover, holding various roles including court councilor and official historian/librarian
- 1686: Writes first major philosophical work, *Discourse on Metaphysics* (published posthumously)
- 1695: Begins writing a major critique of the philosophy of John Locke, *New Essays on Human Understanding* (published posthumously)
- 1699: Becomes embroiled in a dispute with Isaac Newton over who had first invented calculus
- 1710: Publishes important contribution to philosophy of religion, the *Theodicy*
- 1716: Dies in Hanover

One of the few major philosophers prior to the twentieth century who were familiar with the work of Anne Conway was Gottfried Leibniz. Through Conway's friend, Francis Mercury van Helmont, Leibniz received a copy of the *Principles* that remained in his personal collection until his death. It is clear that Leibniz thought very highly of Conway's philosophy, stating in 1697 that his "philosophical views approach somewhat closely those of the late Countess of Conway."[5] However, though they have been grouped together here as idealist monists, it is important to bear in mind that there are significant differences between their respective metaphysical systems.

Before being introduced to Conway's *Principles*, Leibniz had already written his own *Discourse on Metaphysics*, which is the text we will be focusing on here. It is an early attempt by Leibniz to formulate his own (at that moment partial) metaphysical system, including an attempt to move beyond what he saw as the faults of Cartesian dualism. At its basis are simple substances, what he would later call **monads**[†], which are perfect unities, without parts or extension (in other words, they are indivisible and without a shape), and come into being only through the direct creative action of God. In the following extract from the *Discourse*, Leibniz introduces some of the key ideas in his account of these substances and applies them to the question of the relation between the mind and body:

Extract 3.2 — Leibniz, *Discourse on Metaphysics* (Selected Sections)

8. . . . In the first place since activity and passivity pertain properly to individual substances (*actiones sunt suppositorum* [actions are of substantial individuals]) it will be necessary to explain what such a substance is. It is indeed true that when several predicates are attributes of a single subject and this subject is not an attribute of another, we speak of it as an individual substance, but this is not enough, and such an explanation is merely nominal. We must therefore inquire what it is to truly be an attribute of a certain subject.

Now it is evident that every true predication has some basis in the nature of things, and even when a proposition is not identical, that is, when the predicate is not expressly contained in the subject, it is still necessary that it be virtually contained in it, and this is what the philosophers call *in-esse* [being in], which is to say that the predicate is in the subject. Thus the content of the subject must always include that of the predicate in such a way that if one understands perfectly the concept of the subject, he will know that the predicate appertains to it also. This being so, we are able to say that this is the nature of an individual substance or of a complete being, namely, to afford a conception so complete that the concept shall be sufficient for the understanding of it and for the deduction of all the predicates of which the substance is or may become the subject.

Thus the quality of king, which belonged to Alexander the Great, an abstraction from the subject, is not sufficiently determined to constitute an individual, and does not contain the other qualities of the same subject, nor everything which the idea of this prince includes. God, however, seeing the individual concept or haecceity [thisness] of Alexander, sees there at the same time the basis and the reason of all the predicates which can be truly uttered regarding him; for instance, that he will conquer Darius and Porus, and even to the point of knowing *a priori* (and not by experience) whether he died a natural death or by poison—facts that we can learn only through history. When we carefully consider the connections of things we can also see the possibility of saying that there always was in the soul of Alexander marks of all that had happened to him and evidence of all that would happen to him and traces even of everything which occurs in the universe, although God alone could recognize them all.

9. There follow from these considerations several noticeable paradoxes; among others that it is not true that two substances may be exactly alike and differ only numerically, *solo numero* [in number only], and that what St. Thomas [Aquinas] says on this point regarding angels and intelligences (*quod ibi omne individuum sit species infima* [of which all individuals are a lowest species]) is true of all substances, provided that the specific difference is understood as Geometers understand it in the case of figures. In addition, that a substance will be able to commence only through creation and perish only through annihilation; that a substance cannot be divided into two nor can one be made out of two, and thus that the number of substances neither augments nor diminishes through natural means, although they are frequently transformed.

Furthermore, every substance is like an entire world and like a mirror of God, or indeed of the whole world which it portrays, each one in its own fashion; almost as the same city is variously represented according to the various situations of him who is regarding it. Thus the universe is multiplied in some sort as many times as there are substances, and the glory of God is multiplied in the same way by as many wholly different representations of his works. It can indeed be said that every substance bears in some sort the character of God's infinite wisdom and omnipotence, and imitates him as much as it is able to; for it expresses, although confusedly, all that happens in the universe, past, present and future, thus deriving a certain resemblance to an infinite perception or power of knowing. And since all other substances express this particular substance and accommodate themselves to it, we can say that it exerts its power upon all the others in imitation of the omnipotence of the creator.

. . .

12. But to resume the thread of our discussion, I believe that he who will meditate upon the nature of substance, as I have explained it above, will find that the whole nature of bodies is not exhausted in their extension, that is to say, in their size, figure and motion, but that we must recognize something which corresponds to soul, something which is commonly called substantial form, although these forms effect no change in the phenomena, any more than do the souls of beasts, that is if they have souls. It is even possible to demonstrate that the ideas of size, figure and motion are not so distinctive as is imagined, and that they stand for

something imaginary relative to our perception as do, although to a greater extent, the ideas of colour, heat, and the other similar qualities in regard to which we may doubt whether they are actually to be found in the nature of things outside of us. This is why these latter qualities are unable to constitute "substance" and if there is no other principle of identity in bodies than that which has just been referred to a body would not subsist for more than a moment.

The souls and substantial forms of other bodies are entirely different from intelligent souls which alone know their actions, and not only do not perish through natural means but indeed always retain the knowledge of what they are. This is a fact that makes them alone open to punishment or reward, and makes them citizens of the republic of the universe, whose monarch is God. Hence it follows that all the other creatures should serve them . . .

. . .

14. After having seen, to a certain extent, in what the nature of substances consists, we must try to explain the dependence they have upon one another and their actions and passions. Now it is first of all very evident that created substances depend upon God who preserves them and can produce them continually by a kind of emanation just as we produce our thoughts. For when God turns, so to say, on all sides and in all fashions, the general system of phenomena which he finds it good to produce for the sake of manifesting his glory, and when he regards all the aspects of the world in all possible manners, since there is no relation which escapes his omniscience [state of knowing all truths], the result of each view of the universe as seen from a different position is a substance which expresses the universe conformably to this view . . . Now we have said before, and it follows from what we have just said that each substance is a world by itself, independent of everything else excepting God; therefore, all our phenomena (that is, all things which are ever able to happen to us) are only consequences of our being. Now as the phenomena maintain a certain order conformably to our nature, or so to speak to the world which is in us (from whence it follows we can, for the regulation of our conduct, make useful observations which are justified by the outcome of the future phenomena) and as we are thus able often to judge the future by the past without deceiving ourselves, we have sufficient grounds for saying that these phenomena are true and we will not be put to the task of inquiring whether they are outside of us, and whether others perceive them also . . .

It is God alone . . . who is the cause of this correspondence in their phenomena and who brings it about that that which is particular to one, is also common to all, otherwise there would be no relation. In a way, then, we might properly say, although it seems strange, that a particular substance never acts upon another particular substance nor is it acted upon by it. That which happens to each one is only the consequence of its complete idea or concept, since this idea already includes all the predicates and expresses the whole universe. In fact nothing can happen to us except thoughts and perceptions, and all our thoughts and perceptions are but the consequence, contingent it is true, of our precedent thoughts and perceptions . . .

15. Without entering into a long discussion it is sufficient for reconciling the language of metaphysics with that of practical life to remark that we preferably attribute to ourselves, and with reason, the phenomena which we express the most perfectly, and that we attribute to other substances those phenomena which each one expresses the best. Thus a substance, which is of an infinite extension insofar as it expresses all, becomes limited in proportion to its more or less perfect manner of expression. It is thus then that we may conceive of substances as interfering with and limiting one another, and hence we are able to say that in this sense they act upon one another, and that they, so to speak, accommodate themselves to one another. For it can happen that a single change which augments the expression of the one may diminish that of the other.

Now the virtue of a particular substance is to express well the glory of God, and the better it expresses it, the less it is limited. Every thing, when it expresses its virtue or power, that is to say, when it acts, changes to better, and expands just insofar as it acts. When therefore a change occurs by which several substances are affected (in fact every change affects them all) I think we may say that those substances, which by this change pass immediately to a greater degree of perfection, or to a more perfect expression, exert power and act, while those which pass to a lesser degree disclose their weakness and suffer. I also hold that every activity of a substance which has perception implies some pleasure, and every passion some pain, except that it may very well happen that a present advantage will be eventually destroyed by a greater evil, from which comes the fact that one may sin in acting or exerting his power and find pleasure in doing so.

. . .

33. We can also see the explanation of that great mystery, "the union of the soul and the body," that is to say how it comes about that the passions and actions of the one are accompanied by the actions and passions, or else the appropriate phenomena, of the other. For it is not possible to conceive how one can have an influence upon the other and it is unreasonable to have recourse at once to the extraordinary intervention of

the universal cause in an ordinary and particular case. The following, however, is the true explanation. We have said that everything which happens to a soul or to any substance is a consequence of its concept; hence the idea itself or the essence of the soul brings it about that all of its appearances or perceptions should be born out of its nature and precisely in such a way that they correspond of themselves to that which happens in the universe at large, but more particularly and more perfectly to that which happens in the body associated with it; because it is in a particular way and only for a certain time according to the relation of other bodies to its own body that the soul expresses the state of the universe.

This last fact enables us to see how our body belongs to us, without, however, being attached to our essence. I believe that those who are careful thinkers will decide favourably for our principles because of this single reason, viz., that they are able to see in what consists the relation between the soul and the body, a parallelism which appears inexplicable in any other way . . .

[From *Leibniz: Discourse on Metaphysics, Correspondence with Arnauld and Monadology*, translated by Montgomery (Chicago: Open Court, 1908). Translation amended.]

We can begin with the extract from Section 8 of the *Discourse*, where Leibniz offers his account of the notion of **substance**† (partly as a precursor to explaining the mind-body distinction). He starts by offering an initial (but insufficient) definition of substance as something that has predicates (things that can be asserted to be true of something else, such as a property or a power), but is not predicated of anything else: in other words, it is only the ground or foundation of a set of predicates. This links to Descartes's conception of substance, as noted in Chapter 1: one of the ways in which a substance can be an independent being is by not being predicated of anything else, while predicates are dependent beings that would not exist without their corresponding substance. Leibniz wants to go further than this in characterizing the notion of substance, though, and so he investigates what it is for a substance to have something truly predicated of it.

In outlining this relation between subject and predicate, Leibniz turns to his **conceptual-containment theory of truth**†, according to which propositions are true if the predicate in question is contained in the concept of the subject. Such a theory of truth is at least plausible when we are considering a proposition that is true by definition: for example, what makes the statement "This square has four sides" true is arguably that contained within the concept of "square" is the idea of "having four sides." One of

Leibniz's innovations is to extend this model of truth to cover all affirmative predications of particular things, even those propositions that do not appear to be true by definition. So, in speaking of my cat, if I say "Julio is black," what makes that proposition true is that the concept of my cat, Julio, contains the concept of being black.

Leibniz therefore claims that a substance is a subject whose concept contains all its predicates. We can thus gain a sense of what is meant when he states that every true predication "has some basis in the nature of things." All substances have their own inner nature or essence that grounds all things that can be truthfully predicated of them. If we had the infinite intellectual capacities of God, we could grasp this essence or **complete concept**† of a substance and on that basis derive all its predicates *a priori*. So, I could in principle reflect on the concept of "Barack Obama" and derive the predicate "elected President of the United States in 2008" from that concept, without having to resort to my experience of the history of US politics. This is why substances (in the example, "Alexander the Great") are distinct from accidents ("being a king"): the concept of Alexander the Great includes everything that characterizes him as a distinct individual, while the concept of being a king does not exhaust all that can be said about a particular individual (there is more to Alexander the Great than just being a king) and is applicable to other individuals, such as King Henry VIII.

At the very end of Section 8, Leibniz extends his claims regarding the nature of substances even further: not only can we reflect *a priori* upon the concept of a particular individual to derive all things that can be predicated of them throughout their life, but we also find "traces of even everything that happens in the universe" within it. While this might seem a strange claim at first, there is something plausible about it, as all things have some kind of relation to everything else in the universe: for example, it might be part of the concept of "Barack Obama" that he was born 245 years after the death of Gottfried Leibniz, the great German philosopher who was very affable in conversation, had Johann Christian von Boineburg as a patron, was interested in reconciling various parts of the Christian church, and so forth. Thus, in principle, I could reflect upon the concept of any being in the universe and deduce *a priori* the entire history of everything that has happened, that is happening right now, and that will happen. In this sense, every individual substance is a mirror of the rest of the universe, or, as Leibniz puts it at the end of Section 9, it expresses all things in the universe (albeit in a confused way, given that a completely clear perception of everything is not possible for finite beings).

We can now move on to consider Section 12, where Leibniz discusses the notion of material substance. Before we consider what is said here, it is worth noting that Leibniz's account of matter is often seemingly quite ambiguous and perhaps changes a number of times throughout his philosophical works. Nevertheless, we can say generally that, for Leibniz, matter is not understood as a kind of fundamental substance; rather, it exists at an ontological level that is derivative of the fundamental substances that are monads. Leibniz rejects the Cartesian notion of matter as a particular kind of substance that can be fundamentally characterized by its size, shape, and motion. Such a thing could not be a substance, according to Leibniz's account, as these properties do not exhaust everything that can be truthfully attributed to a body, particularly in the case of organic bodies, which seem to have a kind of life and organization that goes beyond its merely mechanical properties. In order to explain such attributes, neither would it be any good to posit a kind of substantial form in the body (which acts as a kind of underlying enlivening and organizing principle for it), on the basis that such a principle has no substantive impact upon the physical behavior of the body in question.

In addition, the physical properties that Cartesians refer to as fundamental to material substances have a kind of indistinct nature to them (such as that had by color or heat, which are sometimes referred to as secondary qualities) that betrays their ultimate foundation in their being perceived. In the same way that color can vary according to the conditions of the perceiver, neither does an object have a precise shape or motion (as, in principle, different perceivers could perceive these properties in the same object differently[6]). Thus, Leibniz concludes, there can be no such distinct substance as that envisioned by Cartesians in their account of matter; rather, matter seems to have an idealist basis in the perception of the fundamental substances, monads.

With these metaphysical assumptions regarding substance in place, we can now move to Section 14 and the question of interaction between mind and body. Leibniz argues that, from what he has claimed so far, we can infer that substances cannot be changed or impacted externally (with the exception of God's creative and sustaining power): each substance is a "world by itself," as he puts it. Recall that everything that happens to a substance is already encoded within its complete concept, such that we could deduce *a priori* from that concept all events in its existence. From this claim, Leibniz argues that all change that a substance undergoes must come from within, rather than without. If a substance changes, that will be due to a purely internal force or principle within it, rather than being grounded in any outside influence from another created substance. Thus, there can be no such thing as causation between distinct substances; rather, all things that happen to us are a result of our inner being or essence. If we are going to follow the Cartesians in holding that mind and body are distinct substances, there is no possible causal interaction between them and therefore the problem of interaction between mind and body never arises.

Why then, does it appear to us as if there is interaction between distinct substances? Leibniz's attempted solution to this problem is that of **pre-established harmony**† between created substances. God has a crucial role here, by ensuring that all changes in substances follow regular patterns or laws, such that our experience of the world gives an appearance of causation between substances. So, for example, it is pre-programmed within my nature that I will feel pain a moment after the hot coffee spills on my hand, rather than there being a causal link between the heat of the coffee and the feeling of pain. Leibniz argues that this does not make causation into an illusion; instead, God's activity in ensuring this harmony between substances is sufficient for relations between substances to have an objective reality. God ensures that all our perceptions agree with each other, such that we inhabit a shared intersubjective framework that constitutes a genuine reality for us.

However, this theory of pre-established harmony may strike some as providing an insufficient notion of causation, or at least not one that accords with what we usually mean when we talk about things having an impact upon each other. Leibniz attempts to deal with this concern in Section 15 by both seeking to give more detail as to how things have an impact upon each other in his account, and arguing that his account does accord with our ordinary language regarding causation. When we talk about one substance having a causal impact upon another, we conceive of the thing that is affected as being under the power of the cause in some respect. Another way of putting it is that the effect has to accommodate itself to the cause, though through the intermediary of God's harmonizing action (as Leibniz has it). As an example, when the white ball hits the yellow ball on the pool table, the two balls cannot occupy the same space and so the white ball displaces the yellow ball from where it was: the yellow ball has "accommodated" itself to the white ball. Leibniz argues that the facilitating role of God in pre-established harmony does not significantly depart from these pre-philosophical ideas regarding the relation between cause and effect, for the reason for the change is still traceable to the cause in a substantial respect.[7]

Curiously, Leibniz also links causation to the notion of growth in perfection and in expression of the glory of God (at least as far as the cause is concerned). There are various ways we can interpret the text here and certainly some confusion may be inevitable, given that we do not normally think about having a causal impact upon things as necessarily entailing an increase in perfection. One way of making sense of this claim is to interpret Leibniz as holding that the power of a substance is an expression of the perfection and glory of God. Given that God has arranged the sequence of events in the universe, whatever brings about a part of that sequence (through its "causal power") will thereby be expressing the glory of God. It is in this way that Leibniz could link causation and perfection within his system. The extent to which this account really accords with our ordinary language regarding causation (which Leibniz seems to think is important to establish) is rather questionable, however. One implication of Leibniz's account, it seems, is that any action expresses the glory of God and increases an individual's perfection. As a result, there does not seem to be any such thing as an evil action. This is just one of many ways in which the connection between power/action and change for the better may force us to depart from our ordinary talk regarding causation.

Finally, we move on to Section 33, which concerns the question of the notion of a "union" between mind and body. Note that Leibniz is not fully committed here to the body being a distinct substance from the mind (he simply seems unsure on this issue in the *Discourse*),[8] so he cannot necessarily use his notion of pre-established harmony to solve the specific problem of interaction between the mind and body. Nevertheless, whether we understand the body as a substance or as merely a "phenomenon," we can construe the supposed unity of body and mind as grounded in a uniquely close correspondence between changes of state in the mind and changes in the body: this is what Leibniz means by stating that the soul expresses itself "more particularly and more perfectly" through its body more than through anything else in the universe. As another way of putting this point, Leibniz adds that the soul relates to the rest of the universe primarily via its body (and so the body is more central than anything else to the *a priori* deductions we could make regarding the state of the universe through reflection upon the complete concept of the particular soul). We can understand this relation between mind and body either in terms of a peculiarly close harmonious relation between two substances or between a soul-substance and a particular phenomenon in the universe, and it is in this sense that we can speak of a union between mind and body.

There are undoubtedly many issues with Leibniz's account that we can consider. First, as already mentioned, it is seemingly important to Leibniz that his account of causation and mind-body interaction respects our ordinary language regarding these topics, but the extent to which he has genuinely achieved this is certainly up for question. When we speak of two events being causally related—for example, when a desire to raise a hand in the air causes the physical act of raising the hand—we naturally intend that there is some sort of *direct* link between them, such that the cause in that moment genuinely brought about that effect. In Leibniz's account, the reality is very different: from the very beginning of time, it was set (by God) within the essence of all things that the physical event of my arm rising in the air at that moment would correlate with the mental act of my volition at the preceding moment. Such a roundabout way of linking causes and effects does not seem entirely consistent with how we ordinarily talk about such matters, particularly in the case of our mind's causal relationship with our body.

There is also a related worry that, in attempting to explain how mental acts can result in bodily actions, Leibniz has ended up ultimately denying the reality of our freedom altogether. If all our actions can be deduced *a priori* from facts regarding our unchanging essences or nature, then it seems that nothing that we do could have been otherwise. Given that all monads are unique, there is no other way that you could have been: if one of your actions had been different, it would have been someone else doing it! So, although there could have been an individual *like* you who, for example, had pizza last night for dinner instead of pasta, that individual *would not have been you*. So, there seems to be no substantive way in which you could have done anything other than what you do at every moment of your life. Thus there seems to be a serious question about whether genuine freedom is possible for us within Leibniz's account.[9]

Key Points

- The "conceptual-containment" theory of truth leads to the claim that everything that happens to a substance is already encoded within its complete concept, such that we could deduce *a priori* from that concept all events in its existence.
- Leibniz rejects the Cartesian notion of matter on the basis that (1) spatial properties alone are unable to account for everything we might want to claim about some bodies, and (2) some properties of bodies are indistinct, which reveals their basis in our subjectivity.

- Leibniz explains apparent interaction between substances on the basis of a pre-established harmony between them.
- The union of body and mind is explained by a uniquely close correspondence between changes of state in the mind and changes in the body.

Suggested Further Reading

Jolley, Nicholas. *Leibniz*, second ed., chs. 1–4. Abingdon: Routledge, 2020.

Phemister, Pauline. "Descartes and Leibniz." In *The Continuum Companion to Leibniz*, edited by Look, 16–31. London: Continuum, 2011.

Rodriguez-Pereyra, Gonzalo. "Leibniz: Mind-Body Causation and Pre-established Harmony." In *Routledge Companion to Metaphysics*, edited by Le Poidevin et al., 109–18. New York: Routledge, 2009.

Rozemond, Marleen. "Leibniz on the Union of Body and Soul." *Archiv für Geschichte der Philosophie* 79 (1997): 150–78.

Shand, John. *Philosophy and Philosophers: An Introduction to Western Philosophy*. Chesham: Acumen, 2002, 93–104.

Questions for Reflection

- If there is a God, could he create "dead" matter?
- Could having our capacity for free will justify the possibility of evil and suffering in the world?
- Could we be free in a universe with pre-established harmony?
- Is a monist approach ultimately successful in offering a solution to the problem of interaction and mind-body union?

4

Materialist Responses
Thomas Hobbes and Margaret Cavendish

Chapter Outline

4a.	Hobbes on Matter and the Limits of Philosophy	88
4b.	Cavendish on the Possibility of Thinking Matter	100
Questions for Reflection		111

As we saw in the previous chapter, some philosophers attempted to avoid the problems faced by **substance dualism**† through the adoption of what we can call a **type monist**† position, according to which there is only one fundamental type of thing in the universe. Of these monists, some (such as Anne Conway and Gottfried Leibniz) opted for a theory that posited thinking, perceiving things as the only type of fundamental thing. The two philosophers we will be considering in this chapter, Thomas Hobbes and Margaret Cavendish, were also monists. However, unlike Conway and Leibniz, they opted for the claim that it is material or corporeal substance that is the only fundamental type. In making such a claim, Hobbes and Cavendish both departed from the views we have discussed so far, all of which hold that at least some **substances**† are incorporeal, lacking material or physical qualities. As we shall see in the following discussion, not only did Hobbes and Cavendish both attack the notion of incorporeal substance, but they also offered positive arguments for **materialism**†, grounded in a new vision of the methods and limits of philosophy.

4A. HOBBES ON MATTER AND THE LIMITS OF PHILOSOPHY

Thomas Hobbes: Brief Chronology

- 1588: Born in Malmesbury, Wiltshire
- 1608: Graduates from Oxford University and enters the service of William Cavendish, future earl of Devonshire (his connection with the Cavendish family would continue for the rest of his life)
- 1629: Publishes first academic work, a translation of Thucydides's *History of the Peloponnesian War*
- 1640: Becomes more active philosophically, writing *The Elements of Law* and objections to Descartes's *Meditations*. Leaves for exile in France to avoid possible civil war
- 1651: Returns from exile and publishes his most famous work, *Leviathan*
- c. 1670: Writes a history of the English Civil War, *Behemoth*, eventually published posthumously
- 1679: Dies on December 4, at Hardwick Hall in Derbyshire

In his main work, *Leviathan*, Thomas Hobbes rejects the notion of incorporeal substance as an "insignificant sound": the idea of an "incorporeal substance" is an example of "when men make a name of two Names, whose significations are contradictory and inconsistent,"[1] on a par with a "round quadrangle." Hobbes is a materialist, who holds that (at least as far as philosophical reasoning is concerned) we can coherently speak only of corporeal, not incorporeal, substance. As a result, we cannot follow the dualist or idealist monist in positing any kind of incorporeal or spiritual substance.

The roots of Hobbes's rejection of the notion of incorporeal substance lie in his empiricism, which he introduces here, in the first chapter of *Leviathan*:

Extract 4.1—Hobbes, *Leviathan* (Chapter I)

Concerning the Thoughts of Man, I will consider them first *Singly*, and afterwards in *Train*, or dependence upon one another. *Singly*, they are every one a *Representation* or *Appearance*, of some quality, or other Accident of a body without us; which is commonly called an *Object*.

Which Object works on the Eyes, Ears, and other parts of man's body; and by diversity of working, produces diversity of Appearances.

The Original of them all, is that which we call SENSE; (For there is no conception in a man's mind, which has not at first, totally, or by parts, been begotten upon the organs of Sense.) The rest are derived from that original.

To know the natural cause of Sense, is not very necessary to the business now in hand; and I have elsewhere written of the same at large. Nevertheless, to fill each part of my present method, I will briefly deliver the same in this place.

The cause of Sense, is the External Body, or Object, which presses the organ proper to each Sense, either immediately, as in the Taste and Touch; or mediately, as in Seeing, Hearing, and Smelling: which pressure, by the mediation of Nerves, and other strings, and membranes of the body, continued inwards to the Brain, and Heart, causes there a resistance, or counter-pressure, or endeavour of the heart, to deliver itself: which endeavour because *Outward*, seems to be some matter without. And this *seeming*, or *fancy*, is that which men call *Sense*; and consists, as to the Eye, in a *Light*, or *Colour figured*; To the Ear, in a *Sound*; To the Nostril, in an *Odour*; To the Tongue and Palate, in a *Savour*; And to the rest of the body, in *Heat*, *Cold*, *Hardness*, *Softness*, and such other qualities, as we discern by *Feeling*. All which qualities called *Sensible*, are in the object that causes them, but so many several motions of the matter, by which it presses our organs diversly. Neither in us that are pressed, are they anything else, but diverse motions; (for motion, produces nothing but motion). But their appearance to us is Fancy, the same waking, that dreaming. And as pressing, rubbing, or striking the Eye, makes us fancy a light; and pressing the Ear, produces a din; so do the bodies also we see, or hear, produce the same by their strong, though unobserved action.

For if those Colours, and Sounds, were in the Bodies, or Objects that cause them, they could not be severed from them, as by glasses, and in Echoes by reflection, we see they are; where we know the thing we see, is in one place; the appearance, in another. And though at some certain distance, the real, and very object seem invested with the fancy it begets in us; Yet still the object is one thing, the image or fancy is another. So that Sense in all cases, is nothing else but original fancy, caused (as I have said) by the pressure, that is, by the motion, of external things upon our Eyes, Ears, and other organs thereunto ordained.

[From *Leviathan, or The Matter, Forme, & Power of a Common-Wealth Ecclesiasticall and Civill* (London: Andrew Crooke, 1651). Some language has been modernized.]

In this extract, Hobbes makes the claim that all our ideas are rooted in sense-experience. Our senses work through mechanism, being impacted upon as part of a physical process traceable back to an external object. Either through a medium or directly, external objects exert a physical pressure upon our senses, which our mind then interprets in order to gain a sense of the environment around us. The physical process does not end at our senses, though: Hobbes characterizes the interpreting work of the mind as consisting itself in a physical process, where the pressure from the senses meets resistance in the physical brain.

In already offering a materialist theory of how the mind experiences the world, it could be argued that Hobbes is unfairly assuming that there is no incorporeal substance involved in operations of the mind such as having experiences. However, there are a couple of things that could be said in response to this possible objection. First, this chapter is just the first of a number of discussions that Hobbes offers in which he offers us a purely material account of how various mental activities could take place. In doing so, it could be argued in his defense that he is offering a cumulative argument in favor of a materialist theory of mind. If Hobbes can offer a comprehensive, ontologically elegant, and plausible theory of mind that does not depend on the rather mysterious notion of incorporeal or spiritual substance, then that would undoubtedly give us good reason to give his theory a fair hearing.

In addition, we can bolster Hobbes's argument by focusing on the very first claim he makes in the extract, namely, that all our ideas are traceable back to the physical processes that involve our senses. Given that our ideas can only come from this source, this acts as a constraint on what we can justifiably reason about: fundamentally, we are constrained to theorize only about things that we can perceive through the senses. In addition, given that Hobbes claims that the only way that our senses can be affected is through the direct or mediate impact of physical bodies, we can only perceive material bodies. As a result, philosophical reflection can only be materialist, insofar as it is constrained to reasoning about material bodies. Dualism or spiritual monism, on the other hand, can only be irrational speculation. All this leads to Hobbes's conclusion that all things in the universe are corporeal: "The World, (I mean not the Earth only, that denominates the Lovers of it Worldly men, but the Universe, that is the whole mass of all things that are) is corporeal, that is to say, body... and consequently every part of the Universe, is Body."[2]

It is worth dwelling a bit more on Hobbes's conception of philosophy, and how this feeds into his materialism. Hobbes outlines his account in more detail in the following extract:

Extract 4.2 — Hobbes, *Elements of Philosophy. The First Section, Concerning Body* (Chapter I, Selected Parts)

2. **Philosophy** *is such knowledge of effects or appearances, as we acquire by true ratiocination from the knowledge we have first of their causes or generation: And again, of such causes or generations as may be from knowing first their effects.*

For the better understanding of which definition, we must consider, first, that although Sense and Memory of things, which are common to man and all living creatures, be knowledge, yet because they are given us immediately by nature, and not gotten by ratiocination, they are not philosophy. Secondly, seeing Experience is nothing but memory; and Prudence, or prospect into the future time, nothing but expectation of such things as we have already had experience of, Prudence also is not to be esteemed philosophy.

By **RATIOCINATION**, I mean *computation*. Now to compute, is either to collect the sum of many things that are added together, or to know what remains when one thing is taken out of another. *Ratiocination*, therefore, is the same with *addition* and *subtraction* . . . So that all ratiocination is comprehended in these two operations of the mind, addition and subtraction.

3. But how by the *ratiocination* of our mind, we add and subtract in our silent thoughts, without the use of words, it will be necessary for me to make intelligible by an example or two. If therefore a man sees something afar off and obscurely, although no appellation had yet been given to anything, he will, notwithstanding, have the same idea of that thing for which now, by imposing a name on it, we call it *body*. Again, when, by coming nearer, he sees the same thing thus and thus, now in one place and now in another, he will have a new idea thereof, namely, that for which we now call such a thing *animated*. Thirdly, when standing nearer, he perceives the figure, hears the voice, and sees other things which are signs of a rational mind, he has a third idea, though it have yet no appellation, namely, that for which we now call anything *rational*. Lastly, when, by looking fully and distinctly upon it, he conceives all that he has seen as one thing, the idea he has now is compounded of his former ideas, which are put together in the mind in the same order in which these three single names, *body, animated, rational*, are in speech compounded into this one name, *body-animated-rational*, or *man*. In like manner, of the several conceptions of *four sides, equality of sides, and*

right angles, is compounded the conception of a *square*. For the mind may conceive a figure of four sides without any conception of their equality, and of that equality without conceiving a right angle; and may join together all these single conceptions into one conception or idea of a square. And thus we see how the conceptions of mind are compounded. Again, whosoever sees a man standing near him, conceives the whole idea of that man; and if, as he goes away, he follows him with his eyes only, he will lose the idea of those things which were signs of his being rational, whilst, nevertheless, the idea of a body-animated remains still before his eyes, so that the idea of rational is subtracted from the whole idea of man, that is to say, of body-animated-rational, and there remains that of body-animated; and a while after, at a greater distance, the idea of animated will be lost, and that of body only will remain; so that at last, when nothing at all can be seen, the whole idea will vanish out of sight. By which examples, I think, it is manifest enough what is the internal ratiocination of the mind without words . . .

4. But *effects* and the *appearances* of things to sense, are faculties or powers of bodies, which make us distinguish them from one another; that is to say, conceive one body to be equal or unequal, like or unlike to another body; as in the example above, when by coming near enough to any body, we perceive the motion and going of the same, we distinguish it thereby from a tree, a column, and other fixed bodies; and so that motion or going is the *property* thereof, as being proper to living creatures, and a faculty by which they make us distinguish them from other bodies.

5. How the knowledge of any effect may be gotten from the knowledge of the generation thereof, may easily be understood by example of a circle: for if there be set before us a plain figure, having, as near as may be, the figure of a circle, we cannot possibly perceive by sense whether it be a true circle or no; than which, nevertheless, nothing is more easy to be known to him that knows first the generation of the propounded figure. For let it be known that the figure was made by the circumduction of a body whereof one end remained unmoved, and we may reason thus; a body carried about, retaining always the same length, applies itself first to one *radius*, then to another, to a third, a fourth, and successively to all; and therefore the same length, from the same point, touches the circumference in every part thereof, which is as much to say, as all the *radii* are equal. We know, therefore, that from such generation proceeds a figure, from whose one middle point all the extreme points are reached unto by equal *radii*. And in like manner, by knowing first what figure is set before us, we may come by ratiocination to some generation of the same, though perhaps not that by which it was made, yet that by which it might have been made; for he that knows that a circle has the property

above declared, will easily know whether a body carried about, as is said, will generate a circle or no.

6. The *end* or *scope* of philosophy is, that we may make use to our benefit of effects formerly seen; or that, by application of bodies to one another, we may produce the like effects of those we conceive in our mind, as far forth as matter, strength, and industry, will permit, for the commodity of human life. For the inward glory and triumph of mind that a man may have for the mastering of some difficult and doubtful matter, or for the discovery of some hidden truth, is not worth so much pains as the study of Philosophy requires; nor need any man care much to teach another what he knows himself, if he think that will be the only benefit of his labour. The end of knowledge is power; and the use of theorems (which, among geometricians, serve for the finding out of properties) is for the construction of problems; and, lastly, the scope of all speculation is the performing of some action, or thing to be done.

-

8. The *subject* of Philosophy, or the matter it treats of, is every body of which we can conceive any generation, and which we may, by any consideration thereof, compare with other bodies, or which is capable of composition and resolution; that is to say, every body of whose generation or properties we can have any knowledge. And this may be deduced from the definition of philosophy, whose profession is to search out the properties of bodies from their generation, or their generation from their properties; and, therefore, where there is no generation or property, there is no philosophy. Therefore it excludes *Theology*, I mean the doctrine of God, eternal, ingenerable, incomprehensible, and in whom there is nothing neither to divide nor compound, nor any generation to be conceived.

It excludes the doctrine of a*ngels*, and all such things as are thought to be neither bodies nor properties of bodies; there being in them no place neither for composition nor division, nor any capacity of more and less, that is to say, no place for ratiocination.

It excludes *history*, as well *natural* as *political*, though most useful (nay necessary) to philosophy; because such knowledge is but experience, or authority, and not ratiocination.

It excludes all such knowledge as is acquired by Divine inspiration, or revelation, as not derived to us by reason, but by Divine grace in an instant, and, as it were, by some sense supernatural.

It excludes not only all doctrines which are false, but such also as are not well-grounded; for whatsoever we know by right ratiocination, can neither be false nor doubtful; and, therefore, *astrology*, as it is now held forth, and all such divinations rather than sciences, are excluded.

Lastly, the doctrine of God's worship is excluded from philosophy; as being not to be known by natural reason, but by the authority of the Church; and as being the object of faith, and not of knowledge.

9. The principal parts of philosophy are two. For two chief kinds of bodies, and very different from one another, offer themselves to such a search after their generation and properties; one whereof being the work of nature, is called a *natural body*, the other is called a *commonwealth*, and is made by the wills and agreement of men. And from these spring the two parts of philosophy, called *natural* and *civil*.

[From *The English Works of Thomas Hobbes of Malmesbury: Vol. I—Elements of Philosophy. The First Section, Concerning Body*, edited by Molesworth (London: John Bohn, 1839). Some language has been modernized.]

According to the conception of philosophy offered here, its scope is limited to what we can learn by reasoning either (i) about what effects will follow, given our knowledge of their causes, or (ii) about what causes must have occurred, given our knowledge of their effects. Though experience offers us the building blocks of philosophical knowledge (insofar as experience is at the basis of all our ideas), it does not itself directly provide us with that knowledge. What is required, in order to gain philosophical knowledge, is for us to engage in what Hobbes calls "ratiocination" or "computation," understood as the combining (addition) or dividing (subtraction) of ideas.

As an example of how this process of the gaining of philosophical knowledge works, Hobbes describes how someone may come to have the concept of "man." If you were approaching such a being for the first time, you might only think of that object as a mere body, just like other bodies you had come across. Then, you notice that the object is moving itself around with apparent purposiveness, so you add the idea of "animated" to the idea of "body" that you were already working with. Finally, you come close to the individual in question and notice various signs that you eventually understand to be reflecting the possession of a rational mind. Through ratiocination, you can therefore add the notions of "body," "animated," and "rational" together to generate the concept of "man," which can then stand as the foundation for further philosophical reflection. In addition, we can also take a concept such as "square" and focus separately on a square's necessary properties (e.g., we can consider the four-sided property of a square without even knowing that its sides and angles will be equal). Through such processes of addition and subtraction of ideas, Hobbes claims that we are able to undertake philosophical reflection that is as secure as a mathematical proof or "demonstration."

However, as Hobbes reiterates in Section 4, we are limited in our reflection to the effects or appearances of the objects of our senses. It is through an object's powers or properties that it is able to affect us through sensation at all, by bringing about the particular motion of an object that has an impact upon us (e.g., our eyes). In the example Hobbes provides, it is our experience of living creatures engaged in (apparently) purposive motion that allows us to have the concept of a living being at all, which permits us to distinguish living beings from non-living ones. However, we cannot legitimately speculate about whether life must involve some immaterial or spiritual aspect (as, say, Henry More and Anne Conway claimed). Our philosophical reflection is limited to considering the causal relationships among things as they appear to our senses, either from cause to effect or effect to cause. In this sense, philosophy is unavoidably materialist, focusing only on bodies and their material causal impact.

It is with these assumptions in mind that Hobbes describes "incorporeal substance" as a name that is an "insignificant sound." If philosophical reflection is limited in the way Hobbes suggests, then the notion of an incorporeal substance looks very suspect. For Hobbes, names are vocal sounds that function as both a mark and a sign.[3] *Marks* are things that aid us in bringing certain ideas from our memory to the forefront of our mind. So, for example, when I think of the name "Barack Obama," the name functions as a mark that brings to mind a complex of thoughts (44th president, born in Hawaii, etc.) that would not be so easily held together otherwise. Such a mark is ultimately arbitrary (the sound of "Barack Obama" is not necessarily the name required to fulfill this function, and indeed Barack Obama could have had a different name). Thus it is possible that different individuals could use different marks for the same complex of thoughts. As a result, a mark that is used by the individual to aid their memory ultimately needs to become a sign that is shared with others: we need to both use the name "Barack Obama" as a mark for the same complex of thoughts in order to effectively communicate about that individual. When a name is successfully shared with others, it becomes a *sign*: it signifies that an individual has certain ideas in their mind that are similar to the ideas held by those they are communicating with.

What makes a name, like "incorporeal substance," an insignificant sound? Given the analysis of Hobbes's position that I have just offered, it may be guessed that a name is an insignificant sound if it fails to signify a genuine idea in the speaker's mind. Further, given that all our ideas are traceable back to the physical processes that involve our senses, there seems to be no way for us to acquire an idea of an incorporeal substance that stands beyond physical processes. Given that we do not have a genuine idea of an incorporeal substance, and that such an idea would be required for the name "incorporeal substance" to be a significant sound, we appear to have a clear Hobbesian argument for his claim that talk of such a substance lacks significance.

As the scholar Stewart Duncan has argued,[4] Hobbes ultimately seems to be drawn between two possible argumentative strategies for establishing the claim that the name "incorporeal substance" is an insignificant sound, linked to two different accounts of the manner in which names signify things. First, we have an object-focused approach, according to which names signify a particular object that it refers to. On this approach, it might be argued that "incorporeal substance" is an insignificant sound on the basis that there is no object for such a name to refer to. We seem to find such an argument in Part III, Chapter 34 of *Leviathan*, where Hobbes seeks to clarify what the names "Body" and "Substance" signify: "The Word *Body*, in the most generall acceptation, signifieth that which filleth, or occupyeth some certain room, or imagined place," while the word "Substance" signifies that thing which has "various accidents,"[5] in other words, a thing that has some properties. On the basis of the signification of these words, Hobbes then argues for the insignificance of "incorporeal substance": "And according to this acceptation of the word, *Substance* and *Body*, signifie the same thing; and therefore *Substance incorporeall* are words, which when they are joined together, destroy one another, as if a man should say, an Incorporeall Body."[6] In this instance, Hobbes's argument seems to be that the name "incorporeal substance" does not mean anything on the basis that there is no object which it signifies (in other words, the attempt to speak of an incorporeal substance fails because there is no such thing that exists).

However, this cannot be all there is to this argument, as Hobbes presumably wants to affirm that we can talk meaningfully about some things which do not exist, such as unicorns. Therefore, in order for Hobbes's argument to reach the conclusion he intends, he must also assume that we know that the names "corporeal" and "substance" apply to the same set of objects (in other words, that these terms are *extensionally equivalent*), and it is on the basis of this knowledge that we can understand the term "incorporeal substance" as nonsensical. However, this assumption implies our knowing that all substances are in fact corporeal. If the argument is construed in this way, as being premised on our knowledge that there is no such thing as an incorporeal substance, this would arguably only ever supply an unsuccessful, circular argument for materialism. Hobbes could not establish that there is no such thing as incorporeal substance as a *conclusion* of his argument if that is already assumed as a *premise* of the argument.

Alternatively, we could read Hobbes as taking an idea-focused approach, according to which names signify particular ideas that we have (he seems to suggest this when he states that "all names are imposed to signify our conceptions"[7]). On this basis, we can take Hobbes's argument regarding the insignificance of "incorporeal substance" as premised on a lack of a genuine conception or idea of an incorporeal substance. While this idea-focused approach is stronger insofar as it is not obviously circular, it is nevertheless still questionable. Even if we grant to Hobbes that we cannot conceive of an *incorporeal body*, the further claim that the notion of an *incorporeal substance* is also inconceivable would perhaps be challenged by many readers. Certainly, Descartes and many other philosophers would reject this view. At the very least, Hobbes would need to supply an argument for why we think we have an idea of an incorporeal substance when we in fact do not. Hobbes's claim that we cannot conceive of an incorporeal substance therefore may just seem like another aspect of his circular assumptions regarding the truth of materialism.

There are a couple more objections to Hobbes's philosophy we can consider before we move on. First, we can question the adequacy of Hobbes's theory of mind. As the account presented in *Leviathan* suggests, various mental processes (such as sensation, imagination, and memory) can be explained in terms of various internal physical motions inside the brain. However, there seems to be something very important left out here—namely, consciousness, or what it feels like to be an experiencing mind. What goes on in the mind is not a process just like any other: there is all the difference in the world between, say, one snooker ball hitting another and my experience of seeing a water bottle bringing about a desire to drink some water. Crucially, we think that there is nothing it feels like to be a snooker ball hit by another snooker ball, though there is something it feels like to be a person looking at a water bottle and feeling thirsty as a result. In philosophical terminology, Hobbes is seemingly leaving out of his account of mind the central notion of "qualia," the idea that there are mental states of various kinds that are introspectively accessible to us as conscious beings, and that these states have a certain feel (or "phenomenal character"). If mental states are reducible to physical processes in the manner Hobbes is proposing, then how do we account for qualia? What is it that makes some physical processes give rise to qualia and that others do not? While later philosophers have attempted in various ways to account for consciousness within a materialist framework, this is an important gap that Hobbes seems to leave in his philosophy.

In addition, we can consider where Hobbes's philosophy leaves us with regard to speaking of God. As we saw earlier, Hobbes argues that our philosophical reasoning is limited to material bodies. At the same time, though, Hobbes also attempts to provide a philosophical argument for the existence of God. In the *Leviathan*, we find a sketch of a cosmological argument for the existence of God, based on the need for the universe to have a cause: "Curiosity, or love of the knowledge of causes, draws a man from consideration of the effect, to seek the cause; and again, the cause of that cause; till of necessity he must come to this thought at last, that there is some cause, whereof there is no former cause, but is eternal; which is it men call God. So that it is impossible to make any profound enquiry into natural causes, without being inclined thereby to believe there is one God eternal."[8] However, it is questionable whether Hobbes can even make this argument by his own understanding of the limits of philosophy, at least without radically altering the traditional understanding of God. At most, it seems that we can only gain a greatly impoverished notion of God in this manner, as a mere "first mover," rather than as the **omnipotent**[†], **omniscient**[†], loving, all-good God that **theists**[†] traditionally believe in. We can know that there is a God, on Hobbes's view, but cannot know anything of his nature or essence. For his part, Hobbes accepts that the nature of God cannot be characterized through philosophical reflection ("philosophy excludes theology, [by which] I mean the doctrine of God"[9]), but this may be an unacceptably strict epistemic restriction upon our knowledge of God for many theists. In addition, given Hobbes's account of motion as equivalent to cause, it would appear that God can only be construed through this argument as having some sort of corporeality, which the later Hobbes does claim.[10] Again, Hobbes's argument leads to a radical notion of God and the limits of philosophy that many religious thinkers would find objectionable.

As we have seen, Hobbes struggles to explain how qualia is possible within the confines of a materialist picture of nature. In more general terms, we can ask: how is it possible that matter can think? In the following section, we shall see how fellow materialist, Margaret Cavendish, tries to answer this question.

Key Points

- Hobbes is a materialist, who argues that the notion of incorporeal substance is an "insignificant sound."
- He offers a physicalist, empiricist account of the origin of our ideas that questions how we could gain a genuine idea of incorporeal substance.
- Given philosophical reflection is limited to considering the causal motion of things as they appear to us, we do not have the ability to reason about incorporeal substance.
- Hobbes's argument for materialism faces charges of circularity, inconsistency, and lacking an explanation for qualia, as well as religious objections.

Suggested Further Reading

Copleston, Frederick. *A History of Philosophy: Volume 5*, ch. 1. New York: Image Books, 1964.

Leijenhorst, Cees. "Sense and Nonsense about Sense: Hobbes and the Aristotelians on Sense Perception and Imagination." In *The Cambridge Companion to Hobbes's Leviathan*, edited by Springborg, 82–108. Cambridge: Cambridge University Press, 2007.

Martinich, A. P. *Hobbes*, chs. 2 and 5. New York: Routledge, 2005.

Sorell, Tom. "Seventeenth-Century Materialism: Gassendi and Hobbes." In *Routledge History of Philosophy: Vol. IV*, edited by Parkinson, 235–72. Abingdon: Routledge, 1993.

Springborg, Patricia. "Hobbes on Religion." In *The Cambridge Companion to Hobbes*, edited by Sorell, 346–80. Cambridge: Cambridge University Press, 1996.

4B. CAVENDISH ON THE POSSIBILITY OF THINKING MATTER

Margaret Cavendish: Brief Chronology

- 1623: Born in Colchester
- 1645: Marries William Cavendish while in exile in Paris, becoming part of an intellectual circle that included Descartes, Mersenne, and Hobbes
- 1653: Publishes first works, *Poems, and Fancies* and *Philosophicall Fancies*
- 1660: Returns to England, upon the restoration of the monarchy
- 1662: Publishes her first collection of plays
- 1666: Publishes one of her most important philosophical works, *Observations upon experimental philosophy to which is added The description of a new blazing world*
- 1667: Becomes first woman to attend a meeting of the Royal Society
- 1672: Dies at home in Welbeck. Buried in Westminster Abbey, with the inscription, "a wise wittie and learned Lady"

Margaret Cavendish was an acquaintance of Thomas Hobbes, the two having met while both were in exile in France during the years following the English Civil War, when England was governed as a republic. Although Cavendish claimed that they only ever exchanged a few words directly and she was never party to any philosophical conversations that involved him,[11] she was clearly familiar with a number of his philosophical texts, including those extracted earlier. Both sought to defend materialist philosophies, with Cavendish providing several distinctive arguments against the notion of an immaterial substance.

As an example, like many critics of dualism, Cavendish pointed to the difficulty of explaining interaction between a corporeal and an immaterial substance: "I cannot understand how an immaterial substance should make a print upon a corporeal substance, for Printing is a corporeal action, and belongs only to bodies."[12] However, in this instance, she places this argument within the context of the metaphysics of pregnancy, by asking how the immaterial soul of a child is produced from their two parents. Immaterial souls were often taken to be indivisible (i.e., incapable of being divided) and so it would be impossible for a part of the parents' respective souls to be sectioned off and used to create a new soul.[13] Further, it is also difficult to understand how a soul could be indivisible if it were produced by two parts coming from both father and mother. One alternative to this view, as Cavendish sees it, is to claim that the soul of a child is a direct creation of God at conception. However, Cavendish argues that this is difficult to square with any commitment to the inherently sinful nature of the human soul: in other words, how could God directly create something that is immediately inherently sinful?[14]

The only way out of this impasse is to accept that we are actually talking about a purely material process (in which case, it is easy to understand, in principle at least, how matter from both parents could interact in order to produce a child, without any need to posit a direct intervention from God). Pregnancy does not involve the production of an immaterial substance from another immaterial substance (or substances); rather, a child is simply a corporeal thing, just like their parents. Connecting this back to the **mind-body problem**[†], it is also difficult for the dualist to explain how a process involving immaterial substances could bring about the material body of the child, given that the "printing" of an image is only a "corporeal action." Again, if there are only corporeal substances involved, it is rather easier to understand how the corporeal body of a child could be produced according to a particular plan, as we see in pregnancy.

This latter argument, though, only carries if we accept Cavendish's assumption that such a process of interaction would have to be a corporeal one, and that all interaction involving material substances is only by contact with other material substances. On that basis, given the further assumption that there is some form of genuine interaction between the mind and body, the mind must be corporeal. Why should we accept these assumptions? While we may not be able to establish with certainty that there is genuine mind-body interaction and that interaction involving material substances is only via corporeal contact, Cavendish might claim strong probabilistic arguments for these assertions. Given the constant experience we have of states of the body affecting states of the mind, and vice versa, our assumption should be that there is genuine mind-body interaction, unless there are sufficiently strong countervailing reasons to abandon such a notion. The incentive for questioning such interaction rests on the assumption that it has to be between two entirely different kinds of substance; if, on the other hand, we accept that such interaction is between material things only, then the metaphysical issues that sparked the debate are resolved. So, the most likely conclusion we come to is that mind-body interaction is a genuine, wholly corporeal process. On that basis, it is also most probable that all interaction in nature is by contact between corporeal substances: while we could posit some other forms of mysterious, incorporeal interaction, we would need overwhelming evidence for such processes before it could rationally supersede our intuitive experience of nature as involving only interaction between material substances by immediate contact.

Alongside her argument regarding the nature of pregnancy, many of Cavendish's arguments for materialism can be found in her book from 1664, *Philosophical Letters*. It is indeed written in the format of letters, from Cavendish to a fictional philosophical correspondent, who had asked for her opinion on some of the most prominent philosophers of the day, including Descartes and More. In addition to offering criticisms of these thinkers, Cavendish also offers a defense of some elements of her philosophy. In the following selections, Cavendish offers arguments against Descartes's and More's respective philosophical dualisms (which were covered in Chapter 1 of this book):

Extract 4.3—Cavendish, *Philosophical Letters* (Section I, Letters XXX and XXXVa; Section II, Letter XXI)

Madam,

I am reading now the works of that Famous and most Renowned *Author, Des Cartes*, out of which I intend to pick out only those discourses which I like best, and not to examine his opinions, as they go along from the beginning to the end of his books; And in order to [do] this, I have chosen in the first place, his discourse of motion, and do not assent to his opinion, when he defines *Motion to be only a Mode of a thing, and not the thing or body itself*; for, in my opinion, there can be no abstraction made of motion from body, neither really, nor in the manner of our conception, for how I can conceive that which is not, nor cannot be in nature, that is, to conceive motion without body? Wherefore Motion is but one thing with body, without any separation or abstraction soever.

Neither does it agree with my reason, that *one body can give or transfer motion into another body; and as much motion it gives or transfers into that body, as much loses it: As* for example, in two hard bodies thrown against one another, where one, that is thrown with greater force, takes the other along with it, and loses as much motion as it gives it. For how can motion, being no substance, but only a mode, quit one body, and pass into another? One body may either occasion, or imitate another's motion, but it can neither give nor take away what belongs to its own or another body's substance, no more than matter can quit its nature from being matter; and therefore my opinion is, that if motion does go out of one body into another, then substance goes too; for motion, and substance or body, as afore-mentioned, are all one thing, and then all bodies that receive motion from other bodies, must needs increase in their substance and quantity, and those bodies which impart or transfer motion, must decrease as much as they increase: Truly, *Madam*, that neither Motion nor Figure should subsist by themselves, and yet be transferable into other bodies, is very strange, and as much as to prove them to be nothing, and yet to say they are something.

The like may be said of all others, which they call accidents, as skill, learning, knowledge etc. saying, they are no bodies, because they have no extension, but inherent in bodies or substances as in their subjects; for although the body may subsist without them, yet they being always with the body, body and they are all one thing: And so is power and body, for body cannot quit power, nor power the body, being all one thing.

But to return to Motion, my opinion is, That all matter is partly animate, and partly inanimate, and all matter is moving and moved, and that there is no part of Nature that have not life and knowledge, for there is no Part that has not a commixture of animate and inanimate matter; and though the inanimate matter has no motion, nor life and knowledge of itself, as the animate has, nevertheless being both so closely joined and commixed as in one body, the inanimate moves as well as the animate, although not in the same manner; for the animate moves of itself, and the inanimate moves by the help of the animate, and thus the animate is moving and the inanimate moved; not that the animate matter transfers, infuses, or communicates its own motion to the inanimate; for this is impossible, by reason it cannot part with its own nature, nor alter the nature of inanimate matter, but each retains its own nature; for the inanimate matter remains inanimate, that is, without self-motion, and the animate loses nothing of its self-motion, which otherwise it would, if it should impart or transfer its motion into the inanimate matter; but only as I said heretofore, the inanimate works or moves with the animate, because of their close union and commixture; for the animate forces or causes the inanimate matter to work with her; and thus one is moving, the other moved, and consequently there is life and knowledge in all parts of nature, by reason in all parts of nature there is a commixture of animate and inanimate matter: and this Life or Knowledge is sense and reason, or sensitive and rational corporeal motions, which are all one thing with animate matter without any distinction or abstraction, and can no more quit matter, than matter can quit motion.

Wherefore every creature being composed of this commixture of animate and inanimate matter, has also self-motion, that is life and knowledge, sense and reason, so that no part have need to give or receive motion to or from another part; although it may be an occasion of such a manner of motion to another part, and cause it to move thus or thus: as for example, A Watch-maker does not give the watch its motion, but he is only the occasion, that the watch moves after that manner, for the motion of the watch is the watch's own motion, inherent in those parts ever since that matter was, and if the watch ceases to move after such a manner or way, that manner or way of motion is nevertheless in those parts of matter, the watch is made of, and if several other figures should be made of that matter, the power of moving in the said manner or mode, would yet still remain in all those parts of matter as long as they are body, and have motion in them.

Wherefore one body may occasion another body to move so and so, but not give it any motion, but everybody (though occasioned by another, to move in such a way) moves by its own natural motion; for self-motion is the very nature of animate matter, and is as much in hard, as in fluid bodies, although your *Author* denies it, saying, *The nature of fluid bodies consists in the motion of those little insensible parts into which they are divided, and the nature of hard bodies, when those little particles joined closely together, do rest*; for there is no rest in nature; wherefore if there were a World of Gold, and a World of Air, I do verily believe, that the World of Gold would be as much interiorly active, as the World of Air exteriorly; for Nature's motions are not all external or perceptible by our senses, neither are they all circular, or only of one sort, but there is an infinite change and variety of motions; for though I say in my Philosophical opinions, *As there is but one only Matter, so there is but one only Motion*; yet I do not mean, there is but one particular sort of motions, as either circular, or straight, or the like, but that the nature of motion is one and the same, simple and entire in itself, that is, it is mere motion, or nothing else but corporeal motion; and that as there are infinite divisions or parts of matter, so there are infinite changes and varieties of motions, which is the reason I call motion as well infinite as matter; first that matter and motion are but one thing, and if matter be infinite, motion must be so too; and secondly, that motion is infinite in its changes and variations, as matter is in its parts. And thus much of motion for this time; I add no more, but rest,

Madam,
Your faithful Friend,
and Servant.

-

Madam,

That the Mind, according to your *Author's* opinion, *is a substance really distinct from the body, and may be actually separated from it and subsist without it*. If he means the natural mind and soul of Man, not the supernatural or divine, I am far from his opinion; for though the mind moves only in its own parts, and not upon, or with the parts of inanimate matter, yet it cannot be separated from these parts of matter, and subsist by itself; as being a part of one and the same matter the inanimate is of, (for there is but one only matter, and one kind of matter, although of several degrees,) only it is the self-moving part; but yet this cannot empower it, to quit the same natural body, whose part it is. Neither can I apprehend, that the Mind's or Soul's seat should be in the *Glandula* or kernel of the Brain, and there sit like a Spider in a Cobweb, to whom the least motion of the Cobweb gives intelligence of a Fly, which he is ready to assault, and that the Brain should get intelligence by the animal spirits as his servants, which run to and fro like Ants to inform it; or that the Mind should, according to others' opinions, be a light, and embroidered all with Ideas, like a Herald's coat; and that the sensitive organs should have no knowledge in themselves, but serve only like peeping-holes for the mind, or barn doors to receive bundles of pressures, like sheaves of Corn; For there being a thorough mixture of animate, rational and sensitive, and inanimate matter, we cannot assign a certain seat or place to the rational, another to the sensitive, and another to the inanimate, but they are diffused and intermixed throughout all the body; And this is the reason, that sense and knowledge cannot be bound only to the head or brain: But although they are mixed together, nevertheless they do not lose their interior natures by this mixture, nor their purity and subtlety, nor their proper motions or actions, but each moves according to its nature and substance, without confusion; The actions of the rational part in Man, which is the Mind or Soul, are called Thoughts, or thoughtful perceptions, which are numerous, and so are the sensitive perceptions; for though Man, or any other animal haves but five exterior sensitive organs, yet there be numerous perceptions made in these sensitive organs, and in all the body; nay, every several Pore of the flesh is a sensitive organ, as well as the Eye, or the Ear. But both sorts, as well as the rational as the sensitive, are different from each other although both do resemble another, as being both parts of animate matter, as I have mentioned before: Wherefore I'll add no more, only let you know, that I constantly remain,

Madam,

Your faithful Friend,

and Servant.

-

Madam,

Your *Author* [now referring to Henry More] endeavours very much to prove the existence of a *Natural Immaterial Spirit*, whom he defines to be an *Incorporeal substance, Indivisible that can move itself, can penetrate contract and dilate itself, and can also move and alter the matter.* Whereof, if you will have my opinion I confess freely to you, that in my sense and reason I cannot conceive it to be possible, that there is any such thing in Nature; for all that is a substance in Nature, is a body, and what has a body, is corporeal; for though there be several degrees of matter, as in purity, rarity, subtlety, activity; yet there is no degree so pure, rare and subtle, that can go beyond its nature, and change from corporeal to incorporeal, except it could change from being something to nothing, which is impossible in Nature. Next, there is no substance in Nature that is not divisible; for all that is a body, or bodily substance, has extension, and all extension has parts, and what has parts, is divisible. As for self-motion, contraction and dilation, these are actions only of Natural Matter; for Matter by the Power of God is self-moving, and all sorts of motion, as contraction, dilation, alteration, penetration etc. do properly belong to matter; so that natural Matter stands in no need to have some Immaterial or Incorporeal substance to move, rule, guide and govern her, but she is able enough to do it all herself, by the free Gift of the Omnipotent God; for why should we trouble ourselves to invent or frame other unconceivable substances, when there is no need for it, but Matter can act, and move as well without them and of itself? Is not God able to give such power to Matter, as to another Incorporeal substance? . . .

[From *Philosophical Letters, or, Modest Reflections upon some opinions in Natural Philosophy*. London: np., 1664. Some language has been modernized.]

In the first letter earlier, we see Cavendish addressing the question of how mind-body interaction is possible, in relation to her account of the nature of motion. As we saw earlier, given that Cavendish believes that mind-body interaction *is* possible, we must view the mind as material in nature (as per her monism). Nevertheless, we do intuitively feel that there is something distinctive about the mind: the substance that makes up my mind is not just like the matter that makes up a simple pebble, for example. Can Cavendish incorporate a sense of the distinctive nature of the mind within her materialist monism, without having to smuggle a kind of dualism in through the back door? In order to achieve this, Cavendish distinguishes between animate (both rational and sensible) and inanimate matter, and argues that all things in nature are made up of a mixture of the two (we can therefore speak of her theory as a kind of "vitalist materialism," reflecting her commitment to a monism that allows for living matter). The animate part of matter is able to direct inanimate matter into particular movements, as well structuring it into the ordered, often intricate forms we find throughout nature: "there be Sense and Reason, which is not only Motion, but a regular and well-ordered self-motion, apparent in the wonderful and various Productions, Generations, Transformations, Dissolutions, Compositions, and other actions of Nature, in all Nature's parts and particles."[15] The order and structure we find in nature requires, as far as Cavendish is concerned, a kind of intelligence within matter itself (distinct from any kind of transcendent intelligence such as God). So, our experience of nature shows that there is animate matter as well as inanimate matter.

With regard to the question of motion and causation, Cavendish claims that the motion of an object derives from within, that is, from the animate part of all matter. This is a version of **occasionalism**† (an account of the relationship between cause and effect as mediated or indirect): it is not that motion transfers from one object to another; rather, one object (the cause) is the "occasion" for another object (the effect) to begin an internal process of self-motion that results in the experience of motion that we can view from the outside. In this way, Cavendish rejects an understanding of motion as a mode or property of a thing (or, in other words, something that a body *has* at a particular moment in time). As far as Cavendish sees it, a body does not *have* motion; rather, it *just is in motion*. If motion were something a body has (which can then be passed on to another body upon impact), then we would be able to conceive of motion as separate from body. Cavendish argues that we cannot make such an abstraction in our conception, and so motion cannot be a mode of a thing (as claimed by Descartes).

More specifically, though, how does mind-body interaction work on Cavendish's account? As we see in the extract earlier, animate matter is able to "force" or "cause" inanimate matter to move in virtue of the two being in a "commixture" with each other. In line with her rejection of the transference account of causation, animate matter does not pass on motion to inanimate matter; rather, because the two are inextricably intertwined with each other, the self-motion of one brings about the motion of another. Clearly, the details of this account are quite sketchy, and we could still raise questions about how it is possible that animate matter is able to interact with inanimate matter (just calling them both "matter" does not necessarily help with this), but it reflects Cavendish's desire to stress the oneness and unity of mind and body, rather than treating them as two entirely separate things.

Cavendish's postulation of animate matter is part of her rejection of the metaphysics of Henry More, as seen in the third letter selected earlier. More had argued that the apparent purpose and organization we find in nature did indeed require an intelligence within nature itself, but that this was a kind of soul that was not part of matter itself, instead directing it from the outside. Cavendish argues here that the postulation of such a soul is unjustified for a number of reasons: for example, there is no reason to believe that God could not create animate matter, and therefore any divine creation of a soul would not serve any function, making nature less simple and elegant. In addition, Cavendish argues that all substances in nature that are extended must be divisible (in other words, could in principle be divided into parts). Thus, More has claimed the existence of an impossible thing, namely, an immaterial soul that is supposed to be indivisible and yet extended. This connects with Cavendish's claim earlier that all parts of a material body require animation, and thus extended and divisible animate matter is required to animate extended and divisible inanimate matter.

Considering the second letter selected earlier, Cavendish claims that Descartes is incorrect in arguing that the mind could be separated and continue to exist apart from the body. Though we can conceptually distinguish between animate and inanimate matter, the two cannot be separated in fact. In other words, they are an inseparable mixture. This is relatedly a rejection of Descartes's principle that we can know that mind and body are distinct because we can conceive of them as having separate existences. Cavendish claims, in contrast to Descartes, that the fact that we can consider animate and inanimate matter as being separate does not imply that they can in fact exist separately. (In other words, she denies that everything that is conceivable is metaphysically possible.) Intriguingly, Cavendish also draws the implication from her theory that the mind is not confined to a particular part of the body, which is partly a rejoinder to views like Descartes's that tried to locate the link between mind and body in the pineal gland[16]. Rather than the mind being confined to the physical brain, even, Cavendish states that the rational and sensitive aspect of matter permeates throughout the body.

One question which Cavendish's views might raise here is that of the afterlife. Cavendish's view of bodily death is expressed in terms of mere rearrangement of matter. All parts of nature have life and retain a life of sorts regardless of the present material structure of which they form part. Thus, while the bodily life of a particular animal may come to an end, the parts of that animal retain their life as they potentially go on to form part of another creature.[17] So, in one sense, we will all "live on," in that all our parts will continue to live and be part of the material structure of other beings to come in the future. However, there is no clear sense in which I, as an individual, will live on, in some sort of afterlife, unless we assume some sort of bodily resurrection in which the material parts that once constituted me will be rearranged as me again at some point in the future.

One of the attractions of substance dualism, at least for some religious believers, is that it neatly explains how an individual can live on after death; namely, the mind, as a separate substance, loses its connection with the physical body and moves on to another sphere of existence. In addition, it helps to avoid a possible commitment to the need for a bodily resurrection, which can be seen as a rather problematic doctrine, given the possibility of two creatures sharing some matter that composed part of them during their respective lifetimes, such as in, for example, cases of cannibalism! In contrast, as we have stated, Cavendish's theory potentially makes the explanation of how the afterlife is possible quite difficult, if one wishes to avoid a doctrine of bodily resurrection.

In reply, it could be argued that, despite seeming quite heterodox to begin with, Cavendish's position is at the very least not antithetical to some common theistic views regarding personal immortality and the afterlife. Nothing in Cavendish's approach ultimately rules out the possibility of an afterlife. It may be that we cannot conceive of an immaterial soul, and how that soul may be linked to a particular individual, but that does not make it the case that they do not exist. We can note that in the extract earlier, Cavendish distinguishes between "the natural mind and soul" and a possible "supernatural or divine" soul. On a more orthodox reading of Cavendish, we could construe her objections to Cartesian dualism as focused on the notion of a *natural* mind or soul, rather than against a supernatural soul that somehow survives bodily death and goes on to a further form of existence. Thus, though it may seem difficult to understand how an afterlife is possible within Cavendish's brand of vitalist materialism, the possibility of such a supernatural soul that cannot be confirmed through our usual bounds of knowledge perhaps makes the question of afterlife one of faith and hope, rather than of philosophy (which may seem quite right to some).

A final issue we might like to consider here is whether Cavendish has indeed moved beyond the dualism that she rejects. In distinguishing between different sorts of matter, has she not merely relabeled "matter" as "inanimate matter" and "spirit" or "mind" as "animate matter"? If this is simply what she has achieved, then she will face all the same objections that she and others posed to dualist philosophies (and arguing that all things in nature are a mixture of these different types of matter will not necessarily help her with this problem). To put a more positive spin on this, though, it could be argued that Cavendish is to some extent attempting to move beyond the simple debate between dualists and monists by offering a distinctive understanding of matter as incorporating features that had traditionally been reserved for either body or spirit. The different levels of activity within nature are inseparably linked in all material beings, with matter at differing degrees of subtlety and purity being able to have an impact upon each other that avoids drawing an overly dualistic picture of reality. Though there are undoubtedly significant philosophical differences between Cavendish and Anne Conway (discussed in the previous chapter), we can view both of their monist ontologies as offering innovative conceptions of matter that does not seek to merely reduce the mental to the material or vice versa; rather, mind and body are taken to sit on a kind of continuum that allows more easily for genuine interaction between the two.

Key Points

- Cavendish is a materialist, who argues against the notion of an indivisible soul.
- The way to avoid the problem of mind-body interaction is to view it as an entirely corporeal process.
- Cavendish postulates a kind of animate matter that has self-motion and is able to direct inanimate matter in various ways.
- The rational aspect (what we might think of as the mind) of an individual permeates throughout the physical body.

Suggested Further Reading

Boyle, Deborah. *The Well-Ordered Universe: The Philosophy of Margaret Cavendish*, chs. 2–3. Oxford: Oxford University Press, 2018.

Broad, Jacqueline. *Women Philosophers of the Seventeenth Century*, ch. 2. Cambridge: Cambridge University Press, 2002.

Cunning, David. *Cavendish: Arguments of the Philosophers*, ch. 2. London: Routledge, 2016.

James, Susan. "The Philosophical Innovations of Margaret Cavendish." *British Journal for the History of Philosophy* 7, no. 2 (1999): 219–44.

Wilkins, Emma. "'Exploding' Immaterial Substances: Margaret Cavendish's Vitalist-Materialist Critique of Spirits." *British Journal for the History of Philosophy* 24, no. 5 (2016): 858–77.

Questions for Reflection

- Can we genuinely think about or conceive of an immaterial substance?
- Can matter think?
- In attempting to explain the mental, can a materialist ultimately avoid slipping back into dualism?
- Can a materialist explain how life after death is possible?

Part II

Sociability and Education

5

The Nature of Love

John Norris, Mary Astell, and Damaris Masham

Chapter Outline

5a.	Norris and Astell on Love of God	116
5b.	Masham's critique of Norris and Astell	127
	Questions for Reflection	137

This second part of the book covers different debates concerning various aspects of social relations. We begin with the discussion concerning the nature of love between Norris, Astell, and Masham. The debates concerning the relation between mind and body (discussed in the first part of the book) led to questions concerning the source of our sensations. Norris argues for an **occasionalist**† viewpoint, from which he thinks it follows that God is the only true cause of pleasure, and as such should be the only object of our love. Astell and Masham both challenge this view, presenting arguments in favor of the conclusion that the material objects of the world can be legitimately loved. Masham, among other things, emphasizes the importance of love between persons for the sustenance of social relations and morality, as well as developing an **empiricist**† methodology, which we will consider in more detail in the following chapter.

5A. NORRIS AND ASTELL ON LOVE OF GOD

John Norris: Brief Chronology

- 1657: Born in Collingbourne Kingston, Wiltshire
- 1676: Begins studies at Exeter College, Oxford
- 1680: Elected a Fellow of All Souls College, Oxford
- 1689: Marries and thus has to leave his Fellowship. Publishes major critique of Locke's *Essay concerning Human Understanding*. Briefly becomes a rector at Newton St Lowe, Somerset, before moving to Bemerton, Wiltshire
- 1701: Publishes the first volume of his major philosophical work, *An Essay towards the Theory of the Ideal or Intelligible World*
- 1711: Dies at Bemerton

John Norris was quite unusual for focusing as a philosopher on the topic of love, but he believed it to be a very important one. He sees the capacity for love (in the broad sense of feeling drawn toward something) as one of the two central aspects of the human condition, alongside the use of our understanding, and argues that only God can be the proper object of this love.[1] Further, Norris claims that it is through love that we are most able to better ourselves and prepare for the afterlife: "Love is not only the shortest and most compendious Way to Perfection, but the greatest Height and Pitch of it. The more we have of love, the nearer Advances we make to GOD, who is Love itself, and who breaths forth from him essential and substantial Love, the more fit we are to taste the Sweetness of Divine Communion."[2] The way in which we love, Norris argues, determines our moral standing:

> For what is the grand intendment and final upshot of Morality but to teach a man to *Love regularly*? As a man *Loves* so is he. Love is not only the *Fulfilling*, but also the *Transgressing* of the Law, and Virtue and Vice is nothing else but the Various Application and Modification of *Love*. By this a good man is distinguished from a bad.[3]

Loving in the right way leads us to do the right thing, while acting immorally stems from loving the wrong things in the wrong way.

In staking out this position, Norris distinguishes between two types of love, "concupiscence" and "benevolence," and discusses the grounding of love in a relation between God and the soul.

Extract 5.1 — Norris, *The Theory and Regulation of Love* (Part I, Section II — excerpts)

5[4][4]. And indeed [love] *needs* [theory and inspection], as well as *deserves* it. For there is nothing that darkens the Nature of things, and obscures the Clarity of our Conceptions more than Ambiguity of Terms, and I know nothing that is more Equivocal and full of Latitude than this word, *Love*. It is given to things whose Ideas are Notoriously different, and men seem to have agreed together not to detect the Fallacy, and from the Identity of the *name* to conclude the Identity of the *thing*. To give one instance out of many, what is there that passes for an Axiom of a more simple, certain and uniform Signification than that Common Proposition in Divinity, that *we must love God for himself, and our Neighbour for God's sake*. But now when we come to examine what Ideas we have under these words, 'tis plain that that Ideas which is expressed by Love in the first part of the Proposition, is not the same with that which is expressed by Love in the Second. For Love in reference to God signifies *Simple Desire*, and in reference to our Neighbour, *wishing well to*, which Ideas are as different as East and West, and yet because of the Commons of the Name, and the Jingling turn of the Proposition, this passes smoothly and unquestionably for one and the same Love.

5. But though this word Love be used to signify Ideas so very different that they seem to have nothing in Common but the Name, yet I think there is one thing wherein they all agree and whereof they all partake, and which may therefore be acknowledged as the *General* and *Transcendental* Notion of Love. And that is, *A motion of the Soul towards good* . . . [This] may as fitly be called *the Moral Gravitation of the Soul*.

6. I further Consider that this *Moral Gravity* is impressed upon the Soul primarily and Originally by *good* in *general*, or by the universal good or Essence of good, that is, by God himself, who is the Sum and Abstract of all goodness, and the Centre of all Love. So that this *Moral Gravity* of the Soul will be its *Connaturality* to all good, or good in general, that is, to God as its primary and adequate object, and to particular goods only so far as they have something of the Common Nature of good, something of Good in them. Whence it will also follow that the *Moral Gravitation* of the Soul does Naturally and Necessarily respect good in Common or God as the Term of its motion and Tendency. So that upon the whole to speak

more *explicitly* the most general and Comprehensive Notion of Love will be found to be, *A motion of the Soul towards God.*

9. But notwithstanding [the variety of different sorts of love] I believe all will be comprehended under these two in general, *Concupiscence* and *Benevolence*. This I take to be the *First* and *great* Division of Love, to which all the several kinds of it may be aptly reduced. For when I consider the Motion of Love, I find it tends to two things, namely to the good which a man wills to any one, whether it be to himself or to another, and to him to whom this good is willed. So that the Motion of Love may be Considered either barely as a *Tendency* towards good, or as a *willing* this good to some person or Being. If it be considered in the first way, then 'tis what we call *Concupiscence* or *Desire*, if in the second, then 'tis what we call *Benevolence* or *Charity*.

[From *The Theory and Regulation of Love* (Oxford: H. Clements, 1688). Some language has been modernized.]

In the most abstract sense, all love is being inclined toward goodness or that which has value. Norris argues, more specifically, that all loving feelings are a result of what he calls the "moral gravitation of the soul" toward God as the ultimate source of all goodness. In analogy with the way in which material objects are attracted to each other by the phenomenon of gravitation, the human soul is ineluctably drawn toward what it naturally finds to be good, namely, the source of all goodness, which is God (the only exception being when the soul is sent off its natural course through sin). The soul naturally likes the good and desires closeness with it, the kind of loving desire that Norris labels as "concupiscence" and as the fundamental type of love. We thus have a general disposition toward loving that manifests itself either toward the source of goodness, God, or in the manner of wishing well to other beings. All "loving motion" is inaugurated by this initial spark of moral gravitation stemming from God. Norris sees this loving action as being undertaken by a partnership between both God and the soul: "First good moves and acts upon the Soul, and then the Soul moves and exerts itself towards good, that so *there* may be the *End* whence was the *Rise* of its motion."[5] There is a sense in which God gives an initial spark to our capacity for loving and striving toward the good, which we can then follow through our loving motion.

With regard to other created beings, one can only suitably feel a secondary kind of love, *benevolence*, toward them. Concupiscence toward another finite being would not be appropriate, as the soul should not be drawn to imperfect beings, but only to the perfect source of goodness, God. Rather, we can only suitably hope for good to also be given to others, which is the feeling of benevolence. Such a benevolence can be felt to oneself (in which case, it is "self-love") as well as to another finite being ("charity").[6] We cannot appropriately feel benevolent toward God as a perfect being, as he does not lack for goodness. Despite being different kinds of love, concupiscence and charity can productively work together to improve the soul. Norris writes,

> I do acknowledge that all Love of *Concupiscence* does proceed from Indigence [a state of lack], and ends in self-Love. For all desire is in order to further Perfection, and Improvement, and did we not *want* something *within*, we should not *endeavour* towards any thing *without*.[7]

Hope for goodness to come to oneself, therefore, can work as a drive toward seeking the source of goodness itself: in other words, self-love can help bring about concupiscence (presumably this is meant as an addition to the natural "moral gravitation of the soul" that draws the soul toward God, though Norris does not make this point entirely clear).

In this account of the nature of love, Norris is drawing upon Plato and the Christian **Platonist**† tradition. Norris emphasizes the manner in which the soul is drawn toward a (re)union with God, having fallen away from his perfect goodness. In the manner of the philosopher in Plato's allegory of the cave, who ascends from underground into the blinding light of higher levels of reality,[8] the soul is on a journey from its current sinful, materially embodied state to a higher unity with God, both ontologically and morally. Part of the Christian Platonic tradition also gives an important role to friendship, as we also find here in Norris's account. As the scholar Catherine Pickstock explains, the experience of friendship is seen as essential preparation for seeking greater unity with the Godhead (or "One" in Platonic terms) on a more transcendent level:

> [F]or Plato, friendship is the necessary exoteric aspect of the esoteric understanding and vice versa. If the cognitive ascent to the form of the Good (or the One) requires the heterogeneity of friendship, then, inversely, the exterior heterogeneity of friendship can promote the tendency to the inner vision of unity.[9]

The overcoming of differences and the recognition of similarities that helps friendships thrive prepares the soul for navigating the difficult path to greater unity with the One, including seeing beyond the mere utility of others for achieving our own selfish ends. In drawing upon these ideas, Norris to a certain extent recognizably stands in the "Christian Platonist" tradition, at least with regard to the theory of love found here.

In addition to taking inspiration from ancient Greek philosophers,[10] one of the most significant influences upon Norris was the French philosopher, Nicolas Malebranche (1638–1715). In particular, Norris is drawn to the theory of occasionalism, which Malebranche had suggested in a series of publications beginning in the 1670s. According to Norris's version of this theory, there is no genuine causal relation between mind and body. In his *Practical Discourses* (1693), Norris argues that a material body could not cause an idea: "But can [physical motion] produce an Effect more Noble and Excellent, and of an Order so very much higher than itself? Can it produce a Thought? Is there any Proportion between such a Cause and such an Effect; between Motion and Thinking, between an Affection of a Body, and a Sentiment of Soul?"[11] The motion transmitted by physical bodies could never produce something as unlike itself as an idea, and besides, it would be impossible for something impenetrable (body) to have an impact upon something that is penetrable (mind): "Can Bodies act upon Spirits? So indeed they must do, if it be true that they produce our Sensations, since the Soul is the only proper Subject of all Perception. But is this possible? Is not Spirit supposed to *penetrate* Body?"[12] This is a familiar restatement of the problem of interaction (or **mind-body problem**†) for substance dualism (see Chapter 2).

Given the lack of a causal link between mind and body, Norris argues that the only explanation for how our sensations correspond to what is taking place in the material world is that God produces our sensations in such a way that it unswervingly follows that pattern. The only thing that could impact a spirit would be another spirit, and the only spirit who would be powerful and knowledgeable enough to achieve this is God: "now what Being can we suppose capable of such a Province as this, but a Being of infinite Understanding and Power, one that need not go abroad for his Intelligence, but sees all things immediately in himself, and produces all things by the immediate Efficacy of his Will?"[13] Physical objects only provide the "occasion" for God's causing the relevant ideas in our mind, including feelings of pleasure and pain, as appropriate for the situation. Any happiness and pleasure we get in life directly comes from God and not from other created beings.

Norris links his occasionalist theory to the nature of love by arguing that we can only legitimately love whatever it is that brings us the goodness of happiness and pleasure. Given that it is only God who is the direct cause of pleasure, this raises the question of whether it is only God who should be loved in the sense of concupiscence. In 1693, Norris began a sustained correspondence on the nature of love with the philosopher, Mary Astell, who we will also consider in this section.

> ## Mary Astell: Brief Chronology
>
> - 1666: Born in Newcastle, and in the following years, receives some tuition from her uncle, Ralph Astell, who had studied at Cambridge
> - 1688: Moves to London, following the death of her parents, which allows her to form intellectual connections with various thinkers
> - 1694: Publishes first part of her first major work, *A Serious Proposal to the Ladies*
> - 1695: Her correspondence with John Norris, *Letters Concerning the Love of God*, is published
> - 1705: Publishes major work of philosophy and theology, *Christian Religion, as Profess'd by a Daughter of the Church of England*
> - 1731: Dies in London

Astell and Norris were both greatly concerned with the nature of love, and they corresponded on this topic for around a year, the result of which was the publication of their co-authored *Letters Concerning the Love of God* in 1695. One major point of discussion in this text is Norris's claim that only God is the proper object of love in the sense of loving desire (as opposed to benevolence, which can properly be felt toward other creatures), and whether the fact that God also causes us to feel pain and displeasure means that we should in fact not love God.

Extract 5.2—Astell & Norris, *Letters Concerning the Love of God* (Letters 1 and 2—excerpts)

> [Astell]: Methinks there is all the reason in the world to conclude, *That GOD is the only efficient Cause of all our Sensations*; and you have made it as clear as the Day; and it is equally clear from the Letter of the Commandment, *That GOD is not only the Principal, but the* sole Object *of our Love*: But the reason you assign for it, namely, *Because he is the only efficient Cause of our Pleasure*, seems not equally clear. For if we must Love nothing but what is Lovely, and nothing is Lovely but what is our Good, and nothing is our Good but what does us Good, and nothing

does us Good but what causes Pleasure in us; may we not by the same way of arguing say, That that which Causes Pain in us does not do us Good, (for nothing you say does us Good but what Causes Pleasure) and therefore can't be our Good, and if not our Good then not Lovely, and consequently not the proper, much less the only Object of our Love? Again, if the Author of our Pleasure be upon that account the only Object of our Love, then by the same reason the Author of our Pain can't be the Object of our Love; and if both these sensations be produced by the same Cause, then that Cause is at once the Object of our Love, and of our Aversion; for it is as natural to avoid and fly from Pain, as it is to follow and pursue Pleasure?

So that if these Principles, *viz. That GOD is the Efficient Cause of our Sensations*, (Pain as well as Pleasure) *and that he is the only Object of our Love*, be firm and true, as I believe they are; it will then follow, either that the being the Cause of our Pleasure is not the true and proper Reason why that Cause should be the Object of our Love, (for the Author of our Pain has as good a Title to our Love as the Author of our Pleasure;) Or else, if nothing be the Object of our Love but what does us Good, then something else does us Good besides what causes Pleasure? Or to speak more properly, the Cause of all our Sensations, Pain as well as Pleasure being the only Object of our Love, and nothing being Lovely but what does us Good, consequently, that which Causes Pain does us Good as well as that which Causes Pleasure; and therefore it can't be true, That nothing does us Good but what Causes Pleasure.

-

[Norris]: I observe therefore first of all, that you grant the two main things contended for, *viz. That God is the only Efficient Cause of all our Sensations*; and that by the Letter of the Commandment, *GOD ought to be the Sole Object of our Love.* Only you say, that the Reason I assign for it seems not equally Clear, by which I suppose you mean, that it does not seem to follow from God's being the only Cause of our Sensations, that he is the only Object of our Love; Or, that GOD is not therefore the only Object of our Love, because he is the only cause of our Sensations; that is in short, you grant the things, but you question the Connection.

Now before I consider the Objection you urge against it, give me leave to tell you that I think it very clear, That not Absolute, but Relative Good is the Formal Object of our Love; that is, that we love a thing not as it is good in itself, but as 'tis good to us; and consequently, GOD is the Object of our Love, not as he is absolutely, but as he is Relatively Good, as he is our Good, or Good to us. For to Love GOD is to desire him as our Good . . .

Now if it be true in the general, that Relative good is the Object of Love, and that GOD is to be loved as, and because he is our *good*, then it will follow, that if GOD only be our *good*, or the Author of *good* to us, then GOD only is to be loved by us. And so the other way, that if GOD only be to be loved by us, it must be, it can be upon no other account than as and because he only is our *good*, as being the only true Cause of our Pleasure. And I cannot imagine upon what other ground you can cast your Obligation to love GOD only, (which you grant to be the literal import of the Commandment) if not upon this, that he only is our *good*. For as the reason why we are to love GOD at all, is because he is our *good*, so the reason why we are to Love him only (which supposition you grant) can be no other, but because he only is our *good*. And since he cannot be our only *good* any otherwise, than as he is the only true Cause of our Pleasure, it follows, that his being the only true Cause of our Pleasure, is the true reason why he ought to be the only Object of our Love . . .

Though I acknowledge Pain to be as truly the Effect of GOD as Pleasure (for I know not what else should cause it) yet it is not after the same manner the Effect of GOD as Pleasure is. Pleasure is the natural, genuine and direct effect of GOD, but Pain comes from him only indirectly and by Accident. For first, 'tis of the proper Nature of GOD to produce Pleasure, as consisting of such essential Excellencies and Perfections as will necessarily beatify and make happy those Spirits, who are, by being in their true rational Order, duly disposed for the Enjoyment of him. But if this same excellent Nature occasion Pain to other Spirits, this is only indirectly and by Accident, by reason of their Moral Indisposition for so Sovereign a Good. Again, as 'tis thus in Reference to the Nature of GOD, so in reference to his Will. GOD's antecedent and primary Design is the Happiness of all his Creatures (for 'twas for this that he made them) but if any of them, in the event prove miserable, 'tis wholly besides his first Design, and only by a subsequent and secondary Will. Again, when GOD causes Pleasure, 'tis because he wills it for itself, and naturally delights in it, as comporting with his primary Design which is the happiness of his Creatures; but when he causes Pain, 'tis not that he wills it from within, or for itself (for so 'tis not at all lovely) but only from without, and for the sake of something else as is necessary to the Order of his Justice. For you are to consider, that if there had been no Sin, there would never have been such a thing as Pain, which is a plain argument that GOD wills our Pleasure as we are Creatures, and our Pain only as we are Sinners. But now in measuring our Devoirs [duties or attention that is owed] to GOD, we are not to consider how he stands affected to us as sinners, but how he stands affected to us as Creatures, how he is disposed towards us as we are *his* Work, and not as we have made our selves. And therefore if as Creatures he Loves us, and Wills our Happiness, that lays a sufficient Foundation for our Love to him; and 'tis not his treating us with Evil as sinners that can overturn it . . .

[All] that you can argue from GOD's being the Author of our *Pain* as well as *Pleasure* will be this, That he is justly to be the Object of our Fear, but not of our Aversion. We are indeed to Fear him, and him only, as being the *true Cause* of all *Pain*, and only able to make us miserable, according to that of our Saviour, *I will forewarn you whom ye shall fear*[14], *etc*. But this is no reason why we should hate him, as never inflicting it but when Order and Justice require it . . .

One consideration more. When you speak of *GOD*'s being the Cause of Pain, either you mean as to this Life, or as to the next. If as to the next, that has nothing to do with the Duty that we owe him here. If as to the present Life, the pain that God inflicts upon us is here is only Medicinal, and in order to our greater good, and consequently from a Principle of Kindness. And I think, setting aside my other Considerations, there will be no more pretence for not loving or hating for this, than for hating our Physician or Surgeon for putting us to pain in order to [provide] our Health or Cure.

[From *Letters Concerning the Love of God* (London: Manship and Wilkin, 1695).]

Astell's argument in this extract focuses on the implication of Norris's occasionalism that, if God is the direct cause of our feelings of pleasure, he must be the cause of our feelings of pain too. Further, if God is the proper object of love on the basis that he is the direct cause of pleasure, surely the fact that he is the direct cause of pain means that he would be the proper object of our hatred too (which Astell would hold to be absurd). Astell's issue with Norris's argument is the intermediate claim that God brings us good by causing us pleasure, and there is no other way of bringing us good. It is by focusing on God's provision of pleasure alone that leaves Norris open to the problem raised by the fact that God is the cause of negative feelings and experiences, as well as positive ones, and thus by his reasoning, we should hate God as much as love him.

In response to Astell's argument, Norris begins by claiming that it is the relative worth of God to us that we love, rather than the absolute value of God in himself (which would seem to follow from the connection he makes elsewhere between love of God and self-love). This may help Norris to answer Astell's argument partly because we are not supposed to be loving God "in the round," taking everything that God does into account; rather, we are focusing on the good that God *does do for us*. So, the fact that God brings about pain, and indeed may need to punish us at some point in the future, does not negate our commitment to loving him for the good that he does in fact do for us. Also, Norris questions whether we can conceive of another reason why we should love God, other than the fact that he is good for us, and why he is good for us, other than that he is the cause of our happiness or pleasure.

Further, Norris seeks to argue that there is an important disanalogy between God's causal role in providing both pleasure and pain, with the effect that one cannot use Norris's reasoning with regard to pain in order to conclude that one should hate God. Pain, Norris argues, is a relatively accidental, indirect effect of God in comparison with pleasure. While God grants us pleasure because it is inherently good and he therefore directly desires to do so, our experience of pain can be ultimately traced back to our sinfulness. God does not directly desire to cause us pain, and yet our sinful actions are such that they inevitably lead these feelings to be appropriate relative to the scheme of divine justice, according to which it is right that sinful behavior be punished (which can only be brought about by causing pain). Thus, we must love God for the fact that he brings us pleasure, and fear him in the rightful way, in recognition of the punishment that can be given in response to our sinfulness in the afterlife. God's role in the divine scheme of justice, including both rewards and punishments, should not hinder us from loving him.

With regard to pain in this life, Norris argues further that such feelings can be useful and good for us, in the manner, for example, that a visit to the dentist may bring about pain, but nevertheless serve a greater function in helping to keep our teeth clean and healthy; or the way in which the pain from touching the hot stove helps us to remove our hand more quickly and avoid sustaining great damage. There are therefore good, loving reasons for God to bring about pain, even if that was not part of his original plan for us. Given this disanalogy between God's provision of pleasure and of pain, we cannot use Astell's argument regarding pain to undermine Norris's conclusion concerning pleasure and the rightness of loving God.

As we have seen, Norris's theory of love is linked to his occasionalism, and the view that our experiences are not directly caused by the material objects around us. To some extent, this can be taken as an anti-empiricist argument, for an **empiricist**[†] like John Locke or Damaris Masham would claim that our ideas are in some sense brought about by what we experience. Thus, as we shall see in the next section, Masham rejects the argument that only God is the proper object of our love, and along the way develops her own empiricist methodology.

Key Points

- Norris argues that the fundamental form of love, concupiscence, can only rightly be felt towards God.
- This claim is grounded in his occasionalist view that God directly produces any feelings of happiness or pleasure we might have.
- In response, Astell claims that the same reasoning would lead us to hate God, on the basis that he directly produces feelings of pain too.
- Norris defends his position by arguing that there are significant disanalogies between God's causing of our feelings of pleasure and his causing of our feelings of pain.

Suggested Further Reading:

Broad, Jacqueline. *Women Philosophers of the Seventeenth Century*, ch. 4. Cambridge: Cambridge University Press, 2002.

Mander, W. J. *The Philosophy of John Norris*, ch. 5. Oxford: Oxford University Press, 2008.

O'Neill, Eileen. "Mary Astell on the Causation of Sensation." In *Mary Astell: Reason, Gender, Faith*, edited by Kolbrener & Michelson, 145–64. Aldershot: Ashgate, 2007.

Squadrito, Kathleen M. "Mary Astell." In *A History of Women Philosophers: Vol. 3*, edited by Waithe, 87–99. Dordrecht: Kluwer, 1991.

Taylor & New. "Introduction." In *Mary Astell and John Norris: Letters Concerning the Love of God*, edited by Taylor & New, 1–49. Aldershot: Ashgate, 2005.

5B. MASHAM'S CRITIQUE OF NORRIS AND ASTELL

> ### Damaris Cudworth Masham: Brief Chronology
>
> - 1658: Born in Cambridge, daughter of the noted Platonist philosopher Ralph Cudworth
> - c. 1681: Meets John Locke, with whom she would have a long-standing intellectual friendship
> - 1685: Marries Sir Francis Masham and takes up residence at Oates Manor, in Essex
> - 1691: Locke takes up semi-permanent residence with the Mashams at Oates, where he would live for the rest of his life
> - 1696: Publishes first philosophical work, *A Discourse Concerning the Love of God*
> - 1704: Begins an extended philosophical correspondence with Leibniz
> - 1705: Publishes *Occasional Thoughts in Reference to a Vertuous or Christian Life*
> - 1708: Dies at Oates

Damaris Cudworth Masham's philosophical works include two published texts and correspondence with prominent thinkers including Leibniz, Jean Le Clerc, and her friend, John Locke. Masham grew up in Cambridge, where the philosophical school of **Platonism**† was largely prevalent, partly due to the influence of her father, Ralph Cudworth. While Masham's works continued to betray evidence of her Platonist background, she also developed Locke's empiricism (which generally sought to trace the origin of our ideas back to experience) in the very early years after the publication of his *An Essay Concerning Human Understanding* (which will be discussed in the next chapter). In her first published work, *A Discourse Concerning the Love of God*, Masham responds to the published *Letters* between John Norris and Mary Astell (discussed in the previous section). In responding to the arguments of both Norris and Astell, Masham shows that she had adopted a largely Lockean empiricist philosophy, though with some interesting developments and additions.

Masham's primary aim in the *Discourse* is to clarify the relation between morality and religion, with a view to protecting Christianity from the threats of atheism (or "irreligion") and irrational superstition (or "enthusiasm"). The discussion begins with a consideration of views that, as far as Masham sees it, undermine the role of morality within religion and true faith in various ways: either by focusing too much on dogma or right belief, rather than right conduct, or by emphasizing one's personal relationship to God in an overly contemplative approach, rather than giving due importance to exercising moral virtue toward other people. Through either approach, moral or social duties toward others become, at best, subsidiary obligations that can be overridden by other considerations, such as duties toward God or the duty to not have heretical beliefs. In contrast to both these approaches, Masham sets herself the task of vindicating social duties as an essential part of a truly religious life.

As part of this, Masham criticizes the argument, canvassed in Norris and Astell's *Letters*, that prioritizes love of God to an extreme degree (as far as Masham sees it), and casts all direct partiality toward other creatures as inescapably sinful: in her words, the view "that mankind are obliged strictly, as their duty, to love with desire, nothing but God only; every degree of desire of any creature whatsoever being sin."[15] Such a theory undermines religion because it is simply impracticable, to the extent that it would mean that religion could not be acceptable to those who are rational.[16] Masham argues that loving the world or some part of it is so natural to us that is almost unavoidable, and so to castigate it as sinful would either "make religion, and the teachers of it, ridiculous to some" or "drive other weaker, but better-minded people into despair."[17] In other words, such a position will lead some to atheism and others to a moral despair that ultimately undermines religion.

Masham also rejects this view on social grounds, insofar as any society composed of individuals who loved *only* God would fall apart and soon die out (which is surely a result that God would not wish). As she puts it: "It is certain, that if we had no desires but after God, the several societies of mankind could not long hold together, nor the very species be continued: for few would give themselves care, and sorrow, in the pursuit of possessions not desirable."[18] As we see in the following extract, for Masham, the sustenance of any kind of social relations relies upon us having love for other creatures and recognizing our duties toward each other. Indeed, the moral law itself includes social duties that must be observed. Masham argues that Norris's claims concerning the love of God inevitably lead to the denunciation of the world entirely and withdrawal from society, and if everyone did that, society would break down.

Extract 5.3—Masham, *A Discourse Concerning the Love of God* (pp. 122-6)

But there can certainly be no greater disparagement to Christian Religion, than to say, That it unfits Men for Society; That we must not only literally become Fools for Christ's sake; but also cease to be Men . . .

[Christ] came Eating and Drinking, Conversing in the World like other Men: And he assures us, That *he came not to destroy, but to fulfil the Law*; viz. The Moral Law, which is the same with the Law of Reason; than which, *Heaven and Earth, shall sooner pass away*; and in which are legibly found those Duties of an active and social Life, that have so much recommended and eterniz'd the Memories of many Philosophers, and Lawgivers, and other great Men of Antiquity; Whose Religion Mankind would be apt to think they had reason to wish for again, if they were persuaded that Christianity were opposite to, and inconsistent with those admired and beneficial Virtues that Support and Profit Society.

There is nothing more evident than that Mankind is designed for a Sociable Life. To say that Religion unfits us for it, is to reproach the Wisdom of God as highly as it is possible; And to represent Religion as the most mischievous thing in the World, dissolving Societies. And there could not be a greater Artifice of the Devil, or Wicked Men to bring Christianity into contempt than this . . .

Nor can there be any stronger Evidence, that (That Notion, of the Love of God, grounded on his Being the immediate Cause of all our Sensations) is false, than this, *viz*. That it Destroys all the Duties and Obligations of Social Life. This indeed is not Mr. [Norris'] deduction from thence, But it is that of his oracle *Pere Malebranche*, and that of Reason; And he will scarce be believed to be Sincere, that shall say he can daily see and enjoy the Creatures as Goods, without desiring them as such; Or that shall deny, that if it be our Duty not to desire any Creature, it must then necessarily be our Duty (as [Malebranche] expressly says it is) to have as little communication with them as is possible; and to betake ourselves for Deserts. But whether it were that Mr. [Norris] has no inclination to this way of Living . . . He can scarcely be presumed not to see that this inevitably follows from the Hypothesis he has embraced.

But yet how injurious soever this Consequence is to Religion, so much is not therefore denied to what [Malebranche] largely insists upon, *viz*. That Retirement is sometimes useful, if not necessary to a Christian Life. Those who live always in the hurry of the World, and the avocations of Worldly Business, without giving themselves time, and retreat, frequently to reflect, being no doubt very likely to enter too much into the Spirit of it; We insensibly giving up our selves to, and uniting our Hearts with what we are constantly engaged in, and with delight apply our selves to. But if in opposition to this, any one should run into the other extreme, of retreating wholly from all commerce and conversation with Men; And should give themselves the Happiness *Pere Malebranche* speaks of, of *attending Eternity in Deserts*; it is to be feared they would not mend the Matter. For whatever Vices they might part with by it, they must necessarily oppose thereby, one great end that they were sent into the World for, *viz.* of doing good; By becoming wholly useless to others: And such a one would certainly, by such a renunciation of all commerce with Men, be likelier to grow Wild, than improve the great Virtue of Christianity, and Ornament of Human Nature, Good Will, Charity, and the being Useful to others.

[From *A Discourse Concerning the Love of God* (London: Awnsham and John Churchill, 1696). Some language has been modernized.]

Masham sees humans as naturally social beings, and so any doctrine that implies the need for removal from society simply ignores the facts of human nature. Given our inherent sociability, and the fact that it is right for us to do good for others, Masham reasons that it is surely not sinful to love things other than God in the true and fullest sense.

In addition to her reservations on religious and practical grounds, Masham objects to the anti-empiricist argument for the claim that only God can be rightly loved, which rests on the premise that "God, not the Creature, is the immediate, efficient cause of our sensations."[19] As we have seen, the argument states that we should only love what gives us pleasure, and given that God is the only direct cause of our sensations (including pleasure), we should only love God. Therefore, we have no duty to love other creatures. Masham disagrees with this view concerning the source of our sensations, by rejecting the Malebranchean view that other creatures only stand as occasional causes for our sensations. According to this account, there is no proper causal link between other created beings and me, so other creatures are unable to bring about pleasure directly in me; rather, following the occasionalist model, God instigates those sensations in me directly in a systematic way, as a consequence of my standing in certain relations to other creatures. Such a theory cuts us off from the kind of causal links with the world that empiricists rely upon to provide us with the ideas and knowledge that we have, and so cannot be acceptable to an empiricist, regardless of other potentially irreligious and immoral consequences that follow.

Masham also argues that there is no competition between love for God and love for other creatures: indeed, these two loves are not only complementary but mutually necessary.[20] In defense of this claim, Masham offers the empiricist argument that we come to know God as an object of love only through our experience of creatures as possible objects of love: "God is an invisible being: And it is by his works, that we are led both to know, and to love him. They lead us to their invisible author. And if we loved not the creatures, it is not conceivable how we should love God."[21] As we cannot gain the ideas necessary to love God without having experience of loving other creatures, our duty is to love God *and* other creatures, and the two cannot be separated.[22] Masham outlines her empiricist account of the source of our idea of God (and its implication for the duties of love that we owe) in the following extract.

Extract 5.4—Masham, *A Discourse Concerning the Love of God* (pp. 62–9)

God is an invisible Being: And it is by his Works, that we are led both to know, and to love him. They lead us to their invisible Author. And if we loved not the Creatures, it is not conceivable how we should love God: at least, how they should have loved him, who not having the Law, yet did by Nature the things contained in the Law. And this, however opposite to what some tell us, seems nevertheless the sense of the above-named Apostle[23], who says (1 John IV.20) *He that loveth not his Brother whom he has seen, how can he love God whom he has not seen?* And I would demand of any one if they could suppose themselves, or any other, never to have loved any Creature, what they could imagine they should love?

I suppose it must be replied by such a one, That as he was not the Author of his own Being, and saw clearly that he could not be produced by nothing; He was thereby led to the Acknowledgement of a Superior Being, to whom he was indebted for his own; and therefore stood obliged to love him. But *Being*, or *Existence*, barely considered, is so far from being a Good, that in the state of the Damned, few are so Paradoxical as not to believe it an intolerable Misery: And many, even in this World, are so unhappy, that they would much rather part with their Existence, than be eternally continued in the State they are in. The Author of our Being therefore merits not our Love, unless he has given to us such a Being as we can Love. Now if none of the Objects that every way surround us, were pleasing to us; How could our Beings, that have a continual Communication with, and necessary Dependence upon these, be so?

But if the objects that surround us do please us; that is, if we do love them; as it is then evident, they must be the first objects of our love, so from their gratefulness, or pleasingness to us, it is also evident that we have both the idea of love, and are led to the discovery of the author of that being, that produces what is lovely. As like as our own existence, and that of other beings, has assured us of the existence of some cause more powerful than these effects; so also the loveliness of his works as well assures us, that the cause, or author, is yet more lovely than they, and consequently the object the most worthy of our love.

But if none of those beings which surround us did move our love, we should then both be ignorant of the nature of the author of all things, and of love itself. For what should then exert it, that it should not lie forever dormant? And which way could we (in the state we are in) receive the idea of love, or lovely? For God as [a merely] powerful [being] (which is all we should know of him, considered barely as a creator) is no more an object of love than of hate, or fear; and is truly an object only of admiration.

It seems therefore plain, that if any could be without the love of the creatures, they would be without the love of God also: for as by the existence of the creatures, we come to know there is a creator; so by their loveliness it is that we come to know that of their author, and to love him.

But it will be said here, That we have Pleasing Sensations ('tis true) as soon as Perception; But that we have them not from the Beings which surround us, but from God. I ask, can we know this, before we know that there is a God? Or, will they say that we know there is a God as soon as ever we have Perception? Let it be true, that the Creatures have received no efficiency from God to excite pleasing Sensations in us, and are but the occasional Causes of those we feel: Yet, does a Child in the Cradle know this? Or is this apparent so soon as it is that the Fire pleases us when we are Cold? or Meat when we are Hungry? No, nor is it at any time a self-evident Truth. We must know many other Truths before we come to know this; which is a Proposition containing many complex ideas in it; and which we are not capable of framing, till we have been long acquainted with pleasing Sensations.

In the meanwhile, it is certain, that till we can make this Discovery, we shall necessarily Love that which appears to us to be the Cause of our Pleasure, as much as if it were really so; It being unavoidably by us the same thing to us: And we are necessitated by God himself to that which Mr. [Norris] says is truly Idolatry, For our Passions are not moved by the reality, but appearance of things. To the prevention of which, this Notion were it true, and received amongst Men as such, could be of no use at all, neither could it teach them not to ascend to the Love of God, by the Love of Creatures: Since it can be of use to none till they are convinced of it, and none are capable of being convinced of it, till sensible Objects by appearing the Causes of their Pleasing Sensations, have gotten Possession of their Love, and have as soon assured them that God is the Object the most worthy of their Love, as they have assured them of his Existence.

It is true, when first in our infancy we feel pleasing Sensations, we are no more capable of being taught by them that there is a Superior Invisible Being that made these things to affect us thus, who therefore ought supremely to be loved; than that this Invisible Being, at the Presence of these Objects, exhibits to us a part of his own Essence, by which these Pleasing Sensations are excited on occasion of those Objects without us, and that therefore he is only and solely to be loved. But though we are incapable of these both alike, when first we cry for the Fire, or the Sucking-Bottle; Yet it is certain, that by the former way we are not only safe, all the time of our Ignorance, from the Sin of Idolatry, and the fatal pre-engagement of a sinful affection; but that our love to God upon that ground is of easier deduction, and earlier apprehended than by the latter. So soon as we do begin to leave off judging by appearances, and are Capable of being convinced that the Diameter of the Sun exceeds that of a Bushel; We are capable also of understanding that there is a Superior Invisible Being, the Author of those things which afford us pleasing Sensations, who therefore is supremely to be loved.

But if we are not capable of escaping Idolatry unless we love God alone, because he immediately exhibits to us a part of his Essence, by which all pleasing Sensations are caused in us, I fear all Mankind (before this present Age) lived and died Idolators, and the greatest part for the future will do so; Since I guess not One of a Thousand will be found capable of apprehending, and being convinced of this new Hypothesis of seeing all things in God. And as, I think, this cannot be denied, so it is also more suitable to the Wisdom, and Goodness of God, that it should be true. For one must say, that the Happiness and Welfare of Mankind were ill taken care for, if it depended upon a Knowledge, which not only few are ever likely to have, but which comes too late to any for much Use to be made of it. For when sensible Ideas have taken Possession of us for Twelve, or Twenty Years, they must be very ignorant of the constitution of Humane Nature, that can think it possible that they should presently, or probably they should ever, be dispossessed by a Notion, although a true one.

[From *A Discourse Concerning the Love of God* (London: Awnsham and John Churchill, 1696). Some language has been modernized.]

In this extract, Masham argues that the experience of love for creatures is the foundation for our love of God. Without recognizing the loveliness of creation, it would be impossible for us to understand that there could be a creator who is even more worthy of our love. When we begin reflecting upon our ideas, it is the things most immediate in our experience that provide the data that is first available to us. Without the experience of loving other beings first, we could never come to the idea of a God who is deserving of love. If we were merely to experience other creatures, without loving them, the only notion we could have of God would be as a being who should be admired as our creator, but not necessarily as one who should be loved. Thus, the experience of loving other created beings is a prerequisite of love for God, and so it cannot be the case that love of other creatures is always sinful. Further, as Masham points out, from a perspective that focuses on the nature of our direct experience, the question of the causal source of our sensations becomes something of a moot point. Even if other creatures are only occasional sources of our sensations, they are still recognized by us as bringing about the situation in which these sensations are had, and so we still love those other beings before we can come to love God. Masham notes that even if occasionalism is true, it is quite a complex notion, and thus only something that can be recognized after we have already loved many creatures, and it would be rather unfair if such an inescapable situation was sinful.[24]

Neither can the two loves (love of God and love of creatures) be distinguished as different kinds of sensation. Our love for other creatures is love just as much as the love we might have for God: "When I say that I love my child, or my friend, I find that my meaning is, that they are things I am delighted in; their being is a pleasure to me. When I say that I love God above all, I find it would express that he is my chiefest good, and I delight in him above all things."[25] To love something is to delight in its existence and the goodness that it brings to you, and we can do that with regard to any other being, be it God or another creature. We should indeed love God above all other things, because "he is infinitely more lovely"[26] than all other beings, but that does not entail that we are essentially cheating God of the love that is due to him by also loving other beings. Masham emphasizes that it is not a waste to love things in this world, even though they may be subject to impermanence and fall significantly short of the perfection of God. She writes,

> For, as short-lived flowers, though they ought not to employ the continual care of our whole lives, may yet reasonably enough be found in our gardens and delight us in their seasons; so the fading good things of this life, though

(for that reason) they are not to be fixed on as the ultimate good of eternal beings, yet there is no reason why we may not rejoice in them, as the good gifts of God, and find all that delight which he has joined with the lawful use of them.[27]

Our duty is to proportion our desires and love correctly according to the relative value of other beings, not to only love or desire God alone.[28] Even though flowers may not last long and so may offer a fleeting source of pleasure to us, they can nevertheless rightfully be loved and affirmed as gifts from God without illegitimately subtracting from our love of God.

Masham further argues that Norris's position is antithetical to our experience of the world around us, as it is presented to us as something absolutely worthy of admiration and love. It is an immense, ordered arena that has numerous living beings who are able to come to know and love God, and thus can be rightly celebrated. In defense of this, Masham points to recent astronomical observations, which has allowed humankind to think beyond "only the compass of our little globe" and discover "further matter for our admiration."[29] For Masham, the view that only God should be loved, and not his creation, shows that a thinker has ignored the evidence of their own senses, as well as what has been learned by the natural sciences, concerning the beauty and majesty of the world around them. Masham argues that reflections upon "the system of the world" and "considering what mathematicians and naturalists offer" shows us "so many regions [of the universe] fit for inhabitants are not empty deserts,"[30] and thus creation is actually most likely full of life. Creation has been shown to be much richer and more wondrous than we ever thought possible, through our own observations, and thus it is nonsensical to state that it cannot be loved (as long as it is loved in the right proportion when set alongside our love for God).

In addition to attacking Norris's view concerning the love of God, Masham also targets his underlying occasionalist metaphysics. One of the arguments she offers begins with the claim that a perfect being would not create anything superfluous or useless, as all things that would be created by such a being would be created for a (good) purpose. On an occasionalist model, though, our apparently expertly crafted sensory faculties become entirely surplus to requirements, as God provides us directly with all the ideas required to have an experience of the world around us, without the need for us to actually use our senses as causal conduits to other things. Masham accuses such a view as "derogating . . .

from the wisdom of God, in framing his creatures like the idols of the heathen, that have eyes, and see not; ears, and hear not," on the basis that "if God immediately exhibits to me all my ideas, and that I do not truly see with my eyes, and hear with my ears; then all that wonderful exactness and curious workmanship, in framing the organs of sense, seems superfluous and vain; which is no small reflection upon infinite wisdom."[31] Indeed, without such a causal requirement for our senses, the need for having a material world at all might come into question, leading to a kind of idealist view utterly opposed to that of the Lockean empiricist (and not something that Norris himself would wish to support). So, Masham argues, Norris needs to explain why God would create such apparently superfluous things (apparently in contradiction with his perfection) if he places ideas directly in our mind without our sensory faculties playing any causal role.

As we have seen, Masham seeks to develop an empiricist approach to moral and religious questions that targets theories (such as Norris's occasionalism) that undermine the importance of observation and empirical evidence in the gaining of our ideas and knowledge. With regard to Norris's theory of love, Masham rejects the view that love in the form of concupiscence should only be directed to God, given our social nature and the beauty of creation. We will continue to see how an empiricist methodology was applied to ethical matters in the following chapter, where we turn to the work of John Locke and Catharine Trotter Cockburn.

Key Points

- In her *Discourse*, Masham rejects the view (proposed by Norris) that you should only love God, and not his creatures.
- Masham argues that our experience of love for other creatures acts as a foundation for our love of God.
- Our experience of the loveliness of creation also entails that it could not be sinful to love other created beings.
- An empiricist account also explains why God has given us the sensory faculties that we have.

Suggested Further Reading

Broad, Jacqueline. *Women Philosophers of the Seventeenth Century*, ch. 5. Cambridge: Cambridge University Press, 2002.

Frankel, Lois. "Damaris Cudworth Masham." In *A History of Women Philosophers: Vol. 3*, edited by Waithe, 73–85. Dordrecht: Kluwer, 1991.

Hutton, Sarah. "Damaris Cudworth, Lady Masham: Between Platonism and Enlightenment." *British Journal for the History of Philosophy* 1, no. 1 (1993): 29–54.

Lascano, Marcy P. "Damaris Masham and 'The Law of Reason or Nature.'" *The Modern Schoolman* 88, nos. 3–4 (2011): 245–65.

Webb, Simone. "Living Philosophy: Self-revelation and Damaris Masham's Philosophical Autobiography." *Journal of Speculative Philosophy* 34, no. 1 (2020): 30–48.

Questions for Reflection

- Can we only at most "wish well to" or feel benevolence toward other human beings?
- Do we only love a thing insofar as it is good to or for us?
- If we are a religious believer, should we only love God?
- What is the relationship between reason and faith? Is it appropriate to use our reason in matters of faith?

6

The Nature of Morality
John Locke and Catharine Trotter Cockburn

Chapter Outline

6a.	Locke on the Source of Moral Knowledge	141
6b.	Cockburn on Locke, God and morality	152
	Questions for Reflection	166

One of the key assumptions made as part of the **empiricist**[†] tradition in philosophy is that, generally speaking, the content of our ideas can be traced back to experience. As a result, one of the main philosophical methods adopted by such thinkers is to examine the source of our ideas and discover whether indeed it is to be found in experience. Part of the rationale for this approach was to undertake a kind of "house cleaning" in the realm of ideas. If we could trace a particular idea back to its source, that is, where we first gain the mental content required to formulate the idea in question, then we may be able to check whether it has a legitimate epistemic ground or is merely a figment of our imagination and empty speculation. This empirical methodology was highly controversial, though. One of the reasons for this was that the source of our moral knowledge is not entirely clear. How do we learn of supposedly universal prescriptive laws that put us under genuine moral obligations? How do we discover, for example, that stealing or murder ought never to be done? While we may examine our experience of those kinds of actions and the effects they have upon the world, there is arguably nothing in our experience that establishes the kind of unconditional obligations that we believe to be involved in morality. While our experience may reveal that a certain sort of action tends to have a particular effect, or that it tends to follow from a particular kind of intention, this on its own does not reveal what we *ought* to do, in a moral sense: arguably, our experience merely reveals what is the case, rather than what ought to be. It was for this reason that empiricist philosophers, with their focus on experience and discovering the source of our ideas, were often accused of taking a dangerous path in undermining our supposed moral knowledge. Thus, one of the tasks facing the empiricist philosophers, John Locke and Catharine Trotter Cockburn, is to explain how our moral knowledge is possible, given the assumption of an empiricist methodology. We will see that the attempt to offer an empiricist account of moral knowledge faced many issues, including questions about the relation between God and morality, about how we are motivated to act morally (sometimes called the **problem of moral motivation**†), and about whether reflection upon our experience and the nature of human beings can give us certain knowledge of moral principles.

6A. LOCKE ON THE SOURCE OF MORAL KNOWLEDGE

John Locke: Brief Chronology

- 1632: Born in Wrington, Somerset
- 1652: Begins studies at Oxford University, though finds the prevailing Aristotelian philosophy there of little interest
- 1667: Following various academic posts at Oxford, a growing interest in medicine leads him to become personal physician to Anthony Ashley Cooper, Lord Ashley
- 1674: Pays an extended visit to France, where he meets with various philosophers and scientists, including Francois Bernier, a noted popularizer of Gassendi's empiricist philosophy
- 1683: Forced into exile in Holland due to his association with Lord Ashley
- 1689: Returns from exile and publishes two important works, *An Essay Concerning Human Understanding* and *Two Treatises of Government*
- 1691: Moves to Oates, a manor house in Essex, residence of the philosopher Damaris Masham and her husband, Sir Francis Masham
- 1704: Dies at Oates

Locke's account of moral knowledge and its source begins with a negative step, namely, a denial of claims that we have access to innate moral principles (that we are born with some common moral knowledge, and thus the source of this knowledge can be solely found within ourselves). This is part of the general attack on the notion of innate knowledge that begins his *Essay concerning Human Understanding*. In this first extract from the *Essay*, Locke argues that our disagreements regarding moral principles and our failure to live up to these standards present overwhelming evidence against innate morality:

Extract 6.1 — Locke, *An Essay concerning Human Understanding* (Book I, Chapter III)

1. If those speculative Maxims, whereof we discoursed in the foregoing Chapter, have not an actual universal assent from all Mankind, as we there

proved, it is much more visible concerning *practical Principles*, that they *come short of an universal Reception*: and I think it will be hard to instance any one moral Rule, which can pretend to so general and ready an assent as, *What is, is*, or to be so manifest a Truth as this, *That it is impossible for the same thing to be, and not to be.* Whereby it is evident, That they are farther removed from a title to be innate; and the doubt of their being native Impressions on the Mind, is stronger against these moral Principles than the other. Not that it brings their Truth at all in question. They are equally true, though not equally evident. Those speculative Maxims carry their own Evidence with them: But moral Principles require Reasoning and Discourse, and some Exercise of the Mind, to discover the certainty of their Truth. They lie not open as natural Characters ingraven on the Mind; which if any such were, they must needs be visible by themselves, and by their own light be certain and known to every Body. But this is no Derogation to their Truth and Certainty, no more than it is to the Truth and Certainty, of the Three Angles of a Triangle being equal to two right ones, because it is not so evident, as *The whole is bigger than a part*; nor so apt to be assented to at first hearing. It may suffice, that these moral Rules are capable of Demonstration: and therefore it is our own faults, if we come not to a certain Knowledge of them. But the Ignorance wherein many Men are of them, and the slowness of assent, wherewith others receive them, are manifest Proofs, that they are not innate, and such as offer themselves to their view without searching.

-

3. Perhaps it will be urged, That the *tacit assent of [criminal] Minds agrees to what their Practice contradicts*. I answer, *First*, I have always thought the Actions of Men the best Interpreters of their thoughts. But since it is certain, that most Men's Practice, and some Men's open Professions, have either questioned or denied these Principles, it is impossible to establish an universal consent (though we should look for it only amongst grown Men) without which, it is impossible to conclude them innate. *Secondly*, 'Tis very strange and unreasonable, to suppose innate practical Principles, that terminate only in Contemplation. Practical Principles derived from Nature, are there for Operation, and must produce Conformity of Action, not barely speculative assent to their truth, or else they are in vain distinguished from speculative Maxims. Nature, I confess, has put into Man a desire of Happiness, and an aversion to Misery: These indeed are innate practical Principles, which (as practical Principles ought) do continue constantly to operate and influence all our Actions, without ceasing: These may be observed in all Persons and all Ages, steady and universal; but these are Inclinations of the Appetite to good, not impressions of truth on the Understanding. I deny not, that there are

natural tendencies imprinted on the Minds of Men; and that, from the very first instances of Sense and Perception, there are some things, that are grateful, and others unwelcome to them; some things they incline to, and others that they fly: But this makes nothing for innate Characters on the Mind, which are to be the Principles of Knowledge, regulating our Practice. Such natural Impressions on the Understanding, are so far from being confirmed hereby, that this is an Argument against them; since if there were certain Characters, imprinted by Nature on the Understanding, as the Principles of Knowledge, we could not but perceive them constantly operate in us, and influence our Knowledge, as we do those others on the Will and Appetite; which never cease to be the constant Springs and Motives of all our Actions, to which, we perpetually feel them strongly impelling us.

-

6. Hence naturally flows the great variety of Opinions, concerning Moral Rules, which are to be found amongst Men, according to the different sorts of Happiness, they have a Prospect of, or propose to themselves: Which could not be, if practical Principles were innate, and imprinted in our Minds immediately by the Hand of God. I grant the existence of God, is so many ways manifest, and the Obedience we owe him, so congruous to the Light of Reason, that a great part of Mankind give Testimony to the Law of Nature: But yet I think it must be allowed, That several Moral Rules, may receive, from Mankind, a very general Approbation, without either knowing, or admitting the true ground of Morality; which can only be the Will and Law of a God, who sees Men in the dark, has in his Hand Rewards and Punishments, and Power enough to call to account the Proudest Offender. For God, having, by an inseparable connection, joined *Virtue* and public Happiness together; and made the Practice thereof, necessary to the preservation of Society, and visibly *beneficial* to all, with whom the Virtuous Man has to do; it is no wonder, that every one should, not only allow, but recommend, and magnify those Rules to others, from those observance of them, he is sure to reap Advantage to himself. He may, out of Interest, as well as Conviction, cry up that for Sacred; which if once trampled on, and profaned, he himself cannot be safe nor secure. This, though it takes nothing from the Moral and Eternal Obligation, which these Rules evidently have; yet it shows, that the outward acknowledgement Men pay to them in their Words, proves not that they are innate Principles: Nay, it proves not so much, as, that Men assent to them inwardly in their own Minds, as the inviolable Rules of their own Practice: Since we find that self-interest and the Conveniences of this Life, make many Men, own an outward Profession and Approbation of them, whose Actions sufficiently prove, that they very little consider the

Law-giver, that prescribed these Rules; nor the Hell he has ordained for the Punishment of those that transgress them.

[From *An Essay Concerning Human Understanding,* 4th edn. (London: Awnsham and J. Churchill, 1700). Some language has been modernized.]

In the previous extract, Locke questions a potential argument for innate moral principles based on the claim that there are some such principles that are universally assented to and that therefore must be innate. Locke argues that knowledge of moral rules cannot be shown to be **innate knowledge**† on the basis of this argument, given that we would expect more general agreement regarding them across different individuals and societies. Locke bases this argument on the claim that an innate moral principle would be so certain that we would be unable to question it, along the lines of a self-evident principle of logic like "A or not A." Such self-evident principles do not have the character of moral principles, which have to be reflected upon before their truth can be grasped. It may be that we can grasp these moral principles as certain following such reflection, but they do not have the kind of immediate certainty that an innate principle would enjoy. If a moral principle *were* as generally agreed-to as "A or not A," that would indeed suggest that it were innate, but this is not something that we find in our experience. There can certainly be great disagreement with regard to key moral issues and dilemmas. In response to Locke's argument, we might question whether the absence of universal assent is sufficient to prove that a moral principle is not innate. Arguably, an innate moral principle that would be self-evident under ideal circumstances could nevertheless be obscured by, for example, (mis)education or countervailing selfish desires. However, it is difficult to settle these matters without leaning into the realm of modern psychology, and so we will leave this point to one side.

In addition, Locke argues that, were general moral principles known innately, criminal behavior would not be as common as it is. Here, too, it is questionable whether this really undermines the notion of innate moral knowledge. Arguably one can know what the right thing to do is and nevertheless fail to live up to one's moral obligations—and for a variety of reasons. Further, there is the important fact of our capacity for self-deception and post hoc rationalization, engaging in tortured logic to convince ourselves that our immoral actions are actually perfectly in line with our moral obligations. In reply to such possible objections, Locke argues that innate practical principles would have to have a positive impact on our behavior. In fact, if we consider human behavior generally, we find that human beings are innately driven by an implicit practical principle, namely, to seek pleasure and avoid pain. However, our following such principles is not to be understood as an instance of having innate knowledge as such; rather, they are an expression of our natural desires. As a result of this account of human motivation, Locke believes that we will be motivated to do the morally right thing through our desire for happiness, rather than by a desire to act for the sake of the good. We see as "good" those things that tend to produce, or at least offer the promise of, happiness, and "evil" those things that threaten its prospect. Locke writes,

> [W]hat has an aptness to produce Pleasure in us, is that we call *Good*, and what is apt to produce Pain in us, we call *Evil*, for no other reason, but for its aptness to produce Pleasure and Pain in us, wherein consists our *Happiness* and *Misery*.[1]

Our motivation to follow our moral principles will therefore come from the hope to attain this sort of happiness. It should not be taken from this, though, that Locke simply defines "good" as "that which is apt to produce pleasure in us"; rather, our capacity for pleasure and pain is meant to explain what *motivates* us to do what we think to be good. The bare knowledge of moral principles in itself would not be sufficient to bring us to follow them. Instead, our consideration of the happiness that might follow from obeying these principles is what brings us to follow them, and it is how we come to such obedience as what is good in the highest sense for us.[2]

So, what kind of ideas are our moral principles, and what is their source? In answering these questions, Locke relies upon the notion of mixed **modes**†, which are complex ideas constructed by the mind, from simple ideas of different kinds drawn from our experience or reflection, and which represent a way in which a substance can be (or alternatively, an attribute or property that a substance can have). Ideas that are mixed modes do not necessarily correspond to anything that really exists: "these *Ideas* are called *Notions*: as if they had their Original, and constant Existence, more in the Thoughts of Men, than in the reality of things; and to form such Ideas, it sufficed, that the Mind put the parts of them together, and that they were consistent in the Understanding, without considering whether they had any real Being."[3] Such notions are composed of cognitive content from different experiences, brought together under a name and expressible sound, for example, the notion of "drunkenness" will be composed from our experiences of drunk people (or, indeed, having been drunk ourselves), along with the name we have chosen in our language for that notion. Thus, morally salient notions such as "duty," "obligation," "murder," and "theft" are constructed by our minds on the basis of a complex of ideas gained from our experience.

This account of the nature of moral ideas may give the initial impression that Locke believes morality to essentially be a human construction, with no basis in reality. However, this would overlook the role that Locke gives to our ability to rationally discern (on the basis of our experience) a law of nature that is instituted by the genuine authority of a divine lawgiver. As Locke argues in this following extract, a moral principle, in addition to the moral rule it prescribes, implicitly involves a relation to a given law, the recognition of which puts us under genuine moral obligations:

Extract 6.2—Locke, An Essay Concerning Human Understanding (Book II, Chapter XXVIII)

4. There is another sort of Relation, which is the Conformity, or Disagreement, Men's voluntary Actions have to a Rule, to which they are referred, and by which they are judged of: which, I think, may be called *Moral Relation*; as being that, which denominates our Moral Actions, and deserves well to be examined, there being no part of Knowledge wherein we should be more careful to get determined *Ideas*, and avoid, as much as may be, Obscurity and Confusion. Humane Actions, when with their various Ends, Objects, Manners, and Circumstances, they are framed into distinct complex Ideas, are, as has been shown, so many *mixed Modes*, a great part whereof have Names annexed to them. Thus supposing Gratitude to be a readiness to acknowledge and return Kindness received; Polygamy to be the having more Wives than one at once: when we frame these Notions thus in our Minds, we have there so many determined *Ideas* of mixed Modes. But this is not all that concerns our Actions; it is not enough to have determined *Ideas* of them, and to know what Names belong to such and such Combinations of *Ideas*. We have a farther and greater Concernment, and that is, to know whether such Actions so made up, are morally good, or bad.

5. Good and Evil . . . are nothing but Pleasure or Pain, or that which occasions, or procures Pleasure or Pain to us. *Morally Good and Evil* then, is only the conformity or Disagreement of our voluntary Actions to some Law, whereby Good or Evil is drawn on us, from the Will and Power of the Law-maker; which Good and Evil, Pleasure or Pain, attending our observance, or breach of the Law, by the Decree of the Law-maker, is that we call *Reward* and *Punishment*.

6. Of these *Moral Rules*, or Laws, to which Men generally refer, and by which they judge of the Rectitude or Pravity of their Actions, there seem to me to be *three sorts*, with their three different Enforcements, or Rewards

and Punishments. For since it would be utterly in vain, to suppose a Rule set to the free Actions of Man, without annexing to it some Enforcement of Good and Evil, to determine his Will, we must, wherever we suppose a Law, suppose also some Reward or Punishment annexed to that Law. It would be in vain for one intelligent Being, to set a Rule to the Actions of another, if he had it not in his Power, to reward the compliance with, and punish deviation from his Rule, by some Good and Evil, that is not the natural product and consequence of the Action itself. For that being a natural Convenience, or Inconvenience, would operate of itself without a Law. This, if I mistake not, is the true nature of all *Law*, properly so called.

7. The *Laws* that Men generally refer their Actions to, to judge of the Rectitude, or Obliquity, seem to me to be these three. 1. The *Divine* Law. 2. The *Civil* Law. 3. The Law of *Opinion* or *Reputation*, if I may so call it. By the relation they bear to the first of these, Men judge whether their Actions are Sins, or Duties; by the second, whether they be Criminal, or Innocent; and by the third, whether they be Virtues or Vices.

8. *First*, The *Divine* Law, whereby I mean, that Law which God has set to the actions of Men, whether promulgated to them by the light of Nature, or the voice of Revelation. That God has given a Rule whereby Men should govern themselves, I think there is no body so brutish as to deny. He has a Right to do it, we are his Creatures: He has Goodness and Wisdom to direct our Actions to that which is best: and he has Power to enforce it by Rewards and Punishments, of infinite weight and duration, in another Life: for no body can take us out of his hands. This is the only true touchstone of *moral Rectitude*; and by comparing them to this Law, it is, that Men judge of the most considerable *Moral Good* or *Evil* of their Actions; that is, whether as *Duties, or Sins*, they are like to procure them happiness, or misery, from the hands of the ALMIGHTY.

-

14. Whether the Rule, to which, as to a Touch-stone, we bring our voluntary Actions, to examine them by, and try their Goodness, and accordingly to name them; which is, as it were, the Mark of the value we set upon them: Whether, I say, we take that Rule from the Fashion of the Country, or the Will of a Law-maker, the Mind is easily able to observe the Relation any Action hath to it; and to judge, whether the Action agrees, or disagrees with the Rule: and so hath a Notion of *Moral Goodness or Evil*, which is either Conformity, or not Conformity of any Action to that Rule: And therefore, is often called Moral Rectitude. This Rule being nothing but a Collection of several simple *Ideas*, the Conformity thereto is but so ordering the Action, that the simple *Ideas*, belonging to it, may correspond to those, which the Law requires. And thus we see, how Moral Beings and Notions, are founded

on, and terminated in these simple *Ideas*, we have received from Sensation or Reflection. For Example, let us consider the complex *Idea*, we signify by the Word Murder: and when we have taken it asunder, and examined all the Particulars, we shall find them to amount to a Collection of simple *Ideas*, derived from Reflection or Sensation, *viz. First*, From Reflection on the Operations of our own Minds, we have the *Ideas* of Willing, Considering, Purposing beforehand, Malice, or wishing Ill to another; and also of Life, or Perception, and Self-motion. *Secondly*, From Sensation, we have the Collection of those simple sensible *Ideas* which are to be found in a Man, and of some Action, whereby we put an end to Perception, and Motion in the Man; all which simple *Ideas*, are comprehended in the word Murder. This Collection of simple *Ideas*, being found by me to agree or disagree, with the esteem of the Country I have been bred in; and to be held by most Men there, worthy Praise, or Blame, I call the Action virtuous or vicious; If I have the Will of a supreme, invisible Lawmaker for my Rule: then, as I supposed the Action commanded, or forbidden by God, I call it Good or Evil, Sin or Duty: and if I compare it to the civil Law, the Rule made by the Legislative of the Country, I call it lawful, or unlawful, a Crime, or no Crime. So that whencesoever we take the Rule of Moral Actions; or by what Standard soever we frame in our Minds the *Ideas* of Virtues or Vices, they consist only, and are made up of Collections of simple *Ideas*, which we originally received from Sense of Reflection: and their Rectitude, or Obliquity [divergence from morality], consists in the Agreement, or Disagreement, with those Patterns prescribed by some Law.

[From *An Essay Concerning Human Understanding,* 4th edn. (London: Awnsham and J. Churchill, 1700). Some language has been modernized.]

We saw earlier that Locke's account of motivation focuses on the question of the prospect of happiness. In the previous extract, Locke links the possibility of moral motivation with the need for a divine moral lawmaker. Our moral principles are understood by us to refer to a rule which is set by a rule-maker. With regard to the highest notion of moral good and evil, our principles ultimately refer to a lawmaker who has the ability and authority to distribute appropriate rewards and punishments in an afterlife, in the form of happiness or misery. While we can consider the relation between our actions and the laws of society—either legally or with regard to how we need to act in order to maintain our reputation—Locke thinks it is clear through reflection that the law of nature is the highest and most authoritative law to follow, at least as far as our moral rectitude is concerned. It is in this way that Locke links our motivation concerning the prospect of happiness with the possibility of following moral principles through our actions. By reflecting upon our experience, we naturally understand that a law of nature has been set for us by an authoritative divine lawmaker, who has the ability to offer us ultimate happiness in another life, and on that basis we have both the obligation and the motivation to do what is morally good and shun what is morally evil.

In this way, Locke is positioned in a longstanding **natural law tradition**[†] in moral philosophy.[4] There is a moral law, Locke writes,

> which each individual can discover by that light [i.e. reason] alone which is implanted in us by nature; to which too he [ought to] show himself obedient in everything, [and] which he perceives as demanding a rational account of his duty . . . [It] can, therefore, be described [as a law] because it is the command of the divine will, knowable by the light of nature, indicating what is and what is not consonant with a rational nature, and by that very fact commanding or prohibiting.[5]

On the basis of our reflection, we can come to understand that God exists and has created us with a rational faculty that reveals the way we ought to live, in line with our divinely created rational nature. Our reason, however, ultimately relies on the senses for the cognitive content required to formulate its ideas of moral principles that conform with the law of nature:

> Yet without the help of the senses and their service, reason can produce nothing more than can a workman in the dark behind closed shutters. Unless the ideas of things penetrate [the mind] from the outside, there will be no matter for reasoning, nor could the mind erect a structure of knowledge any more than could an architect erect buildings, if he had no stones, timber, sand, and other building materials.[6]

Reason and the senses thus must work together to give us the moral principles required to discern what God has commanded us to do, with the prospect of eternal reward offered as motivation for following this law.

Locke's account of the nature of our moral knowledge has attracted a number of objections. For one thing, it seems to attribute a decidedly selfish ground for our being motivated to undertake morally good actions. While the natural law gives us a reason to act morally, the prospect of future happiness is supposedly required to motivate us to act in that way. Can we really be said to be morally good if we only do the right thing because we think it is going to bring us future happiness in the afterlife? On such an account, the moral good for us seems to become merely the pleasure that we can expect for following the law of nature, which is arguably quite an impoverished conception of what goodness is really about.

In response to this objection, the scholar Patricia Sheridan has defended Locke and argued that he holds a rather more complicated account of moral motivation than it may seem at first glance. While Locke's settled account of motivation does seem to be a hedonistic one, he nevertheless allows for us to be motivated by the intrinsic pleasure to be found in doing and being good, in addition to the possible extrinsic pleasure offered by rewards in the afterlife.[7] In an unpublished manuscript from 1692, Locke discusses the possible pleasure derived from offering food to someone in dire need: "Whoever spared a meal to save the life of a starving man, much more a friend, which all men are to us whom we love, but had more and much lasting pleasure in it than he that eat it. The other's pleasure died as he eat and ended with his meal. But to him that gave it him 'tis a feast as often as he reflects on it."[8] Sheridan argues that this quote reveals a more nuanced understanding of the motivation underlying the morally good act of providing a meal to a starving person, because such a person is not acting for an expected reward; rather, there is a pleasure that is received by the individual just in virtue of having done something good, beyond the shallow pleasure they would have gained from eating the meal themselves. On this reading, Locke follows an Aristotelian line that sees virtue partly as finding the pleasure that is intrinsic to being virtuous, which can act as a motivating factor in our deciding to undertake morally good actions.[9] On this basis, Locke is not positing a simple account of moral motivation based on expected pleasure; rather, we at least partly do the right thing because we learn to take pleasure directly from pursuing the good.

However, it is not clear here whether Locke is indeed moving away from an account of motivation based on expected pleasure, if we take into account the wider context of the quote provided above. Locke is speaking in quite a self-interested way here about how to secure the most intense and long-lasting pleasures for ourselves. We do good to others in the expectation that "all the good we do to them redoubles upon ourselves and gives us an undecaying and uninterrupted pleasure."[10] The reason to give the meal to the starving man rather than to ourselves is that we will be able to reflect upon our action in the future and repeatedly derive satisfaction from having done this good act. While eating the meal ourselves may provide a fleeting satisfaction based on our immediate appetites, there is an "immaterial pleasure" to be had from doing good and later remembering the good that we had done. Thus, there is still a sense in which it is the expectation of pleasure that is driving us to do good things on Locke's account, and such a hedonistic grounding for moral motivation will always seem questionable to some. We will return to this objection in the following section.

Locke was often accused of offering an undeveloped or unsatisfactory treatment of religion and morality in his *Essay*, and so it was up to supporters of Locke, such as Catherine Cockburn, to attempt to defend him in these matters. However, in filling in these gaps in Lockean empiricism, they were able to positively develop the theory beyond that proposed in the *Essay*. Thus, Cockburn should not merely be understood as a defender of Locke, but as an innovative and original thinker in her own right, as we shall see in the following section.

Key Points

- The lack of agreement on moral principles, and our inability to largely live in accordance with those principles, leads Locke to deny innate moral knowledge.
- Our experience gives us the opportunity to rationally discern a moral law of nature that is prescribed by God for all to follow.
- Moral ideas are "mixed modes," constructed by the mind on the basis of our experience.
- Though Locke's account of moral motivation is not entirely clear, he gives an important role to the expectation of divine reward or punishment in the afterlife.

Suggested Further Reading

Ayers, Michael. *Locke: The Arguments of the Philosophers, Vol. 2: Ontology*, chs. 14 and 15. Abingdon: Routledge, 1991.

Darwall, Stephen. "Locke and Butler." In *The Cambridge History of Moral Philosophy*, edited by Sacha Golob and Jens Timmermann, 311–19. Cambridge: Cambridge University Press, 2017.

Garrett, Aaron. "Locke's Metaethics." In *The Lockean Mind*, edited by Jessica Gordon-Roth and Shelley Weinberg, 341–50. Abingdon: Routledge, 2022.

Schneewind, J. B. *The Invention of Autonomy: A History of Modern Moral Philosophy*, ch. 8. Cambridge: Cambridge University Press, 1998.

Wilson, Catherine. "The Moral Epistemology of Locke's *Essay*." In *The Cambridge Companion to Locke's "Essay Concerning Human Understanding,"* edited by Lex Newman, 381–405. Cambridge: Cambridge University Press, 2007.

6B. COCKBURN ON LOCKE, GOD AND MORALITY

Catherine Trotter Cockburn: Brief Chronology

- *c.* 1674: Born in London
- 1693: Publishes first novel, *The Adventures of a Young Lady*
- 1695: Writes her first play, *Agnes de Castro*, one of many that she would compose in her youth
- 1702: Publishes her first philosophical work, *A Defence of Mr. Locke's Essay of Human Understanding*
- 1707: Announces her conversion from Catholicism to the Church of England in *A Discourse Concerning a Guide in Controversies*
- 1708: Marriage to clergyman Patrick Cockburn, leading to a temporary break in her literary activities
- 1726: Resumes her philosophical activities with another defense of Locke, *A Letter to Dr. Holdsworth Occasioned by his Sermon*
- 1740s: Publishes a series of works in defense of the philosopher and theologian Samuel Clarke (1675-1729)
- 1749: Dies in Northumberland, following work on a collected edition of her writings
- 1751: Collected works are published, edited by Thomas Birch

In the previous section, we considered the outlines of Locke's empiricist project, as outlined famously in his *An Essay Concerning Human Understanding*. Though Lockean empiricism gathered many supporters, it also drew its fair share of critics, who published numerous books and pamphlets criticizing Locke's philosophical project in the following decades. As Locke was not always willing or able to defend himself in print, a number of empiricist philosophers wrote defenses of him, often in response to a particular critic. However, in offering such defenses, these empiricist philosophers often developed his account in new and interesting directions, in order to fill in argumentative and theoretical gaps.

Catherine Trotter Cockburn's aim in her philosophical works has often been described as offering a defense of John Locke's empiricism, as presented in his *Essay*. However, though Cockburn does seek to answer some of Locke's critics on his behalf, she substantially develops Lockean empiricism, partly by seeking to fill in some of the gaps left in the philosophy presented by Locke.

One of the debates that Cockburn responds to is between two competing visions of the relation between God and morality. Both sides are attempts to answer the question of where morality comes from, or, in other words, what the ground of morality is. It is generally agreed by both sides that morality came from God in some way, but they disagreed about the particulars. According to **voluntarism**†, morality depends on the arbitrary will of God. What makes it the case that stealing or murder, for example, are wrong is simply that God declares or commands them to be so, and thereby places us under an obligation not to commit those kinds of acts. According to **intellectualism**†, on the other hand, morality is grounded in God's immutable nature. On this view, God's commands to refrain from stealing or murder are a response to an antecedent recognition of what is unchangeably good given the intrinsic nature of goodness.

Both voluntarism and intellectualism face significant objections. One of the main objections to intellectualism is that it seems to constrain God's freedom. One of God's attributes is absolute or maximal freedom: in other words, God is the most free being there could be. Intellectualism suggests that, for a maximally free being, God is remarkably unfree, in the sense that his will is entirely constrained to only act according to a pre-existing eternal law (albeit one grounded in his own intrinsic nature). Voluntarists argue that the suggestion of such a constraint on divine freedom does not do justice to the majesty and power of the divine, and thus intellectualism cannot be the correct view.

On the other hand, voluntarism faces its own objections. From the empiricist standpoint, it suggests a limit to our sources of moral knowledge that many find overly restrictive. The reason for this is that voluntarism seems to entail that God's commands could have been different, so although in fact God has decreed murder to be wrong and this decree is immutable once issued, nevertheless God *could* have decreed that murder is permissible. Even setting aside the fact that it seems intuitively false that murder could have been morally permissible, this possibility poses a problem specific to the empiricist approach. If morality could have been drastically different than it is without any other change to the world, it is unclear how we could garner knowledge of moral principles from studying stable features of our experience (such as, for example, the nature of rationality or of human nature). By holding that moral properties are attached extrinsically to individuals, intentions and actions by a divine act of will, rather than through the intrinsic nature of those things themselves, it becomes more difficult to see how our empirical observations could reliably teach us moral principles. Experience therefore turns out to be an insufficiently stable source for us to use as a basis for moral knowledge (and so a natural law theory such as Locke's could not offer a legitimate account of the source of moral knowledge). We would instead have to rely on some kind of divine revelation (that is, God directly communicating his will to us in some way) for any moral knowledge. As this is an implication that many empiricists would not accept, they typically reject voluntarism and argue for intellectualism.

However, despite Locke's empiricism, he was nevertheless accused of upholding voluntarism by the anonymous author of a series of three pamphlets, entitled *Remarks upon an Essay Concerning Humane Understanding, in a Letter adress'd to the Author* (1697–9). The author of these pamphlets, who I shall refer to as the "Remarker" (given the current uncertainty as to their identity[11]), in addressing Locke states, "you seem to ground your demonstration [of morality] upon future punishments and rewards and upon the arbitrary will of the lawgiver... If things were so, there would be no fixed notion of holiness, and God might be the author of sin."[12] The Remarker essentially has a two-pronged attack here: (1) Locke is accused of promoting a voluntarism that, at least in principle, allows for absurd situations such as God commanding horrendous actions and punishing us for actions such as giving money to charity; and (2) Locke is said to hold a **prudential account**[†] of moral motivation, that is, to hold that the reason for our observing moral obligations is merely the prospect of future rewards or punishment in the afterlife. Neither view is fitting for the majesty of God and the sacrosanct nature of morality, as far as the Remarker is concerned.

As both an empiricist and a defender of Locke, Cockburn wishes to argue that an empiricist account of the grounds of moral knowledge can be given without committing oneself to voluntarism or a prudential account, and that Locke has been misinterpreted by the Remarker. In the following extract, we see Cockburn reacting to the charge of voluntarism that has been leveled at Locke, in connection with the promise he offers in the *Essay* of being able to offer certainty in moral knowledge through empiricist principles:

Extract 6.3—Cockburn, *A Defence of Mr. Locke's Essay of Human Understanding* (pp. 53–9)

[It is] clear to me, that whatever we can know at all, must be discoverable by Mr. *Locke's* principles; for I cannot find any one idea not derived from sensation and reflection. But let us see, how those points may be established on them, for which the Remarker doubts their force; and first of morality, or natural religion; of which, he thus begins:

"As to morality, we think the great foundation of it is the definition of good and evil, virtue and vice.—And I do not find, that my eyes, ears, nostrils, or any other outward senses, make any distinction of these things, as they do of colours, sounds, etc.—Nor from any ideas taken in from them, or from their reports, am I conscious, that I do, or can conclude, that there is such a distinction in the nature of things."

In which words, he says, he thought he had taken in enough to comprehend both Mr. *Locke*'s principles of knowledge, *sensation and reflection*, which I should not have thought; but since he owns he designed them to do so, we will suppose both expressed, and proceed with him.

"I allow, that we may infer from observation and reason, that such a distinction is useful to society, but both philosophers and divines, you know, make a more immutable and intrinsic distinction, which is that I cannot make out from your principles.—This I am sure of, that the distinction, suppose of gratitude and ingratitude, fidelity and infidelity, justice and injustice, and such others, is as sudden without any ratiocination, and as sensible and piercing, as the difference I feel from the scent of a rose and *asafoetida*."

One would think here, he were doubting, whether upon Mr. *Locke*'s principles we can distinguish *gratitude* from *ingratitude*, *fidelity* from *infidelity*, etc. that is, know that breaking a trust is not keeping a trust, etc. which (as all other moral virtues, as Mr. *Locke* has shown) are a collection of simple ideas, received from sensation and reflection. But since he allowed above, that *we can from observation and reason, infer such a distinction to be useful to society*, and by consequence, that we can by them perceive such a distinction, we will guess his meaning here, to be, that the perception of the *morality* and *immorality* of these things is as sudden, etc. *as the difference he feels from the scent of a rose, and* asafoetida; though I do not know what it is, to perceive the *morality and immortality* of these things *without any ratiocination*.

Justice and injustice, I think, depend upon the rights of men, whether natural, or established by particular societies; and therefore to know what they are, it is necessary to know what right is, which sure requires some *reflection*. But to know, that *injustice* is *evil*, without any *reflection*, seems to me no more than to know, that the term *injustice* stands for something that we do not know, which is evil; unless it will be said, that we know it to be a detaining of any one's right, without knowing what right is, which will be a very insignificant knowledge.

But if the Remarker means, that as soon as he knows what it is to have a right to a thing, he perceives, that to detain from a man what he has such a right to, is evil, without any farther reflection, I understand him, but see not how it can be objected against the force of Mr. *Locke*'s principles, being only a perception of the disagreement of these two ideas, of one man's having a right to a thing, and another's having a right to take it away: but this is only by the way.

Let us now consider that, for which this sudden perception without ratiocination is brought as a proof, *viz.* that the ground of the distinction of moral good and evil is in the *nature of the things themselves*, abstracted from the good of society; which is that he cannot make out from Mr. *Locke*'s principles. By which distinction in the nature of things, if he means, that without respect to men, or to society, though mankind has never been, or never been designed, justice, gratitude, fidelity, etc. had been good, and their contraries evil; I confess myself incapable of having a notion of these virtues abstract from any subject to conceive: For example, that it would have been good to be faithful to a trust, though there had never been any one to trust, or be trusted: nor do I find, that the assertors of this distinction in the nature of things have any real idea of them more abstracted than I have, which will appear in examining their particular instances.

I will take that, which the Remarker gives, being one of the most incontested principles in morality, "That it is a wicked thing, for a man maliciously to kill his friend, or his father, or any other innocent person. The truth of this," he says, "seems to him as clear and eternal, as any proposition in mathematics"; and it seems to me as clear, that it cannot possibly be conceived at all, either *true* or *false*, in itself, *i.e.* without any relation to man. I desire any one, to try, whether he can conceive it to be an eternal truth, that it is a wicked thing, for a man to kill his father, or his friend, though there never had been, or designed to be, such a thing as friend, father, or man. But whether he can or not, it will still be a truth as *certain and immutable*, as any proposition in mathematics. No mathematician, that I know of, thinks it necessary to establish the immutability of this truth, that the three angles of a triangle are equal to two right ones; to affirm, that it is true, without any relation to angles or triangles. Either of these propositions are sufficiently established, if it is, and always must be true, supposing those things, to which it relates to exist.

But here the Remarker's question will be made, upon what grounds must it be [that moral truths are as certain and immutable as propositions in mathematics]? If good and evil, virtue and vice, are not such in their own nature, they must be so from the arbitrary will of God; and all things are indifferent, until he declare this or that to be fine, according to his pleasure: that is, he might, if he had so pleased, have made virtue, vice; and vice, virtue:

To which, I answer, that God having made man such a creature as he is, it is as impossible, that good and evil should change their respects to him, as that pleasure can be pain, and pain pleasure, which no one in his senses will affirm; and yet, I think, nobody has supposed them to be real existences, independent of any subject. And if the relation, which moral good and evil has to natural good and evil, were sufficiently observed, there would be as little dispute about the nature and reality of virtue and vice. Those, who think they are only notions in the mind, would be convinced they are as real as natural good and evil; all moral good consisting in doing, willing, or choosing, for one's self or others, whatever is a natural good; and all moral evil, in doing, willing, or choosing whatever is a natural evil, to one's self or others.

This, I doubt not, will appear a full definition, when tried by every instance of moral good and evil, to all who reflect on it; unless there are any, who do not place the perfection and imperfection, the advantages and disadvantages of the *mind*, in their account of *natural good* or *evil*; which I believe no rational man will own.

And as this unalterable relation makes the real and immutable nature of virtue and vice undeniable; so also from thence it is plain, *that the nature of man is the ground or reason of the law of nature*; *i.e.* of moral good and evil. But if the Remarker will rather have it, that the nature of these things is the reason of the nature of man, that they are essentially in the nature of God, which is the rule of his will, and according to which he formed man; let it be so, as it is unquestionable, that he cannot will any thing contrary to his nature. But, however the moral attributes of God, goodness, justice, etc., are in him (who is infinitely beyond the reach of our narrow capacities) this I say (which Mr. *Locke* has observed of our idea of their infinity) that we have no idea of them, but what carries with it a respect to their objects, *the natural good or evil of his creatures*; and we could have no idea of them at all without reflection upon ourselves; for whatever is the original standard of good and evil, it is plain, we have no notion of them but by their conformity, or repugnancy to our reason, and with relation to our nature; and that what according to it we perceive to be good, we ascribe to the Supreme Being; for we cannot know, that the nature of God is good, before we have a notion of good. It must be then by reflecting upon our own nature, and the operations of our minds, that we come to know the nature of God; which therefore cannot *be to us* the rule of good and evil; unless we will argue in a circle, that by our notion of good, we know the nature of God, and by the nature of God, we know what is good.

From whence it will follow, that the nature of man, and the good of society, are *to us* the reason and rule of moral good and evil; and there is no danger of their being less immutable on this foundation than any other, whilst man continues *a rational and sociable creature*. If the law of nature is the product of human nature itself . . . it must subsist as long as human nature; nor will this foundation make it the less sacred, since it cannot be doubted, that it is originally the will of God, whilst we own him the author of that nature, of which this law is a consequence.

If then, in Mr. *Locke*'s way, we can perceive what is conformable, or not, to our own nature, which cannot be doubted; if by reflecting on ourselves, we can come to know there must be a Supreme Being, the source of all others, which he has admirably shown; we have a sacred and immutable foundation for natural religion, on his principles; this being a plain and infallible inference, that the Author of our being does require those things of us, to which he has suited our nature, and visibly annexed our happiness, which he has made the necessary motive of all our actions. For it is inconsistent with that divine wisdom, which we see has fitted all other things to their proper and certain end, to have formed us after such a manner, that if we employ those faculties, which he has given us, we cannot but judge, that such things are fit to be done, and others to be avoided, and this to no end at all. Much less can we suppose he has designed us to act contrary to the necessary motives of our actions, and judgement of our minds; it being a flat contradiction, that infinite wisdom and power should form any of his works so disproportionate to their end.

[From *The Works of Mrs. Catherine Cockburn: Volume 1* (London: J & P Knapton, 1751). Some language has been modernized.]

In this extract, Cockburn defends an empiricist approach that views our knowledge of moral principles as grounded in our experience of what it is like to be human, such as what we find brings us pain or pleasure. The Remarker's argument (at least, as Cockburn reads him) is that if we gain our knowledge in this manner, it cannot be certain or unchangeable, for certain knowledge cannot be gained through experience and human nature could, at least in principle, change. Further, if certain and **immutable**[†] moral knowledge is not possible, this would potentially entail that moral principles themselves are not true simply in themselves (otherwise there would be no possibility of them changing); rather, they must depend for their determination on some other source. The only possible ground for these principles would be the arbitrary will of God, and so Locke's empiricist project of grounding moral knowledge in observations upon human nature leads to problematic voluntarism.

Cockburn's response to this challenge has a few different aspects. First, she states that human nature is a stable foundation for moral knowledge. On the basis of a set of stable facts about human nature that we discover in our experience, we can identify a natural moral law that could not have been otherwise (at least, not without human nature having been different). So, in response to the Remarker's argument that certain or unchangeable moral knowledge cannot be garnered from experience, Cockburn argues that in fact, given the unchanging features of our experience (which is conditioned by our own nature), we can have an epistemically stable foundation for knowledge regarding the moral law. As an analogy, Cockburn points to the respective natures of pleasure and pain. Given the nature of our constitutions, it simply could not be the case that pleasure is felt as pain, or pain is felt as pleasure (though, of course, the two can sometimes go together). Rather, our intrinsic nature sets what pain and pleasure are for us and what they feel like. Cockburn argues that in the same way that what is pleasure and what is pain for us cannot change (as grounded in human nature), neither can be what is morally good or bad for us change.

Further, Cockburn notes that even though we do not think that pain and pleasure are interchangeable, we are not thereby led to think of them as having their own separate existence in principle. We can only conceive pleasure and pain as being had by a particular individual; we cannot think of a "free-floating" pleasure or pain that is not had by someone in a particular moment. In an analogous way, our moral principles can be both unchangeable and grounded in the particularity of human nature and the society in which we live. Cockburn expands on this point by arguing for an essential connection between *moral* goodness and *natural* goodness. What is morally good for us to do is what we are most fitted to do given our intrinsic human nature. It is up to us to reflect upon our experience as human beings and the way in which humans interact with each other to gain knowledge of what is most fitting for us to do as the kinds of beings we are.[13] On this experiential basis, we are thus able to gain knowledge of what is naturally good for us.

The key to this process is a particular account of reflection, according to which we are able to gain knowledge through reflection by discerning the agreement (or disagreement) between our ideas: for example, if I reflect upon my idea of "property" and my idea of "theft," I can come to see the affinity or "congruity" between them. On that basis, I can reason that there can be no theft without property, and I have thus gained some moral knowledge—"Where there is no property, there is no theft."[14] Through this process of reflection, we are able to generate a system of moral knowledge, as well as the knowledge that there is a God who wills us to follow moral principles. As Cockburn argues, "we could have no idea [of moral principles and the moral nature of God] at all without reflection upon ourselves; for whatever is the original standard of good and evil, it is plain, we have no notion of them but by their conformity, or repugnancy to our reason, and with relation to our nature."[15] So, with experience and reflection working in tandem, I am able to gain all the moral knowledge I need without relying upon innate knowledge or some kind of supernatural intervention.

However, why should we think that knowledge of our natural good is sufficient to give us a complete system of moral knowledge? We might particularly wonder this if we view our current natural state as only the first part of our existence, prior to an afterlife where we have left our bodies behind. There are a couple of strands to Cockburn's moral theory that help to answer this question. First, there is the question of moral obligation: why is it that, upon recognizing what the natural good is for us, we are thereby morally obliged to promote it as far as we are able? It could be that I recognize, for example, that it is most fitting for me as a human being to help others, but then wonder why I should not prioritize my self-interest in the decisions I make. Cockburn argues that, as part of our reflection upon what is fitting for us to do, we naturally recognize the obligatory nature of the principles of natural good that follow. In other words, we are naturally able to see that we are morally obliged to promote the natural good. So, asking why we are obliged to promote the natural good is an empty question, because as soon as you identify the natural good, you also recognize your obligation to promote it.

One important implication of this view is that we are no longer put under moral obligation directly through knowledge of God's will (as voluntarists would be inclined to claim). Rather, *we put ourselves under moral obligation* through our natural recognition of what we ought to do. In this way, we can see Cockburn's leanings toward the emphasis upon the autonomy of the self, in other words, the ability of an individual to engage in self-determination apart from the overwhelming influence or power of external authority (which became increasingly important in the era of the Enlightenment in the early modern period). However, this is not to say that God does not have a role to play, and this leads us to the second strand of answering the question of how knowledge of the natural good gives us moral knowledge. God's creative action (through his will) is undertaken with the prior recognition of moral goodness in mind, so the natural order of things was created with the goal of the promotion of moral ends. In other words, God created us in such a way that our natural good *reflects* the moral good. Further, Cockburn argues that God can act in no other way than to create a world that conforms to his own perfect nature. If God were to fail to do so, then this would be to allow an imperfection in God, which is nonsensical. In this way, God acts as an archetype of sorts for our own created nature, and thus we are able to read off something about morality and God's perfect nature through reflection upon ourselves. Due to this connection, brought about by God, we are able to use our reflection upon the natural good to come to moral knowledge.

However, linking the natural good to moral goodness in such a way invites another charge that the Remarker levels at Locke: namely, that this position ultimately devolves into a kind of hedonism, where all value is ultimately located in pleasure or mere self-interest. The Remarker states that an empiricist approach could only give us a value system based on self-interest (either individual or social), rather than a true system of morality:

> I will take the liberty to say that the author cannot, upon those [empiricist] principles, give us, as is pretended, a demonstrative morality as clear as mathematics. He may give us a set of prudential maxims for the conveniences of life, or a kind of political righteousness, but will never reach what is most sacred and divine either in morality or religion.[16]

The Remarker further claims that Locke's hedonism is confirmed by the role granted in the *Essay* to the prospect of future rewards and punishments in the afterlife. As we saw in the previous section, Locke writes that "what Duty is, cannot be understood without a Law; nor a Law be known, or supposed without a Law-maker, or without Reward and Punishment."[17] This comment by Locke might be taken to suggest that our understanding and recognition of the moral law depends upon the prospect of possible reward or punishment in the afterlife, which would potentially make our observance of what is morally good depend upon non-moral self-interest. In this passage, the Remarker accuses Locke of reducing love of God and morality to mere love of self:

> I think you should tell us what is the love of God, the fountain of virtue and piety, according to your principles, and how it is distinguished from self-love ... We love God: but why? Not for His sake, but for our own sake, because He will reward our love and obedience. Without this motive you seem to leave no argument to love Him, or virtue, or piety.[18]

In defense of Locke on this point, Cockburn seeks to argue that the Remarker has simply misinterpreted the *Essay*. When considering morality, we can distinguish between what grounds morality (in other words, what determines what is morally good and what is morally bad) and what gives morality the force of law. Cockburn explores this distinction in the following extract.

Extract 6.4 — Cockburn, *A Defence of Mr. Locke's Essay of Human Understanding* (pp. 60–2)

But the Remarker will object, that Mr. *Locke* does not establish morality upon the nature of man, and the nature of God, but *seems to ground his demonstration upon future punishments and rewards, and upon the arbitrary will of the law-giver; and he does not think these the first grounds of good and evil.* To which I answer, first, supposing it were so, the question is not what Mr. *Locke* thinks, but what may be proved from his principles. But secondly, I say, that Mr. *Locke* does ground his demonstration upon the *nature of God and man* . . .

Nothing can be clearer than this; and in all those places, which the Remarker quotes out of Mr. Locke, where he seems to establish morality upon *the will of God, and rewards and punishments*, he is speaking of it, as it has the force of a law; and the Remarker cannot deny, whatever he thinks, *the first grounds of good and evil*, or however clearly we may see the *nature of these things*, we may approve or condemn them; but [moral principles] can only have the force of a *law* to us, considered as *the will of the Supreme Being*, who can, and certainly will, reward the compliance with, and punish the deviation from that rule, which he has made knowable to us by the light of nature.

But that we can only know these things to be his will by their conformity to our nature, and that therefore they cannot be arbitrary, I have before shown; and that he will punish or reward us according to our obedience or disobedience to it, is a consequence of his nature. So that, though Mr. *Locke* says, that the will of God, rewards and punishments, can only give morality the force of a law; that does not make them the *first grounds* of good and evil, since by his principles, to what the will of God is (antecedently to revelation) we must know what is good by the conformity it has to our nature, by which we come to know the nature of God, which therefore may be to him the first ground or rule of good; though *the will of God* [through the promise of rewards or punishments] can only enforce it as a *law*.

[From *The Works of Mrs. Catherine Cockburn: Volume 1* (London: J & P Knapton, 1751). Some language has been modernized.]

As we see in this extract, Cockburn claims that Locke does not seek to ground morality upon the will of God and promise of rewards or punishments in the afterlife; rather, Locke holds that the will of God is what gives morality "the force of a law" to us. However, what exactly does Cockburn (and presumably Locke, if she is interpreting him correctly) mean by giving morality "the force of a law"? One way of interpreting Cockburn on this question is to say that the prospect of rewards and punishment is part of what allows us to recognize morality as binding on all of us. If God punishes me for undertaking a particular action, that is an unmistakable sign that morality is non-negotiable and that I must observe it. In addition, being rewarded for a particular action is a sign that what I did had inherent value and brought credit upon myself. On this view, the divine system of justice built on rewards and punishments becomes a reflection of the seriousness and obligatory nature of morality, rather than being the ground of morality itself. We might think of an analogy with laws laid down by the government. In the UK, laws are passed by Parliament on behalf of the Crown. Those laws are then enforced by the Police force, and transgressions of the laws are punished by the justice system. It is the Crown and Parliament who are the sources of obligation to follow certain rules for behavior, not those who enforce the laws (the Police and the justice system). In the same way, God's will and the divine system of rewards and punishments are not the source of moral principles; rather, they enforce and reflect the obligatory nature of morality.

So, when referring to God's will and the prospect of rewards and punishment, Locke is not arguing that this is what grounds morality (and thus morality does not reduce to mere self-interest). Rather, these are factors that are a consequence of the nature of morality, and they may function as part of the motivational structure that brings us to act morally. (At least, that interpretation is how Cockburn reads Locke, though it is an open question whether or not this is indeed the position taken in the *Essay*.) Cockburn's view is that self-interest may have a role to play in moral motivation, but this does not mean that self-interest is the essence of morality.

Before we conclude, we can reflect upon just why this debate concerning God and the nature of morality mattered to Locke, Cockburn, Masham, and others at the time. The power of the Church in public life during this period was significant indeed, with strong links to both the government and the justice system that allowed it to have a significant influence upon how individuals were able to act. Through this influence upon government, and thereby shaping the laws that were passed and the way in which they were enforced, the Church was able to impose its values upon the populace in a manner that reinforced its power. The justification for acting in such a way was that it helped to ensure the realization of God's will and true morality in society, and so the question of the nature of morality and its relation to God became of great social importance.

With this in mind, we can see that a voluntarist account of morality might be particularly useful for the Church, in terms of maintaining its moral and political authority. If morality is grounded in God's will, and we have to rely upon special revelation to gain moral knowledge, this helps to secure the Church's status as the worldly authority in moral matters, due to its self-proclaimed status as the sole historical receptacle of special revelation from God. If, however, morality is not grounded in God's will, and if individuals are able to come to genuine knowledge of moral principles themselves (through the autonomous action of their individual faculties), as Locke, Masham and Cockburn claim, then the Church's status as a moral and political authority is undermined. So, there are two strands of Cockburn's thought, intellectualism and Lockean empiricism, that were each potentially of great social and political significance.

Some of the implications of empiricism were particularly potent for thinkers such as Cockburn and Masham, who would have been shut out of the Church's ecclesiastical hierarchy and were denied any kind of political power. If all individuals have the possibility of gaining the experience required, and they are able individually to use their powers of reflection to come to genuine knowledge of moral principles, this has profound egalitarian implications, for the Church's status as an unquestioned arbiter of moral issues would be significantly undermined. It is also possible to see intellectualism as a kind of philosophical rebellion against the idea that arbitrary power could be used to settle matters of right and wrong—placing intellectualism against the political reality at the time, namely, an undemocratic society that was governed by the whims of royalty and a very small elite. From an intellectualist standpoint, there is not *just* power, with rewards and punishments that follow for doing what you are told. Rather, there is a genuine essence of morality that is unchangeable and is not subject to the whim of any being, not even God.

The idea that morality is demonstrable through reason was important to Locke from a social standpoint. The scholar Catherine Wilson writes that this notion

> communicated his expectation that law and government power could be constructed on a reasonable and non-authoritarian, nonsectarian basis. He thinks of "indifference and attention" as capable of raising the study of morality from doxology to science, in much the way that the seventeenth century raised the study of nature from doxology to science.[19]

With the possibility of coming to a system of values that could achieve a wide consensus in society, through demonstration and the individual efforts of all reflecting rationally upon their own experience, Locke looked forward to a society that had moved away from arbitrary power and constant factional infighting. Instead, a new, rational society could be built that was more open and less stuck on the customs and ideas of the past. These were hopes shared by Cockburn and Masham, who also argued that a more rational religion and system of values would help undermine the superstition and fanaticism that had led to great suffering, such as the recent English Civil War and the various upheavals that had followed it.[20] Though the question of whether morality is grounded in God's will or the divine nature may seem relatively unimportant today, it was an issue that struck at the very heart of the social hierarchy at the time.

As a final note, some readers may be surprised by Cockburn's thought with regard to the way in which it fits into the divide that is often discussed by philosophers between empiricism and **rationalism**[†], construed as a strict distinction between those thinkers who claim that the content of our ideas can be ultimately traced back to experience and those who deny such a claim. While Cockburn clearly follows empiricist principles by grounding our knowledge in experience, she nevertheless posits an innate ability to recognize moral obligation in a manner that looks rather close to the kind of rational insight often proposed by rationalists that can give us *a priori* knowledge. What Cockburn shows us is that the dividing-line between rationalists and empiricists is ultimately not clear-cut, and trying to separate thinkers of the past into these two camps (though it can sometimes be helpful) can ultimately mislead. The fact is that many thinkers of Cockburn's time had elements of both empiricism and rationalism in their respective philosophies, and this should be borne in mind as we read them so that we do not miss some of the more nuanced aspects of their views.

Key Points

- In her *Defence*, Cockburn seeks to show (among other things) that an empiricist account of the nature of religious belief does not lead to theological voluntarism
- Against "the Remarker," Cockburn argues that our observations of human nature can be used as a stable basis for moral knowledge
- In addition, she argues for an intellectualist view, according to which morality is grounded in God's immutable nature

- Cockburn also argues that the Remarker misinterprets Locke as a voluntarist, as his appeals to the divine will are intended to show what gives morality the force of law, and not to characterize the fundamental ground of our moral obligations

Suggested Further Reading

Bolton, Martha Brant. "Some Aspects of the Philosophical Work of Catharine Trotter." *Journal of the History of Philosophy* 31, no. 4 (1993): 565–88.

Broad, Jacqueline. *Women Philosophers of the Seventeenth Century*, ch. 6. Cambridge: Cambridge University Press, 2002.

Gordon-Roth, Jessica. "Catherine Trotter Cockburn's *Defence* of Locke." *The Monist* 98 (2015): 64–76.

Sheridan, Patricia. "Reflection, Nature, and Moral Law: The Extent of Catharine Cockburn's Lockeanism in her *Defence of Mr. Locke's Essay*." *Hypatia* 22, no. 3 (2007): 133–51.

Waithe, Mary Ellen. "Catharine Trotter Cockburn." In *A History of Women Philosophers: Vol. 3*, edited by Mary Ellen Waithe, 101–26. Dordrecht: Kluwer, 1991.

Questions for Reflection

- Can an empiricist successfully explain how we get moral knowledge?
- Are we only motivated to do good by the prospect of pleasure?
- If theism is true, does the divine will decide what is morally right?
- What is the relationship between reason and faith? Is it appropriate to use our reason in matters of faith?

7

The Nature of Education
Anna van Schurman and Mary Astell

Chapter Outline

7a.	Anna Maria van Schurman on Education	169
7b.	Mary Astell's Serious Proposal	180
Questions for Reflection		190

Though the educational system a person grows up in often strikes them as inevitable, history abounds with alternative models of human education. Each such model implicitly takes a stance on some difficult philosophical questions about education. In this chapter, we will focus on three such questions: Who should receive an education? What subject matter ought they be taught? And what ultimately is the purpose of education? Although these are not the only questions that philosophers of education are interested in, they are surely among the deepest philosophical questions one can raise about the topic.

This chapter examines how two early modern philosophers, Anna Maria van Schurman (1607–1678) and Mary Astell (1666–1731), answered such questions. The question of the aims and scope of education are politically charged today; they were no less so in early modern Europe. Both Van Schurman and Astell have explicitly political aims in their writings on the topic: they both hope to change the popular attitude in seventeenth- and early eighteenth-century Europe that women need not (and, according to many at the time, *ought* not) receive a formal education beyond the basic literacy required for reading the Bible and writing letters or notes.

What did education look like in early modern Europe? A full answer to this question would require a volume all its own, and there was a great deal of variety from country to country (and indeed from town to town). Nevertheless, as a general rule, the public was better educated during this period than at any previous era in European history, though education had not yet become a fully state-sponsored institution in any European country. The case of the Netherlands is an interesting one. Although primary schools did receive some money from the state to take in students who couldn't afford to pay tuition, the motive was mainly to keep such children off the streets during the day.[1] Whatever the motive, it seems that most young men and women received a primary education, and the Netherlands in this period had a famously high rate of literacy across all classes and genders. Many young men went on to receive secondary schooling until the age of 18, at which point some went on to study at a university. However, young women typically did not receive secondary schooling, and they were also actively barred from attending university—and thereby prevented from studying the topics introduced at that level of the curriculum, including medicine, anatomy, physics, and (most) philosophy. While there were exceptions to this restriction, ordinarily the only way for a woman to study these subjects was under private tutelage (including at one of the many private French schools run by immigrants who had fled France in the aftermath of the Reformation).

In the cultural context of early modern Europe, then, Van Schurman and Astell's arguments that women ought to be permitted to pursue a higher education are strikingly bold. Their points of *disagreement* with one another, however, are no less interesting: although Van Schurman and Astell concur in their views about who ought to receive an education—namely, any man or woman who is willing and even modestly capable—they deeply disagree about the primary purpose of education, as well as about what material students ought to be taught.

7A. ANNA MARIA VAN SCHURMAN ON EDUCATION

Van Schurman was highly educated in the arts and humanities from a young age: she learned to read at four, and her family was keen to help hone her gift for language.[2] During her youth, she learned Latin, Greek, French, and several other languages; in adolescence, she quickly achieved renown for her poetry and, later, for her art. At the age of twenty-nine, she was asked by an influential professor at the newly founded Utrecht University to deliver a poem on the occasion of the school's opening. The poem was well received, and—presumably on the basis of this public demonstration of her abilities—she was permitted to take classes at the new university. She appears to have been the first woman to attend university classes, and new seating arrangements were introduced specifically for her: she sat in a booth with dark curtains so that the other students wouldn't see her.

Anna Maria van Schurman: Brief chronology

- 1607: Born in Cologne, Germany.
- c. 1623: Due to religious intolerance toward Calvinists, the Van Schurman family moves to Utrecht in the Netherlands.
- 1636: Becomes the first woman to attend a European university, taking classes at Utrecht University (which opened that same year).
- 1639: Publishes *On the End of Life*.
- 1641: Publishes a Latin treatise, *Dissertation on women's ability for learning and aptitude for scholarship*, including the text that is later translated into English as "The Learned Maid."
- 1648: An unauthorized volume of her works is published, *Short Works in Hebrew, Greek, Latin, and French, in prose and meter*, which includes a republication of her earlier *Dissertation*.
- 1650: The unauthorized *Short Works* is reprinted due to popularity.
- 1652: Publishes her authorized version of the *Short Works*.
- 1662: Meets Jean de Labadie, a prominent French **Pietist**[†].
- 1669: Joins the Labadist community, renouncing her view of the value of humanistic education.
- 1670-72: With the Labadists, lives under the protection of Princess Elisabeth of Bohemia at Herford Abbey in Germany.

- 1673: Publishes an autobiography entitled *Eukleria, or Choosing the Better Part*.
- 1674: After Jean de Labadie's death, becomes one of the leaders of the Labadist community. The following year, they move back to the Netherlands.
- 1678: Dies in Wiuwert.

In spite of the circumstances, she was eager to attend classes and seems to have flourished in her time at university. The experience clearly motivated her to make a public case for the education of women. She published a number of works in the ensuing decades, but the most influential was her *Dissertatio de ingenii muliebris ad doctrinam et meliores litteras aptitudine*, which included a series of arguments for the thesis that "A maid may be a scholar" and refutes the most popular objections to that thesis. First published in 1641, it was republished several times in different editions, and was eventually translated into English in 1659. The following extract is taken from that English translation.

Extract 7.1 Anna Maria van Schurman, *The Learned Maid*

A Logical Exercise upon this Question: *Whether a* Maid *may be a Scholar?*

We hold the affirmative and will endeavour to make it good.

These *Praecognita* [previously known facts] we permit: First on the part of the *subject*, and then of the *predicate*.

By a *Maid or Woman*, I understand her that is a *Christian*, and that not in Profession only, but really and indeed.

By a *Scholar*, I mean one that is given to the study of *Letters*, that is, the knowledge of *Tongues* and *Histories*, all kinds of learning, both superior (entitled *Faculties*) and inferior (called *Philosophy*). We except only *Scriptural Theology*, properly so named, as that which without controversy belongs to all Christians.

When we enquire, *whether she may be*, we mean whether it be *convenient*, that is, expedient, fit, decent. [. . .]

Wherefore we make use of these limitations:

First [limitations] of the subject; and first, that our *Maid* be endowed at least with an indifferent good wit, and not unapt for learning.

Secondly, that she be provided of necessaries and not oppressed with want: which exception I therefore put in, because few are so happy to have parents to breed them up in studies, and teachers are chargeable.

Thirdly, that the condition of the times, and her quality be such that she may have spare hours from her general and special calling, that is, from the exercises of piety and household affairs. To which end will conduce, partly her immunity from cares and employments in her younger years, partly in her elder age either celibate, or the ministry of handmaids, which are wont to free the richer sort of matrons also from domestic troubles.

Fourthly, let her end be, not vain glory and ostentation, or unprofitable curiosity: but beside the general end, God's glory and the salvation of her own soul; that both her self may be more virtuous and the more happy, and that she may (if that charge lie upon her) instruct and direct her family, and also be useful as much as may be to her whole Sex.

Next, limitations of the predicate, Scholarship, or the study of Letters, I so limit that I clearly affirm all honest discipline. . . , the Circle and Crown of liberal Arts and Sciences (as the proper and universal Good and Ornament of Mankind) to be convenient for the Head of our Christian Maid . . . according to the Dignity and Nature of every Art or Science, and according to the capacity and condition of the Maid herself . . . But especially let regard be had unto those Arts which have nearest alliance to Theology and the Moral Virtues, and are Principally subservient to them. In which number we reckon Grammar, Logic, Rhetoric; especially Logic, fitly called the Key of All Sciences: and then, Physics, Metaphysics, History, etc., and also the knowledge of Languages, chiefly of the Hebrew and Greek. All of which may advance to the more facile and full understanding of Holy Scripture: to say nothing now of other books. The rest, i.e., Mathematics (to which is also referred Music), Poesie, Picture, and the like, not illiberal Arts, may obtain the place of pretty Ornaments and ingenious Recreations.

Lastly, those studies which pertain to the practice of the Law, Military Discipline, Oratory in the Church, Court, University, as less proper and less necessary, we do not very much urge. And yet we in no wise yield that our Maid should be excluded from the Scholastic knowledge or Theory of those; especially not from understanding the most noble Doctrine of the Politics, or Civil Government.

And when we say a Maid may be a scholar, it is plain we do not affirm Learning to be . . . requisite, and precisely needful to eternal salvation: no, nor as such a good thing which makes to the very Essence of Happiness in this life: but as a very useful tool, conferring much to the integrity and perfection thereof: and as that, which by the contemplation of excellent things will promote us to a higher degree in the Love of God, and everlasting Felicity. . . .

I. Argument from the property of the subject

Whosoever is, is naturally endowed with the Principles, or powers of the principles, of all Arts and Sciences, may be a student in all Arts and Sciences: But Maids are naturally endowed with the Principles, etc. Therefore, etc.

The proposition is thus proved: They that may have the knowledge of Conclusions deduced from Principles may be students, etc. But they that are naturally endowed with the Principles may have the knowledge of Conclusions deduced from those Principles. Therefore, etc.

The assertion may be proved both from the property of the form of this Subject, or the rational soul: and from the very acts and effects themselves. For it is manifest that Maids do *actually* learn any Arts and Sciences. . . .

II. Argument. Again from the property of the subject.

Whosoever naturally has a desire of Arts and Sciences, may study the Arts and Sciences. But a Maid naturally has a desire of Arts and Sciences. Therefore, etc.

The reason of the major premise is manifest: because Nature does nothing in vain.

The minor premise is thus confirmed: That, which is in the whole Species or kind, is in every Individual or particular person, [and] in Maids also. But all Mankind have in them by Nature a desire of knowledge (Aristotle, *Metaphysics* I.2). Therefore, etc.

III. Argument, from the external property, or adjunct.

Whosoever is by God created with a sublime countenance, and erected toward Heaven, may (and ought) give himself to the contemplation and knowledge of sublime and heavenly things. But God has created woman also with a sublime and erected countenance: *Os homini sublime*, etc. Therefore, etc. . . .

IX. Argument from the end of Sciences.

Whatsoever perfects and adorns the intellect of Man, that is fit and decent for a Christian woman. But Arts and Sciences do perfect and adorn the intellect. Therefore.

The reason for the major premise is that all creatures tend unto their last and highest perfections as that which is most convenient for them. The minor premise is plain, because Arts and Sciences are *habits*, and by these habits are the natural powers and faculties of the soul proved and perfected.

X. Argument.

The things that by their nature conduce to the greater Love of God, and the exciting of his greater reverence in us, are convenient and fit for a Christian Woman. But Arts and Sciences by their nature conduce, etc. Therefore.

The truth of the major premise is clearer than the Light. For the most perfect love and reverence of God becomes all mankind, so that none can here offend in the excess.

The minor premise is thus confirmed: That which exhibits and proposes God and his works to be seen and known by us in a more eminent degree, naturally conduces to the stirring up in us the greater love of God and reverence. But Arts and Sciences exhibit and propose God and his Works, etc. . . .

XIV. Argument.

That which affects and replenishes the Mind with honest and ingenuous *delight* is convenient for a Christian Woman. But, Learning does so. Therefore.

The reason for the major premise is that nothing is more agreeable to human nature than honest and ingenuous delight, which represents in Man a certain similitude of Divine gladness. . . .

The minor premise is proved thus: Because there is no delight or pleasure (except that of Christians which is supernatural) either more worthy of an ingenuous soul, or greater than this, which arises from the study of Letters: as by examples and various reasons might easily be evinced.

XV. Argument from the Opposite.

Where ignorance and want of knowledge is not convenient, there the study of knowledge is convenient. But ignorance and want of knowledge is not convenient for a Christian Woman. Therefore.

The minor premise is confirmed thus: That which is of itself not only the cause of error in the understanding, but of vice in the will or action, is not convenient for a Christian Woman. But ignorance and want of knowledge is of itself the cause of error, etc. Therefore.

The major premise of this syllogism is demonstrated, first, in respect of error in the understanding. Because ignorance in the understanding (which is called the Eye of the Soul) is nothing else but blindness and darkness which is the cause of all error. Secondly, [it is demonstrated] in respect of vice in the Will or Action: because whatsoever makes men proud, fierce, etc., that is the cause of Vice in the will or action. But ignorance and want of knowledge makes men proud, etc. Therefore.

The major premise is evident, the minor premise is proved hence: the less a man knows himself, the more will he please himself and condemn others. And he who knows not how much he is ignorant of, will be wise in his own conceit. And then (as to fierceness) nothing is more intractable than ignorance, as Erasmus upon much experience testifies. . . .

Lastly, the danger of ignorance, in respect of vice, may be shown from the nature of vice and virtue. For, whereas to every virtuous action is required such exactness that it must be conformable on every part to the rule of right reason, to the Nature of vice even the least inordination, which follows ignorance, may be sufficient. . . .

The Thesis of the Adversaries.

A Christian Maid (or Woman) except she be perhaps divinely excited to it by some peculiar motion or instinct, may not conveniently give herself to the study of Letters.

I. Argument. On the part of the subject.

Whosoever has a weak wit may not give herself to the study of Letters. But women are weak of wits. Therefore.

They will prove the major premise because, to the study of Letters is required a wit firm and strong: unless we will labor in vain, or fall into the danger of a disease of the Intellect.

The minor premise, they think, needs no proof.

We answer to the major premise that by our limitation such are exempted, which by imbecility of their wit are altogether unapt for studies; when we state it, that at least indifferent good wits are here required. Then, we say, not always heroical wits are precisely necessary to studies. For the number even of learned Men, we see, is made up in good part of those that are of the middle sort.

To minor premise we answer: It is not absolutely true, but only *comparatively* true, in respect of the male Sex. For, though Women cannot be equalled for their wit with those more excellent Men . . . yet, the matter itself speaks thus much: Not a few are found of so good wit, that they may be admitted to studies, not without fruit. But

On the contrary we infer:

They that are less able by dexterity of wit, may most conveniently addict themselves to studies. But women are less able by dexterity of wit. Therefore.

We prove the major premise because studies do supply us with aids and helps for our weakness. Therefore.

II. Objection.

Whose mind is not inclined to studies, they are not fit to study. But the minds of Women are not inclined to studies. . . .

We answer to the major premise. It should be thus: "Whose mind, *after all means duly tried*, is not inclined to studies, they are not fit to study." Otherwise it is denied.

To the minor premise we say, no man can rightly judge of our inclination to studies before he has encouraged us by the best reasons and means to set upon them, and withal has given us some taste of their sweetness . . .

[Anna Maria van Schurman, *The Learned Maid, or Whether a Maid May Be a Scholar?* translated by Clement Barksdale (London: John Redmayne, 1659). Some of the language has been modernized.]

Van Schurman's answer to the first of our guiding questions is carefully formulated. Who ought to receive an education? Any "maid" or "Christian woman" who wants to learn and who meets certain minimal requirements of ability and circumstance. The prospective student must have:

(i) a basic capacity to learn the material in question,
(ii) basic life necessities taken care of (e.g., food and shelter),
(iii) the time to study, and
(iv) an appropriate, virtuous motive for learning.

Each of these requirements seems straightforwardly to apply just as well to men as to women, however. They describe conditions that would need to be in place in order for anyone to profitably pursue scholarship. Notably, condition (iv) is a *moral* requirement: the prospective student must have a virtuous motive in order for her education to genuinely improve her and make her more helpful to her community. If the motivation for one's studies is merely "vain glory and ostentation, or unprofitable curiosity," Van Schurman apparently believes that one would be better off not pursuing them. (This may explain why her thesis is only that *Christian* women are suited to receive an advanced education: she might hold that women without a firm commitment to religion would lack an appropriately virtuous motive for their studies. For simplicity's sake, we typically elide this restriction on Van Schurman's thesis in what follows.)

Van Schurman offers numerous arguments for the conclusion that, if these conditions are met, it is "expedient, fit, decent" for any woman who is inclined to pursue an education to receive one. She divides her arguments into two categories. Some are based on "the property of the subject," that is, the property of *being a woman*. Others are based on "the property of the predicate," which is the property of *being a scholar* or *being learned*. These two categories correspond to two different sorts of reasons that motivate her conclusion. The arguments based on the property of *being a woman* generally aim to show that there is nothing intrinsic about being a woman that is incompatible with learning, or that would make it inappropriate for women to pursue scholarship. The arguments based on the property of *being a scholar*, on the other hand, are intended to show that whatever reasons we might offer in support of a man's pursuit of knowledge are no less applicable to a woman.

The preceding extract from *The Learned Maid* includes a small but representative selection of the arguments she proposes in each of these categories. The first argument is that women naturally possess "the Principles, or powers of the principles, of all Arts and Sciences," that is, the basic mental capacity to study whatever discipline they wish. There is no field of study that by its very nature is beyond the ability of women to grasp. Why should we think that? Van Schurman wryly observes that "it is manifest that Maids do *actually* learn any Arts and Sciences"—that is, we know women have the capacity to become scholars because, as a matter of fact, women have actually been scholars. There may be individuals who lack the capacity to pursue the study of, say, advanced mathematics, but this inability cannot be due to their gender.

Where the first argument focuses on women's capacity or ability, the second argument turns to their desire for learning. Learning is appropriate for anyone who naturally desires to learn, she argues, and "a Maid naturally has a desire of Arts and Sciences." Here Van Schurman is addressing the possibility that, even if women can become scholars, they naturally lack the desire to do so. That is (an opponent might object), even if a woman wants to pursue advanced studies, that could only be an unnatural and therefore inappropriate desire. Van Schurman addresses this by appealing to no less an authority than Aristotle. In his *Metaphysics*, Aristotle writes that "All men [ἄνθρωποι] by nature desire understanding" (*Metaphysics* 980a). Van Schurman, a famously prolific student of language, notes that Aristotle's claim here is supposed to apply to humans *in general*, not strictly to men.

The third argument draws on similar themes as the first two, but with a religious audience in mind. According to the Book of Genesis, human beings were created in God's image—which, among other things, is supposed to confer upon human beings the ability to appreciate the glory of creation (and its creator), an ability that nonhuman creatures lack. In the early modern period, many held that this is one of the main reasons learning is valuable: through the study of creation, one becomes more directly acquainted with the glory of the creator. Thus, as Van Schurman summarizes the idea, anyone with "a sublime countenance . . . erected toward Heaven, may (and ought) give himself to the contemplation and knowledge of sublime and heavenly things." But, Van Schurman argues, women have been created in God's image no less than men, so the same justification for the pursuit of knowledge ought to apply to women as well.

This last line of reasoning is reiterated in subtly different ways when Van Schurman presents arguments based on the property of *being a scholar*. Studying the arts and sciences serves to "perfect and adorn the intellect" (Argument IX), and the arts and sciences "by their nature conduce to the greater Love of God" (Argument X). Both of these effects, again, are just as salutary for women as for men. They are reasons that scholarship is appropriate for any human being (or at least, on Van Schurman's view, for any *Christian*).

While some of these ideas may seem unsurprising to us today, they were highly unconventional in seventeenth-century Europe. Thus, in the second part of her essay, Van Schurman describes and addresses some objections she expects her contemporaries will make. The first of these is based on the simple, misogynistic premise that "women are weak of wits," a premise that Van Schurman wryly notes, "they think, needs no proof." As she understands the objection, it is that women ought not to pursue scholarship because scholarship requires a keen mind, and this is a feature that women generally lack (with some few, divinely inspired exceptions). The line of reasoning is easily dismantled in Van Schurman's reply. If all scholarship required especially "heroical wits," then most *men* ought not to pursue scholarship either. Since most actual scholars are men of merely average intellects, she points out, it is not reasonable to require more than that of women scholars either.

She does concede that in order for it to be "convenient" for a person to pursue scholarship in a given domain, that person must have a basic capacity to study the material in question. People whom "by imbecility of their wit [*imbecillitatem ingenii*] are altogether unapt for studies" are, Van Schurman notes, not included in the scope of her argument. Thus, if it *were* true that people of a particular gender truly did lack the basic capacity to learn and understand some subject, Van Schurman would be committed to the conclusion that people of that gender ought not to pursue that course of study. However, it is important to recognize that this is a far cry from the common view that she is opposing. For instance, consider the stereotype (still prevalent today) that women are in general worse at advanced mathematics than men. According to the view of Van Schurman's opponents, this difference in degree of ability would (if true) on its own be a reason to exclude women from the study of advanced mathematics. On Van Schurman's view, however, it is simply irrelevant whether women are on average worse at mathematics than men. As long as women have *some* capacity to learn the subject, they will benefit from studying it, and so they ought to be permitted to do so.

The second objection she discusses is based on the stereotype that women generally are not "inclined" or motivated to study. Since (the opponent argues) it turns out that women don't *want* to study, it is moot whether women have the *ability* to do so. And, the opponent argues, the sociological fact that women scholars are so rare—at least in early modern Europe—is evidence that most women lack the inclination to scholarship. This argument might seem to be a relic of history, since there are today women working at the highest ranks in every academic discipline. However, even today, men continue to vastly outnumber women in certain disciplines. For instance, in the United States in 2019–2020, 76 percent of bachelor's degrees in engineering were awarded to men.[3] Just like Van Schurman's early modern opponent, someone today might take such disparities to indicate a natural disinclination of women to study engineering.

Van Schurman's response to this sort of objection is incisive. The rarity of women scholars is not necessarily due to some innate disinclination toward study. She does not propose any specific alternative explanation for the sociological facts, but it is easy to imagine some. If a person grows up in a culture that discourages them from seeing advanced studies as an open possibility for them, they are unlikely to retain any inclination to pursue those studies. At any rate, there are multiple possible explanations for the sociological facts; the opponent would need to rule out these alternative explanations before they could be justified in assuming that women have an innate disinclination to study. Thus, Van Schurman concludes, the opponent's argument is unfounded until such time as women have been "encouraged ... by the best reasons and means to set upon [studies], and withal has given us some taste of their sweetness."

Key Points

- The purpose of education, on van Schurman's view, is to improve students intellectually in order to make it easier for them to live virtuously.
- Van Schurman argues that anyone with the basic mental capacity and means to study a subject ought to be permitted to do so, if their intentions are good.
- Notably, even if there *were* sex-based differences in intellectual ability, van Schurman thinks this would be irrelevant: individual people would still be improved through study, regardless of such differences.
- But van Schurman is skeptical of such differences: she suggests that any differences in performance among the sexes likely have alternative explanation.

Suggested Further Reading

Beek, Pieta van. *The First Female University Student: Anna Maria van Schurman (1636)*. Translated by Anna-Mart Bonthuys and Dineke Ehlers, ch. 1. Utrecht: Igitur, 2010.

Larsen, Anne R. *Anna Maria van Schurman: "The Star of Utrecht," the Educational Vision and Reception of a Savante*, chs. 1–2. Oxford: Routledge, 2016.

Pal, Carol. *Republic of Women: Rethinking the Republic of Letters in the Seventeenth Century*, chs. 2–3. New York: Cambridge University Press, 2012.

Uckelman, Sara L. "Bathsua Makin and Anna Maria van Schurman: Education and the Metaphysics of Being a Woman." In *Early Modern Women on Metaphysics*, edited by Emily Thomas, 95–110. Cambridge: Cambridge University Press, 2018.

7B. MARY ASTELL'S SERIOUS PROPOSAL

The picture that Van Schurman's arguments suggest is that, in general, anyone with a basic ability and inclination to study a given academic discipline ought to be permitted to do so. Such study improves one's mind and inculcates a better appreciation of the author of nature. Even if we accept these arguments, however, they leave open many questions about how to construct our educational institutions so as to best satisfy these goals. We turn next to the arguments of Mary Astell (an author we first met back in Chapter 5). Astell is another proponent of the idea that women ought to receive an advanced education—at least in certain subject areas. However, unlike Van Schurman, Astell discusses questions of institutional design: What would an appropriate curriculum include, and how would a good academic institution be structured?

Extract 7.2: Mary Astell's *A Serious Proposal to the Ladies*, Part I

> I doubt not, Ladies, but that the age, as bad as it is, affords very many of you who will readily embrace whatever has a true tendency to the glory of God and your mutual edification, to revive the ancient spirit of piety in the world and to transmit it to succeeding generations . . . I have therefore no more to do but to make the proposal, to prove that it will answer these great and good ends, and then it will be easy to obviate the objections that persons of more wit than virtue may happen to raise against it.
>
> Now as to the proposal, it is to erect a *monastery*, or if you will . . . we will call it a *religious retirement*, and such as shall have a double aspect, being not only a retreat from the world for those who desire that advantage, but likewise an institution and precious discipline to fit us to do the greatest good in it. Such an institution as this (if I do not mightily deceive myself) would be the most probable method to amend the present, and improve the future age. For here those who are convinced of the emptiness of earthly enjoyments, who are sick of the vanity of the world and its impertinencies, may find more substantial and satisfying entertainments, and need not be confined to what they justly loathe. Those who are desirous to know and fortify their weak side, first do good to themselves, that hereafter they may be capable of doing more good to others . . .
>
> You are therefore Ladies invited into a place where you shall suffer no other confinement but to be kept out of the road of sin: You shall not be

deprived of your grandeur but only exchange the vain pomp and pageantry of the world, empty titles and forms of state, for the true and solid greatness of being able to despise them. You will only quit the chat of insignificant people for an ingenious conversation; the froth of flashy wit for real wisdom; idle tales for instructive discourses. . . . Here are no serpents to deceive you, whilst you entertain yourselves in these delicious gardens. No provocations will be given in this amicable society, but to love and to good works, which will afford such an entertaining employment that you'll have as little inclination as leisure to pursue those follies, which in the time of your ignorance past with you under the name of love . . .

We have hitherto considered our retirement only in relation to religion, which is indeed its *main*, I may say its *only* design. Nor can this be thought too contracting a word, since religion is the adequate business of our lives, and largely considered, takes in all we have to do, nothing being a fit employment for a rational creature, which has not either a *direct* or *remote* tendency to this great and *only* end. But because, as we have all along observed, religion never appears in its true beauty except when it is accompanied with wisdom and discretion; and that without a good understanding, we can scarce be *truly*, but never *eminently* good; being liable to a thousand seductions and mistakes . . . Therefore, one great end of this institution shall be to expel that cloud of ignorance which custom has involved us in, to furnish our minds with a stock of solid and useful knowledge, [so] that the souls of women may no longer be the only unadorned and neglected things. It is not intended that our *religious* should waste their time, and trouble their heads about such unconcerning matters as the vogue of the world has turned up for learning . . . , but busy themselves in a serious enquiry after *necessary* and *perfective* truths, something which it *concerns* them to know, and which tends to their real interest and perfection . . . Such a course of study will neither be too troublesome nor out of the reach of a female virtuoso, for it is not intended she should spend her hours in learning *words* but *things*, and therefore no more languages than are necessary to acquaint her with useful authors. Nor need she trouble herself in turning over a great number of books, but take care to understand and digest a few well chosen and good ones. . . . And thoroughly to understand Christianity as professed by the *Church of England*, will be sufficient to confirm her in the truth, though she have not a catalogue of those particular errors which oppose it. . . .

There is a sort of learning indeed which is worse than the greatest ignorance: A woman may study plays and romances all her days and be a great deal more knowing but never a jot the wiser. Such a knowledge as this serves only to instruct and put her forward in the practice of the greatest follies, yet how can they justly blame her who . . . won't afford the opportunity of better? A rational mind *will* be employed, it will never be satisfied in doing nothing, and if you neglect to furnish it with good materials, it's like to take up with such as come to hand. . . .

The ladies, I'm sure, have no reason to dislike this proposal, but I know not how the men will resent it to have their enclosure broke down, and women invited to taste of that tree of knowledge they have so long unjustly *monopolized*. But they must excuse me if I be as partial to my own sex as they are to theirs, and think women as capable of learning as men are, and that it becomes them as well. . . .

[Mary Astell, *A Serious Proposal to the Ladies, Part I* (London: Richard Wilkin, 1697).]

The first part of Astell's *Serious Proposal* is framed as an advertisement for a novel educational institution: a kind of monastery or retreat specifically designed for women to advance their education. While it is a commonplace today that university is a distinctive social space with some distance from the "real world," Astell's proposal is for an institution even more radically separated from everyday life. The institution that Astell envisions is one where those who are "sick of the vanity of the world and its impertinencies, may find more substantial and satisfying entertainments"—and this will require a different sort of separation from the outside world than one finds at schools and universities today. For one thing, while most schools and universities today are secular institutions, Astell's educational monastery is explicitly a religious one: after all, she writes, "religion is the adequate business of our lives, and largely considered, takes in all we have to do . . ." All of Astell's subsequent proposals for how the institution should be designed are informed by her belief in the central importance of religion. It also informs her responses to the guiding questions about the philosophy of education that we raised at the outset of this chapter.

What is the purpose of education, on Astell's view? Her proposal has some common ground with van Schurman's views, already discussed. Education is not an intrinsic good, something valuable for its own sake. However, where van Schurman holds that one valid reason for pursuing an education is simply that it gives you a better appreciation of the glory of the creator, Astell's vision of education is more pragmatic. The primary purpose of study at Astell's monastery would be to acquire enough wisdom to avoid being led into sin. The monastery itself would be "a place where you shall . . .

be kept out of the road of sin," and its curriculum would be designed to help students to avoid "being liable to a thousand seductions and mistakes." Thus, although both Astell and van Schurman focus on the instrumental value of an education—that is, both view education as valuable because of the effects it produces—Astell has a much more narrow view about *which* effects we ought to aim at.

This in turn leads her to adopt a more narrow view of an appropriate curriculum for her monastery. Here the contrast between Astell and van Schurman could not be more dramatic. While van Schurman herself was famous for her knowledge of a stunning range of languages, Astell writes that a student needs "no more languages than are necessary to acquaint her with useful authors." The rationale for this striking claim is clear enough: if English authors can convey the wisdom necessary to live well and avoid sin, there is no need to learn other languages to achieve the goal of this educational monastery.

Again, where van Schurman argues for the value of the study of arts and sciences generally (they "perfect and adorn the intellect"), Astell takes a dim view of any such study that does not directly lead to wisdom. For this reason, she condemns much of the study of literature: "A woman may study plays and romances all her days and be a great deal more knowing but never a jot the wiser." This is a surprising verdict. One might object that the study of literature—even popular literature!—is likely to give students a more expansive understanding of the human condition, and this seems a helpful preparation for the sort of wisdom Astell is concerned with. For example, studying romance novels may not directly lead the student to knowledge of how to live well, but it will convey information about (among other things) the wide range of motivations, habits, quirks, and characters that a person can have. It is hard to see how someone could be called wise without that sort of background knowledge about humanity.

Astell would likely reply to this objection by drawing upon her deeply pragmatic view of the purpose of education. Although it may be that a student *could* acquire this sort of information about the diversity of the human condition from the study of romance novels—or horror novels, or comic books, or video games, for that matter—some genres and works of literature will be better at inculcating these lessons than others. Given that (as Astell sees it) the purpose of education is solely to train students to be able to lead morally upright lives, the objection amounts to the suggestion that we should train them less efficiently. And it is hard to see why we should design a curriculum to do *that*—unless, that is, education has some broader or more expansive goal.

A similar objection might be raised about her views about what religious traditions students ought to learn about. Again, Astell takes a narrow view on this question: students need only be taught the doctrines of Christianity, and specifically the Church of England; they need not learn "a catalogue of those particular errors which oppose it"—that is, information about other religious traditions is otiose. Yet one might object here that the study of other religious traditions is likely to instill a better understanding of one's own. This is particularly true when one's religious doctrines include mysteries that are difficult or impossible to comprehend literally. Perhaps the most famous mystery of this sort is the doctrine of the Trinity, the claim that God, Jesus Christ, and the Holy Spirit are three distinct persons with one shared substance or being. To understand the meaning and significance of such a doctrine, it is likely to be helpful to study the arguments of those who have rejected it. Among other things, such arguments will typically make clear what the stakes are: What are the intellectual and practical consequences of accepting such a doctrine? The question is hard to answer without knowing something about those who have rejected it.

Again, though, Astell's narrow view of the purpose of education suggests how she would likely reply. One can clearly understand the doctrines of the Church of England well enough to live virtuously without plumbing their metaphysical depths. Thus, although theological disputes do bear on religion ("the adequate business of our lives"), they don't bear on it in the specific way that is required for cultivating virtue and avoiding vice. For this reason, teaching such debates—or, indeed, information about any other religious traditions—to the students at the proposed monastery would simply slow down their progress toward the desired goal. So, Astell seems to think, it would be better for the students to focus on more directly morally edifying lessons.

The Second Part of Astell's *Serious Proposal* provides a more detailed discussion of the sorts of things that she believes *ought* to be studied, in light of this pragmatic view of the goals of education.

Extract 7.3, Mary Astell's *A Serious Proposal to the Ladies,* Second Part

Chapter II, §4.

Whoever would act to purpose must propose some end to themselves, and keep it still in their eye throughout their whole progress. Life without this is a disproportionate unseemly thing, a confused huddle of broken, contradictory actions, such as afford us nothing but the being ashamed of them. But do we need to be taught our end? One would rather think there were no occasion to mention it, did not experience daily convince us how many there are who neglect it. What end can creatures have but their creator's glory? And did they truly understand their own happiness, 'tis certain they would have no other, since this is the only way of procuring their own felicity. But it is not enough to have barely an implicit and languid desire of it; it would be much better to hold it ever in view, and [so] that all our actions had in their proportion a warm and immediate tendency thither. . . . We are not made for ourselves, nor was it ever designed [that] we should be adored and idolized by one another. Our faculties were given us for use, not ostentation—not to make a noise in the world, but to be serviceable in it, to declare the wisdom, power and goodness, of that all-perfect being from whom we derive *all* our excellencies, and in whose service they ought *wholly* to be employed. If our knowledge served no other purpose than the exalting us in our own opinion, or in that of our fellow creatures, the furnishing us with materials for a quaint discourse, an agreeable conversation, it would scarce be worth while to go to the trouble of attaining it. But when it enlarges the capacity of our minds, gives us nobler ideas of the majesty, the grandeur and glorious attributes of our adorable creator, regulates our wills and makes us more capable of imitating and enjoying him, 'tis then a truly sublime thing, a worthy object of our industry: And she who does not make this the end of her study, spends her time and pains to no purpose or to an ill one.

We have no better way of finding out the true end of anything, than by observing to what use it is most adapted. Now the art of *Well-Living*, the study of the divine will and law, that so we may be conformable to it in all things, is what we're peculiarly fitted for and destined to; whatever has not such a tendency, either directly or at least remotely, is besides the purpose. Rational studies therefore next to GOD's Word bid fairest for our choice because they best answer the design above mentioned. Truths merely speculative and which have no influence upon practice, which neither contribute to the good of soul or body, are but idle amusements, an impertinent and criminal waste of time. To be able to speak many Languages, to give an historical account of all ages' opinions and authors, to make a florid harangue, or defend right or wrong the argument I've undertaken, may give me higher thoughts of myself but not of GOD; this is the *knowledge that puffeth up*, in the words of the Apostle, and seldom leads us to that *charity which edifieth*.

And as the understanding so [also] the will must be duly directed to its end and object. Morality is so consonant to the nature of man, so adapted to his happiness, that had not his understanding been darkened by the Fall, and his whole frame disordered and weakened, he would naturally have practiced it. And according as he recovers himself, and casts off those clouds which eclipse his reason, so proportionably are his actions more agreeable to moral precepts, and tho we suppose him ignorant of any higher end, he will however do such things as they enjoin him, to the intent that he may be easy, obtain a good reputation, and enjoy himself and this world the better. Now were we sure that reason would always maintain its ground against passion and appetite, such an one might be allow'd to be a good neighbour, a just ruler, a plausible friend or the like, and would well enough discharge the relative duties of society, and do nothing misbecoming the dignity of human nature. But considering how weak our reason is, how unable to maintain its authority and oppose the incursions of sense, without the assistance of an inward and spiritual sensation to strengthen it, 'tis highly necessary that we use due endeavours to procure a lively relish of our true good . . .

The Conclusion.

Thus you have, Ladies, the best method I can at present think of for your improvement . . . It is not my intention that you should seclude yourselves from the world, I know it is necessary that a great number of you should live in it; but it is unreasonable and barbarous to drive you into it before you are capable of doing good in it, or at least of keeping evil from yourselves. Nor am I so fond of my proposal, as not to lay it aside very willingly, did I think you could be sufficiently served without it. But since such seminaries are thought proper for the men, since they enjoy the fruits of those noble ladies' bounty who were the foundresses of several of their colleges, why should we not think that such ways of education would be as advantageous to the ladies? . . . [I]t is altogether beside the purpose, to say 'tis too reclus[ive], or prejudicial to an active life; 'tis as far from that as a lady's practicing at home is from being a hindrance to her dancing at court. For an active life consists not barely in *being in the world*, but in *doing much good in it*. And therefore it is fit we retire a little, to furnish our understandings with useful principles, to set our Inclinations right, and to manage our passions, and when this is well done, but not till then, we may safely venture out. . . .

[Mary Astell, *A Serious Proposal to the Ladies, Part II: Wherein a Method is offer'd for the Improvement of their Minds* (London: Richard Wilkin, 1697). Some of the language has been modernized.]

The Second Part of Astell's *Serious Proposal* reiterates some of the central points of the First Part. The reason that education is valuable is that it "enlarges the capacity of our minds," yes—but this intellectual improvement is only important because of its practical effects. Intellectually, the purpose of education is to enable students to better understand what morality and religion demands of them, as well as how best to satisfy those demands. Purely theoretical knowledge is not an apt means to these ends. So, as in the First Part, Astell's picture of education centers on the importance of conveying to students "the art of *Well-Living*," where this is construed in religious terms. The goal of the religious monastery for women that Astell has proposed is, ultimately, to inculcate Christian virtues in students, and to prepare them to help others achieve these virtues in turn. However, the Second Part adds more detail about how to achieve this goal.

In line with many early modern philosophers, Astell views the mind as possessing two distinct faculties or powers: the *intellect* (or understanding) is a power to form and compare ideas; and the *will* is a power to affirm or deny the ideas or comparisons formed in the intellect. To form a judgment about something requires both faculties working in tandem. In order for a person to judge that (to use one of her examples) wealth does not guarantee happiness, two things must happen: the intellect compares the ideas of wealth and happiness, identifying differences between them to establish that neither of them implies the other; and the will then affirms that they are different.

With this familiar picture of the mind's faculties in the background, Astell distinguishes between two intellectual vices that corrupt or "disease" the mind. Prejudice is a vice of the intellect—she does not define the term, but she indicates that she takes prejudice to make ideas that are widely accepted or promulgated by authorities to seem more certain than they really are. Thus, although the intellect does not really have a clear and distinct understanding of an idea, that idea may nevertheless *feel* certain.

Astell distinguishes prejudice in general from *custom*, a second vice. Whereas prejudice afflicts the intellect, custom serves as a "manacle" on the will. Custom operates both internally and externally to restrict what sorts of ideas a person can consider critically, so that the will "scarce knows how to divert from a Track which the generality around it take, and to which it has it self been habituated." Externally, claims that are widely accepted by one's community will tend to be passed on without critical reflection or justification. To call such claims into question is to invite the scorn of the crowd, and so one is from a young age given incentive not to deviate from judgments customarily accepted in one's community. This external influence of custom is then reinforced by internal custom, or habituation. When someone becomes accustomed or habituated to affirm (or to deny) some claim, it becomes more and more difficult for them to refrain from affirming (or denying) that claim. The longer an idea has been uncritically accepted, the harder it is to call it into doubt. These external and internal forms of custom work together to corrupt the will from its true purpose, namely, to affirm only what we have good reason to believe.

Astell's proposed monastic retreat for women is intended to address the problem of prejudice by providing an education that cultivates rather than confines the intellect. And to combat the pernicious effects of custom, the proposed educational institution must be one that removes or shields students from the social forces that prop up customary, unjustified beliefs. This is why Astell's proposal is for a monastery where students are intended to stay for an extended period—a stay measured in years rather than months. Earlier, we saw that the proposed monastic institution would involve a much more dramatic form of separation from ordinary life than one finds in colleges or universities today. Now we can see why this is necessary, from Astell's perspective. There are strong social pressures guiding people to focus on style rather than substance, on passing trends rather than abiding wisdom. These pressures will continue to exert their effect when students return to ordinary life, so it is crucial to her project that students be kept at a remove from ordinary life for the duration of their studies. (Indeed, insofar as prejudices are reinforced by custom, the separation of students from the pressures of custom is vital for combating prejudice as well.)

The *Serious Proposal* is, of course, a proposal "to the Ladies," but some of Astell's recommendations seem to apply to any educational institution, regardless of the gender of the students. It is worth trying to tease apart these threads in her proposal. Scholars have observed that the proposed monastic retreat is similar in certain respects to traditional nunneries, and that the institution Astell describes would have played a social function that was sorely lacking in early-eighteenth-century England. The last of the nunneries in England closed in 1539, over a century and a half before Astell penned her *Serious Proposal*. In the intervening time, the rate of unmarried women in England rose dramatically, which for many women foreclosed a traditional seventeenth-century path to security and stability: marriage.[4] If marriage was not in the cards for many women in this period, what course of life ought they to pursue instead? The alternative that Astell envisions is a life dedicated to charity and good works, supported by a network of likeminded Christian women.

Key Points

- Astell broadly agrees with van Schurman about the purpose of education as intellectual improvement for the sake of living more virtuously.
- However, Astell believes that an educational institution ought to focus on actively fighting against vices of the mind, especially prejudice and custom.
- *Prejudice* is a vice of the intellect: it makes ideas seem more plausible than is warranted by our understanding.
- *Custom* is a vice of (or "manacle on") the will: it makes us more inclined to agree or disagree with some claim just because we have formed the habit of doing so.

Suggested Further Reading

Broad, Jacqueline. *The Philosophy of Mary Astell: An Early Modern Theory of Virtue*, "Introduction" and ch. 1. New York: Oxford University Press, 2015.

Broad, Jacqueline. "Mary Astell's Malebranchean Concept of the Self." In *Early Modern Women on Metaphysics*, edited by Emily Thomas, 211–26. Cambridge: Cambridge University Press, 2018.

Detlefsen, Karen. "Liberty and Feminism in Early Modern Women's Writing." In *Women and Liberty, 1600–1800*, edited by Jacqueline Broad and Karen Detlefsen, 17–32. New York: Oxford University Press, 2017.

Hill, Bridget. "A Refuge from Men: The Idea of a Protestant Nunnery." *Past & Present* 117 (1987): 107–30.

Perry, Ruth. "Radical Doubt and the Liberation of Women." *Eighteenth-Century Studies* 18, no. 4 (1985): 472–93.

Questions for Reflection

- What in your view is the ultimate purpose of education? What goals should our educational institutions focus on, and why?
- Should someone *ever* be prevented from receiving a formal education on a certain topic or discipline that they wish to study? For what reasons?
- Universities typically require all students to take courses on certain topics. In your view, are there any courses that ought to be required of all students? Why?
- Should one of the goals of an educational institution be to shape students to become more virtuous (courageous, wise, temperate, generous, and so on)? Why, or why not?

8

Sympathy and Morality
Sophie de Grouchy and David Hume

Chapter Outline

8a.	Sophie de Grouchy on Sympathy and Morality	193
8b.	David Hume on Sympathy and Morality	203
	Questions for Reflection	216

It is difficult to explain the motivation to do the right thing. Often, our self-interest conflicts with the demands of morality: in order to act rightly, we often have to sacrifice some other good that we desire. You see someone's lost wallet, flush with cash; you could return it, or you could keep the money for yourself. In spite of the temptation to keep the money, many of us would be inclined—apparently contrary to our own interest—to try to return the wallet to its owner. But *why*? As we saw in our examination of John Locke's moral philosophy (Chapter 6), this is typically called the **problem of moral motivation**†: How does our knowledge that an action is morally right motivate us to take that action, even when it is not in our interest to do so?

Many philosophers in the eighteenth century believed that the solution to the problem of moral motivation could be built on a proper understanding of the psychology of sympathy. Sympathy, or the capacity to share the emotions we observe or imagine in others, seems to provide an easy explanation of the drive to do the right thing. When you think about keeping the lost wallet, it's all too easy to imagine and sympathize with the frustration of the person who lost it. Conversely, when you think about returning the wallet, it's equally easy to sympathize with the owner's relief and gratitude. Your anticipation of, and sympathy with, their emotional response thereby gives you a motive to return the wallet.

Notably, this approach uses facts about human psychology to provide a *naturalistic* solution to the problem of moral motivation: we are ultimately motivated to do the right thing by the same natural impetus to seek pleasure and avoid pain that motivates all the rest of our actions. Now, not every philosopher would agree with this. (Immanuel Kant famously argued that, for your action to have any moral worth at all, you must do it solely *because* it is the right thing to do. So, if your motivation to return the wallet is that sympathy with the owner makes you feel bad about keeping it, then your action has no moral worth, on Kant's view.) However, a wide range of early modern philosophers did adopt this naturalistic approach to morality. This chapter examines two prominent authors in this tradition, the French philosopher Sophie de Grouchy (1764–1822) and the Scottish philosopher David Hume (1711–76).

Grouchy and Hume broadly agree that the psychology of sympathy is a crucial component in the explanation of morality. However, they disagree about (i) whether sympathy is the product of nature or nurture, (ii) how sympathy functions, and (iii) whether we also need to appeal to *reason* in the explanation of morality. The following extracts display the different theories of sympathy, and different accounts of moral motivation, advanced by these authors.

8A. SOPHIE DE GROUCHY ON SYMPATHY AND MORALITY

Sophie de Grouchy: Brief chronology

- 1764: Born in Château de Villette, in Condécourt, France.
- 1782: Attends school at Neuville-les-Dames in Normandy, a finishing school where she practiced translating works from English and Italian.
- 1785(?): Meets the Marquis de Condorcet (then 43 years old) through her uncle.
- 1786: Marries the Marquis de Condorcet and moves to his apartments in the Hotel des Monnaies.
- 1789: With her husband, becomes associated with the Girondins, a revolutionary faction that favored a republican government with relatively limited state power.
- 1791(?): Composes the *Letters on Sympathy*, in response to Adam Smith's *The Theory of Moral Sentiments* (published in English in 1759).
- 1793: The Girondins fall out of favor among the French revolutionaries; Grouchy's husband goes into hiding, and Grouchy moves just outside of Paris.
- 1794: The Marquis de Condorcet has his property confiscated, is arrested, and dies in prison. Grouchy takes up artistic and literary jobs to support herself.
- 1798: Publishes her translation of Smith's *Theory of Moral Sentiments*, to which was appended her *Letters on Sympathy*.
- 1822: Dies after brief illness. Per her wishes, she is buried among the poor, without ceremony, in Père-Lachaise in Paris.

Sophie de Grouchy composed the *Letters on Sympathy* in response to the account of sympathy and its relation to morality given by the famous Scottish philosopher Adam Smith in his *Theory of Moral Sentiments*. She translated Smith's *Theory* into French and published it (along with her *Letters*) in 1798. Smith, although now primarily known for his influence in the history of economics, was in the eighteenth century recognized primarily for his philosophical works. In particular, his account of the origins of morality in the interplay of our reason and our "sentiments" or emotions was widely viewed as a landmark contribution to moral philosophy. Like the other authors to be discussed in this chapter, he ultimately finds the psychology of sympathy to be the root cause of our motivation to be moral. His description of sympathy's power over the mind is poetic:

> Whatever is the passion which arises from any object in the person principally concerned, an analogous emotion springs up, at the thought of his situation, in the breast of every attentive spectator. Our joy for the deliverance of those heroes of tragedy or romance who interest us, is as sincere as our grief for their distress, and our fellow-feeling with their misery is not more real than that with their happiness. We enter into their gratitude towards those faithful friends who did not desert them in their difficulties; and we heartily go along with their resentment against those perfidious traitors who injured, abandoned, or deceived them. In every passion of which the mind of man is susceptible, the emotions of the by-stander always correspond to what, by bringing the case home to himself, he imagines should be the sentiments of the sufferer.[1]

Smith later makes the case that sympathy is the initial ground of our concern for morality, for it causes us to share in the pain or pleasure we observe in other people. Yet he also argues that "It is by reason that we discover those general rules of justice by which we ought to regulate our actions."[2] Both sympathy and reason are required to explain human morality, then; neither is sufficient on its own.

As we will see, Grouchy agrees with much of this picture. She, too, thinks that moral motivation is grounded in sympathy, but that we must apply reason and reflection to derive general principles of morality and justice. However, her *Letters on Sympathy* are intended to flesh out details that she thinks Smith's discussion of sympathy neglects, as well as to spell out disagreements she has with certain technical points of Smith's moral psychology. The extract below sets out Grouchy's solution to the problem of moral motivation, as well as her views about how precisely reason and reflection are involved in the development of the ideas of good and evil. In earlier letters, though, Grouchy explains the origins of our capacity for sympathy. Other authors in this period tended to treat sympathy as a capacity innate to human beings, part of human nature itself. For instance, Adam Smith takes sympathy to be among the "principles in [human] nature, which interest him in the fortune of others."[3] By contrast, Grouchy believes that sympathy is the product of nurture rather than nature. Before analyzing the following selection from her Letters V and VI, it will be helpful to summarize her account of how human beings develop the capacity for sympathy.

The first part of Grouchy's account of the origin of sympathy is based on her model of the experience of pleasure and pain. Each experience of pleasure or of pain is composed of two elements: it includes both (i) a particular pleasure or pain in some specific organ, as well as (ii) a general sensation of well-being or discomfort. So, for example, if you accidentally burn your hand, there is simultaneously a particular sensation of pain in your hand, as well as a general feeling of discomfort or suffering. These two feelings can come apart. To continue our example, even after the particular burning sensation has subsided in your hand, you might still retain the general feeling of discomfort. Grouchy suggests that, when we reflect on the idea of pain or injury, this can revive the general feeling of discomfort without necessarily making us feel any particular pain we've experienced in the past (Letter I).

The second part of the explanation is based on the dependence all humans have on their parents during infancy. The joy or suffering of our parents tend to correlate nearly directly to our own joy or suffering, so infants quickly become sensitive to the behaviors that signal the presence of those sentiments. A mother's smile indicates good times ahead, while a furrowed brow and pursed lips suggest trouble is in store. The infant thus has a strong natural incentive to attend to such things, and they come to do so habitually.

These two points combine to explain the initial origins of sympathy in infants. Even though an infant will not usually be capable of comprehending the particular causes of their parents' emotions, they can still associate the parents' emotions with their own general feeling of well-being or discomfort. When the infant observes the behavioral signs of pleasure or joy in the parent, this activates the infant's general feeling of pleasure. Likewise, when the infant detects signs of pain or sadness in the parent, their general feeling of discomfort is activated. Notably, this does not require the infant to understand the particular cause of their parents' emotions. Grouchy believes that the infant's response will be all the stronger if indeed they are able to comprehend the particular cause of their parent's joy or suffering (if, for instance, they see that their parent has tripped and fallen, a cause of suffering that infants know all too well). But the infant doesn't *need* to comprehend the particular cause of their parents' emotions in order for their sympathy to be activated. The mechanism Grouchy has described can operate even if the infant has no notion of the particular cause of the emotion they detect. The parents could be celebrating their tax return or mourning the cancellation of their favorite series—concepts an infant has no grasp of whatsoever—and this basic form of sympathy could still operate.

Thus, on Grouchy's view, humans typically cultivate sympathy during their infancy as an adaptive response to our dependence on our parents and other adults around us. This basic form of sympathy can be (and ideally is) further developed as part of a child's education. A child gradually comes to recognize the importance of other human beings outside the family—a neighborhood, a classroom, a village, a city. Only gradually do they develop a capacity to sympathize with humanity in general, on Grouchy's view. Although sympathy is powerful, it is also delicate: a bad education can and does cause it to wither on the vine during childhood.

The following selection from Letter V, however, focuses less on the origins of sympathy and more on the mechanisms by which it leads to what she calls the ideas of moral good and evil. As we've seen, it's no guarantee that someone will have a well-developed capacity for sympathy. But suppose that we're dealing with someone who has indeed cultivated an adequate sense of sympathy. How does their sympathy lead them to be motivated to act morally or justly?

Extract 8.1: Sophie de Grouchy's Letters on Sympathy

Letter V: On the Origins of Moral Ideas

[A]lthough the immediate influence of vice and virtue on our well-being has been praised often and eloquently, it has not sufficiently been argued that the principles of virtue and the personal happiness they procure are a necessary consequence of our moral constitution, and that the need to be virtuous is practically irresistible for those who are ruled by wise laws and raised without prejudices.

Because witnessing the pleasure of others, or even the idea of someone else's pleasure naturally satisfies us, it necessarily follows that we experience pleasure when we are the cause of it in another. It is stronger than the sort of pleasure we cause in others because it is more thoughtful and deliberate, and because it is anticipated, which always increases the mind's activity. If we get more pleasure from contributing to others' happiness than we do from witnessing it, then that pleasure must be greater still when we relieve someone of their trouble. . . .

Performing good deeds, therefore, naturally brings us pleasure. But another sentiment is born out of that pleasure: the satisfaction of having done good. This is similar to the way physical pain, as well as a local and present impression, creates a painful impression through-out our body. We find, therefore, a personal pleasure in the memory of somebody else's happiness. But in order for this memory to be often present in our minds, it must be tied to our existence, to our thought processes, and this is what happens when we are the cause of another's happiness. Then, that memory becomes part of our intimate conception of ourselves; and like that conception, it becomes a habit, and it produces in us a pleasant feeling which reaches much further than the specific pleasure that instigated it. . . .

Here, my dear C***, we have a distinction, already established through sentiment alone, between our actions. Some come with a pleasurable feeling and the mind is satisfied by them, while others come with pain and are followed by a sentiment that is always unpleasant, and often painful also.

But the more lasting sentiment of satisfaction or pain, which comes with the memory of the good or bad we have done to others, is necessarily altered by reflection. And it is those adjustments that lead us to the idea of moral good and evil, this first and eternal rule with its judgment which is prior to that of human laws . . . When, for instance, we give a person pleasure that will last but a short time, and will have no influence on the rest of their life, if our motivation is not that of particular sympathy, then we will receive less satisfaction than we would had we given that person pleasure that was also a lasting benefit. Perhaps we will repent, even, for having left that person in the grip of real hardship, when we only offered them temporary help, and instead of satisfaction, we will feel remorse. Here we see, therefore, the beginning of a distinction between the good deeds we do through luck and those we do through reflection, the good we are drawn to do by a particular sympathy and that we do from general sympathy. When we follow a particular sympathy, we obey, in doing so, the instinct of our hearts. But if we act out of general sympathy, when we are indifferent among several possible good deeds, or cannot decide between one inspired by our inclination and another, greater deed toward which we are not inclined, we weigh the benefits to others and we choose according to that which will bring us, if not the greatest present pleasure, the more lasting satisfaction.

From this point, our actions, which were before simply beneficial and humane, acquire moral goodness and beauty, and from this is born the idea of virtue—that is, *of actions that give others pleasure in a way that is sanctioned by reason*.

The idea of a distinction between the moral and physical harm inflicted on someone is more difficult to grasp, but no less precise. When it happens that a small harm done to one individual would prevent a greater harm done to another, or an equal harm to many others, then if we do not inflict this small harm, we will be afflicted by the remorse of not having prevented the greater harm much more than we would have allowed had we inflicted the smaller harm. By contrast, the regret of having inflicted the lesser harm will be softened by the stronger satisfaction of having prevented the more serious harm. The same is true in relation to any pleasure we may derive from harming someone else: such pleasure will be weak and will not compensate us for the remorse that comes with inflicting this harm. In all those circumstances, we become used to consulting our reason as to what the best course of action is, and we settle on the one that will give us the greatest satisfaction afterwards, and thus we acquire the idea of moral evil—that is, of *an act that is harmful to others and which is prohibited by reason*. . . .

Letter VI: The Same Subject Continued

[W]hen we harm or benefit others, we experience sentiments that, joined with reflection, give us the abstract idea of moral good and evil. This idea gives birth to that of justice and injustice. And that idea differs from the first only in the following way: reason's endorsement of a just action must be guided by the idea of right—that is, a preference ordered by reason itself in favor of a person and because of which we must prefer that person's interest even when particular circumstances may make it seem weaker than somebody else's interest. Thus, a man who, in the state of nature, has taken pains to cultivate a field, to supervise its harvest, has a right to this harvest. That is, reason demands that it be his because he bought it through his labor, because by taking it away from him, and making his work useless, depriving him of what he had long looked forward to and of the possession he deserved, we hurt it more than we would if we were to deprive him of a similar harvest that just happened to be within his reach. Reason demands that we give him preference even when he does not need all his harvest while another has a real need of some harvest—and this is precisely what constitutes right. It is grounded in reason, on the necessity of general laws to rule over actions, common to all men, and makes it unnecessary for us to examine the motives and consequences of each particular act. It is also grounded in sentiment, for since the effect of injustice is more harmful for its victim than just the effects of mere harm, it must inspire in us a greater repugnance. . . .

A right such as property right is positive: it consists in a preferment grounded in reason for the enjoyment of a particular thing. A right such as liberty is in some ways negative. It only exists because of the possibility that it might be in someone's interest to threaten my liberty. In this case, it would be reasonable to defer to that person's interest—my own in preserving it—because there are no reasons why this person should hold over me a power I do not hold over him. The same is true concerning equality. If another claims a preference over me that is not grounded in reason, reason demands that I should give preference to my interest in maintaining that equality rather than give preference to his claim. This is because submitting to another's will and being inferior in any respect is a greater evil than subjugating another's will and achieving superiority is a good. The idea of moral good and evil requires us to submit the natural sentiment of sympathy to reason so that it is directed towards the more pressing interests. The ideas of justice and injustice require that we submit to reason, which is itself led by general rules, by a preference grounded in general and reasoned concerns that aim at the greatest good—that is, in a preference for rights. . . .

It was necessary to establish the first grounds, to show that our moral sentiments originated in natural and unthinking sympathy for others' suffering, that our moral thoughts originated in reflection. It had to be shown, especially, that assenting to a moral truth differs from assenting to a mathematical or physical truth, in that what naturally follows from such assent is a desire to behave in conformity with it, to see others do the same, fear of not conforming to it, and regret not having done so. We cannot say, however, that morality is grounded in sentiment alone, as it is reason that teaches us what is just and unjust. But it is even less arguable that it be grounded solely in reason, as reason's judgment is nearly always preceded by and followed by a sentiment that asserts and ratifies it. And it is even originally from sentiment that reason acquires moral ideas and derives principles.

[Sophie de Grouchy, Sophie de Grouchy's Letters on Sympathy: *A Critical Engagement with Adam Smith's* The Theory of Moral Sentiments, translated by Sandrine Bergès, with an introduction, glossary, and commentary by Sandrine Bergès and Eric Schliesser (New York: Oxford University Press, 2019).]

We've already seen that, on Grouchy's view, our sympathy for creatures like ourselves causes us to feel pleasure or pain when we observe in others behaviors that we have learned are characteristic of pleasure or pain. When we treat others well, this typically brings them pleasure and elicits the behaviors that activate a sympathetic response in us. Grouchy infers that "Performing good deeds, therefore, naturally brings us pleasure." And, notably, this pleasure is even greater insofar as we ourselves are the cause of the resulting pleasure. It feels good to see your neighbor find and rescue their lost kitten, but it feels even better if you helped them to find the kitten.

The sympathetic pleasure we derive from doing good deeds thus provides a natural motivation to do them.

On the face of it, this looks like a promising solution to the problem of moral motivation. However, there are many cases in which sympathy seems to be a bad guide to what we ought morally to do. And if there are cases where our sympathetic responses tell us one thing while morality tells us another, that would undermine the idea that pure sympathy could be the basis for moral motivation.

One kind of problem case arises when you are considering how best to help someone whose immediate pleasure or pain does not track their best interest in the long term, all things considered. Such cases are common enough. Suppose your friend asks how their outfit looks; it looks bad, but you can tell your friend wants you to admire it. What ought you to do? Here, your immediate sympathy would seem to motivate you to lie to your friend, since you expect they'll be pleased by the lie. Yet it also seems that you are doing them a disservice rather than genuinely helping them. It certainly isn't obvious that it's the right thing to do.

Or suppose a parent is trying to have his child hold still while receiving a necessary immunization shot. At the sight of the needle, the child bursts into tears and struggles to escape. Sympathy with the child's immediate fear and imminent pain makes the parent feel anguish at holding the child still for the shot. Nevertheless, in spite of his sympathy with the child's pain, the parent is bound to care for the child's long-term health. If he succumbed to the child's wish not to receive the shot, it would be a form of vice. Thus—sometimes at least—being virtuous requires tempering one's sympathy. This is difficult to understand if virtue is ultimately grounded in sympathy.

The second kind of problem case involves rights. The question of whether a person has a right to do or to possess something seems to have nothing to do with whether we find that person sympathetic. Grouchy uses the example of a farmer whose work yields a large harvest: even though others have a greater interest in the part of the harvest that goes beyond the farmer's needs, the farmer's right to the possession and use of it makes the interest of others morally irrelevant. They may want the harvest badly—and we may sympathize greatly with them—but they have no right to it. So, once again, the verdict encouraged by our sympathetic response does not seem to align with our ordinary moral judgments.

To summarize, we have two kinds of problem case: (1) scenarios in which a person's immediate interest isn't consistent with their well-being in the long term; and (2) scenarios in which a person's immediate interest isn't consistent with the moral rights of all involved parties. Our sympathy is activated by their immediate interest, but morality demands us to resist that sentimental response. How can situations like these be reconciled with the idea that sympathy is the basis for morality?

Grouchy proposes more or less the same solution to both sorts of problem. In such cases, she acknowledges, we feel an immediate particular sympathy—for instance, our sympathy for the crying child who doesn't want to receive a shot. Yet this particular sympathetic response is not the only relevant emotion we feel: we also have a *general* sympathy that is activated by our *rational* evaluation of the various outcomes that are open to the person we're considering. The child may be crying out of fear right now, but it is rational to infer that the child will fare much better after receiving the shot than were they not to receive it. The parent's general sympathy for the child's overall well-being, combined with his ability to draw rational inferences about what courses of action will best improve that well-being, lead him to hold the child steady for the shot.

More or less the same response applies to the problem about moral rights. There are, of course, cases in which we sympathize with someone who is not in the right. The mythical version of Robin Hood is a nice case in point: it's hard not to sympathize with someone who robs from the rich to give to the poor, even when we would acknowledge that the rich have a right to their property. Grouchy's proposal is that our general sympathy counterbalances and—when we are reasoning clearly—outweighs this particular inclination to violate someone's rights. However, in this case, it is not necessarily the interest of the rights-holder that we sympathize with. Rather, reason allows us to recognize the general good that is promoted by a system of rights. Even if we regard it as a tragedy that some particular person has the rights that they have, Grouchy thinks we can rationally infer that it is better to uphold the general system of rights than to subvert it in any particular case. In this way, we are motivated to act morally "by a preference grounded in general and reasoned concerns that aim at the greatest good—that is, in a preference for rights."

This, then, is her solution to our problem: although our *particular* sympathies can sometimes be activated in a way that would lead us to do something contrary to what morality demands, we also have a *general* sympathy for a person's overall well-being—and for the well-being of our community as a whole—that can override those more immediate, particular sympathies.

Key Points

- Grouchy proposes that our experience of pleasure and pain includes both a particular sensation as well as a general feeling of well-being or discomfort.
- We naturally *sympathize* with others like ourselves: when we observe behaviors in them that indicate pleasure or pain, we ourselves feel to some degree that pleasure or pain, or at least the general feeling of well-being or discomfort.
- Sympathy provides a natural motivation to be moral: we get pleasure from seeing others benefited and are pained by seeing others harmed.
- In cases where our particular sympathies don't track morality, reason can correct our moral evaluations.

Suggested Further Reading

Berges, Sandrine. "Sophie de Grouchy." In *Stanford Encyclopedia of Philosophy*, Winter 2019 edition, edited by Edward N. Zalta. https://plato.stanford.edu/archives/win2019/entries/sophie-de-grouchy/

Forget, Evelyn L. "Cultivating Sympathy: Sophie Condorcet's *Letters on Sympathy*." *Journal of the History of Economic Thought* 23, no. 3 (2001): 319–37.

Schliesser, Eric. "Sophie de Grouchy, Adam Smith, and the Politics of Sympathy." In *Feminist History of Philosophy: The Recovery and Evaluation of Women's Philosophical Thought*, edited by E. O'Neill and M. Lascano. Springer: Cham, 2019.

Stephens, Winifred. *Women of the French Revolution*, ch. 2. London: Chapman and Hall Limited, 1922, 193–219.

8B. DAVID HUME ON SYMPATHY AND MORALITY

David Hume: Brief Chronology

- 1711: Born in Edinburgh
- 1722?: Begins studies at the University of Edinburgh, initially considering a legal career
- 1729: Decides to dedicate his life to philosophical and other academic studies
- 1734: Moves briefly to Bristol to work for a merchant, but soon travels to France to continue his studies
- 1739: Publication of the first volume of his most significant philosophical work, *A Treatise of Human Nature*
- 1745: Refused an academic post at the University of Edinburgh due to his suspected atheism
- 1752: Appointed as librarian of the Advocate's Library in Edinburgh, giving him the resources to write his *History of England*, for which he was best-known in his own lifetime
- 1763: Returns to Paris as private secretary to the British Ambassador, where he forged friendships with many prominent intellectuals, including Jean-Jacques Rousseau (with whom he would famously fall out)
- 1776: Dies in Edinburgh
- 1779: An important later work, *Dialogues concerning Natural Religion*, is published posthumously

David Hume was among the most influential philosophers in the eighteenth century. In his most widely read philosophical works—the *Treatise of Human Nature* and *Enquiry Concerning Human Understanding*—he presents a thoroughgoing **empiricist**[†] philosophy. For an empiricist, in order for us to be justified in some belief, we must be able to trace it back to some set of experiences (or, as Hume refers to them, "impressions") that support that belief. One category of beliefs that proves troubling for an empiricist is our beliefs about morality. We have already seen (especially in Chapter 6) some of the philosophical problems faced by other attempts to explain how experience could teach us about morality. Hume, too, was aware of the difficulty. What set of experiences gives rise to and justifies our belief that lying is morally wrong, or that charity is morally right?

With this problem in mind, Hume's goal in the third and final part of his *Treatise of Human Nature* is to present an account of how we acquire moral knowledge and why we are naturally motivated to act morally. In this, he has similar aims as philosophers such as Sophie de Grouchy. However, as we have seen, Grouchy (as well as Adam Smith) thinks that sympathy alone isn't enough to explain our natural drive to follow the rules of morality. Reason, they argue, can motivate us to pursue what is right or good in cases where our particular sympathies conflict with morality. Hume denies this. Indeed, he argues, not only is reason not required to explain morality, it cannot motivate us to do *anything*. Although reason allows us to see what consequences will follow from our actions, it does not tell us whether those consequences are good or bad, right or wrong.

In the following extract, Hume makes his case against viewing reason as playing a role in explaining morality. The alternative view he presents is that our experiences of sympathetic reactions and other natural emotional responses are alone sufficient for explaining why and how we are motivated to adhere to moral rules.

Extract 8.2: David Hume's *A Treatise of Human Nature*

Part 1. Section 1. Moral distinctions not deriv'd from reason

It has been observ'd, that nothing is ever present to the mind but its perceptions; and that all the actions of seeing, hearing, judging, loving, hating, and thinking, fall under this denomination. The mind can never exert itself in any action, which we may not comprehend under the term of *perception*; and consequently that term is no less applicable to those judgments, by which we distinguish moral good and evil, than to every other operation of the mind. To approve of one character, to condemn another, are only so many different perceptions. . . .

Those who affirm that virtue is nothing but a conformity to reason; that there are eternal fitnesses and unfitnesses of things, which are the same to every rational being that considers them; that the immutable measures of right and wrong impose an obligation, not only on human creatures, but also on the deity himself: All these systems concur in the opinion that morality, like truth, is discern'd merely by ideas, and by their juxta-position and comparison. In order, therefore, to judge of these systems, we need only consider, whether it be possible from reason alone, to distinguish betwixt moral good and evil, or whether there must concur some other principles to enable us to make that distinction.

If morality had naturally no influence on human passions and actions, 'twere in vain to take such pains to inculcate it; and nothing wou'd be more fruitless than that multitude of rules and precepts, with which all moralists abound. Philosophy is commonly divided into *speculative* and *practical*; and as morality is always comprehended under the latter division, 'tis suppos'd to influence our passions and actions, and to go beyond the calm and indolent judgments of the understanding. And this is confirm'd by common experience, which informs us, that men are often govern'd by their duties, and are deter'd from some actions by the opinion of injustice, and impell'd to others by that of obligation.

Since morals, therefore, have an influence on the actions and affections, it follows, that they cannot be deriv'd from reason; and that because reason alone, as we have already prov'd, can never have any such influence. Morals excite passions, and produce or prevent actions. Reason of itself is utterly impotent in this particular. The rules of morality, therefore, are not conclusions of our reason. . . .

Reason is the discovery of truth or falshood. Truth or falshood consists in an agreement or disagreement either to the *real* relations of ideas, or to *real* existence and matter of fact. Whatever, therefore, is not susceptible of this agreement or disagreement, is incapable of being true or false, and can never be an object of our reason. Now 'tis evident our passions, volitions, and actions, are not susceptible of any such agreement or disagreement; being original facts and realities, compleat in themselves, and implying no reference to other passions, volitions, and actions. 'Tis impossible, therefore, they can be pronounc'd either true or false, and be either contrary or conformable to reason.

This argument is of double advantage to our present purpose. For it proves *directly*, that actions do not derive their merit from a conformity to reason, nor their blame from a contrariety to it; and it proves the same truth more *indirectly*, by showing us, that as reason can never immediately prevent or produce any action by contradicting or approving of it, it cannot be the source of the distinction betwixt moral good and evil, which are found to have that influence. Actions may be laudable or blameable; but they cannot be reasonable or unreasonable: Laudable or blameable, therefore, are not the same with reasonable or unreasonable. The merit and demerit of actions frequently contradict, and sometimes control our natural propensities. But reason has no such influence. Moral distinctions, therefore, are not the offspring of reason. Reason is wholly inactive, and can never be the source of so active a principle as conscience, or a sense of morals.

Part 3. Section 1. Of the origin of the natural virtues and vices

To discover the true origin of morals, and of that love or hatred, which arises from mental qualities, we must take the matter pretty deep, and compare some principles, which have already been examin'd and explain'd.

We may begin with considering anew the nature and force of *sympathy*. The minds of all men are similar in their feelings and operations; nor can any one be actuated by any affection, of which all others are not, in some degree, susceptible. As in strings equally wound up, the motion of one communicates itself to the rest; so all the affections readily pass from one person to another, and beget correspondent movements in every human creature. When I see the *effects* of passion in the voice and gesture of any person, my mind immediately passes from these effects to their causes, and forms such a lively idea of the passion, as is presently converted into the passion itself. In like manner, when I perceive the *causes* of any emotion, my mind is convey'd to the effects, and is actuated with a like emotion. Were I present at any of the more terrible operations of surgery, 'tis certain, that even before it begun, the preparation of the instruments, the laying of the bandages in order, the heating of the irons, with all the signs of anxiety and concern in the patient and assistants, wou'd have a great effect upon my mind, and excite the strongest sentiments of pity and terror. No passion of another discovers itself immediately to the mind. We are only sensible of its causes or effects. From *these* we infer the passion: And consequently *these* give rise to our sympathy. . . .

The same principle produces, in many instances, our sentiments of morals, as well as those of beauty. No virtue is more esteem'd than justice, and no vice more detested than injustice; nor are there any qualities, which go farther to the fixing the character, either as amiable or odious. Now justice is a moral virtue, merely because it has that tendency to the good of mankind; and indeed is nothing but an artificial invention to that purpose. The same may be said of allegiance, of the laws of nations, of modesty, and of good-manners. All these are mere human contrivances for the interest of society. The inventors of them had chiefly in view their own interest. But we carry our approbation of them into the most distant countries and ages, and much beyond our own interest. And since there is a very strong sentiment of morals, which has always attended them, we must allow, that the reflecting on the tendency of characters and mental qualities, is sufficient to give us the sentiments of approbation and blame. Now as the means to an end can only be agreeable, where the end is agreeable; and as the good of society, where our own interest is not concern'd, or that of our friends, pleases only by sympathy: It follows, that sympathy is the source of the esteem, which we pay to all the artificial virtues.

Thus it appears, *that* sympathy is a very powerful principle in human nature, *that* it has a great influence on our taste of beauty, and *that* it produces our sentiment of morals in all the artificial virtues. From thence we may presume, that it also gives rise to many of the other virtues; and that qualities acquire our approbation, because of their tendency to the good of mankind. This presumption must become a certainty, when we find that most of those qualities, which we *naturally* approve of, have actually that tendency, and render a man a proper member of society: While the qualities we *naturally* disapprove of, have a contrary tendency, and render any intercourse with the person dangerous or disagreeable. . . .

That many of the natural virtues have this tendency to the good of society, no one can doubt of. Meekness, beneficence, charity, generosity, clemency, moderation, equity, bear the greatest figure among the moral qualities, and are commonly denominated the *social* virtues, to mark their tendency to the good of society. . . .

The only difference betwixt the natural virtues and justice lies in this, that the good which results from the former, arises from every single act, and is the object of some natural passion: Whereas a single act of justice, consider'd in itself, may often be contrary to the public good; and 'tis only the concurrence of mankind, in a general scheme or system of action, which is advantageous. When I relieve persons in distress, my natural humanity is my motive; and so far as my succour extends, so far have I prompted the happiness of my fellow-creatures. But if we examine all the questions, that come before any tribunal of justice, we shall find, that, considering each case apart, it wou'd as often be an instance of humanity to decide contrary to the laws of justice as conformable to them. Judges take from a poor man to give to a rich; they bestow on the dissolute the labour of the industrious; and put into the hands of the vicious the means of harming both themselves and others. The whole scheme, however, of law and justice is advantageous to the society and to every individual; and 'twas with a view to this advantage, that men, by their voluntary conventions, establish'd it. After it is once establish'd by these conventions, it is *naturally* attended with a strong sentiment of morals; which can proceed from nothing but our sympathy with the interests of society.

Part 3. Section 6. Conclusion of this book

Thus upon the whole I am hopeful, that nothing is wanting to an accurate proof of this system of ethics. We are certain, that sympathy is a very powerful principle in human nature. We are also certain, that it has a great influence on our sense of beauty, when we regard external objects, as well as when we judge of morals. We find, that it has force sufficient to give us the strongest sentiments of approbation, when it operates alone, without the concurrence of any other principle; as in the cases of justice, allegiance, chastity, and good-manners. We may observe, that all the circumstances requisite for its operation are found in most of the virtues; which have, for the most part, a tendency to the good of society, or to that of the person possess'd of them. If we compare all these circumstances, we shall not doubt, that sympathy is the chief source of moral distinctions; especially when we reflect, that no objection can be rais'd against this hypothesis in one case, which will not extend to all cases. Justice is certainly approve'd of for no other reason, than because it has a tendency to the public good: And the public good is indifferent to us, except so far as sympathy interests us in it. We may presume the like with regard to all the other virtues, which have a like tendency to the public good. They must derive all their merit from our sympathy with those, who reap any advantage from them: As the virtues, which have a tendency to the good of the person possess'd of them, derive their merit from our sympathy with him.

Most people will readily allow, that the useful qualities of the mind are virtuous, because of their utility. This way of thinking is so natural, and occurs on so many occasions, that few will make any scruple of admitting it. Now this being once admitted, the force of sympathy must necessarily be acknowledg'd. Virtue is consider'd as a means to an end. Means to an end are only valu'd so far as the end is valu'd. But the happiness of strangers affects us by sympathy alone. To that principle, therefore, we are to ascribe the sentiment of approbation, which arises from the survey of all those virtues, that are useful to society, or to the person possess'd of them. These form the most considerable part of morality.

[David Hume, *A Treatise of Human Nature* (London: John Noon, 1739–1740).]

One of Hume's most controversial philosophical claims is that *reason is motivationally inert*: when you consider a possible course of action, your reason never gives you any new motivation either to take or refrain from taking that action. All of our reasoning, on Hume's view, is neutral about the value (or cost) of different outcomes of a course of action. Reasoning about your situation may allow you to see how best to satisfy the desires or passions that you already have, but it does not tell you what you ought to desire or what passions you *ought* to have. For example, you might rationally infer from what you know about spiders that you're likely to find some if you go looking in the dark corners of an abandoned shack in the woods. But reason doesn't tell you how you ought to use this information: if you're an arachnophobe, you might respond by avoiding that shack you see on your hike; but if you love to observe the local spider population, you'll head over to begin searching without delay. Reason doesn't tell you that either of these courses of action is right or wrong—it just tells you what's likely to happen if you do them.

That example illustrates that reason is sometimes silent about what we ought to do. But why should we think that reason is *always* motivationally inert in this way? Hume believes that this follows from the very nature of reason and emotion. First, what is reason? On Hume's view, "Reason is the discovery of truth or falshood," that is, the ability to discern whether some idea or claim is true or false. There are many different kinds of reasoning—logical reasoning, causal reasoning, and probabilistic reasoning, most prominently—but they are all unified in their shared goal of distinguishing the true from the false. Whether we are checking a mathematical proof, solving a murder, or interpreting a political survey, we are in each case trying to find out whether something is true or false.

Hume next suggests that truth is a matter of "agreement" or correspondence between our ideas and reality. Roughly, when we say that some idea or claim is true, we mean that it agrees with the way things really are. Sometimes, we aim for our ideas to agree with **matters of fact**[†] about the world—for instance, the detective wants her idea of the murderer's identity to line up with the murderer's actual identity, and there is some matter of fact about which person committed the crime. However, on other occasions, our goal is for our ideas to agree with what Hume calls **relations of ideas**[†], or necessary connections among our concepts themselves. When the math student is checking his proof of the side-angle-side theorem of Euclidean geometry, he is not trying to see whether his idea of that theorem agrees with some contingent fact about this or that triangle. Rather, he is trying to see whether his idea agrees with a relationship that is inherent to our geometrical concepts themselves (*side, angle, congruence*, etc.).

If we now turn to the psychological forces that motivate us to act—our desires, emotions, urges, and the like—Hume thinks it is clear that these objects cannot be appropriately ascribed either truth or falsity. When you feel an emotion, that emotion is neither true nor false, it just *is*. Emotions are in this way very different than beliefs. Suppose you see a spider in the corner. Your beliefs that the spider is big, that it is hairy, that it is dangerous—all of these are either true or false. That is, on Hume's view, these beliefs either agree with the way the spider really is (if in fact it is big, hairy, dangerous) or they do not (if it turns out to be tiny, hairless, and harmless). By contrast, your *fear* of the spider is neither true nor false. The reason is that, on Hume's view, it doesn't make sense to say that your fear either agrees or disagrees with the way the spider really is. It doesn't even matter whether the spider you fear actually exists—the fear of it remains real enough either way. This is what Hume means when he says that emotions are "original facts and realities, compleat in themselves."

The same rationale also applies to **volitions**[†] and actions, Hume thinks. Recall that a volition is a particular exertion of the will, such as when you decide to stand up from your chair. Volitions may be successful or unsuccessful: a volition to do something may or may not bring about the intended action. When you decide to stand up, you might discover that you're tied to the chair, in which case your volition would fail to bring about the action it aims at. But this doesn't make the volition *false*. As it happens, your volition is frustrated in this case—yet for all that, the volition still really occurs, your exertion of will leads to some real effort on the part of your body. Likewise for actions: the actions you take neither agree nor disagree with any matters of fact about the world. Indeed, it seems closer to the mark to say that your actions generate new matters of fact in the world. So, again, it seems that actions are not apt for either truth or falsity.

Hume thinks that these observations support the general conclusion that "actions do not derive their merit from a conformity to reason, nor their blame from a contrariety to it." Insofar as an action is particularly effective at satisfying some desire I have, it may be rational for me to take that action. Yet actions considered in themselves are neither rational nor irrational, since they neither agree nor disagree with any matters of fact or relations of ideas. Drinking water if I am thirsty may be rational, but the action of drinking water *considered independently of my interests and goals* is neither rational nor irrational. So, likewise, actions such as murder, theft, or parental negligence are not in themselves either rational or irrational. Thus, Hume concludes, the fact that these actions are immoral—and that we are generally averse to doing them—cannot be due to their irrationality.

So far, the argument has focused entirely on the negative claim that reason is *not* the source of our moral beliefs, nor does it motivate us to do the right thing. What *does* explain these phenomena, then? Hume's answer focuses on how people end up approving of, and wanting to cultivate, moral virtues—and he thinks sympathy plays the crucial role in this process. His account is divided in two parts, one which pertains to what he calls "artificial virtues" and the other which pertains to the so-called "natural virtues."

The **artificial virtues**†, as Hume uses the term, are "mere human contrivances for the interest of society," intentionally invented by human beings because of the positive effects they would have for society as a whole. For example, we view it as virtuous to be law-abiding and polite, but it is clear that civil laws as well as the rules of etiquette or politeness are the inventions of human beings. These artificial virtues had to be imposed on people initially. Yet over time, their value to society has become evident (or at least taken for granted). As a consequence, Hume suggests, when we see people behave in ways that are law-abiding or polite, our sympathy with society is activated and we feel approval toward those people. Likewise, when we see people break the law or behave rudely, our sympathy with society causes us to regard them disapprovingly.

Justice, too, is an artificial virtue on Hume's account. This may seem surprising, but Hume argues that justice must have been an invention because "a single act of justice, consider'd in itself, may often be contrary to the public good; and 'tis only the concurrence of mankind, in a general scheme or system of action, which is advantageous." Hume's point here is similar to an observation that we saw in Sophie de Grouchy's analysis. Strict adherence to a system of principles of justice may often lead to outcomes in particular cases that we regard as bad, yet it is still better for society to adhere to such a system. For Hume, this is a sign that justice is artificial. Humans have a natural inclination to give unjust preference to some people over others—for instance, a judge is likely to feel inclined to side with his friends or benefactors even when the law is clear that his friends are in the wrong. Yet this sort of injustice or corruption has a huge social cost, so we collectively have a strong interest in minimizing and preventing it. The virtue of justice was intentionally inculcated to that end, claims Hume. It allows our sympathy with the whole of society to counteract our sympathy for particular people we are especially close to.

The **natural virtues**† differ from the artificial ones with respect to their origin. Where the artificial virtues are based on human conventions—the social value of which is not always obvious—the natural virtues are not the product of convention. They are recognized as virtues because their benefit either to the community or to the person who has them is immediately apparent. Hume lists "Meekness, beneficence, charity, generosity, clemency, moderation, equity" as examples of natural social virtues: when we observe these character traits in ourselves or others, their value to the community is evident. This is the most salient mark that differentiates natural from artificial virtues, and it is easy to observe in practice. If you see a parking attendant writing a ticket, you probably don't immediately feel any positive emotion about the parking attendant, even if you recognize their actions as part of a system of rules that have been justly enforced and that we would all probably be worse off without. By contrast, if you find out that someone spends their time in the evenings helping to cook or serve food at a homeless shelter, the feeling of approval is easy and immediate.

Despite these differences, the natural social virtues have a similar structure to the artificial ones. The natural virtues, too, elicit our approval only by activating our sympathy. Take generosity, for instance, as in the case of a person who gives their time and labor at a homeless shelter. Your approval of such generosity doesn't depend on your knowing anyone who directly benefits from it. In general, our approval of someone's generous character doesn't depend on our sympathy with any of the particular people who directly benefit from it. Instead, Hume thinks, it depends on our sympathy with the whole of society: whoever *directly* benefits from a generous character will also be part of society as a whole, and so a generous character will always be of indirect benefit to that whole. Generosity can therefore elicit approbation even when we can't see (for instance) expressions of gratitude from the people who it directly benefits.

Are there any virtues that *don't* depend on sympathy in this way? Hume does allow that there are some natural virtues that aren't social virtues. These character traits are not viewed as virtuous on the grounds of their benefit to society, but because of their benefit to the person who possesses them. For example, confidence and a quick wit are virtues. These traits tend to elicit our approval, and someone who lacks self-assurance or who is slow to connect the dots will tend to elicit disapproval, at least with respect to those traits. Yet Hume thinks the reason that we approve of these character traits is not because we feel that they benefit society as a whole. Indeed, sometimes the fact that a person has these traits makes things *worse* for society as a whole: a confident, quick-witted tyrant might well be worse for society as a whole than a tyrant who lacks those character traits. (Notice that this is not true of the social virtues. A meek, charitable, generous tyrant is always better than a brash, selfish, unkind one.)

For this reason, Hume refers to traits like confidence and quick-wittedness as virtues with "a tendency to the good ... of the person possess'd of them ..." Even if the fact that someone is clever, courageous, or ambitious doesn't necessarily benefit society as a whole, these traits will tend to be beneficial to someone who has them. Our sympathy with that person will arouse in us a feeling of approval that corresponds to the self-esteem we would feel if we ourselves had these character traits. Thus, the reason we view these characteristics as virtues is not our sympathy with the whole of society, but with the person who has these traits. Nevertheless, the mechanism of sympathy is still ultimately responsible for our approval of these virtues.

Given that sympathy plays such a central role in Hume's account of morality, he faces the same sorts of difficulties that we saw attended Grouchy's explanation of moral motivation in the previous section. There are obviously cases in which our personal sympathies don't align with the demands of morality. Moreover, unlike Grouchy, Hume has explicitly ruled out the possibility of using reason to adjudicate between sympathy and moral principle. Reason can reveal to us whether something we wish to do conflicts with certain moral principles. It allows us to see, for example, that lying about one's work history to get a job interview conflicts with the principle that one ought to be honest. But reason can't motivate a dishonest job candidate to adhere to that principle if he doesn't already want to. Hume thus seems to have painted himself into a corner. Sympathy for others is the ultimate source of our motivation to do the right thing, *and* reason cannot correct our sympathies when they don't track morality. How then can we explain the fact that we ought to (and frequently do!) act against the demands of our personal sympathies when they conflict with morality? And what about the fact that we sympathize more strongly with people who are close to us (in space, time, culture, and other respects) than with those who are remote from us, even though morality doesn't vary in this way?

Hume's solution to these problems is developed elsewhere in the *Treatise*, but it is worth summarizing here. He observes first that there are two distinct points of view that we can take up when we are evaluating someone's character or actions. We can consider things from our personal, purely subjective point of view, or we can consider them from a more general point of view, one that could be shared by other people making the evaluation. For instance, suppose your friend fails an exam. You drag the sorry tale out of them over dinner: they didn't study, failed the exam, and now are likely to fail the course. Their situation evokes your sympathy: you feel genuine sadness, anger, and anxiety on their behalf. Your friend asks you whether they should make a special appeal to the professor to raise their grade. After all, if your friend fails the class, they may need to retake the course, which in turn could cause them to take a semester longer to finish college. Although your personal sympathy has led you to share in your friend's grief, you now reflect on what their situation would look like from the general point of view—the point of view of someone who isn't personally close to them. You imagine what it would feel like to hear the story of a student (not your friend!) who didn't study for an important exam, failed it, and then sought a higher grade by appealing to the pity of the professor. From *that* point of view, you see that your friend's story isn't likely to evoke much sympathy out of those not already personally interested in them.

The ability to adopt this general point of view is what allows us to make properly moral judgments, as distinct from whatever purely subjective sympathetic reactions we may personally have. One's personal sympathy for a friend might incline one to overlook—or even to help with—their cheating on an exam, stealing a luxury handbag, or even covering up a murder. But from the general point of view, things look much different. Someone doing these things is unlikely to evoke pity in a relatively unbiased, disinterested observer. Instead, from the general point of view, such actions suggest that your friend is probably in the grip of a number of moral vices, and that it would be best to avoid helping with these projects.

In general, the thought is that our moral judgments are grounded not in whatever sympathetic responses we *actually* have, but in the sympathetic responses that we *would* have if we were looking at the matter from the general point of view. This is why we can (grudgingly) admit that our enemy is charitable or courageous, even though his charity and courage inspire no sympathy in us. It is why the responsible parent holds their child steady while the child receives necessary immunization shots, even while grimacing in sympathy with the child's tears. And it is why we tend to be critical of injustice even in cases where such injustice is to our personal benefit. Although our personal interests and sympathies in these cases might incline us away from doing the right thing, a well-educated and morally competent adult will be aware of and sympathetic to the reaction that someone would have from the general point of view.

Hume's account neatly addresses the problem cases in which our personal sympathies don't align with our moral judgments. However, there is a theoretical difficulty here—one that Hume himself does not address. When we form judgments about how we would evaluate some person or action from the general point of view, it seems that we must engage in reasoning. For example, in order for the parent to decide whether to resist their immediate sympathy for the child's cries and hold them steady to receive a shot, the parent needs to consider what the situation calls for from the general point of view. And to make that evaluation, the parent needs to (for example) weigh the child's present pain and fear against their expected benefit down the line from receiving this immunization. Thus, it seems, the parent must use their reason to estimate the expected benefits and weigh them against the present costs. The problem is that Hume has come down about as stridently as possible against the idea that there is any role for reason in our practical or moral evaluations.

Perhaps the best reply on Hume's behalf here is to distinguish the claim that reason cannot provide any motivation for us to act morally from the claim that reason cannot play any role in our judgments about what is morally right or wrong. Hume is clearly committed to the first of these claims: the initial section of the previous extract provides a pointed argument for this conclusion. Without that initial urge to do the right thing—ultimately derived from our capacity to sympathize with other people and with society as a whole—we would not have any concern for morality. But once that initial motivation to be moral is in the picture, we do also use reason to (for instance) predict the likely outcomes of a given action, and to factor these outcomes into our evaluation of the situation.

In spite of their disagreement about details such as the role of reason in moral judgment, the ideas of Grouchy and Hume should make us optimistic about the possibility of understanding morality as a natural phenomenon, not as something supernatural or ultimately mysterious. On the basis of features of human nature that we have all experienced in our own lives—in particular, the pervasive sympathy that we feel for other people and for our community—these authors have pointed the way to plausible accounts how we come by our moral beliefs and why we care about morality.

> ## Key Points
> - Hume argues that reason cannot motivate us to act. It can only show us how best to attain goals we already have.
> - On Hume's view, this implies that our desire to do the right thing cannot be grounded in reason: it must have some source in our passions.
> - For Hume, *sympathy* is the source of moral motivation. We value moral virtue because we sympathize with the community that benefits when people have those traits.
> - In cases where our individual sympathies don't track morality, we draw on our capacity to imagine things from a relatively unbiased, general point of view.
> - Moral evaluations are evaluations based on the sympathetic reactions that a person would have from this general point of view.

> **Suggested Further Reading**
>
> Brown, Charlotte R. "Hume on Moral Rationalism, Sentimentalism, and Sympathy." In *A Companion to Hume*, edited by Elizabeth S. Radcliffe. Malden: Blackwell, 2008, 219–239.
>
> Garrett, Don. *Hume*, ch. 8. New York: Routledge, 2014.
>
> McHugh, John. "Hume's General Point of View, Smith's Impartial Spectator, and the Moral Value of Interacting with Outsiders." *Journal of Scottish Philosophy* 19, no. 1 (2020): 19–37.
>
> Taylor, Jacqueline. *Reflecting Subjects: Passion, Sympathy, and Society in Hume's Philosophy*, ch. 4. Oxford: Oxford University Press, 2015.

Questions for Reflection

- Sophie de Grouchy believes that sympathy, our capacity to feel what others like us appear to feel, is learned—it is the product of nurture rather than mere nature. Do you agree?
- Do you agree with Grouchy that every particular sensation of pleasure or pain is accompanied by a general feeling of well-being or suffering in the whole body?
- Hume thinks that reason can never motivate us to act. Can you think of any cases where your actions were motivated purely by your reason, not by your emotions?
- On Hume's view, justice is an "artificial virtue," in the sense that it depends on human conventions. Do you think that's true? Why, or why not?

9

The Debate about Slavery Jacobus Capitein and Ottobah Cugoano

Chapter Outline

9a. Jacobus Elisa Johannes Capitein on Religion and
   Slavery   219
9b. Ottobah Cugoano on Slavery and Race   230
Questions for Reflection   242

The transatlantic slave trade, begun in the middle of the fifteenth century, quickly became one of the defining features of the politics and economy of Europe. Different nations participated in the slave trade to varying degrees at various times during the roughly 400 years that would pass before its abolition. Some countries got into the business later, and some got out of it sooner. However, during the period definitive of early modern philosophy—the seventeenth and eighteenth centuries—the trafficking and use of slaves was a major business for almost every country in Western Europe. Britain, France, Spain, Portugal, the Dutch Republic, and the Holy Roman Empire were all heavily invested in the colonization of either Africa or the Americas as well as in the slave trade that emerged during these colonial projects.

As a result, every philosopher discussed in this book was born, lived, and died in a world where slavery was more or less commonplace. It is tempting to suppose that, because slavery was *so* commonplace at the time, nobody regarded it as problematic. Some have also been tempted by the further thought that, since nobody during this period regarded slavery as problematic, the people during the period who bought or sold slaves shouldn't be judged so harshly for it. Yet the assumption is false: the morality of slavery was the subject of heated philosophical debate for much of the early modern period. When James Tobin, a plantation owner, describes the debate at the outset of his 1785 defense of slavery, he sounds almost weary: "this subject has been repeatedly, and amply, discussed, by many writers of extensive abilities, whose arguments have been long before the public, for its decision."[1] Europeans during this period were indeed aware of the moral arguments against the sale and ownership of human beings. Of course, it is one thing to be aware of the arguments and another to be persuaded by them.

Perhaps unsurprisingly, a number of the early modern philosophers who participated in this debate were themselves of African descent. Indeed, the first African to receive a PhD from a European university, Anton Wilhelm Amo (discussed in Chapter 1), wrote his dissertation on the legal limits of slavery. Though the text of that dissertation has not survived, a contemporary journal describes it as including an investigation into "how far the freedom or servitude of Moors purchased by Christians extends in Europe according to the commonly accepted laws."[2] As this brief description already suggests, the debate about slavery drew upon considerations about religion, about law, and on still-evolving notions of race and ethnicity.

Fortunately, although Amo's dissertation is not extant, other works on the topic survive. This chapter will examine two such entries in the early modern debate about the morality and legality of slavery.

9A. JACOBUS ELISA JOHANNES CAPITEIN ON RELIGION AND SLAVERY

Jacobus Elisa Johannes Capitein: Brief Chronology

- 1717: Born in Elmina on the Gold Coast, in what is now Ghana.
- ~1724-25: Orphaned and sold into slavery.
- 1728: Travels to the Netherlands with his owner, Jacob van Goch, an employee of the West India Company (WIC).
- ~1730: Begins studying at The Hague in preparation for Christian missionary work.
- 1735: Receives his baptism; continues his studies at The Hague.
- 1737: Delivers a public lecture on missionary work, titled "On the calling of the heathen." Enters the University of Leiden as a theology student.
- 1742: Delivers his *Political-theological dissertation* as a public lecture. Ordained into the Dutch Reformed Church. The WIC appoints him as the minister for the colony at Elmina.
- 1745: Marries Antonia Ginderdros, a Dutch woman sent to Elmina by the WIC.
- 1747: Dies in Elmina of unknown causes.

Jacobus Capitein (1717–1747) was a former slave, originally from the Gold Coast, who went on to work for the Dutch West India Company.[3] Surprisingly, Capitein is not strictly opposed to slavery. After becoming a Christian minister, he went on to study theology at the University of Leiden, where he wrote the short treatise that is excerpted here (Extract 9.1). The treatise, originally delivered as a public lecture, defends the thesis that the political institution of slavery is compatible with the moral and spiritual demands of Christianity.

Before we examine Capitein's arguments for this thesis, it is important to differentiate his position from another, even older argument in defense of slavery—an argument that Capitein explicitly rejects. In his *Politics*, the ancient Greek philosopher Aristotle argues that some people "are so disposed that their best function is the use of their bodies," so that they "are by their nature slaves, and it is better for them to be ruled despotically."⁴ Aristotle's argument takes slavery to be justified by the fact that some people are *naturally* inferior and suited to be ruled over by others, and so it is often referred to as the doctrine of **natural slavery**†. For those who accepted the doctrine of natural slavery, there was no special difficulty in justifying slavery as a political institution or the slave trade as a legitimate market.

However, the case for natural slavery was not generally viewed as compelling in the seventeenth and eighteenth centuries, as the natural equality of all human beings had become more and more widely accepted by political thinkers. For instance, in his extraordinarily influential 1651 treatise, *Leviathan*, the political philosopher Thomas Hobbes famously expresses this thought:

> Nature hath made men so equal in the faculties of body and mind as that, though there be found one man sometimes manifestly stronger in body or of quicker mind than another, yet when all is reckoned together the difference between man and man is not so considerable as that one man can thereupon claim to himself any benefit to which another may not pretend as well as he.⁵

Hobbes concedes that there are clearly natural differences among human beings. Yet, on his view, none of these differences are significant enough to amount to a natural difference in *kind* of the sort Aristotle envisions. There is no natural characteristic that makes some humans fit to be subjugated to others. If the practice of enslaving human beings is to be justified, then, it must be justified in a different way.⁶

Numerous other important political philosophers in the period—even those that would disagree with Hobbes about much else—converged on this thought. In his 1762 work, *The Social Contract*, Jean-Jacques Rousseau reasons that "Since no man has any *natural* authority over his fellow men, and since might is not the source of right, conventions remain as the basis of all lawful authority among men."⁷ Likewise, in a 1768 dialogue, Voltaire has a bombastic English character exclaim,

> In truth, we don't have the natural right to go and capture a citizen of Angola, take him off and beat him into working in our sugar plantations in Barbados in the same way that we have the natural right to take a dog we have fed hunting; but we have the right by convention [to do it].⁸

Although it was not universally rejected, these examples at least indicate that the doctrine of natural slavery was typically viewed as implausible by political philosophers in this period, especially in the eighteenth century.

This is the position that Capitein adopts in his 1742 *Treatise* as well: "The most learned people propose that . . . every human being is under his own authority according to natural law, and that the common condition of early humankind permitted equal freedom to all humans."[9] Therefore, there is not any difference in nature among human beings that could underwrite the practice of slavery.

Nevertheless—as the passage from Voltaire highlights—even those who rejected the doctrine of natural slavery could still embrace slavery as an acceptable political institution, such that the right of slaveholders over their slaves is grounded in social convention. Authors who took up this view often appealed to the long history of the institution as a defense of its continued practice, and Capitein's *Treatise* is a case in point. Its second chapter "explores the ancient origin of slavery and shows that nearly all societies made use of it."[10] The general strategy behind such historical analyses is to defend the use of slaves in early modern colonies by connecting this practice to older forms of forced servitude and serfdom. Insofar as these older practices were legitimated by the political circumstances of their day (the argument goes), likewise there is no difficulty in principle with accepting it today, given the needs and goals of the various empires involved. Even if there is no *natural* basis by which one human could claim the right of ownership over another, this right could still be legitimately conferred by *law*.

A serious problem for this general defense of slavery, however, is that it appears to conflict with very basic tenets of Christianity. In particular, a number of passages of the Bible were interpreted by early modern theologians to imply that once a person had been baptized as a Christian, they ought to be thereby freed from slavery as well. Some of the passages that the debate was oriented around include II Corinthians 3:17, which states that "where the spirit of the lord is, there is freedom," and Galatians 5:1, "For freedom Christ has set us free; stand fast therefore, and do not submit again to a yoke of slavery." And perhaps most significantly, there is the so-called "golden rule" set out at Matthew 7:12: "Therefore all things whatsoever ye would that men should do to you, do ye even so to them . . ." It is hard to see how the act of enslaving another human being could be made compatible with this moral rule. Since Christianity was the majority religion of early modern Europe and its colonies, any defense of slavery had to contend with this religious objection.

This was not the first time that Christian philosophers had been forced to reconcile religious belief with the institution of slavery. After the Roman emperor Constantine made Christianity the official religion of the Empire, Christian authorities had to take a position on the Roman institution of slavery. As historian Lester Scherer notes in his account of the relationship between Christianity and slavery, "In that situation a body of theology and church law arose that justified and protected slavery while asserting the essential humanity of slaves."[11] Early modern advocates of slavery drew on these precedents from antiquity to respond to Christian abolitionists.

This is the tradition that Capitein's *Political-Theological Dissertation* falls within: Capitein seeks to show that there is a viable way of interpreting the moral and theological commitments of Christianity such that slavery is a permissible institution for Christians to uphold. The following extract presents the core of Capitein's argument for this thesis.

Extract 9.1: Capitein's *Political-theological Dissertation*.

Chapter Three, which proves that slavery and Christianity are not antithetical.

(1) It is clear beyond doubt that most Netherlanders wish to persuade themselves and others in in the exchange of debate that Christian freedom can in no way walk in step with slavery in the proper sense. For now in our time it is thought that the worship of God must necessarily be cultivated not only with a pure mind, which does not allow itself under the devil's control to be reduced from the spiritual basis that gives it life, but indeed also with a free body. If this opinion, as I would label it, is not on the right lines, at least it can be linked somehow to the views and sayings of fanatics, by which they, charged up with meaningless spirit and arguing that every magistrate in the Christian world should be removed, were unable to proclaim that slavery does not contradict Christianity. This incorrect view would never have occupied the minds of our adversaries had they not formed preposterous ideas of all sorts about the nature of the New Covenant, and were they not ignorant of the ways of the early Christians, or of their own regions, of ancient law and of the more significant customs.

(2) Concerning the nature of the New Covenant they believe that this freedom promised to believers is just as much corporeal as spiritual. And so, as the Old Covenant was transformed into the New, slavery which flourished under the Old . . . now in our age would be thrown out together with the other repealed practices of Mosaic law. All of this is affirmed, they allege, by the witness of II Corinthians 3:17; Galatians 5:1; I Corinthians 7:23 and John 8:32, among other sacred writings.

(3) They think that support and corroboration for their opinion derives from the custom of their regions: on the grounds that slavery is unknown in the Netherlands, since it is forbidden for any person to be cast into slavery, nay more, that every slave who is brought to live here in the

Netherlands from some other place is granted bodily freedom as if by tacit consent, and even more if he formally embraces Christianity, so much so that he can no longer be sold by his master at will.

(4) Although these reasons may seem specious to some, still after being called back to a just weighing with a balanced scale, they will easily be found to lack in weight. For my part, I freely assert that the New Covenant gives freedom to people who, through the special grace of the Most High God, are or become participants in it. But how should it be understood? As spiritual and bodily simultaneously? Decidedly not. It is only the spiritual which shakes off from Christian shoulders the burden of ceremonial law which according to Paul and Peter, the fathers were not able to bear, and liberates them so they may undergo the mild yoke of Christ. . . .

(10) But nobody who pursues the truth can ignore the fact that each person is the best interpreter of his or her own words. . . . Christ makes absolutely clear what he wished to signify by liberty, that is liberty from the sin by which the devil rules all those who have not yet fled to Christ the savior through his health-giving faith. In this way the person who has been devoted to sin, that is to pleasure and desire, is called a slave of sin par excellence. . . .

(11) And so we distinguish between slavery of conscience or sin and civil slavery; between heavenly law and the law of the courtroom; between freedom of the spirit and freedom of the body. Christ talks about heavenly law and about slavery of conscience or the spirit, from which we are defended by the New Covenant . . . Henry More of Cambridge discusses what freedom under the New Covenant involves, in his *Opera theologica* . . . :

(i) The faithful are freed from the fussy and excessive encumbrances of ritual observance, so that we are no longer caught up in the toils of silly superstition and its practices, things which are of such a nature that they cannot show the way to everlasting life or extend Christ's kingdom on earth.

(ii) The faithful are freed from their sins, that is, from pride, envy, hatred, anger, grief, avarice, and every desire, so that this freedom can lead us to justice, which cannot fail to presuppose the effective persuasion of truth. Therefore it seems that I was not wrong to conjecture that Christ, our heavenly teacher, means with the phrase, *The truth will make you free* (John 8:32) that believers would be sanctified through truth in the word of God, as John says (17:17). Anyone who wishes to learn more fully about the nature and aspects of Christian freedom should look at John Calvin's *Institutes* (3.19).

(12) But if anyone does not agree with these solutions, let them read the brief letter of Paul to Philemon, and they will recognize with me that "where there is evidence there is no need for words." From this letter it is more clearly elucidated than the light of noon that a slave named Onesimus who secretly fled from his master Philemon to Rome was there initiated by Paul into the rudiments of Christian doctrine, and afterwards sent back to his master. As one can infer from the context of the letter, Philemon is beseeched humanely through prayers to take Onesimus back without flogging him, not in terms of his rights but out of brotherly love, on account of the shared faith which will make Onesimus more fit than before to perform his future duties.

From these things it is abundantly clear, as we wished, that the nature of the New Covenant demands only *spiritual* freedom in order that we can worship God, not necessarily *external* freedom. As a result, differences of status in Christianity by no means have to be removed. . . .

(26) To be sure, the most learned and meritorious persons in the state do not hesitate to wish that personal slavery, which in our time has been partly or completely abolished among most Christians, should be reinstituted, inasmuch as it is extremely useful to the state, but restored in such a way that it is in keeping with Christian clemency, rather than brutality. For it is absolutely certain that countless troubles, such as cannot be enumerated easily, would result from the discontinuation of slavery. The most esteemed Busbecq leans toward this view in his *Turkish Letter* 3, pp. 160–1 (Leiden 1633):

I do not know whether the person who first abolished slavery did us a favor. If run justly, leniently, and according to the precepts of Roman law, public slavery in particular could have remained . . . Freedom without possessions does not always promote honorable activity. Not everybody's nature can endure resourceless freedom and not everyone is born so that they can have control over themselves and know by their own judgment what is right. They need the leadership and rule of their betters, like a prop; in no other way will they put an end to their misdeeds. . . .

On the other hand Potgiesserus, relying on the judgments and opinions of great people, especially Busbecq, proves . . . not only that humankind reaps greater benefits from slave than from hired labor; but also, in particular, that there would be a massing of dishonest and lazy people who would wander around and consume the food of their fellow-citizens and others, thereby weakening them, an evil that would come about unless slavery continues to proliferate on a large scale among all Christians.

(27) Lest I continue indefinitely, I can, I think, safely draw the following conclusion from the above discussion, even though I by no means concur with every opinion of the most learned writers mentioned above: that slavery in no way contradicts Christian freedom—slavery, which indeed has been repealed here in the Netherlands out of some sense of benevolence and clemency or for political expediency, not because of divine law. From this it follows naturally that slavery does not impede the spread of the Gospel in those Christian colonies where it prevails right up to the present day. For this reason, a kingdom most amicable and pleasing to God can and should be built for both masters and slaves, educated in the better religious practices. This is what Paul recommends to Philemon (v. 16). And in this way slaves will certainly in the end be as prepared as possible for the will of their masters, as we read in Ephesians 6:5-8: *Slaves, be obedient to those who are your earthly masters, with fear and trembling, in singleness of heart, as to Christ.* On these lines, another passage will grow deep roots in the minds of those masters who have not cast off the character of a Christian gentleman (v. 9): *Masters, do the same to them, and forebear threatening, knowing that he who is both their master and yours is in heaven, and that there is no partiality with him.*

[Jacobus Elisa Johannes Capitein, *Political-theological Dissertation Examining the Question: Is Slavery Compatible with Christian Freedom or Not?* In *The Agony of Asar: A Thesis on Slavery by the Former Slave, Jacobus Elisa Johannes Capitein 1717-1747,* edited and translated by Grant Parker (Princeton: Markus Wiener, 2001).]

The basic problem for early modern Christian advocates of slavery, as we've seen, is that there are a number of Bible passages that suggest Christians will be liberated or set free through their faith. Capitein accepts this, but he insists that these passages only apply to *spiritual* forms of bondage. We must distinguish, he thinks, "between slavery of conscience or sin and civil slavery; between heavenly law and the law of the courtroom; between freedom of the spirit and freedom of the body." The slavery that Christianity is essentially opposed to is *only* spiritual slavery or sin, on Capitein's view. Read this way, the Bible passages that indicate Christians will be liberated from bondage do not imply that, say, slaves who convert to Christianity thereby become free people. They will be spiritually liberated from sin, but they may still be "unwillingly subjected to the authority of another," Capitein's definition of civil or external slavery.

What does it mean to be liberated spiritually in the way Capitein alludes to? In answer to this question, Capitein approvingly quotes Henry More (whom we previously encountered back in Chapter 1). On Capitein's reading, More identifies two kinds of freedom that are bestowed upon Christians under the New Covenant—that is, roughly, the promise that those who believe in Christ will attain a special spiritual relationship or communion with God.[12] (This is the idea after which the New Testament of the Bible receives its name: "New Covenant" in Latin is *Novum Testamentum*.)

The first kind of freedom established by the New Covenant is a freedom from the requirement to adhere to various "fussy" ritualistic practices or "superstitious" beliefs. Neither More nor Capitein explains precisely what rituals or beliefs they have in mind, but they are almost certainly thinking of the numerous rituals of purification described in various passages of the Old Testament. For example, Leviticus 12 outlines certain rituals that must be observed by a mother after childbirth:

> [W]hen the days of her purifying are fulfilled ... she shall bring a lamb of the first year for a burnt offering, and a young pigeon, or a turtledove, for a sin offering, unto the door of the tabernacle of the congregation, unto the priest.

The New Covenant is supposed to release Christians from the obligation to observe such rituals and sacrifices; they are not required for spiritual purification and communion with the divine.

It is the second kind of freedom, however, that bears directly on the debate about slavery. For in addition to unburdening the faithful from the obligation to observe such rituals, Christian faith is supposed to unburden people from their sins. Capitein (still paraphrasing Henry More) enumerates a number of specific sins he takes Christian faith to ameliorate: "The faithful are freed from their sins, that is from pride, envy, hatred, anger, grief, avarice, and every desire ..." Here, sins are not identified with particular wicked *actions*, such as theft or murder. Instead, they are identified with the vices or wicked *character traits* that tend to lead to such actions, such as avarice or hatred. The spiritual freedom that Christian faith provides, on Capitein's view, is freedom from the grip of these vices. Yet even someone who is free from such spiritual vices could nevertheless be forced to obey the commands of another person.

Thus, Capitein has proposed an interpretation of Christianity according to which it is compatible with external slavery, or chattel slavery as a social institution. What is the evidence in favor of this interpretation? Capitein frequently relies on arguments from authority. For instance, after he presents the quotation from Henry More discussed earlier, he also refers readers to John Calvin's *Institutes of the Christian Religion*. And there are indeed passages in Calvin's *Institutes* that support Capitein's interpretation. Calvin writes that "it must be carefully observed, that Christian liberty is in all its branches a spiritual thing; all the virtue of which consists in appeasing terrified consciences before God . . ."[13] In context, Calvin's point is that "Christian liberty" does not license Christians to do whatever they want without repercussion. To be freed from the sin of avarice, for example, is not supposed to imply that one is permitted to hoard wealth. Still, it is easy to see how Calvin's proposal suits Capitein's needs: if "Christian liberty is in all its branches a spiritual thing," then it is a form of liberty that a person could enjoy even while enslaved.

Perhaps more interesting, however, is the argument Capitein draws from the biblical story of Philemon and Onesimus. Onesimus was a slave of Philemon, who fled his owner and made his way to Rome. In Rome, he met the apostle Paul, and Paul apparently converted Onesimus to Christianity. Although Paul considered the possibility of retaining Onesimus to assist him in the work of spreading the Christian religion (Philemon 1:13), he eventually decided that Onesimus should return to his owner. Paul then wrote a letter to Philemon—the text of which forms the New Testament book of Philemon—asking that Philemon take Onesimus back without punishment. Paul writes:

> For perhaps he therefore departed for a season, that thou shouldest receive him for ever; Not now as a servant, but above a servant, a brother beloved, specially to me, but how much more [beloved] unto thee, both in the flesh, and in the Lord? If thou count me therefore a partner, receive him as myself. If he hath wronged thee, or oweth thee ought, put that on mine account . . .[14]

What exactly is Paul asking of Philemon here? It is tempting to interpret Paul's letter as suggesting that Onesimus should be freed from slavery—that he should not be "a servant" but "a brother beloved" instead. However, this interpretation makes it difficult to understand why Paul would bother sending the escaped slave back to his previous master. For reasons such as this, Capitein infers that Paul does *not* intend that Onesimus should be freed from slavery upon his return to Philemon. Rather, Capitein suggests, Paul's argument is that "shared faith . . . will make Onesimus more fit than before to perform his future duties" for his owner. Philemon is to accept Onesimus back without punishment, yes—but to accept him as a slave, not as a free man. And this suggests that the freedom conferred by Onesimus's newfound faith is purely the spiritual freedom described above. If conversion to Christianity also involved freeing the converted person from chattel slavery, then Paul wouldn't have sent the runaway slave back to his master—or so Capitein infers.

Capitein closes his argument with an approving summary of reasons that other authors had given for thinking that slavery, as a civil institution, "is extremely useful to the state" so long as it is practiced without "brutality." To this end, he quotes a letter written by the diplomat Ogier Ghiselin de Busbecq (1522–92), who—based on his observations of the use of slaves in the Ottoman Empire—argues that many people would be better off enslaved. By nature, Busbecq argues, many people "need the leadership and rule of their betters" in order to avoid "misdeeds." When they are free to choose their own path, such people are more harmful both to themselves and to society. From this, Capitein seems to conclude not only that slavery is compatible with Christianity, but that the continued proliferation of slavery would be a net good.[15]

Needless to say, these arguments are unpersuasive. Although they are unpersuasive, these arguments are indicative of the efforts of advocates of slavery to resist the growing tide of abolitionist sentiment in the eighteenth century. And this debate is an important one, even if it seems obvious to us today how it must play out. For the eventual abolition of slavery was not the inevitable result of economic forces, but of a change in public attitude toward the practice. As Grant Parker notes in his commentary on Capitein's work, "[T]he economic viability of slavery is now widely accepted by scholars. . . . [I]t is simply not the case that slavery was abolished because it failed to benefit slave-owners financially."[16] Slavery was still profitable at the time of its abolition, so there must be some other explanation of the fact that the tide turned against it. And at least one reasonable possibility is just that the philosophical and theological arguments in its defense were bad, while the arguments against it were good. If that is so, then this is an especially important case in which philosophical debate had a substantial impact on society at large.

What *were* the arguments against slavery, though? In the next section, we turn to the other side of the debate: the case for abolition.

Key Points

- According to the doctrine of natural slavery, some people are by their nature suited to be slaves; however, some advocates of slavery (like Capitein) rejected this doctrine.
- Capitein holds that slavery as a civil institution is compatible with Christianity.
- He distinguishes *spiritual* from *external* freedom: spiritual freedom consists primarily in freedom from sin, while external freedom consists in freedom from coerced servitude.
- Capitein's main argument is that Christian faith only confers spiritual freedom, and coerced servitude is consistent with that sort of freedom.

Suggested Further Reading

Amponsah, David Kofi. "Christian Slavery, Colonialism, and Violence: The Life and Writings of an African Ex-Slave, 1717–1747." *Journal of Africana Religions* 1, no. 4 (2013): 431–57.

Jorati, Julia. *Slavery and Race: Philosophical Debates in the Eighteenth Century*, ch. 5.1. New York: Oxford University Press, 2024, 268–280.

Parker, Grant. "An Introduction to the Life and Work of Capitein." In *The Agony of Asar: A Thesis on Slavery by the Former Slave, Jacobus Elisa Johannes Capitein 1717–1747*, edited and translated by Grant Parker. Princeton: Markus Wiener, 2001, pp. 3–78.

Sommar, Mary E. *The Slaves of the Churches: A History*, ch. 8. New York: Oxford University Press, 2020, pp. 244–262.

9B. OTTOBAH CUGOANO ON SLAVERY AND RACE

Ottobah Cugoano: Brief Chronology

- 1757: Born somewhere in Africa.
- 1772: Taken to England.
- 1773: Baptized (under the name "John Stuart") and set free; takes a job as a servant for Richard Cosway, the Painter to the Prince of Wales.
- ~1786: Becomes seriously involved in the abolitionist movement in London.
- 1787: Publishes *Narrative of the Enslavement of a Native of Africa* and sends copies to leading political and intellectual figures, including George III. This fails to win them over; in the same year, he publishes *Thoughts and Sentiments on the Evil and Wicked Traffic of the Slavery and Commerce of the Human Species.*
- 1791: Publishes a shortened version of his previous work under a shorter title: *Thoughts and Sentiments on the Evil of Slavery.*

Like Capitein, Ottobah Cugoano was a freed slave. Unlike Capitein, however, Cugoano argues unequivocally *against* slavery. His book begins by addressing a number of claims made by the pro-slavery writer James Tobin. Before we turn to Cugoano's text, then, it's helpful to see a few of the key passages that Cugoano is responding to. As we'll see, the arguments Tobin offers are not especially novel ones—some of them are similar to those proposed by Capitein that we discussed in the previous section.

Tobin agrees with the thesis advanced by Capitein that Christianity is compatible with slavery. However, he argues for this thesis by pointing to the state of peasants (also called "boors") in various European countries:

> [D]o the blessings of Christianity and liberty so constantly go hand in hand? Let the author ask these questions of the Christian boors of Russia, Poland, Livonia, Lithuania, and other extensive provinces; will they not all join in telling him, that they continue, to this day, in a state of the most abject slavery, constantly transferred, with the soil, from the oppressions of one capricious tyrant to those of another, who have absolute power over their lives and

properties, and who daily abuse it in the most cruel and merciless manner. Let him even come nearer home, and make the same inquiries among the *protestant* peasants of Denmark and Norway, and they will inform him that their situation is scarcely a shade better.[17]

The basic idea is that, if Christianity is compatible with such treatment of peasants in early modern Europe, then it also permits such treatment of African slaves in the colonies.

As an Englishman, the case Tobin is most interested in is the case of English peasants or workers. Unlike the boors of Russia or Poland, the English peasant is not legally bound to serve a particular feudal lord or to live and work on a particular plot of land. Still, Tobin thinks the situation of the slaves in the colonies is in many cases better than the situation of an English peasant. To make his case, he compares the material goods that the peasant and the slave have access to. For instance, here he calculates the amount of food that a peasant is able to afford with his labor and compares it with the amount of food allotted to a slave:

> [T]he general allowance, on a tolerably well regulated plantation, is as follows, viz. out of crop-time, from six to nine pints of flour, oatmeal, rice, pease, &c. and from six to eight salted Scotch herrings, for a week . . . [C]ompare this allotment of food with what may be purchased by the weekly earnings of an English labourer. A negro, for himself, his wife, and four children, receives thirty-six pints of flour, &c. and thirty-six herrings. The labourer earns six shillings a week, to support himself, his wife, and his four children. With his six shillings, he purchases a bushel of wheat . . . He has, therefore, at most, but forty-eight pints of flour to divide among his family, or two pints a week, each, more than the negro; which difference is amply made up by the negro's herrings.[18]

Tobin does not precisely spell out the point of this comparison, but it's easy to see what he's thinking. If the English peasant's situation doesn't lead us to reject the economic and political institutions of England, and the peasant's life is materially on par with that of an African slave in the colonies, it follows (he thinks) that we likewise have no reason to reject the institution of slavery.

Of course, one obvious disanalogy between these two cases is the fact that an English peasant is *free*, while a slave is not. Tobin anticipates this objection. He denies that the English peasants are free in any substantive sense of that word:

> They are absolutely bound either to work, or starve; nor do they, in fact, enjoy the privilege of changing the scene of their labour . . . so that such of the poor

as raise families in a parish, are, in reality, nearly as much fixed to the soil they cultivate, as the boors of Russia or Poland.[19]

Since the English peasant is free in name only, not in reality, Tobin concludes that the situation of the African slave is not really worse than that of the English peasant. For this reason, he thinks, we have no principled basis for opposing chattel slavery. (He does not consider the possibility that, in light of the comparison, we might take *both* sets of institutions to be unacceptable or unjust.)

Recall that another argument that Capitein offered was that "humankind reaps greater benefits from slave than from hired labor" and that if slavery were abolished, "there would be a massing of dishonest and lazy people . . ." Tobin echoes this argument as well. He claims that in colonial communities where slaves have been freed, they do not go on to become productive members of society. For example, he writes:

> In Jamaica, it is well known, there are several different communities of negroes, who are to all intents and purposes already free, and have been so for a series of years; many of them, at least as many as are so inclined, are also christians. Yet do any of them labour in the field for hire? not one.[20]

Tobin appears to believe that this is a natural racial characteristic of the African slaves and their descendants. Though he does not make this point explicit, it appears to be a version of the doctrine of natural slavery: Black people are taken to be naturally unproductive or unsociable, and this is supposed to justify enslaving them.

This version of the doctrine of natural slavery makes explicit the racial aspect of early modern chattel slavery, in a way that most of the other arguments we've examined did not. The modern concept of race was not fully developed in this period, but the variation in traits associated with different racial or ethnic groups was the subject of much interest.[21] Most philosophers in the early modern period believed that all human beings descended from the same ancestors, a view today known as **monogenism**[†]. One of the main reasons for this was simply that the biblical story of Noah and the flood implies that every living human being is a descendant of Noah himself. This made the alternative view—known today as **polygenism**[†]— unpopular among early modern Europeans. However, monogenism naturally raises questions about how human differences come about. Different groups of people share among themselves certain skin coloration, facial features, and other characteristics, which are not universal to all human beings. If monogenism is true, what explains this variation among human beings? In the debate about the transatlantic slave trade, the difference that drew the most attention was skin color: why do Africans typically have dark skin, while Europeans typically have pale skin? As we shall see, one explanation that pro-slavery writers favored was that the Africans' darker skin was in fact the result of a biblical curse—a curse that marked them as worthy to be enslaved.

Cugoano addresses each of these arguments. In the first part of the following extract, he briefly but decisively refutes Tobin's analogy between slaves in the West Indies colonies and laborers in Europe. He then turns to the idea that blackness of skin is itself a marker of natural inferiority or subjugation. By way of refuting this idea, he presents a naturalistic account of the origins of skin color differences in human beings. Finally, the extract concludes with an evaluation of the argument that slavery is justified by the fact that it is an ancient and widespread tradition. Cugoano rejects this. He offers his own historical account of the origins of slavery—an account that makes clear its fundamental injustice.

Extract 9.2: Cugoano's Case against Slavery

But again, when [an advocate of slavery] draws a comparison of the many hardships that the poor in Great-Britain and Ireland labour under, as well as many of those in other countries; that their various distresses are worse than the West India slaves—It may be true, in part, that some of them suffer greater hardships than many of the slaves; but, bad as it is, the poorest in England would not change their situation for that of the slaves. And there may be some masters, under various circumstances, worse off than their servants; but they would not change their own situation for theirs: Nor as little would a rich man wish to change his situation of affluence, for that of a beggar: and so, likewise, no freeman, however poor and distressing his situation may be, would resign his liberty for that of a slave, in the situation of a horse or a dog. The case of the poor, whatever their hardships may be, in free countries, is widely different from that of the West India slaves. For the slaves, like animals, are bought and sold, and dealt with as their capricious owners may think fit, even in torturing and tearing them to pieces, and wearing them out with hard labour, hunger and oppression; and should the death of a slave ensue by some other more violent way than that which is commonly the death of thousands, and tens of thousands in the end, the haughty tyrant, in that case, has only to pay a small fine for the murder and death of his slave. [Animals] in general may fare better than man, and some dogs may refuse the crumbs that the distressed poor would be glad of; but the nature and situation of man is far superior to that of beasts; and, in like manner, whatever circumstances poor freemen may be in, their situation is much superior, beyond any proportion, to that of the hardships and cruelty of modern slavery. . . .

"Some pretend that the Africans, in general, are a set of poor, ignorant, dispersed, unsociable people; and that they think it no crime to fell one another, and even their own wives and children; therefore they bring them away to a situation where many of them may arrive to a better state than ever they could obtain in their own native country." This specious pretence is without any shadow of justice and truth, and, if the argument was even true, it could afford no just and warrantable matter for any society of men to hold slaves. But the argument is false; there can be no ignorance, dispersion, or unsociableness so found among them, which can be made better by bringing them away to a state of a degree equal to that of a cow or a horse. . . .

But the supporters and favourers of slavery make other things a pretence and an excuse in their own defence; such as, that they find that it was admitted under the Divine institution by Moses, as well as the long continued practice of different nations for ages; and that the Africans are peculiarly marked out by some signal predication in nature and complexion for that purpose.

This seems to be the greatest bulwark of defence which the advocates and favourers of slavery can advance, and what is generally talked of in their favour by those who do not understand it. I shall consider it in that view, whereby it will appear, that they deceive themselves and mislead others. Men are never more liable to be drawn into error, than when truth is made use of in a guileful manner to seduce them. Those who do not believe the scriptures to be a Divine revelation, cannot, consistently with themselves, make the law of Moses, or any mark or predication they can find respecting any particular set of men, as found in the sacred writings, any reason that one class of men should enslave another. In that respect, all that they have to enquire into should be, whether it be right, or wrong, that any part of the human species should enslave another; and when that is the case, the Africans, though not so learned, are just as wise as the Europeans; and when the matter is left to human wisdom, they are both liable to err. But what the light of nature, and the dictates of reason, when rightly considered, teach, is, that no man ought to enslave another; and some, who have been rightly guided thereby, have made noble defences for the universal natural rights and privileges of all men. . . .

But this will appear evident to all men that believe the scriptures, that . . . they afford us this information: "That all mankind did spring from one original, and that there are no different species among men. For God who made the world, hath made of one blood all the nations of men that dwell on all the face of the earth." Wherefore we may justly infer, as there are no inferior species, but all of one blood and of one nature, that there does not an inferiority subsist, or depend, on their colour, features, or form, whereby some men make a pretence to enslave others; and consequently, as they have all one creator, one original, made of one blood, and all brethren descended from one father, it never could be lawful and just for any nation, or people to oppress and enslave another.

And again, as all the present inhabitants of the world sprang from the family of Noah, and were then all of one complexion, there is no doubt, but the difference which we now find, took its rise very rapidly after they became dispersed and settled on the different parts of the globe. . . . [A]s the bodies of men are tempered with different degree to enable them to endure the respective climates of their habitations, so their colours vary, in some degree, in a regular gradation from the equator towards either of the poles. However, there are other incidental causes arising from time and place, which constitute the most distinguishing variety of colour, form, appearance and features, as peculiar to the inhabitants of one tract of country, and differing in something from those in another, even in the same latitudes, as well as from those in different climates. Long custom and the different way of living among the several inhabitants of the different parts of the earth, has a very great effect in distinguishing them by a difference of features and complexion. . . .

According, as we find that the difference of colour among men is only incidental, and equally natural to all, and agreeable to the place of their habitation; and that if nothing else be different or contrary among them, but that of features and complexion, in that respect they are all equally alike entitled to the enjoyment of every mercy and blessing of God. But there are some men of that complexion, because they are not black, whose ignorance and insolence leads them to think, that those who are black, were marked out in that manner by some signal interdiction or curse, as originally descending from their progenitors. To those I must say, that the only mark which we read of [in the Bible], as generally alluded to, and by them applied wrongfully, is that mark or sign which God gave to Cain, to assure him that he should not be destroyed. . . . The denunciation that passed upon Cain was, that he should be a fugitive and a vagabond on the earth, bearing the curse and reproach of his iniquity . . . But allow the mark set upon Cain to have consisted in a black skin, still no conclusion can be drawn at all, that any of the black people are of that descent, as the whole posterity of Cain were destroyed in the universal deluge. . . .

[It also] came to pass, in the days of Noah, that an interdiction, or curse, took place in the family of Ham, and that the descendants of one of his sons should become the servants of servants to their brethren, the descendants of Shem and Japheth. . . . But the prediction and curse rested wholly upon the offspring of Canaan, who settled in the land known by his name, in the west of Asia, as is evident from the sacred writings. . . .

But it may be reasonably supposed, that the most part of the black people in Africa, are the descendants of the Cushites . . . [and] of the Phutians [rather than the Canaanites] . . .; and the various revolutions and changes which have happened among them have rather been local than universal; so that whoever their original progenitors were, as descending from one generation to another, in a long continuance, it becomes natural for the inhabitants of that tract of the country to be a dark black, in general. The learned and thinking part of men, who can refer to history, must know, that nothing with respect to colour, nor any mark or curse from any original prediction, can in anywise be more particularly ascribed to the Africans than to any other people of the human species, so as to afford any pretence why they should be more evil treated, persecuted and enslaved, than any other. Nothing but ignorance, and the dreams of a viciated imagination, arising from the general countenance given to the evil practice of wicked men, to strengthen their hands in wickedness, could ever make any person to fancy otherwise, or ever to think that the stealing, kidnapping, enslaving, persecuting or killing a black man, is in any way and manner less criminal, than the same evil treatment of any other man of another complexion.

But again, in answer to another part of the pretence which the favourers of slavery make use of in their defence, that slavery was an ancient custom, and that it became the prevalent and universal practice of many different barbarous nations for ages: This must be granted; but not because it was right, or any thing like right and equity. . . . For while civil society continued in a rude state, even among the establishers of kingdoms, when they became powerful and proud, as they wanted to enlarge their territories, they drove and expelled others from their peaceable habitations, who were not so powerful as themselves. This made those who were robbed of their substance, and drove from the place of their abode, make their escape to such as could and would help them; but when such a relief could not be found, they were obliged to submit to the yoke of their oppressors, who, in many cases, would not yield them any protection upon any terms. Wherefore, when their lives were in danger otherwise, and they could not find any help, they were obliged to sell themselves for bond servants to such as would buy them, when they could not get a service that was better. But as soon as buyers [of slaves] could be found, robbers began their traffic to ensnare others, and such as fell into their hands were carried captive by them, and were obliged to submit to their being sold by them into the hands of other robbers, for there are few buyers of men, who intend thereby to make them free, and such as they buy are generally subjected to hard labour and bondage. Therefore, at all times, while a man is a slave, he is still in captivity, and under the jurisdiction of robbers; and every man who keeps a slave, is a robber, whenever he compels him to his service without giving him a just reward. The barely supplying his slave with some necessary things, to keep him in life, is no reward at all, that is only for his own sake and benefit; and the very nature of compulsion and taking away the liberty of others, as well as their property, is robbery; and that kind of service which subjects men to a state of slavery, must at all times, and in every circumstance, be a barbarous, inhuman and unjust dealing with our fellow men.

[Ottobah Cugoano, *Thoughts and Sentiments on the Evil and Wicked Traffic of the Slavery and Commerce of the Human Species* (London, 1787). Some of the language has been modernized.]

The first point of debate that Cugoano considers is Tobin's contention that the circumstances of the West Indies slaves are on par with those of English peasant laborers. Cugoano argues that this is obviously *not* the case, insofar as the laborers are free but the slaves are not. As we saw earlier in this section, Tobin himself anticipated this objection and denied that the peasant laborers are free in any significant sense. Cugoano, however, thinks that there's an easy thought experiment that shows Tobin's claim to be false. All we have to do, Cugoano argues, is ask the peasant laborers whether they would swap places with the slaves. It is clear that "no freeman, however poor and distressing his situation may be, would resign his liberty for that of a slave," Cugoano notes. What does this show? Although it may be true that in many material respects the free peasant is no better off than the slave, nevertheless freedom itself has a value that is incomparable: for this reason, "whatever circumstances poor freemen may be in, their situation is much superior, beyond any proportion, to that of the hardships and cruelty of modern slavery."

It's worth examining this idea that the kind of freedom the peasant enjoys, and that the slave lacks, makes the peasant's situation "superior, beyond any proportion," to the slave's. Exactly what kind of freedom is it that the slave lacks, on Cugoano's view, and why does that freedom make the peasant's situation so much better than the slave's? He repeatedly compares the treatment of the slaves in the West Indies to the treatment of nonhuman animals: they are "in the situation of a horse or a dog," in the sense that they, "like animals, are bought and sold, and dealt with as their capricious owners may think fit. . ." These comparisons with animals suggest a couple of elements of the slave's situation that Cugoano wants to draw our attention to. Perhaps the central point is that, whereas the peasant's *labor* is assigned some monetary value, the slave's very *life* is assigned merely monetary value. This in turn is connected with the freedom of self-determination. A free laborer working for someone who treats them badly can decide to take their work elsewhere. By contrast, a slave with an owner who treats them badly is not free to opt for a different owner—any more than a dog, horse, or cow could do so (to use Cugoano's examples).

This helps to clarify why Cugoano thinks the free person is better off than the slave simply in virtue of being free. But Cugoano's claim is even stronger than this: freedom is better than slavery "beyond any proportion," he says. What does this mean? One plausible interpretation of Cugoano's point is that freedom is *incommensurable* with other goods, especially with material goods like money, food, clothing, shelter, and so on, in the sense that there is no way to measure how much more valuable freedom is than these other goods. Many things that we value are incommensurable in this way. For example, imagine that you have a dear friend—someone who you've known for years, and who has been with you through all the ups and downs of your life. Suppose also that you have quite a taste for popcorn. In some broad sense, both of these are goods that you value: you value that friendship, and you also value having popcorn. But they are not comparable goods, in the sense that there is no amount of popcorn you would accept in exchange for the loss of that friendship. Your friendship is not just better than popcorn: no amount of popcorn could offset the loss of the friendship. In other words, we might say, the value this friendship has for you is "superior, beyond any proportion" to the value popcorn has for you. Similarly, Cugoano's point is that no amount of material goods could offset the freedom that one loses when enslaved.

Another line of argument that Cugoano responds to is that Africans and their descendants are naturally unsociable or unproductive, so that they are actually better off enslaved. Cugoano denies the premise that Africans by nature have these traits, but he also adds that even if Africans *did* have these characteristics, the argument is straightforwardly absurd. Chattel slavery essentially treats human beings as beasts of burden, and nobody is improved "by bringing them away to a state of a degree equal to that of a cow or a horse." Cugoano's suggestion is that there is a morally significant difference in kind between any human being and any nonhuman animal that the defender of slavery asks us to ignore.

Still, even if there is a morally significant difference between human beings and nonhuman animals, monogenist advocates of slavery argued that there is *also* a morally significant difference among the different races of human beings. One idea that appears to have appealed to pro-slavery writers is that the darker skin color that Africans tended to have was originally due to a curse placed on their ancestors. The key text drawn upon to support this claim is a selection from the book of Genesis (9:21-25) that describes Noah's curse of his son, Ham:

> [Noah] drank of the wine, and was drunken; and he was uncovered within his tent. And Ham, the father of Canaan, saw the nakedness of his father, and told his two brethren without.... And Noah awoke from his wine, and knew what his younger son had done unto him. And he said, Cursed be Canaan; a servant of servants shall he be unto his brethren.

The idea, then, was that (sub-Saharan) Africans are the descendants of Ham and Canaan, and that their skin color differs from that of Europeans because they were marked by Noah's curse. Since Noah's curse specifies that Canaan and his descendants will be bound in servitude, advocates of slavery thought this story suited their position well.

Cugoano responds that this proposal is not really consistent with what is said in the Bible. The idea that Africans are the descendants of Canaan does not explain the fact that they have darker skin than Europeans, since the story of the so-called "curse of Ham" does not mention any such "mark" of the curse. (Indeed, he points out, the only biblical curse that involves a mark of this sort is the curse placed on Caine for murdering his brother Abel—but that's irrelevant, since even if Caine had descendants, the Bible says that none survived the flood.) Finally, Cugoano suggests that based on what we are told of the descendants of Canaan in the Bible, there is reason to think they did *not* settle in Africa. Adding all of this up, he concludes, there is absolutely no basis for thinking that the darker skin of Africans is the mark of a biblical curse that would justify enslaving them.

Intriguingly, though, Cugoano goes even further than this: he proposes that there is a better explanation of human variation in characteristics such as skin color. On the one hand, we observe that, corresponding to the different climates in which people live, "their colours vary, in some degree, in a regular gradation from the equator towards either of the poles." On the other hand, there is also variation of skin color and other features among people "even in the same latitudes, as well as from those in different climates." This, he suggests, is due not to climate, but to differences of "custom" and "way of living." He does not propose a specific mechanism by which differences in climate and custom bring about racial differences. (He is writing over half a century before the publication of Darwin's *On the Origin of Species*.) However, his position is that there are plausible natural explanations of such differences, and we ought to seek such explanations rather than appeal to supernatural curses and the like. And—this is the real point—there simply is no natural explanation of human variation that would license the practice of slavery.

The final argument Cugoano refutes is grounded in slavery's status as a widespread tradition with ancient roots. He concedes that it "must be granted" that slavery is an ancient tradition, but he denies that this fact has any moral weight. Mere tradition does not provide moral justification, since immorality and injustice can clearly be enshrined in tradition. To see this in the case of slavery, Cugoano asks us to imagine how people came to be enslaved in the first place, back at the beginning of this admittedly ancient practice. He proposes that they must have been unjustly deprived of their own peaceful homes, due for example to violent attacks from bands of raiders. This in turn forced them to become "bond servants"—that is, slaves—either to their oppressors or to someone who could protect them from their oppressors. Once people began to retain bond servants, Cugoano reasons, a market for them would naturally begin to form. Finally, after the practice of owning and trading slaves had arisen, the purchase of a slave came to *appear* perfectly consistent with the demands of law and justice. By the mediation of the market, someone could buy a human being without appearing to kidnap or wrong them.

This appearance is an illusion, of course. If the enslavement of a person was originally wrong, its perpetuation remains wrong. Cugoano thus concludes that "at all times, while a man is a slave, he is still in captivity, and under the jurisdiction of robbers; and every man who keeps a slave, is a robber..." Not only must the institution of slavery in general be overthrown, but also everyone should treat slaveholders the way they treat robbers. A slave therefore has every right to resist their owner—to evade, injure, and possibly even kill them—just as one has every right to resist a robber in self-defense. Cugoano's conclusion is radical indeed, especially for a book penned half a century before Britain, his adopted country, would legally abolish slavery.

Key Points

- Cugoano argues that freedom is a good that is incomparably more valuable than material goods, since people who are poor but free would not trade their freedom for wealth.
- Against pro-slavery writers who claim that Africans have darker skin because of a biblical curse, Cugoano proposes that environment and custom can explain racial variation.
- Against the idea that slavery is legitimate because it is an ancient, pan-cultural tradition, Cugoano argues that its widespread acceptance does not make it morally right.
- Since slavery is no better than robbery, Cugoano concludes that slaves have a right to rebel against their masters and that masters have an obligation to free their slaves.

Suggested Further Reading

Bernasconi, Robert. "Ottobah Cugoano's Place in the History of Political Philosophy: Slavery and the Philosophical Canon." In *Critical Philosophy of Race: Essays*. New York: Oxford University Press, 2023, pp. 123–141.

Carretta, Vincent. "Introduction." In Quobna Ottobah Cugoano, *Thoughts and Sentiments on the Evil of Slavery and Other Writings*, edited by Vincent Carretta. New York: Penguin, 1999, ix–xxviii.

Jeffers, Chike. "Rights, Race, and the Beginnings of Modern Africana Philosophy." In *The Routledge Companion to the Philosophy of Race*, edited by Paul Taylor, Linda Alcoff, and Luvell Anderson. New York: Routledge, 2017, pp. 127–139.

Jorati, Julia. *Slavery and Race: Philosophical Debates in the Eighteenth Century*, ch. 3.6. New York: Oxford University Press, 2024, 180–187.

Questions for Reflection

- Capitein holds that someone could be spiritually free even while they are enslaved or imprisoned, or spiritually enslaved while they are physically free. What are some examples of situations like this?
- Cugoano holds that the value of freedom is incommensurable with other goods. Is this true? Why?
- Cugoano argues that the fact that slavery was an ancient tradition doesn't make it right. Are there practices or institutions today that we accept solely because of tradition, but that we should reject?

Part III

Mind and Reality

10

God and World
Baruch Spinoza and George Berkeley

Chapter Outline

10a.	Spinoza's Substance Monism	247
10b.	Berkeley's Theistic Idealism	260
	Questions for Reflection	272

Many early modern European philosophers were **theists**[†]: they held that there exists an **omnipotent**[†], **omniscient**[†], and benevolent God. They typically held that the universe came into being for some divine purpose and with design. Many also held that this God in some sense transcends the cosmos he creates. That is, although the world of space, time, bodies, and minds is brought about by an act of divine creation, the creator himself exists beyond that world while remaining present to it.

Yet beneath such general points of consensus, disputes roiled about the precise nature of God's relationship with the world. For instance, in what specific *way* does the created world depend upon God? And what exactly is it that God *does* when creating the world? Religious texts tend to speak about this relationship metaphorically. For instance, the Bible suggests that the relationship between God and the world is like the relationship between a potter and some clay: "But now, O LORD . . . we *are* the clay, and thou our potter; and we all *are* the work of thy hand."[1]

Some early modern philosophers hoped to develop a clearer understanding of the meaning of such metaphors by fleshing out in more detail the metaphysical relation between God and the created world. This chapter examines two philosophers who developed especially extreme accounts of the world's dependence on God: Baruch Spinoza (1632–77) and George Berkeley (1685–1753).

10A. SPINOZA'S SUBSTANCE MONISM

Baruch Spinoza: Brief Chronology

- 1632: Born in Amsterdam in the Dutch Republic.
- 1656: Exiled from the Jewish community due to "abominable heresies."
- 1661: Begins corresponding with European scientists and philosophers, including Henry Oldenburg, Robert Boyle, and Gottfried Leibniz.
- 1666: Correspondence with John Hudde indicates that Spinoza has begun work on his masterpiece, the *Ethics*.
- 1670: Publishes the *Theological-Political Treatise*, which provokes strong backlash.
- 1675: Correspondence with Oldenburg indicates that the *Ethics* is complete, but Spinoza decides not to have it published.
- 1676: Meets with Leibniz to discuss philosophy; no record of the meeting survives.
- 1677: Dies in The Hague. A volume of his works is published soon after by his devoted friends.

Baruch Spinoza's life was marked by controversy from a young age. He grew up in Amsterdam as part of a community descended from Portuguese Jews who had been exiled during the Inquisition. However, at the age of twenty-four, Spinoza was himself exiled from this religious community; the exact reasons for his exile are unknown, though they appear to be related to his wildly unorthodox views about God and the afterlife (about which more will be said herein). He appears to have accepted this with equanimity, recognizing that life outside of any religious community would enable him to pursue philosophy and the sciences without interference.

Since he could no longer continue in his family's business after his exile, he became a lens grinder by day, as well as an occasional tutor of philosophy, and he wrote philosophical treatises by night. He also cultivated a circle of friends among the more liberal and philosophically inclined Christians in the Netherlands, who held small reading groups to discuss his work and ask him questions about it. These friends are the only reason that his most famous work, the *Ethics*, ever saw print. In 1670, he published a book on political philosophy (the *Theological-Political Treatise*), but it provoked a terrible backlash; he realized after this that he could never publish his *Ethics*. In the years leading up to his death in 1677, he continued to revise and complete the *Ethics*, but made no attempt to publish it. Upon his death, his friends arranged to have it published on his behalf. And, as he had anticipated, it scandalized the whole of early modern Europe.

Spinoza's *Ethics* is written using the geometrical method. That is, he begins by setting out the *definitions* of the key technical terms he will use, along with a collection of *axioms* or principles to be assumed without argument. These definitions and axioms are then used to prove *propositions*, the philosophical claims he hopes to persuade us of. Sometimes, a proposition will have attached a *corollary* (a consequence that he takes to follow immediately from a given proposition) or *scholium* (a note intended to further explain the proposition).

The geometrical method is difficult to read, as Spinoza himself admits. Why use it, then? One reason for embracing it is the clear success the method had had in mathematical thinking. By proceeding in roughly this manner, the ancient Greek mathematician Euclid definitively established results that remain absolutely essential to mathematics and the sciences even today, such as the Pythagorean Theorem. (Pythagoras may have first *postulated* the Theorem, but Euclid *proved* it.) Given that so much of philosophical argumentation seems speculative and unstable, it is easy to see why someone might try to match the successes of mathematics by imitating its methods.

A second reason for taking up this method has to do with the nature of Spinoza's conclusions. The view he develops is unorthodox in the extreme. As we have seen, he decided not to publish the *Ethics* in his lifetime because he knew the backlash against it, and him, would likely be violent. Now, the more surprising and unorthodox one's conclusion, the clearer and stronger one's arguments must be. An argument presented in the geometrical method may be difficult to read, but it also eliminates much of the obscurity that bogs down an argument presented in ordinary language. Spinoza's proof of any given proposition cites certain prior propositions, as well as certain definitions and axioms, which he takes to entail his conclusion. In order to escape his conclusions, we cannot just say, "This is obviously false," and close the book. Instead, we are forced to reflect on those prior propositions, definitions, and axioms used in the proof. And what we may find—what many of Spinoza's friends found—is that the conclusions which initially seemed outlandish begin to strike us as reasonable after all.

What are these outlandish conclusions? At least in the first part of the *Ethics*, they principally concern God and God's relationship to the world. The *Ethics* opens without preamble or preface: Spinoza jumps right into the definitions of the key terms he will use throughout his work. Those terms include **substance**†, *attribute*, and **mode**†, the categories most crucial to his metaphysics. In adopting these categories, Spinoza is consciously drawing on Descartes and the Cartesian tradition. Indeed, his definition of 'substance' is clearly inspired by Descartes's own. In Descartes's most systematic presentation of his philosophy, a work titled *The Principles of Philosophy*, he writes that a substance is "a thing which exists in such a way as to depend on no other thing for its existence."[2] As we saw in Chapter 1, Descartes argues on this basis that it is legitimate to treat the mind and body as distinct substances: it is *conceivable* that your mind could exist apart from your body, therefore (he argues) it is *possible* that your mind could exist apart from your body, therefore (he finally concludes) your mind is a substance distinct from your body.

Spinoza will reject this Cartesian conclusion. But he does not reject the Cartesian notion of substance. Spinoza, too, takes the term "substance" to refer to an independent being: a substance does not depend on anything else for its existence, nor is it explained by or "conceived through" anything else. This implies that many of the things we might ordinarily call a substance would not actually count. For instance, water is not a substance, according to this definition: in order for water to exist, hydrogen and oxygen must exist; and in order to explain what water is, we need to draw on our knowledge of those elements. By contrast, the term "mode" refers to a being that is dependent in these ways. The term "mode" is a fairly literal translation of one sense of the Latin *modus*, which in this context means something like *a manner of being*. A mode is literally a modification of the way some substance is. On Descartes's view, for example, a particular candle is a substance, and the way that candle is shaped is a mode. The candle could exist without being shaped the way that it presently is. After all, its shape will begin to change if we light it. But if the candle didn't exist, the entity that is the-present-shape-of-that-candle would not exist either.

That is an example that Descartes would be happy with. However, when Spinoza first sets out his definitions of these terms, he is sparse on the details. He does not include any examples of substances or modes at the outset. Only gradually does it become clear that, although he takes up Descartes's basic terminology and starting assumptions, he takes them to entail a radically different picture of the world than the one Descartes arrived at.

Since Spinoza's arguments are sometimes difficult to follow, it is easier to begin by describing his conclusions. This will make it easier to see the purpose of each step he takes en route to his destination.

In broad outline, the picture that he develops is a version of an idea we have discussed in Part 1 of the textbook: **substance monism**[†]. The monistic ontologies we have examined each posited that all substances were of the same type or kind (e.g., the materialists held that all substances are material or corporeal). As we shall see, Spinoza goes further than the other monistic philosophers we have encountered, for he holds not just that there is a single *type* of substance, but that there exists only a single substance in the universe. In this sense, Spinoza disagrees with all of the other monistic views we have considered, whether idealist or materialist. Those philosophers all held that there are multiple distinct substances that could exist apart from one another. This plurality of substances is what Spinoza denies.

What is his alternative position? Although we ordinarily carve the world up into distinct objects (tables, chairs, beer mugs, etc.), these objects do not qualify as substances. They are, Spinoza argues, merely modifications of a single, universal substance that underlies them all. Just as for Descartes, the candle's shape is a mode that inheres in the candle, likewise for Spinoza *the candle itself* is a mode of the one substance. Nor is there anything special about the candle, in this regard. None of the finite, particular objects we identify in our ordinary experiences—including we humans ourselves—are actually substances. Such "objects" are more like local variations in a single, universal field that is pervasive throughout the cosmos.

It is natural at this point to wonder about the characteristics of this single universal substance. Spinoza says that this substance is God: "No substance besides God can exist or be conceived." Yet as the *Ethics* proceeds, it becomes clear that Spinoza's God has few features in common with the God of Christianity, Judaism, or Islam. In those religions, God is described in ways that include personal characteristics. He has plans and desires, feels emotions such as love and anger, and is benevolent towards humanity. Spinoza's God has none of these personal characteristics. God makes no plans and has no desires, for these would imply that God was not *already* complete and perfect. God feels neither love nor anger toward creation, for these emotional connections would involve a form of dependence that is incompatible with God's independence and self-sufficiency. Nor is God particularly benevolent toward us. Human beings are simply another part of the natural world, on Spinoza's view, and the world was no more designed for us than for (say) flesh-eating bacteria. In an encounter between humans and flesh-eating bacteria, Spinoza's God is entirely indifferent about who comes out alive.

This lack of personal characteristics suggests that God's relationship to the world must be strikingly different to many traditional views of that relationship. The cosmos is described in a number of religious traditions as the product of an intentional act of creation by a divine being—analogous to the clay shaped by the potter in the passage from Isaiah quoted earlier. But the creation of the world cannot really be like this, on Spinoza's view. Unlike a potter, God does not create with a plan in mind or for the sake of producing some previously unrealized good. Also unlike the potter, God does not exist separately from the things he has created. If God is the only substance, it follows that neither the world nor any of the finite things that compose it are entities in their own right, really distinct from God.

Spinoza uses quite a different analogy to explain the relationship between God and the world. The cosmos is said to "flow" from God's nature in the same way that "from eternity to eternity it follows from the nature of a triangle that its three angles are equal to two right angles" (Prop. XVII, Schol.) And since God's nature could not be otherwise, neither could any particular link in the infinite chain of events that follows from God's nature be any different than it is. Your existence right now, at this moment in the history of the universe—as well as the fact that you are reading this sentence right now, and whatever thoughts you have in response to reading it—all follow with absolute necessity.

The foregoing picture of the cosmos is a radical one. Yet Spinoza believes it can be supported by rational demonstration. After defining his terms, he lists a series of axioms (only one of which is necessary for the propositions to be considered in our selection) and then proceeds to argue for his view.

Extract 10.1. Spinoza's *Ethics*

Definition 3. By 'substance' I understand that which is in itself and conceived through itself; that is, that the concept of which does not depend on the concept of another thing in order to be formed.

Definition 4. By 'attribute' I understand that, which the intellect perceives of a substance as constituting its essence.

Definition 5. By 'mode' I understand the affections of a substance, or [alternatively] that, which is in, and also conceived through, another.

Definition 6. By 'God' I understand an absolutely infinite being, that is, a substance containing infinite attributes, of which each [attribute] expresses an eternal and infinite essence. . . .

Axiom 1. Everything that is, is either in itself or in another. . . .

Axiom 6. A true idea must agree with its object. . . .

Proposition 4. Two or more distinct things are distinguished from one another either by a difference of attributes, or by a difference of their affections.

Demonstration. Everything that exists is either in itself or in another (by axiom 1), that is (by definitions 3 and 5), outside of the intellect there is nothing except substances and their affections. Therefore, there is nothing outside the intellect by which many things can be distinguished from one another except substances—or, what is the same (by definition 4), their attributes—and their affections. Q.e.d.

Proposition 5. In nature, there cannot be two or more substances with the same nature or attribute.

Demonstration. If there were multiple distinct substances, they must be distinguished from one another either by a difference of attributes, or by a difference of affections (by the preceding proposition). If only by a difference of attributes, it is thus conceded that there is but one substance of the same attribute. However, if by a difference of affections, then—since substance is prior in nature to its affections (by Prop. 1)—the affections may therefore be put aside and [the substance] considered in itself, that is (by definition 3 and axiom 6) considered truly, it will not be possible to conceive of one distinguished from the other. That is (by the preceding proposition) there cannot be many [of the same attribute], but only one. Q.e.d. . . .

Proposition 11. God, or a substance containing infinite attributes, each of which expresses eternal and infinite essence, necessarily exists.

Demonstration. . . . To each thing must be assigned a cause or reason, either for why it exists or for why it does not exist. . . . If therefore no reason or cause can be given that prevents God from existing, or which takes his existence away, it is wholly to be concluded that he necessarily exists. Yet if there is some such reason or cause, it must either be in God's very nature, or . . . it must be in another substance of another nature. For if that substance was of the same nature, it would thereby be conceded that God exists. Yet a substance with another nature would have nothing in common with God . . . , so it would neither be able to posit nor to prevent his existence. Since therefore a reason or cause that prevents God's existence cannot be found outside the divine nature, if he does not exist, the reason must be in his nature itself—that is, his nature must involve a contradiction. However, this is absurd to affirm of a being absolutely infinite and most perfect; therefore neither in God nor outside of God is there a cause or reason that prevents his existence, and hence God necessarily exists. Q.e.d. . . .

Prop. 14. Besides God, no substance can either be or be conceived.

Demonstration. Since God is a being absolutely infinite, lacking no attribute that expresses an essence of substance . . . if there were another substance besides God, it must be explained by some attribute of God. Thus, two substances of the same attributes would exist, which (by proposition 5) is absurd . . .

Proposition 15. Whatever is, is in God, and nothing can either be or be conceived without God.

Demonstration. Besides God, no substance can either be or be conceived (by proposition 14) . . . Modes, however, (by definition 5) can neither be nor be conceived without substance; because of this, they can only exist in the divine nature and through it alone can they be conceived. Yet besides substances and modes, there is nothing (by axiom 1). Therefore, nothing can either be or be conceived without God. Q.e.d.

Proposition 16. From the necessity of the divine nature must follow an infinite infinity of modes (that is, everything that can be comprehended by an infinite intellect).

Demonstration. This proposition must be manifest to everyone, if only they attend to this: from the given definition of any thing, the intellect infers many properties, which in fact necessarily follow from it (that is, from the thing's essence); and the more reality the definition of the thing expresses . . . the more properties are inferred from it. Since however the divine nature has absolutely infinite attributes (by definition 6), each of which also expresses infinite essence in its own kind, from the necessity of God's nature therefore must necessarily follow an infinite infinity of modes (that is, everything that can be comprehended by an infinite intellect). Q.e.d.

Proposition 17. God acts from the laws of his nature alone, and he is constrained by no one.

Demonstration. We have shown in proposition 16 that from the necessity of the divine nature alone, or (what is the same) from the laws of nature alone, there follows an absolute infinity of modes. And in proposition 15, we demonstrated that nothing can either be or be conceived without God, and that all things are in God. From which it follows that there can be nothing outside him, by which his action is determined or constrained, and so God acts from the laws of his nature alone and is constrained by no one. Q.e.d.

Corollary 1. From this it follows . . . that there is no cause that incites God to action, either extrinsically or intrinsically, besides the perfection of his nature. . . .

Scholium. . . . [F]rom the perfect power or infinite nature of God, an infinite infinity of modes—that is, all things—have necessarily flowed or always follow by the same necessity, in the same way that from the nature of a triangle it follows from eternity to eternity that its three angles are equal to two right angles. . . .

Proposition 25. God is not only the efficient cause of the existence of things, but also of their essence. . . .

Scholium. This proposition more clearly follows from proposition 16. For from that proposition it follows that from the given divine nature, both the essence and the existence of a thing must necessarily be inferred; and, to say it in a word, in the same sense in which God is said to be the cause of himself, so also he is said to be the cause of all things, which will be rendered even more clear by the following corollary.

Corollary. Particular things are nothing but affections of God's attributes, or modes by which God's attributes are expressed in a certain and determinate way. The demonstration is evident from proposition 15 and definition 5. . . .

[Benedictus de Spinoza, Ethica, Ordine Geometrico demonstrata, in Spinoza Opera, edited by Carl Gebhardt (Heidelberg: Carl Winters, 1925). Translation by John Grey.]

There are three key argumentative moves that Spinoza makes in the selection included earlier. First, he argues that there cannot be two substances that share an essential characteristic or "attribute." Next, he argues for the existence of "a substance containing infinite attributes, each of which expresses an infinite and eternal essence" (E1d6), that is, God. Finally, with both of those claims having been proved, he concludes that God must be the only substance. God has all the attributes, so any other substance would share some attribute with God. But no two substances can share any attribute. So, he reasons, God is the only substance.

The first key claim is given at E1p5, "there cannot be two or more substances of the same nature or attribute." The argument for this proposition is worth examining in detail. (Spinoza's peers, especially Gottfried Leibniz, were quick to recognize it as a crucial proposition in the development of his system.) The argument is a proof by contradiction. It begins with the assumption that there are two substances that share an attribute, then derives a contradiction from this assumption:

(1) Suppose there are two substances of the same attribute (call them *a* and *b*).

How does this assumption lead to contradiction? Spinoza invites us to consider what *makes* these substances distinct from one another. In ordinary cases, if we're asked why we think two objects are distinct from one another, we can point to some feature or characteristic that one has and the other lacks. These characteristics could be essential ones, in which case they are what Spinoza and Descartes call "attributes." Or they could be inessential characteristics, in which case they are what Spinoza sometimes calls "affections" and sometimes (as we've already seen) calls "modes." And this leads Spinoza to his next premise:

(2) If *a* and *b* are distinct substances, then they are distinguished by their attributes or distinguished by their modes.

For instance, if you asked Descartes, "How do you know that your mind is distinct from your body?" he would say, "My body is spatially extended, but my mind is not." That is, he would point to a difference in their attributes. And if you asked Descartes, "How do you know that your mind is distinct from my mind?" he might say, "The thoughts I'm having right now are different to the thoughts you're having right now." That is, he might point to a difference in their modes.

But wait: we've assumed that we're dealing with two substances that *share* an attribute. We can't very well use that attribute to distinguish them. So, Spinoza infers:

(3) *a* and *b* can't be distinguished by their attributes.

It seems, then, that they must be distinguished by their modes. Yet, Spinoza objects, that's not possible either. If we say that the modes are what make our two substances distinct from one another, then the very identity of those substances turns out to be contingent upon their modes. And this is inconsistent with the very definitions of these terms. Substances are "prior in nature" to their modes: the modes depend on their substances, but the substances don't depend on their modes. Thus, the modes of our two substances can't be what differentiate them either:

(4) *a* and *b* can't be distinguished by their modes.

At this point, lines (2)–(4) entail:

(5) *a* and *b* are not distinct substances.

And this contradicts line (1), our starting assumption. Of course, there's nothing special about *a* and *b*—the same problem will arise for any two substances with the same attribute. For this reason, Spinoza concludes:

(6) There are not two substances of the same attribute.

This is the first key claim that Spinoza will rely upon to establish substance monism. The second is the claim that God exists.

Spinoza's argument for the existence of God at E1p11 is an inversion of the traditional **ontological argument**† for God's existence. That traditional argument can be glossed briefly as follows. As a matter of definition, God is an absolutely perfect being. Yet existence is a perfection, such that it is more perfect to exist than not to exist. Therefore, it is inconsistent to deny God's existence—it amounts to denying the existence of something that is defined as existing. This traditional argument has a number of flaws. Perhaps the most important of these flaws is that, when some object has some characteristic as part of its essence, this implies only that *if* that object exists, then it has that characteristic. For instance, to say that Harry Potter is essentially a wizard implies only that *if Harry Potter exists*, he's a wizard. But we can agree that Harry Potter is essentially a wizard even if we deny that there are any wizards. The reason is simple: Harry Potter doesn't exist. Likewise, to say that God is an absolutely perfect being entails that *if God exists*, then God is absolutely perfect. And this is logically consistent with denying that God exists.

Spinoza's argument for the existence of God is related to this ontological argument, but avoids the logical pitfall just outlined. The argument requires one bold assumption: **the Principle of Sufficient Reason**†, that is, the principle that everything that exists must have an explanation of its existence, and everything that does not exist must have an explanation for its nonexistence. That is, roughly speaking: every fact about what exists or does not exist must be explicable or intelligible. Spinoza does not refer to the Principle by this name—the name was coined by Leibniz some decades later—but it is clear that he accepts it. With the Principle in hand, Spinoza develops the following argument.

The Principle of Sufficient Reason entails that if God does not exist, there must be some explanation of that fact. So, Spinoza asks, supposing that God doesn't exist, what would explain God's nonexistence? There are two possible cases to consider, he thinks. **Case 1:** Perhaps God is prevented from coming into being by some other substance. In that case, God's failure to exist would be like a unicorn's failure to exist: there's nothing logically inconsistent about the notion of a unicorn, but the actual evolutionary history of the world happened to rule out their existence. **Case 2:** Perhaps God does not exist because the very nature of God is logically inconsistent. In that case, God's failure to exist would be like a square circle's failure to exist. The very nature of a square circle is such that it cannot be realized in existence—so too, perhaps, with God.

Yet neither of these cases is really possible, Spinoza argues. Take Case 1. If God were prevented from existing by some other substance, that other substance must have a nature different to God's nature. This follows from E1p5: if the other substance shared God's nature, it would just *be* God. However, on the assumption that this other substance differs in nature from God, it would have "nothing in common with God" (E1p11 alt. dem.) and therefore couldn't prevent God's existence. We should here be reminded of the mind-body problem as developed in Chapter 2. Interaction between the mind and body seemed impossible on the Cartesian model because, on that model, the mind and body shared no common attributes. Spinoza here applies similar reasoning to this hypothetical substance that prevents God from existing: it can't share an attribute with God, so there is no way for it to interact with God.

This leaves open the second case. If God does not exist, the explanation must be that there is a contradiction contained in the very nature of God itself. Unfortunately, Spinoza's treatment of this possibility is glib: "to affirm this of the absolutely infinite and perfect being is absurd" (E1p11 alt. dem.) In other words, Spinoza does not take this case to reflect a genuine possibility. It is not clear *why* he adopts this attitude, though. Many things that seem to have consistent definitions turn out to harbor hidden contradiction—think, for instance, of perpetual motion machines. Couldn't the definition of 'God' contain a surreptitious contradiction? Scholars have suggested different ways that Spinoza *could* have addressed this concern, but the text itself gives little indication of his actual reasoning on this point.

However, if we grant that the definition of 'God' is not contradictory, Spinoza's proof is complete at this point. Every fact has an explanation. Yet if God did not exist, there would be no possible explanation of that fact. So,

God must exist after all. Putting the argument in such stark terms serves to highlight how central the Principle of Sufficient Reason is to Spinoza's reasoning. The entire proof depends on it, for without that principle, it could simply be a brute, inexplicable fact that God does not exist.

The remaining passages in the selection are about how everything other than God is related to God and, as has already been indicated, the consequences are striking. Since God has every attribute, and no two substances can share an attribute, it follows that there is no other substance than God (E1p14)—that is, substance monism obtains. Everything else that exists, including human beings, are "modes by which the attributes of God are expressed in a certain and determinate manner" (E1p25c). When we think, our thoughts are modifications of God's infinite intellect. When we act, our actions are simultaneously God's actions. It is hard to imagine a picture that makes God's relationship to the world any closer than this.

Nevertheless, Spinoza's view was reviled by most of his peers and his name was synonymous with "atheist" for over a hundred years after his death. There is a paradox here. Spinoza clearly believed in God; indeed, he took the existence of God to be a central tenet of his philosophical system. How could someone who believes that God exists be reckoned an atheist? One possible answer is that, since Spinoza excises all personal characteristics from his notion of the divine, the "God" that he believes in is incompatible with any form of Christianity, the most politically influential version of theism in Western Europe during this period.

Key Points

- Spinoza, like Descartes and many other early moderns, embraces a *substance-mode ontology:* everything is either a substance or a mode of some substance.
- Spinoza accepts *substance monism,* the thesis that there exists only one substance.
- Although Spinoza argues for the existence of God, it is a God without any personal characteristics: it does not care about us nor have any plan for creation.
- A distinctive feature of Spinoza's writing is his use of the geometrical method: he sets out a series of definitions and axioms, and uses them to prove his conclusions.

Suggested Further Reading

Carlisle, Clare. "Introduction." In *Spinoza's Ethics*, translated by George Eliot and edited by Clare Carlisle. Princeton: Princeton University Press, 2020.

Della Rocca, Michael. *Spinoza*, chs. 1–2. New York: Routledge, 2008.

Lin, Martin. "Spinoza's Arguments for the Existence of God." *Philosophy and Phenomenological Research* 65, no. 2 (2007): 269–97.

Nadler, Steven. *Spinoza: A Life*. Cambridge: Cambridge University Press, 2018 [1999].

Shein, Noa. "Spinoza's Theory of Attributes." In *Stanford Encyclopedia of Philosophy*, edited by Edward N. Zalta. https://plato.stanford.edu/entries/spinoza-attributes/

10B. BERKELEY'S THEISTIC IDEALISM

George Berkeley (1685–1753) was born in Ireland, and he attended Trinity College, Dublin, where the curriculum included a number of the most famous modern philosophers, including René Descartes and John Locke, as well as the groundbreaking scientific works of authors such as Isaac Newton. Berkeley was a talented student and was elected a junior fellow of Trinity College. Shortly thereafter, in 1709, he also took orders in the Church of Ireland as a deacon. A year later he was ordained as a priest.

However, his interests were as philosophical as they were religious. During the same years he was taking up positions of increasing responsibility in the Church of Ireland, he also wrote, in rapid succession, several of his most influential philosophical works. These included a short book on vision and the philosophy of perception (*Essay towards a New Theory of Vision*) as well as a book advocating a radical form of idealism, the view that there are no mind-independent material substances. The extracts contained in this section are taken from that work, *A Treatise Concerning the Principles of Human Knowledge*. The work was not well received upon its publication, so a few years later Berkeley attempted to present his arguments in a more digestible format in *Three Dialogues between Hylas and Philonous*. This work, although it did not win over many converts to idealism, presented his views in a fashion at once more engaging and more comprehensive than in the earlier *Treatise*.

George Berkeley: Brief Chronology

- 1685: Born near Kilkenny in the southeast of Ireland.
- 1707: Elected a junior fellow of Trinity College, Cambridge.
- 1709: Publishes *An Essay towards a New Theory of Vision*.
- 1710: Publishes *Treatise Concerning the Principles of Human Knowledge*.
- 1713: Publishes *Three Dialogues between Hylas and Philonous*, which presents many of the ideas from the *Principles* in more popular form.
- 1724: Appointed Dean of Derry. Begins plans to found a college in Bermuda.

- 1728: Travels to Newport, Rhode Island, with his wife, Anne Forster, to begin implementing his plans for the new college.
- 1731: When his plan fails to secure funding, the couple travel back to London.
- 1734: Publishes *The Analyst*. Appointed Bishop of Cloyne; returns to Ireland.
- 1753: Dies in Oxford, England.

Later in his life, Berkeley began to develop plans for a radical new educational venture. He viewed European culture as falling into spiritual decline; thus, he hoped to start a college across the ocean in Bermuda.³ While he attempted to secure a grant for the project, in 1728 he and his new wife, Anne Forster, moved to Newport, Rhode Island. Berkeley hoped to use his Rhode Island house as a base of operations as they continued to make plans for the new college. They lived in Newport for three years before it became clear that he would not receive the grant he had been pursuing. He returned to Ireland in 1731 to resume his ordinary duties for the Church, and he was eventually made Bishop of Cloyne.

In an ironic twist of fate, although Berkeley's attempt to found a college in the Americas failed, he is the namesake of one of the most famous American universities. During his time in Rhode Island, he befriended some of the philosophers at Yale. When he left Newport, he donated his property to Yale so that the university could use proceeds from it to support graduate scholarships. He also donated over 800 books to Yale's library. And so, when a number of Yale alumni a century later made the trip to California to establish a college of their own, it was natural for them to name it *Berkeley*.

There is a darker side to Berkeley's legacy, however, that should not be neglected. His dim view of the state of European culture led him, somewhat perversely, to promote the expansion of the British Empire into the Americas. The famous line, "Westward the course of empire takes its way," comes from one of Berkeley's poems. And there is evidence that Berkeley was willing to go to great lengths to help empire "take its way." In his plans for the Bermuda college, he suggests that Native American students might be trained as missionaries. Where would these students come from, though? "The young Americans necessary for this purpose, may, in the beginning be procured, either by peaceable methods from those savage nations . . . or by taking captive the children of our enemies."[4] This is in line with Berkeley's considered views about slavery: other passages of the Bermuda plan indicate his support for the institution, and he owned at least four slaves himself. Thus, in spite of his important contributions to philosophy and education, recent historians have tended to paint a bleak picture of the man himself.

In the following extract, Berkeley argues against the very idea of a mind-independent material world. The concept, he concludes, is a "manifest contradiction." The objects we ordinarily take to populate the world are "collections of ideas," and nothing more. This conclusion may initially seem outlandish, but Berkeley does not merely *assert* it. He provides a series of increasingly challenging arguments for his view. And even if we reject those arguments after due consideration, they do at least force us to reflect seriously on our reasons for believing in a mind-independent material reality.

Extract 10.2. Berkeley's Case against Matter.

1. It is evident to anyone who takes a survey of the *objects* of human knowledge, that they are either ideas actually imprinted on the senses; or else such as are perceived by attending to the passions and operations of the mind; or, lastly, ideas formed by help of memory and imagination—either compounding, dividing, or barely representing those originally perceived in the aforesaid ways. By sight I have the ideas of light and colours with their several degrees and variations. By touch I perceive hard and soft, heat and cold, motion and resistance . . . Smelling furnishes me with odours; the palate with tastes; and hearing conveys sounds to the mind in all their variety of tone and composition. And as several of these are observed to accompany each other, they come to be marked by one name, and so to be reputed as one thing. Thus, for example, a certain colour, taste, smell, figure, and consistence having been observed to go together, are accounted one distinct thing, signified by the name *apple*; other collections of ideas constitute a stone, a tree, a book, and the like sensible things . . .

2. But, besides all that endless variety of ideas or objects of knowledge, there is likewise something which knows or perceives them, and exercises divers operations, as willing, imagining, remembering about them. This perceiving, active being is what I call *mind, spirit, soul* or *myself*. By which words I do not denote any one of my ideas, but a thing entirely distinct from them, wherein they exist, or which is the same thing, whereby they are perceived—for the existence of an idea consists in being perceived. . . .

4. It is indeed an opinion strangely prevailing among men, that houses, mountains, rivers, and in a word all sensible objects have an existence

natural or real, distinct from their being perceived by the understanding. . . . [Y]et whoever shall find in his heart to call it in question, may, if I mistake not, perceive it to involve a manifest contradiction. For, what are the aforementioned objects but the things we perceive by sense? and what do we perceive besides our own ideas or sensations? and is it not plainly repugnant that any one of these, or any combination of them, should exist unperceived? . . .

8. But, say you, though the ideas themselves do not exist without the mind, yet there may be things like them whereof they are copies or resemblances, which things exist without the mind in an unthinking substance. I answer, an idea can be like nothing but an idea; a colour or figure can be like nothing but another colour or figure. If we look but never so little into our thoughts, we shall find it impossible for us to conceive a likeness except only between our ideas. Again, I ask whether those supposed originals or external things, of which our ideas are the pictures or representations, be themselves perceivable or no? If they are, then they are ideas, and we have gained our point; but if you say they are not, I appeal to anyone whether it be sense, to assert a colour is like something which is invisible; hard or soft, like something which is intangible; and so of the rest. . . .

18. But, though it were possible that solid, figured, moveable substances may exist without the mind, corresponding to the ideas we have of bodies, yet how is it possible for us to know this? Either we must know it by sense or by reason. —As for our senses, by them we have the knowledge only of our sensations, ideas, or those things that are immediately perceived by sense, call them what you will: but they do not inform us that things exist without the mind, or unperceived, like to those which are perceived. . . . It remains therefore that if we have any knowledge at all of external things, it must be by reason, inferring their existence from what is immediately perceived by sense. But what reason can induce us to believe the existence of bodies without the mind, from what we perceive, since the very patrons of Matter themselves do not pretend, there is any necessary connexion betwixt them and our ideas? I say it is granted on all hands . . . that it is possible we might be affected with all the ideas we have now, though there were no bodies . . . resembling them. Hence it is evident the supposition of external bodies is not necessary for the producing our ideas . . .

22. I am afraid I have given cause to think I am needlessly prolix in handling this subject. For, to what purpose is it to dilate on that which may be demonstrated with the utmost evidence in a line or two, to anyone that is capable of the least reflection? It is but looking into your

own thoughts, and so trying whether can conceive it possible for a sound, or figure, or motion, or colour, to exist without the mind, or unperceived. This easy trial may perhaps make you see that what you contend for is a downright contradiction. Insomuch that I am content to put the whole upon this issue:—If you can but conceive it possible for one extended movable substance . . . to exist otherwise than in a mind perceiving it, I shall readily give up the cause . . .

23. But, say you, surely there is nothing easier than for me to imagine trees, for instance, in a park, or books existing in a closet, and no body by to perceive them. I answer, you may so, there is no difficulty in it; but what is all this, I beseech you, more than framing in your mind certain ideas which you call books and trees, and at the same time omitting to frame the idea of any one that may perceive them? But do not you yourself perceive them all the while? This therefore is nothing to the purpose: it only shews you have the power of imagining or forming ideas in your mind; but it does not shew that you can conceive it possible the objects of your thought may exist without the mind. To make out this, it is necessary that you conceive them existing unconceived or unthought of, which is a manifest repugnancy. When we do our utmost to conceive the existence of external bodies, we are all the while only contemplating our own ideas. . . . A little attention will discover to any one the truth and evidence of what is here said, and make it unnecessary to insist on any other proofs against the existence of *material substance*. . . .

[George Berkeley, *A Treatise Concerning the Principles of Human Knowledge* (Philadelphia: J. B. Lippincott & Co., 1874).]

Berkeley advances three key arguments against the existence of mind-independent material substance in this extract. The first of these, presented in section 4, is straightforward. We directly perceive ordinary objects such as houses, mountains, and rivers. Yet we only directly perceive our ideas; our ideas are the immediate objects of our thoughts and perceptions. So, ordinary objects such as houses, mountains, and rivers must *be* ideas in our minds.

So stated, this argument is not especially compelling. However, responding to it requires us to reflect on the nature of perception. Suppose that on a clear summer day, you are standing at the foot of the Matterhorn looking up at it. Its distinctive figure stands out starkly against the blue sky beyond. When you gaze at it, do you directly perceive the mountain itself? Or do you only directly perceive a representation of the mountain in your mind? The appropriate response to Berkeley's initial argument depends on our answer to this question. A common view among Berkeley's contemporaries was that our perception of external objects is always mediated by some manner of mental representation. Such views are typically referred to as **indirect realism**† about perception. For instance, a simple version of indirect realism would say that you have a mental image or model of the mountain that partially resembles it—something like a mental photograph of the object—and that you (indirectly) perceive the mountain by means of (directly) perceiving this mental image.

This indirect realist view of perception strikes some as paradoxical, for it implies that the very processes that make perception possible also prevent us from directly perceiving mind-independent external objects. A comparison might make the position seem less strange. Imagine that you are remotely controlling a robot arm in a warehouse and you make the robot arm place a box on a shelf. Did *you* place the box on the shelf? There is a sense in which you did, but only indirectly; all you did directly was push some buttons. By analogy, if you look at a mountain and your brain constructs a mental model of it that you use in all your thinking and reasoning about the mountain, there *is* a sense in which you perceive the mountain, but only indirectly. However, all you directly perceive is your mental image or model of it.

In any case, if we accept indirect realism, this gives us a reason to reject Berkeley's first premise. We don't directly perceive mind-independent material objects, only our mental representations of them. To the extent that our mental representations resemble their objects, they permit us to successfully navigate our environment—though we never directly apprehend the objects themselves.

Berkeley considers and objects to this position in section 8 of the *Principles*. To respond to it, he introduces a claim that subsequent scholars have dubbed the *likeness principle*: "an idea can be like nothing but an idea." In order for you to judge that, say, the white peaks of the mountain are similar in color to the clouds, you must have ideas both of the peaks and of the clouds. After all, in order to make such a judgment, you must be able to compare your ideas of the two objects to one another.[5] This point leads to trouble for indirect realism. The indirect realist says that even though your ideas mediate your knowledge of your environment, nevertheless you *do* have such knowledge. The world is in many respects just as we perceive it to be, and our ideas more or less resemble their objects. But Berkeley's likeness principle challenges this claim. The idea of the mountain cannot resemble the mountain itself, since (on the realist's hypothesis) the mountain itself is not an idea. How could you mentally compare a representation in your mind with an object external to your mind? This is impossible, Berkeley thinks, and so undermines the indirect realist's contention that our ideas resemble their objects in certain respects. Even if there were a mind-independent reality, we could never know what it is like.

An alternative account of perception, known as **direct realism**[†], has it that when you look at the Matterhorn, you directly perceive the mountain itself. On this view, the analogy of the remote-controlled robot is misleading. The causal processes involved in perception are more like the causal processes involved in moving *your own arms* to place a box on a shelf. Just as you can (directly) place the box on the shelf by performing a complex series of muscle movements, you can (directly) perceive the mountain by means of a complex series of neural or mental processes. Now, if this view is correct, then we have no reason to accept Berkeley's second premise: our ideas are not the immediate objects of perception after all. We directly perceive mind-independent material objects, not ideas.

Yet Berkeley holds that the very idea of "mind-independence" itself is inconceivable—that is, literally, we cannot have an idea of mind-independence. When someone says that the Matterhorn is a mind-independent object, their words are without meaning. Sections 22 and 23 set out the argument for this position in a series of passages that have come to be called Berkeley's "master argument" (so called because Berkeley himself insists that "A little attention will discover to any one the truth and evidence of what is here said and make it unnecessary to insist on any other proofs against the existence of material substance" [Sect. 23]).

He frames the argument as a kind of challenge to the reader: see for yourself whether you can conceive of "trees, for instance, in a park, or books existing in a closet, and no body by to perceive them" (Sect. 23). It's easy enough to call such images to mind. However, as Berkeley dryly continues, "do not you yourself perceive them all the while?" (ibid.). His suggestion is that there is an implicit contradiction involved in the attempt to form the idea that something could exist unperceived by any mind.

What is the contradiction, exactly? Spelling this out proves difficult, and scholars continue to disagree about how to interpret Berkeley's argument.[6] Here is one interpretation. Suppose you try to imagine a tree as unperceived by anyone. Now, in the act of imagining the tree, you perceive it; a mental image of the tree is formed in your mind, with particular features and from a particular perspective. (Perhaps you visualize a lone, small tree from a great distance, so you can better represent the absence of anyone around to see it.) In that case, you must imagine the tree both as perceived (as from that particular perspective) and as unperceived (by anyone, from any perspective). And this is, on the face of it, impossible.

Berkeley takes this to show us that the very *concept* of a mind-independent material object is, at its core, incoherent. It is not possible even to imagine such a thing without generating contradiction. If Berkeley is right about this, it will sink even direct realism about perception. The claim that we directly perceive mind-independent material objects surely requires that the concept *mind-independent material object* is not contradictory.

The result, if Berkeley is right, is that we must abandon the view that the world exists as a mind-independent material reality. Does that make Berkeley some sort of radical skeptic? He insists that it does not: the ordinary objects we perceive *do* exist, just not as mind-independent matter. They are nothing more than "collections of ideas" (Sect. 1) perceived by the mind. Everything you knew about objects based on your experiences of them remains intact: that apple really is red, shiny, and round. When you cut it open, the flesh inside really is white, moist, and sweet. All Berkeley rejects is the idea that, beneath all of the qualities of the apple that you experience, there is some additional thing, the apple itself, which could exist without any of these perceivable qualities.

Of course, there's a reason most of us believe that there are "unthinking" material objects. They help us make sense of the difference between reality and our imagination, and they help explain the lawlike patterns in our experiences. How can Berkeley explain such things? The next extract presents his response: what we think of as mind-independent objects are really ideas, not dependent on *our* minds, but on *God's* mind.

Extract 10.3. Berkeley's *Principles of Human Knowledge,* continued.

> 27. A Spirit is one simple, undivided, active being—as it perceives ideas, it is called the *understanding*, and as it produces or otherwise operates about them it is called the *will*. Hence there can be no *idea* formed of a soul or spirit; for all ideas whatever, being passive and inert . . . cannot represent unto us, by way of image or likeness, that which acts. . . . [Though it must be owned at the same time that we have some *notion* of soul, spirit, and the operations of the mind; such as willing, loving, hating—inasmuch as we know or understand the meaning of these words.][7]
>
> 28. I find I can excite ideas in my mind at pleasure, and vary and shift the scene as oft as I think fit. It is no more than willing, and straightway this or that idea arises in my fancy; and by the same power it is obliterated

and makes way for another. This making and unmaking of ideas doth very properly denominate the mind active. This much is certain, and grounded on experience . . .

29. But, whatever power I may have over my own thoughts, I find the ideas actually perceived by Sense have not a like dependence on my will. When in broad daylight I open my eyes, it is not in my power to choose whether I shall see or no, or to determine what particular objects shall present themselves to my view; and so likewise as to the hearing and other senses, the ideas imprinted on them are not creatures of my will. There is therefore some *other* Will or Spirit that produces them. . . .

30. The ideas of Sense are more strong, lively, and distinct than those of the imagination; they have likewise a steadiness, order, and coherence, and are not excited at random, as those which are the effects of human wills often are, but in a regular train or series—the admirable connexion whereof sufficiently testifies the wisdom and benevolence of its Author. Now the set rules or established methods wherein the Mind we depend on excites in us the ideas of sense, are called the *laws of nature*; and these we learn by experience, which teaches us that such and such ideas are attended with such and such other ideas, in the ordinary course of things. . . .

32. And yet this consistent uniform working, which so evidently displays the goodness and wisdom of that Governing Spirit whose Will constitutes the laws of nature, is so far from leading our thoughts to Him, that it rather sends them wandering after second causes. For, when we perceive certain ideas of Sense constantly followed by other ideas, and we know this is not of our own doing, we forthwith attribute power and agency to the ideas themselves, and make one the cause of another, than which nothing can be more absurd and unintelligible. Thus, for example, having observed that when we perceive by sight a certain round luminous figure we at the same time perceive by touch the idea or sensation called heat, we do from thence conclude the sun to be the cause of heat. . . .

33. The ideas imprinted on the Senses by the Author of nature are called *real things:* and those excited in the imagination being less regular, vivid, and constant, are more properly termed *ideas*, or *images of things*, which they copy and represent. But then our sensations, be they never so vivid and distinct, are nevertheless ideas, that is, they exist in the mind, or are perceived by it, as truly as the ideas of its own framing. The ideas of Sense are allowed to have more reality in them, that is, to be more strong, orderly, and coherent than the creatures of the mind; but this is no argument that they exist without the mind. . . .

[George Berkeley, *A Treatise Concerning the Principles of Human Knowledge* (Philadelphia: J. B. Lippincott & Co., 1874).]

After having pulled the curtain away from the doctrine of mind-independent matter, Berkeley now turns to the basic explanatory problems that matter is traditionally used to solve. He hopes to address these problems without appealing to matter at all. And, in doing so, he takes himself to establish a remarkable conclusion about the intimate relationship between God and our sensory experiences of the world. Rather than a picture on which God creates the world out of matter, which in turn causes us to form ideas of the sensible qualities of objects, Berkeley argues that God *directly* wills us to have the sensory experiences that we do.

To see why Berkeley thinks God must play this role, we need to consider two explanatory problems that we face after eliminating the concept of matter from our philosophical thought. First, we ordinarily distinguish (i) ideas that represent real objects from (ii) ideas that we have produced by applying our imagination. There is an important difference between seeing something (a horse grazing in a pasture) and imagining something (a unicorn grazing next to the horse). Ordinarily, we might think that part of the difference lies in the fact that there really is a horse in the pasture—that is, there is a material object there, whether one sees it or not. By contrast, there is not really a unicorn in the pasture; the imagination generated that image without any corresponding material object. The problem for Berkeley is that, having forsworn the concept of matter, he cannot use this method to differentiate ideas of real things from ideas of imaginary things. If every object is just a collection of ideas, what's the difference between the (real) horse and the (imaginary) unicorn?

The second problem is that the concept of a mind-independent material world is usually used to explain lawlike regularities in our experience. When you toss an apple into the air, why doesn't it ever disappear, or transform into a butterfly? Typically, the concept of matter could be used to explain these regularities: insofar as the material substance of the apple is what causes it to have the sensible qualities you perceive, those sensible qualities won't change in such dramatic ways unless you change the underlying matter of the apple. Berkeley has ruled out that sort of explanation, though. What's his alternative?

Berkeley thinks he can explain both of these phenomena, and without the aid of matter. Sections 28 and 29 briefly address the first problem. The reason that the concept of matter seemed like a good way to explain the difference between real and imaginary objects is that our ideas of real objects are not subject to our will in the way that merely imagined objects are. If you look at the horse in the pasture and it appears to you to be brown, simply wishing it were pink will not make it so. By contrast, it requires only a modest effort to turn your imagined unicorn into a pink unicorn. Proponents of matter can explain this by appealing to the fact that the matter of the horse is not dependent on your mind in the way that the unicorn is.

Berkeley likes the general point that there is a difference between your sensation of the horse (which is not subject to your will) and your idea of the unicorn (which is subject to your will). But since the concept of mind-independent matter is bankrupt, he turns to an alternative explanation for the fact that your sensations are not "creatures of [your] will" (Sect. 29): they are ideas caused in you by "some *other* Will or Spirit" (ibid.) As subsequent passages reveal, Berkeley takes this other spirit to be God, "the Author of nature" (Sect. 33). That is, the sensation you have of the horse as you look at it is generated by the will of God; the mental image you form of the unicorn, by contrast, is generated by your own will. Moreover, our sensations can be said to be of real things insofar as they are "more strong, lively, and distinct" (Sect. 30) than ideas we merely imagine—and the reason they are stronger, livelier, and more distinct is that they are produced in us by a will greater than our own.

This also gives Berkeley a straightforward (albeit supernatural) way to explain the lawlike regularities we observe in our ordinary sensory experiences. The patterns we observe in the unfolding of our experiences are not due to *our* will, but to that of the "Governing Spirit whose Will constitutes the laws of nature" (Sect. 32). These laws Berkeley takes to reflect God's wisdom and benevolence, as their "constant, uniform working" permit us to identify what courses of action will tend to produce beneficial effects and what will lead us to harm.

To sum up, Berkeley's position is that, since the concept of mind-independent matter is incoherent, the ideas we have from sensory experience must be produced by a mind, instead. And, as our sensations are not controlled by our will, it must be some other mind that produces them. The force or vivacity of our sensations (as compared with our own imaginings) indicate that they are generated by a will more powerful than ours; and their predictable, lawlike succession in our experience indicates that they are generated by a wise and benevolent mind (as compared with our own rather capricious minds). God, Berkeley concludes, is the mind best suited to explain these phenomena.

Objections remain. For one thing, Berkeley's proposal takes what we had thought of as a naturalistic explanation of our experience and transforms it into a supernatural one: it is the will of God, not the stability of material objects, that explains our sensory experiences. Indeed, it seems that Berkeley's view rules out any genuine distinction between the natural and the supernatural. For another, Berkeley's argument doesn't seem to give us any reason to assume that the divine spirit responsible for our experiences corresponds to the God of any particular religious tradition. (On the face of it, these arguments might even be compatible with an *animistic* picture of the cosmos, with innumerably many divine spirits animating the natural world to produce our sensations.) Though Berkeley himself takes the relevant deity to be the God of Christianity, his arguments don't on their own establish this.

Still, Berkeley's arguments are worth our consideration. They challenge the complacent but common assumption that there exists a material reality independent of any mind, and they seem to force us into a radical alternative—that what we think of as mind-independent reality is really a collection of ideas willed by some *other* mind, not our own.

Key Points

- Berkeley argues for the existence of God on the basis of his rejection of the very possibility of mind-independent material substance.
- In the absence of unthinking matter, Berkeley thinks some other mind must be producing our sensations of the world.
- The difference between the ideas of the imagination and of sensation is that the former are less vivid in their force and lawlike in their succession.
- For this reason, Berkeley thinks we can still treat ideas of sensation as ideas of "real" objects—even though they depend on the mind.

Suggested Further Reading

Atherton, Margaret. "'The Books are in the Study as Before': Berkeley's Claims about Real Physical Objects." *British Journal for the History of Philosophy* 16, no. 1 (2008): 85–100.

Downing, Lisa. *Berkeley*. New York: Routledge, 2014.

Fields, Keota. *Berkeley: Ideas, Immaterialism, and Objective Presence*. Plymouth: Lexington Books, 2010.

> West, Peter. "Why Can An Idea Be Like Nothing But Another Idea? A Conceptual Interpretation of Berkeley's Likeness Principle." *Journal of the American Philosophical Association* 7, no. 4 (2021): 530–48.
> Winkler, Kenneth. *Berkeley: An Interpretation*. Oxford: Oxford University Press, 1989.

Questions for Reflection

- If substance monism is true, and we are all modes of a single underlying substance, do you think this would have any practical implications for how we ought to live?
- Given what we've learned about Spinoza in this chapter, do you think he is best understood as an atheistic thinker? Why?
- Do you think the concept of *mind-independence* is something we can acquire from experience? If so, what kinds of experience do we derive it from?
- In what ways do you think the hypothesis of mind-independent matter better fits with our experience than the idealist hypothesis? In what ways do you think it fares worse?

11

The Nature of Space
Samuel Clarke and Émilie du Châtelet

Chapter Outline

11a.	The Leibniz–Clarke Correspondence	275
11b.	Émilie du Châtelet on Space	289
	Questions for Reflection	301

The overthrow of medieval science in favor of the mechanistic view of nature advanced by Galileo and others (as described back in Chapter 2) led to new philosophical problems. Earlier in this book, we considered just one of these problems at length: How does conscious experience—mind—fit into the picture of the world as a vast mechanism in which each body is an interlocking part? But another set of problems had to do with the basic concepts of this new picture of the world. Space, time, and motion were central concepts in the mechanical vision of nature. Yet, from a philosophical point of view, these remained puzzling notions. For instance, it seems innocent enough to say that each body occupies some region of space, or that the parts of a body include any bodies that spatially overlap it. What *is* space, though? When we say of a body that it has a location in space, what exactly are we saying about it? This metaphysical question captured the interest of many early modern authors, and the present chapter examines the two main accounts of space that were developed in response to it.

The two main early modern views about the nature of space are easy to state. Some viewed space as a container: it is an entity that bodies may be placed in, but that could exist even if there were no bodies at all. Though we can only measure space by comparing bodies to one another—for example, by holding a ruler up to a wall—the spatial regions we measure don't depend on those bodies, and the region occupied by the ruler would still exist, and have the same distance, even if it were void of any body. On this view, if we were to write a comprehensive list of everything that exists, our list would not only need to include all of the bodies that exist in space; it would also need to include space itself as a distinct existing thing. Because this treats space as something like a substance, it is today frequently called the **substantival view of space**[†].

Others, by contrast, rejected the substantival view, arguing that space was nothing more than the spatial properties of, and relations among, bodies. Bodies do stand in spatial relationships with other bodies—they are larger or smaller, contiguous, overlapping, and so on. However, on this view, there is nothing to space over and above these relations, which in turn depend on the bodies that bear them. When we say that a body, such as a ruler, is "in" space, this only means that the ruler bears certain spatial relations to each other existing body; for instance, each other body is either *longer than*, *less long than*, or *the same length as* the ruler. But these properties and relations do not require us to postulate a further entity, space, distinct from and independent of all bodies: if all the bodies in space suddenly ceased to exist, space would also vanish. Since this view takes space to be nothing more than a set of relations among bodies, it is often called the **relational view of space**[†].

Early modern authors, especially in the eighteenth century, offered intriguing arguments both for and against the substantival view. This chapter first examines these arguments as they figured in the correspondence of Gottfried Leibniz (a figure discussed much earlier in Chapter 3) and Samuel Clarke, a friend and neighbor of Isaac Newton. Clarke, like Newton, embraced the substantival view of space, and the extract focuses on his reasons for this. The second part of the chapter turns to the work of the philosopher and mathematician Émilie du Châtelet, who attempted to defend the relational view of space against Clarke's (and Newton's) attacks.

11A. THE LEIBNIZ–CLARKE CORRESPONDENCE

In 1715, Leibniz sent a brief letter to Caroline, Princess of Wales, who was a long-standing acquaintance of his. In the letter, Leibniz criticized certain theological views that he attributed to John Locke and Isaac Newton. Caroline shared the letter with the English philosopher and theologian Samuel Clarke (1675-1729), a friend and confidant of Newton. Clarke penned a reply to Caroline, initiating an indirect exchange of letters between Leibniz and Clarke. Although their correspondence begins with a discussion of theology, it quickly turns to the nature of space and time. This is not surprising: Clarke in his letters represents himself as a defender of Isaac Newton's ideas, and Newton's groundbreaking *Mathematical Principles of Natural Philosophy* contains an extraordinarily influential presentation of the substantival view of space.

Samuel Clarke: Brief Chronology

- 1675: Born in Norwich, England.
- 1695: Receives BA degree from University of Cambridge based on a thesis defending Newton's physics.
- 1697: Publishes a popular translation of the then-prominent textbook, Rohault's *Treatise of Physics*, annotated with critical notes on the work.
- 1698: Becomes chaplain to the bishop of Norwich.
- 1699–1702: Publishes a series of minor works on theology.
- 1705: Publishes *A Demonstration of the Being and Attributes of God*, a systematic work that attempted to prove the existence of God.
- 1706: Publishes *A Discourse Concerning the Unchangeable Obligations of Natural Religion*, an attempt to derive moral principles on the basis of reason alone.
- 1706: Becomes chaplain to Queen Anne; publishes a Latin translation of Newton's *Opticks*.
- 1715: Initiates a correspondence with Leibniz about the nature of space and time, which would unfold over the course of two years (until Leibniz's death in 1716).
- 1729: Dies in Leicestershire, England.

Since Newton's position shaped so much of the debate to follow, it is worth briefly discussing his own description of the idea before turning to the extract from Leibniz and Clarke's correspondence. Newton distinguishes between what he calls "absolute" and "relative" space, with two corresponding, distinct accounts of motion:

> Absolute space, of its own nature without reference to anything external, always remains homogeneous and immovable. Relative space is any movable measure or dimension of this absolute space… Absolute motion is the change of body from one absolute place to another; relative motion is change of position from one relative place to another.[1]

Newton believes that a body may be at rest with respect to relative space but nevertheless in motion with respect to absolute space. For example, if you are sitting still while reading this chapter, you might occupy the same relative space for the duration of your reading. That is, your position relative to (say) the furniture in the room, and the building you're in, remains unchanged. However, as the earth rotates, your position in *absolute* space is continually changing. So, Newton thinks, that which is relatively at rest may be in motion with respect to absolute space.

Likewise, it is possible (Newton thinks) for a body to be in relative motion even though it is absolutely at rest. Imagine that you are at absolute rest—that is, your position in absolute space is unchanging—and a bird flies by. Your position relative to the bird would change as it flies, so you would be in relative motion; from the bird's point of view, it might even appear as though you're the one moving. But, by hypothesis, you would not be in absolute motion, for you would be at rest with respect to absolute space. So, once again, absolute and relative space come apart.

However, while we can directly perceive spatial relations among objects, and thereby perceive their relative motion, Newton acknowledged that we can only abstractly conceive of a body's position and motion in absolute space. He writes:

> But since these parts of [absolute] space cannot be seen and cannot be distinguished from one another by our senses, we use sensible measures in their stead. For we define all places on the basis of the positions and distances of things from some body that we regard as immovable, and then we reckon all motions with respect to these places, insofar as we conceive of bodies as being changed in position with respect to them. Thus, instead of absolute places and motions we use relative ones, which is not inappropriate in ordinary human affairs, although in philosophy abstraction from the senses is required.[2]

In other words, we approximate observations of absolute space and motion by treating certain bodies—such as distant stars—as though they were immobile. Those bodies stand in for the (genuinely immobile but imperceptible) parts of absolute space: in practice, we say that other bodies are absolutely in motion or at rest if they are in motion or at rest with respect to the "fixed stars," though in fact this, too, is merely a relative form of motion or rest.

This creates a philosophical difficulty for Newton. Given that we only ever observe relative space and motion, why should we think that there is also an unobservable *absolute* space which underlies these observable phenomena? Are there any reasons that can be offered for or against it? In the following extracts, Leibniz offers a reason against this idea, while Clarke responds by further clarifying his (and Newton's) notion of absolute space and providing a brief but important argument in its favor.

Extract 11.1. Leibniz's Third Letter to Clarke

3. These gentlemen maintain, therefore, that space is a real absolute being. But this involves them in great difficulties, for such a being must be eternal and infinite. Hence, some have believed it to be God himself, or one of his attributes, his immensity. But since space consists of parts, it is not a thing that can belong to God.

4. As for my own opinion, I have said more than once that I hold space to be something merely relative, as time is; that I hold it to be an order of coexistences, as time is an order of successions. For space denotes, in terms of possibility, an order of things that exist at the same time, considered as existing together, without inquiring into their manner of existing. And when many things are seen together, one perceives that order of things among themselves.

5. I have many demonstrations to confute the fancy of those who take space to be a substance, or at least an absolute being. But I shall use at present only one demonstration, which the author [Clarke] here gives me occasion to insist upon. I say, then, that if space were an absolute being, something could happen for which it would be impossible there is a sufficient reason, which is against my axiom [the **Principle of Sufficient Reason**[†]]. And I prove it thus. Space is something absolutely uniform, and without the things placed in it, one point of space does not absolutely differ in any respect whatsoever from another point of space. Now from this it follows (supposing space to be something in itself, besides the order of bodies among themselves) that it is impossible there should be a reason why God, preserving the same situations of bodies among themselves, should have placed them in space in one particular manner

and not otherwise—why everything was not placed in the exact opposite way, for instance, by changing east into west. But if space is nothing but that order or relation, and is nothing at all without bodies but the possibility of placing them, then those two states—the one such as it is now, the other supposed to be quite the contrary way—would not at all differ from one another. Their difference therefore is only to be found in our chimerical supposition of the reality of space in itself. But in truth the one would be exactly the same thing as the other, they being absolutely indiscernible.

[Gottfried Leibniz, "Mr. Leibnitz's Third Paper," in *A Collection of Papers Which Passed between the Late Learned Mr. Leibnitz, and Dr. Clarke, In the Years 1715 and 1716. Relating to the Principles of Natural Philosophy and Religion*, edited and translated by Samuel Clarke (London: Knapton, 1717). Some of the language has been modernized.]

In the main argument of this extract, Leibniz tries to establish that the notion of absolute space conflicts with the principle of sufficient reason. According to that principle, which we've already encountered in previous chapters, every fact has a complete explanation ("sufficient reason"), even though we typically do not know what that explanation is in its entirety. This entails that there are no brute facts, no phenomena that cannot—at least in principle—be explained. If absolute space exists, however, Leibniz believes that there would be facts that cannot be completely explained.

To demonstrate this, he asks us to imagine that the world is as Clarke and Newton say. In addition to all of the purely relative ways we might identify the position of a body—for instance, by measuring its distance from some other body—that body also has a position in absolute space. If that were true, Leibniz notes, then the entire physical universe could have been rotated 180° along an axis of symmetry, such as by "changing east into west" and vice versa, and this would involve a real difference in the place of those bodies. Although each body would still bear all the same spatial relations to each other body, nevertheless each would occupy a different position in absolute space than it occupies in the actual world. So, these would be two distinct worlds: the actual world and the rotated world.

However, as Newton acknowledged earlier, we cannot detect a body's position in absolute space. Thus, the actual world and the rotated world would be *indiscernible* from one another: bodies in the rotated world would have the same spatial relationships to one another that the corresponding bodies have in the actual world, so there would be no way for us to tell which of these two worlds we occupy. The difference between the worlds would be like the difference between an ordinary map and a copy of that map printed upside-down.

Are the actual world and the rotated world *really* different, then? Leibniz argues that they are not—and, indeed, that any two indiscernible worlds are really one and the same world, described in different ways. As we shall see, Leibniz holds that there cannot be two or more distinct objects that have all the same intrinsic features. However, in this extract, he offers a more specific reason for rejecting the possibility of multiple indiscernible but distinct worlds: if such a situation *were* possible, there would be no possible explanation for why God would choose to create one of those worlds rather than the other. Everything that exists at one of them would also exist at the other, and everything that happens at each world is entirely similar. The *only* differences would be undetectable differences with respect to absolute space. So, Leibniz concludes, God's choice to create the actual world rather than the rotated world would be a brute fact, a fact without a complete explanation. In this way, the substantival view of space is incompatible with the principle of sufficient reason.[3]

It is worth noting that although God figures prominently in Leibniz's version of the argument, this is not essential to show the conflict between absolute space and the principle of sufficient reason. If absolute space exists, it makes sense to ask why the rotated world didn't come to exist rather than the actual world. Even though there is no observable difference between them, they are nevertheless (on the substantival view of space) different situations. But, because they are indiscernible, there is no possible explanation why the world came to be one way rather than the other. And so—regardless of what view of the origins of the cosmos one endorses—the substantival view of space entails that there are physical facts that cannot in principle be explained.

In his reply to Leibniz, Clarke advances a weaker version of the principle of sufficient reason that, in his view, is compatible with cases of distinct but indiscernible possibilities. He also offers an initial version of an argument against the relational view that he will further flesh out in later letters—an argument based on the effects of absolute motion.

Extract 11.2. Clarke's Third Reply to Leibniz

2. Undoubtedly nothing *is*, without a sufficient reason why it is, rather than not; and why it is *thus*, rather than otherwise. But in things in their own nature indifferent, mere will, without anything external to influence it, is alone that sufficient reason. As in the instance of God's creating or placing any particle of matter in one place rather than in another, when all

places are originally alike. And the case would be the same even if space were nothing real, but only the mere order of bodies: For still it would be absolutely indifferent, and there could be no other reason but mere will, why three equal particles should be placed or ranged in the order *a, b, c*, rather than in the contrary order. And therefore no argument can be drawn from this indifference of all places to prove that no space is real. For different spaces are really different or distinct, one from another, though they be perfectly alike. And there is this evident absurdity in supposing space not to be real, but to be merely the order of bodies; that, according to that notion, if the earth and sun and moon had been placed where the remotest fixed stars now are (provided they were placed in the same order and distance they now are with regard to one another), it would not only have been (as this learned author rightly says) *la même chose*, the same thing in effect, which is very true; but it would also follow, that they would then have been in the same *place* too, as they are now, which is an express contradiction. . . .

3. Space is not a *being*, an eternal and infinite being, but a *property*, or a consequence of the existence of a being infinite and eternal. Infinite space is immensity, but immensity is not God; therefore, infinite space is not God. Nor is there any difficulty in what is here alleged [by Leibniz] about space having parts. For infinite space is one, absolutely and essentially indivisible. And to suppose it parted is a contradiction in terms, because there must be space in the partition itself, which is to suppose it parted and yet not parted at the same time. The immensity or omnipresence of God is no more a dividing of his substance into parts, than his duration or continuance of existing is a dividing of his existence into parts. . . .

4. If space was nothing but the order of things coexisting, it would follow that if God should [move] in a straight line the whole material world entire, with any swiftness whatsoever, yet it would still always continue in the same place; and that nothing would receive any shock upon the most sudden stopping of that motion. . . .

5. The argument [Leibniz offers] is that, because space is uniform or alike, and one part does not differ from another, therefore the bodies created in one place, if they had been created in another place (supposing them to keep the same situation with regard to one another) would still have been created in the same place as before; which is a manifest contradiction. The uniformity of space does indeed prove that there could be no (external) reason why God should create things in one place rather than in another; but does that hinder his own will from being to itself a sufficient reason of acting in *any* place, when all places are indifferent or alike, and there be good reason to act in *some* place?

[Samuel Clarke, "Dr. Clarke's Third Reply," in *A Collection of Papers Which Passed between the Late Learned Mr. Leibnitz, and Dr. Clarke, In the Years 1715 and 1716. Relating to the Principles of Natural Philosophy and Religion*, edited and translated by Samuel Clarke (London: Knapton, 1717). Some of the language has been modernized.]

Clarke here makes three points in response to Leibniz's critique of the substantival view of space. First, although he claims to accept the principle of sufficient reason, he insists that it must be restricted in its scope. It does not apply, he argues, to cases in which free agents are choosing between two options that are "in their own nature indifferent." For example, if you are choosing between two apples that look to you exactly the same—that is, they are qualitatively indiscernible to you—part of what is involved in your being a free agent is that you can arbitrarily pick one rather than the other. If someone asked why you picked *that* apple rather than the other, you might just say, "I had to pick one, and both seemed equally good, so I just chose." And in such a case, Clarke thinks, no further explanation of your choice is required. Rather, your choice would be completely explained by what you said: you had a reason to pick *some* apple, but no reason to pick any *specific* apple. Thus, in such a case, Clarke holds that "mere will, without anything external to influence it, is alone that sufficient reason" of your choice.

How does this apply to Leibniz's argument against absolute space? Leibniz had wished to show that God could have no reason to create the actual world rather than the rotated world, and so they ought not to be construed as distinct physical possibilities after all. Clarke's reply is that when confronted with a choice between two such indiscernible outcomes, God (like any free agent) can simply choose one rather than the other; and that alone would be a complete explanation of why the rotated world was not made actual.

Notice that this reply is only effective against the version of the rotated-world argument that is based upon Leibniz's and Clarke's shared belief that the world was created by a wise and benevolent God. For an author such as Spinoza, whom we encountered in the previous chapter, Clarke's reply would be unacceptable. Clarke has attempted to address Leibniz's argument by rejecting some of Leibniz's assumptions about what counts as a sufficient reason for a free choice. But if the universe is not the freely chosen creation of a divine agent, these considerations are irrelevant. The question, "Why isn't everything rotated 180° in absolute space?" will remain unanswered.

The second issue Clarke addresses is the question of what exactly absolute space is. Leibniz had raised a dilemma about the religious implications of absolute space. If space is a substance, then it is an infinite and eternal substance—so God would not be the only such substance. Alternatively, if it is a property or attribute of God, then God would be divisible into parts (which both Leibniz and Clarke take to be absurd). Clarke here denies that space is a substance and instead accepts the alternative that it is an attribute of God. Does this imply that God is divisible into parts? No, he argues: although bodies are divisible, *space itself* "is one, absolutely and essentially indivisible."

Finally, Clarke sketches an argument against the relational view. He invites us to consider what would happen if each body in the universe were moved uniformly the same distance in the same direction at the same time. On the assumption that space is nothing more than the various spatial relations among existing bodies, there would be no way to detect such a motion: as you moved, all of the bodies around you would move in exactly the same way, and so it would not seem to you as though you were moving at all. Indeed, on the relational view of space, you wouldn't really be moving at all. If all motion is relative to other bodies, then simultaneously and uniformly moving all bodies at once is equivalent to moving nothing at all. However, Clarke points out, there is a real difference between these two situations. If God moved the "whole material world entire" exactly three feet in one direction, when that motion ceased, we would feel "shock upon the most sudden stopping of that motion." That is, although the *motion* might be undetectable, the *acceleration* would be felt. This is an argument to which Clarke returns later in the correspondence.

In response, Leibniz rejects Clarke's attempt to delimit the principle of sufficient reason as well as the possibility of two completely indiscernible individuals or situations.

Extract 11.3. Leibniz's Fourth Letter.

> 3. Tis a thing indifferent to place any three bodies, equal and perfectly alike, in any order whatsoever. Consequently, they will never be placed in any order by Him, who does nothing without wisdom. But then, He being the author of things, no such things will be produced by him at all; and consequently there are no such things in nature.
>
> 4. There is no such thing as two individuals indiscernible from each other. An ingenious gentleman of my acquaintance, discoursing with me in the presence of her electoral highness, the Princess Sophia, in the Garden of

Herrenhausen, thought he could find two leaves perfectly alike. The princess defied him to do it, and he ran all over the garden a long time to look for some; but it was to no purpose. Two drops of water, or milk, viewed with a microscope, will appear distinguishable from each other. . . .

6. To suppose two things indiscernible is to suppose the same thing under two names. And therefore to suppose that the universe could have had at first another position in time and place than that which it actually had—and yet that all the parts of the universe should have had the same situation among themselves as that which they actually had—such a supposition, I say, is an impossible fiction. . . .

8. If space is a property or attribute, it must be the property of some substance. But what substance will that bounded empty space be an affection or property of, which the persons am I arguing with, suppose to be between two bodies? . . .

10. If space is an absolute reality, far from being a property or an accident opposed to substance, it will have a greater reality than substances themselves. God cannot destroy it, nor even change it in any respect. It will be not only immense in the whole, but also immutable and eternal in every part. There will be an infinite number of eternal things besides God. . . .

13. To say that God can cause the whole universe to move forward in a right line, or in any other line, without making otherwise any alteration in it, is another chimerical supposition. For two states indiscernible from each other are the same state; and consequently, it is a change without any change. Besides, there is neither rhyme nor reason in it. But God does nothing without reason, and it is impossible there should be any here. . . .

[Samuel Clarke, "Mr. Leibnitz's Fourth Letter," in *A Collection of Papers Which Passed between the Late Learned Mr. Leibnitz, and Dr. Clarke, In the Years 1715 and 1716. Relating to the Principles of Natural Philosophy and Religion*, edited and translated by Samuel Clarke (London: Knapton, 1717). Some of the language has been modernized.]

In this letter, Leibniz draws heavily upon what he elsewhere calls the **Principle of the Identity of Indiscernibles**[†]. According to this principle, whenever two individuals share exactly the same qualities (i.e., they are indiscernible from one another) it follows that they are really "the same thing under two different names," as Leibniz puts it in the extract. Even when two things appear to us to be qualitatively identical, Leibniz insists, they must bear *some* differences to one another—even if those differences are microscopic.

This point is connected to Clarke's proposal that we ought simply to accept a certain degree of arbitrariness in our explanations of the way things are. For example, if three particles all share exactly the same qualities, Clarke had proposed, then the fact that they were created in one spatial arrangement (*a*, *b*, *c*) rather than the reverse (*c*, *b*, *a*) is unavoidably arbitrary. Likewise, Clarke thinks, we shouldn't worry that there would be some arbitrariness in where God decided to place the material universe in absolute space. However, if the Identity of Indiscernibles is admitted, then the assumption involved in Clarke's thought experiment is an impossible one. There cannot be three indiscernible particles. Nor could there be another possible world, indiscernible from the actual world, at which all bodies are uniformly shifted in absolute space.

Given that Clarke would clearly reject the Identity of Indiscernibles—indeed, he *does* reject it explicitly at the beginning of the next extract—this leaves the debate about Leibniz's rotated-world objection to absolute space at an impasse. Roughly, Clarke is willing to accept that there are infinitely many physical situations that are in principle indiscernible from one another: all the different places in absolute space that the material universe could have occupied. For instance, the situation in which everything is rotated 180° around some axis from its actual position is, on Clarke's view, a physical situation that is genuinely distinct from the actual world even though there would be no way to tell the difference. The same could be said for any other degree of rotation (179°, 178°, etc.), as well as for shifting everything one foot in the same direction (or two feet, or three feet, etc.). There is no way to discern among all these physical situations since they all preserve the same observable spatial relations among bodies. Yet the substantival view of space requires treating them as distinct. Leibniz has objected that this would make it inexplicable why our world, rather than any of the others, actually exists. Clarke thinks that fact is explained by God's having made an arbitrary choice among these different possibilities, while Leibniz denies that this explanation is sufficient.

What of Clarke's objection to the relational view of space? If God pushed the entire material universe uniformly, wouldn't the associated acceleration and deceleration be felt even if all the spatial relations among bodies remained fixed? Leibniz has said little to address this objection, and Clarke presses it further in his reply.

Extract 11.4. Clarke's Fourth Reply

5. and 6. Two things, by being exactly alike, do not cease to be two. The parts of time are as exactly like to each other as those of space. Yet two points of time are not the same point of time, nor are they two names of

only the same point of time. Had God created the world but this moment, it would not have been created at the time it was created. And if God has made (or can make) matter finite in dimensions, the material universe must consequently be in its nature movable, for nothing that is finite is immovable. To say therefore that God could not have altered the time or place of the existence of matter is to make matter necessarily infinite and eternal, and to reduce all things to necessity and fate. . . .

8. Space, void of body, is the property of an incorporeal substance. Space is not bounded by bodies, but exists equally within and without bodies. Space is not enclosed between bodies, but bodies, existing in unbounded space, are—themselves only—terminated by their own dimensions. . . .

10. Space is not a substance, but a property, and if it is a property of that which is necessary, it will consequently (as all other properties of that which is necessary must be) exist more necessarily . . . than those substances themselves which are not necessary. Space is immense, and immutable, and eternal, and so also is duration. Yet it does not at all follow that anything is eternal *hors de Dieu* [outside of God]. For space and duration are not *hors de Dieu*, but are caused by, and are immediate and necessary consequences of his existence. And without them, his eternity and ubiquity [or omnipresence] would be taken away. . . .

13. If the world is finite in dimensions, it is moveable by the power of God, and therefore my argument drawn from that moveableness is conclusive. Two places, though exactly alike, are not the same place. Nor is the motion or rest of the universe the same state, any more than the motion or rest of a ship is the same state because a man shut up in the cabin cannot perceive whether the ship sails or not, so long as it moves uniformly. The motion of the ship, though the man does not perceive it, is a real different state, and has real different effects, and upon a sudden stop it would have *other* real effects. And so likewise would an indiscernible motion of the universe. To this argument, no answer has been given. It is largely insisted on by Sir Isaac Newton in his *Mathematical Principles* (Definition 8) where, from the consideration of the properties, causes, and effects of motion, he shows the difference between *real motion*, or a body's being carried from one part of space to another, and *relative motion*, which is merely a change of the order or situation of bodies with respect to each other. This argument is a mathematical one, showing from real effects that there may be real motion where there is none relative, and relative motion where there is none real. And this is not to be answered by simply asserting the contrary. . . .

18. The uniformity of all the parts of space is no argument against God's acting in any part, after what manner he pleases. God may have good reasons to create finite beings, and finite beings can be but in particular

places. And, all places being originally alike (even if place were nothing but the situation of bodies), God's placing one cube of matter behind another equal cube of matter—rather than the other behind that—is a choice in no way unworthy of the perfections of God, though both these situations may be perfectly equal. Because there may be very good reasons why both the cubes should exist, and they cannot exist but in one or other of equally reasonable situations.

[Samuel Clarke, "Dr. Clarke's Fourth Reply," in *A Collection of Papers Which Passed between the Late Learned Mr. Leibnitz, and Dr. Clarke, In the Years 1715 and 1716. Relating to the Principles of Natural Philosophy and Religion*, edited and translated by Samuel Clarke (London: Knapton, 1717). Some of the language has been modernized.]

Several of the ideas from Clarke's previous letters are reiterated here, including his view that some degree of arbitrariness in the world is inevitable, given "the uniformity of all the parts of space." For our purposes, though, the most important part of this letter is the expanded version of the argument based on the "real effects" of absolute motion, presented in section 13.

How does the argument go? Suppose, again, that the entire material universe were moved with respect to absolute space in a straight line—by exactly three feet over the course of a minute, say—such that all of the spatial relationships among all bodies were preserved intact. Given that all of those spatial relationships remain unchanged, none of the bodies would be subject to any relative motion. So, as we observed above, on the relational view of space that Leibniz advocates, such a situation would be equivalent to a world in which the entire material universe were *not* moved at all in absolute space. However, Clarke notes, although bodies in the three-foot-shifted world would retain all the same spatial relations as they have in the actual world, there would be a real difference between them. Clarke compares such a world to a ship traveling smoothly on a calm sea. Even if a passenger on the ship couldn't tell that the ship was in motion, there is a real difference between the ship's being in motion and its being at rest. As Clarke puts it, "The motion of the ship, though the man does not perceive it, is a real different state, and has real different effects, and upon a sudden stop it would have *other* real effects."

What are these "real effects"? In the version of this thought experiment we've imagined, when the material universe finished moving three feet over the course of that minute, we would all feel the resulting inertial force as our motion with respect to absolute space came to a halt. Again, the analogy with the ship is instructive: although a passenger on a ship might not be able to tell when the ship is in motion, they *would* certainly notice if the ship suddenly stopped. Thus, the actual world and the three-foot-shifted world are genuinely distinct physical situations. This is a problem for the relational view of space: if all of the spatial relations among bodies are held fixed, there is no way to explain the difference between these two physical possibilities.

One might object that Clarke's thought experiment is too hypothetical to tell us anything useful about the nature of space. How can we really know what would happen "if God should [move] in a straight line the whole material world entire"? Yet this argument from the "real effects" of absolute motion is explicitly based on a famous experiment discussed in Newton's *Principles*—an experiment that Newton appears actually to have performed, and that we ourselves can perform to test the hypothesis of absolute space. In Newton's famous bucket experiment, a bucket of water is attached to a rope hanging from the ceiling. The bucket is rotated until the rope attached to it is twisted up. When the bucket is released, it will begin to revolve as the rope unwinds. What happens to the water in the bucket? Newton writes, "the surface in the water will at first be level, just as it was before the vessel began to move."[4] Thus, at the beginning of the experiment, the bucket is in motion relative to the water. However, as the bucket spins, the water gradually begins to move with it, revolving in the same direction as the bucket itself. As the process unfolds, "the water will gradually recede from the middle and rise up the sides of the vessel, assuming a concave shape."[5] Eventually, the water revolves around the axis in the same time as the bucket does; that is, the water and bucket are at rest relative to one another. Nevertheless, the shape of the water's surface is deformed—it continues to press up against the sides of the bucket even though it is at rest relative to the bucket.

What explains the deformation of the water's surface? It cannot be the relative motion of the water with respect to the bucket, for the water *is not moving* relative to the bucket. And it doesn't seem as though any other bodies in the vicinity could explain the deformation of the water's surface either—the bucket is the only body that seems relevant in the context of this experiment. There seems to be no explanation of this experimental result in terms of purely relative motion. Thus, Clarke (following Newton) thought that this experiment clearly vindicated the existence of absolute space. The water's surface is concave not because of any relative motion it is undergoing, but because it is moving with respect to absolute space.

Is this argument decisive? As we'll see in the next section, although many early modern authors found it persuasive, not everyone was convinced by it.

Key Points

- According to the *substantival view of space*, space is like a substance in that it could exist even if there were no bodies occupying it.
- According to the *relational view of space*, space has no being over and above the set of spatial relations among bodies; it couldn't exist without bodies.
- Leibniz argues against the substantival view by showing that, if space had an absolute existence independent of bodies, then there would be many distinct physical possibilities that are completely indiscernible from one another.
- Clarke argues against the relational view by showing that there are situations in which we can detect the "real effects" of motion, even though all the bodies involved are at rest relative to one another.

Suggested Further Reading

Cohen, I. Bernard. "A Guide to Newton's *Principia*." In *The Principia: Mathematical Principles of Natural Philosophy*, edited and translated by I. Bernard Cohen and Anne Whitman, ch. 4. Berkeley and Los Angeles: University of California Press, 1999, pp. 85–108.

Grosholz, Emily. "Space and Time." In *The Oxford Handbook of Philosophy in Early Modern Europe*, edited by Desmond M. Clarke and Catherine Wilson. Oxford: Oxford University Press, 2011, pp. 51–70.

Meli, D. Bertoloni. "Caroline, Leibniz, and Clarke." *Journal of the History of Ideas* 60, no. 3 (1999): 469–86.

Vailati, Ezio. *Leibniz and Clarke: A Study of Their Correspondence*, ch. 4. New York: Oxford University Press, 1997, pp. 109–137.

Yenter, Timothy. "Samuel Clarke." In *Encyclopedia of Early Modern Philosophy and the Sciences*, edited by D. Jalobeanu and C. T. Wolfe. Springer Nature Switzerland AG, 2020.

11B. ÉMILIE DU CHÂTELET ON SPACE

Émilie du Châtelet (full name: Gabrielle-Émilie Le Tonnelier de Breteuil, marquise du Châtelet) was for several centuries primarily remembered for her intellectual and romantic partnership with one of the most famous figures of the Enlightenment, Voltaire (1694–1778). However, in her own lifetime, she was widely acknowledged to be one of the greatest scientists and philosophers then living.[6] Her most influential work—at first published anonymously, then in a second edition under her own name—is the *Foundations of Physics* [*Institutions de Physique*]. In the preface to that work, she suggests that her goal is partly to explain the Newtonian picture of the world, but partly to identify places where that picture stands on shaky ground.

Émilie du Châtelet: Brief Chronology

- 1706: Born in Paris, France.
- 1725: Marries the Marquis Florent du Châtelet and moves to Semur-en-Auxois in eastern France. The couple goes on to have three children.
- 1733: After her third child dies in infancy, she unofficially separates from her husband and returns to Paris to pursue the study of mathematics and physics. The same year, she meets Voltaire and begins a long-standing relationship with him.
- 1734: Voltaire's *Philosophical Letters* are published; to dodge legal and political fallout from them, the couple move out of Paris to a château of Du Châtelet's.
- 1738: Voltaire's *Elements of the Philosophy of Newton* is published, in which he acknowledges Du Châtelet's contributions to the work.
- 1738: Submits her *Dissertation on the nature and propagation of fire* to a prize competition by the French Academy of Sciences. Receives honorable mention.
- 1740: Publishes *Institutions de Physique* (variously translated "Lessons in Physics" or "Foundations of Physics"), which critically examines extant physical theories.

- 1744: The French Academy publishes her *Dissertation*, making Du Châtelet the first woman to have scientific work published by that institution.
- 1746: On the basis of her contributions to physics, she is made a member of the Academy of the Sciences of the Institute of Bologna.
- 1749: Completes a translation of and commentary on Newton's *Mathematical Principles of Natural Philosophy*. Dies in Lunéville, France.

Newton famously disdained metaphysical hypothesizing. For example, although he popularized the view that gravity is a universal force binding all bodies to one another, he refused to postulate about how it might work or where it might come from. Nevertheless, Newton was willing to embrace certain metaphysical claims when he thought the experimental evidence clearly supported them—as in the case of his claim that space exists independently of bodies. In the following extract, Du Châtelet objects to this metaphysical component of the Newtonian picture of the world. Taking Leibniz's side in the debate, she argues that space is best construed as an abstraction, like number, rather than a concrete reality.

Extract 11.5. Émilie du Châtelet's Foundations of Physics

72. The question of the nature of Space is one of the most famous that has divided ancient and modern Philosophers alike. It is also one of the most essential because of its influence on the most important truths of Physics and of Metaphysics.

Some have said: *Space is nothing over and above things, it is a mental abstraction, an ideal Being, it is nothing other than the order of things as they coexist, and there is nothing to Space except bodies.* Others have, on the contrary, maintained that *Space is an absolute Being, real, and distinct from the bodies it contains, that it is an intangible, penetrable extension, lacking solidity, the universal vessel that receives the Bodies that are placed in it; in a word, a sort of immaterial and infinitely extended fluid, in which Bodies swim.* The former group has put forward several metaphysical reasons in support of their opinion. The others have put forward the idea of Space that the imagination is able to form, and they have supported this idea using many objections against the contrary opinion; these objections are taken from the Phenomena, and above all from the difficulty there is with Bodies moving in the absolute plenum.

73. In the past, the view that Space is distinct from matter was held by Epicurus, Democritus, and Leucippus, who regarded Space as a Being that is incorporeal, intangible, and incapable of action or passion. In our day, Gassendi has revived this opinion, and in his *Essay Concerning Human Understanding* the renowned Locke does not distinguish pure Space from the Bodies that fill it, except by penetrability: this Philosopher derives the true notion of Space from sight and touch because, he says, we can neither see nor touch it, but we see and touch Bodies. . . .

Several mathematicians have embraced the opinion of the absolute void on the authority of Mr. Newton. This great man believed, in line with Mr. Locke, that one can explain the creation of matter through Space, envisaging that God would have rendered several regions of Space impenetrable. One sees in the General Scholium, which is at the end of Mr. Newton's *Principia*, that he believed that Space was God's immensity; in his *Opticks* he calls it God's Sensorium; that is to say, the means by which God is present in all things.

74. Mr. Clarke has taken great pains to support the opinions of Mr. Newton, as well as his own views on absolute Space, against Mr. Leibniz, who maintained that Space was nothing but the order of coexisting things.

Certainly if one consults the principle of sufficient reason that I established in the first chapter, one cannot help but acknowledge that Mr. Leibniz was right to banish absolute Space from the Universe, and to regard the idea that several Philosophers believe they have as an illusion of the imagination. For . . . if Space is a real Being and subsistent without the Bodies that could be placed in it, it makes no difference in which part of this homogeneous Space one places them, as long as they keep the same order among themselves: therefore there would not have been any sufficient reason why God would have placed the Universe in the place where it is now, rather than in any other, since he could have placed it 10,000 leagues further away, and put the East where the West is; or indeed he could have reversed it, so long as he kept things in the same situation among themselves.

Mr. Clarke was well aware of the force of this argument, and he was unable to counter it with anything other than that the simple will of God was the sufficient reason for the place of the Universe in Space, and that there was nothing more to it. But one can easily see that this admission undermines his view, and lays bare the weakness of his case; for God would not be able to act without reasons within his own Understanding, and his will must always be determined by reason. Thus being obliged to resort to an arbitrary will of God, which is not based upon sufficient reason, is to be reduced to the absurd. Therefore, since the reason for the place of the Universe in Space and the reason for the limit of extension are neither in the things themselves nor in the will of God, one has to conclude that the hypothesis of the void is false, and that there is no such thing in Nature.

Mr. Leibniz's reasoning against absolute Space is therefore irrefutable, and one is forced to abandon this Space, if one does not wish to renounce the principle of sufficient reason; that is to say, to renounce the foundation of all truth. . . .

77. It will not be without use to examine here how we came to form our ideas of extension, Space, and continuity; this examination will reveal to you the source of the mistakes that have been made about the nature of Space, and prevent you from making them in the future.

We feel that, once we consider two things as different, and when we distinguish them the one from the other, in our minds we place one external to the other; thus, everything that we consider to be different from us we see as external to us; there are many examples of this. If in our imagination we represent to ourselves a structure that we have never seen before, we represent it as external to ourselves, even though we know well that the idea we have of it exists within us, and that there is perhaps nothing of this structure existing external to our idea. But we still represent it as being external to ourselves because we know that it is different from us; likewise, if we represent two men ideally, or even the same man twice, we place them external to one another, because we cannot force our mind to imagine that they are *one*, and *two*, at the same time.

It follows from this that we cannot represent to ourselves several different things as being one, without this resulting in a notion that is attached to this diversity and to this union of things, and this notion we call *Extension*. Thus we give extension to a line, insofar as we pay attention to several diverse parts which we see as existing external to one another, which are united together and which are for this reason a single whole. . . .

Since we represent to ourselves in extension several things that exist external to one another and are *one* through their union, all extension has parts that exist external to one another and are *one*; and once we represent to ourselves parts both diverse and unified we have the idea of an extended Being.

78. Once we pay attention to this notion of extension, we perceive that the parts of extension, when considered abstractly and without taking into account either their limits or their shapes, must not have any internal differences; they must be similar, and differ only in number. For since, in order to form the idea of extension, we consider only the plurality of things and their union (from which their existence external to one another originates), and we exclude every other determination (all the parts being the same with respect to plurality and unity), we can substitute one in the place of another without destroying these two determinations, the plurality and the unity (which are the only determinations to which we are paying attention), and so any two parts of extension can differ from each other only in being two and not one. So all of extension must be conceived of as being uniform, homogeneous, and having no internal determination that distinguishes one part from another, since if we place these parts howsoever we wish, the result will always be the same Being, and that is how we arrive at the idea of absolute Space, which we consider to be homogeneous and indiscernible. . . .

79. When we have thus formed a Being in our imagination from the diversity of the existence of several things and of their union, extension, which is this imaginary Being, seems to us distinct from all that is real, from which we have separated it by abstraction. We envisage that this extension can subsist by itself, because in conceiving it we have no need of the other determinations that the Beings can contain, since we consider these Beings only insofar as they are diverse and united. Because our mind perceives these determinations separately (those which constitute this ideal Being that we call *extension*), and then conceives the other qualities (that we have mentally separated from it, and that are no longer part of the idea we have of this Being), it seems to us that we import all these things into this ideal Being, and that we house them there, and that extension receives and contains them as a vessel receives liquid that is poured into it. Thus, as long as we consider the possibility that several different things can exist together in this abstract Being we call *extension*, we form the notion of Space, which is nothing other than the notion of extension joined to the possibility of restoring to the coexistent and unified Beings (from which the notion was formed) the determinations that we had previously stripped from them by abstraction. Thus, we are right to define Space, *the order of coexisting things*, that is to say, the resemblance in the manner in which Beings coexist. For the idea of Space originates from our attending solely to their manner of existing external to one another, and representing to ourselves that this coexistence of several Beings produces a certain order or resemblance in their manner of existing; so that once one of these Beings is taken to be the first, another becomes the second, another the third, and so on.

80. We see well that this ideal Being, extension, that we form from the plurality and the union of all these Beings, must appear to us to be a substance. For, insofar as we envisage several things existing together, and stripped of all internal determinations, this Being appears to us to be enduring. And insofar as it is possible by an act of our understanding to restore to these Beings the determinations that we have stripped from them by abstraction, it seems to the imagination that we are importing something that was not there before. And so this Being appears to us to be modifiable. Thus, we are led to represent Space as a substance independent of the Beings that are placed in it. . . .

87. We could consider Extension without paying attention to the determinations of the Beings that constitute it, and in this way would acquire our idea of Space. However, since the Abstract cannot subsist without anything Concrete, that is to say without a real and determined Being from which we are abstracting, it is certain that there is Space only insofar as there are real and coexistent things; and without these things there would be no Space. However, Space is not the things themselves; it is a Being formed by abstraction from them that does not subsist external to things, but yet is not the same thing as the subjects from which we abstracted it, for these subjects contain an infinity of things that we ignored in forming the idea of Space. Thus, Space is to real Beings as Numbers are to numbered things, which become alike and each form a unit with respect to their Number, because we abstract the internal determinations of these things, and consider them only insofar as they make a multitude, that is to say, several units. For without a multitude of things that we count, there would be no real and existing Numbers, but only possible Numbers. Thus, just as there are no real units more than there are actually existing things, neither are there any actual parts of Space except for those designated by actually existing extended things. And we can admit parts into actual Space only insofar as there exist real Beings that coexist together. Therefore, those who wanted to apply to actual Space the demonstrations that they had deduced concerning imaginary Space could not help but lose themselves in labyrinths of errors from which they could find no way out.

[Émilie du Châtelet, *Foundations of Physics* (Paris, 1740). Translated by Katherine Brading, Monica Solomon, Anne Seul, and Penelope Brading, www.kbrading.org.]

In her brief survey of the debate between Leibniz and Clarke, Du Châtelet here comes down decisively in agreement with Leibniz. Clarke (and, by extension, Newton) have no good response to the argument that absolute space is incompatible with the principle of sufficient reason. Du Châtelet herself is a staunch advocate of that principle. Early in the *Foundations*, she argues that if you reject the principle of sufficient reason—that is, if you hold that things may come to exist, or events to occur, without a complete explanation or cause—then you could never be certain in any of your knowledge. In the context of her account of physics, one important consequence of rejecting the principle of sufficient reason is that it would undermine the legitimacy of **inductive inferences**† (roughly, inferences from observed cases to unobserved cases). Without that principle, for instance, the fact that all bodies we've observed have been attracted to one another by the force of gravity would not justify our belief that all bodies in general are subject to that force, or even that the bodies we've observed will continue to gravitate toward one another as they have in the past. It is with this point in mind that she here described the principle as "the foundation of all truth." Thus, Du Châtelet argues, if the belief in absolute space turns out to conflict with the principle of sufficient reason, so much the worse for absolute space.

Recall the problem: if all bodies ("the material universe entire") really were contained in absolute space, then there would be countless other ways those bodies might have been placed in that space, holding fixed all of their spatial relationships to one another. For example, Du Châtelet remarks, the material universe could have been created "10,000 leagues away" from its actual location in absolute space. Yet each such possibility corresponds to an apparently inexplicable fact—namely, the fact that bodies occupy their actual positions in absolute space rather than this other possible set of positions. Given that there is no observable difference between all these physical possibilities, there is in principle no way to give any reason or explanation for such facts.

Du Châtelet finds Clarke's attempt to appeal to the arbitrary will of God unsatisfying. To say that God simply chooses arbitrarily from among the possible places that the material universe could be located in absolute space does not give us a sufficient reason for that outcome. After all, the very same explanation would apply if God had chosen to create one of those alternative possibilities instead. That is, on Clarke's proposal, the answer to the question "Why did God create things *here* rather than *there*?" is that he was indifferent between the two options and so exercised his "mere will" to select one rather than the other. But that question would have precisely the same answer even if God had chosen the other option instead. Such an explanation is incomplete in ways that Leibniz and Du Châtelet find objectionable. If we are trying to explain some fact, we ought not to settle for an explanation that would apply even if that fact didn't obtain. Thus, Clarke's view entails that God makes choices without sufficient reason—which, Du Châtelet claims, "is to be reduced to the absurd."

For such reasons, Du Châtelet rejects a substantival view of space. There is no absolute space, on her view, there are only spatial relations among bodies. However, where Leibniz was content simply to refute the substantival view, Du Châtelet thinks it is important to go further and diagnose the source of the error that the substantival view makes. Suppose we have shown that there is no such thing as absolute space. Why then are people so inclined to believe that space exists independently of the things contained within it? A significant portion of Du Châtelet's chapter on space is dedicated to answering this question. She proposes an account of how we initially acquire the concept of space that is intended to explain why people tend to mistakenly treat it as something substantial.

Du Châtelet believes our concept of absolute space originally derives from our mental representation of bodies standing in relationships of spatial extension. On her view, conceiving of two bodies as parts of a single physical system involves recognizing both their distinction from one another as well as their unity as coexisting parts of a single system. For example, when you consider the moon as a body that orbits the earth, you represent the earth and moon as (i) distinct from one another, differing in many properties, but also (ii) unified with one another by certain relations of extension (e.g., being a certain distance from one another). The concept of extension in general arises from considering a collection of bodies as distinct from, but coexisting with, one another. However, this concept does not presuppose that the extended field delineated by a collection of bodies could exist *without* those bodies. That possibility requires a further act of mental abstraction, which Du Châtelet thinks is required to generate the concept of absolute space.

How do we move from the (innocent) idea of extension to the (erroneous) idea of absolute space? Rather than conceiving of the diversity and unity of the parts of a particular set of bodies, we can consider "the parts of extension . . . abstractly and without taking into account either their limits or their shapes . . ." For example, suppose you are presented in sensation by a particular set of bodies: a cherry tree, leaves and fruit hanging from its outward-reaching branches, standing in front of a small house with a sharply angled roof above a single ground level. These bodies and their parts all bear certain spatial relationships to one another, and the sensible qualities of the bodies—for example, the colors and shapes of the various parts of the cherry tree—permit us to perceive those spatial relationships. But it is possible for us to remove or "abstract" away the sensible qualities from our mental image of the scene. (Imagine the cherry tree and the small house set against a blue sky; then remove the tree; then remove the house; then remove the sky.)

What remains is an extended field composed of parts that are intrinsically featureless. The parts of this pure, featureless extended field are each distinct, but the only differences among them are differences in their spatial relationships to one another. And this, on Du Châtelet's view, is the source of the concept of absolute space: we form the idea of an extended field that is "uniform, homogeneous, and having no internal determination that distinguishes one part from another..., and that is how we arrive at the idea of absolute Space."

Once it is possible to distinguish the idea of a system of extended bodies from the idea of this featureless extended field, it becomes possible to suppose that the field exists prior to, and independently of, the bodies themselves—that it "contains them as a vessel receives liquid that is poured into it," as Du Châtelet puts it. But this is a mistake. The idea of spatial extension was ultimately derived from actual experiences of external bodies. Then the idea of empty, absolute space was formed by abstracting away all of the qualities of those bodies. Finally, Du Châtelet thinks, this abstract idea of absolute space was supposed to be a real entity, something that could exist even if there were no bodies whatsoever. This conclusion is simply not warranted, she argues, since the idea of absolute space is merely the product of mental abstraction.

Now, Clarke and Newton both admit that we do not directly observe or experience absolute space. They would both agree that the idea of absolute space is something we derive only by abstraction. What exactly is *wrong* with this kind of abstraction, though? As Newton put it in a passage already quoted, "in philosophy abstraction from the senses is required."[7] That is, Clarke and Newton simply accept that abstraction is an acceptable cost of doing business. From their point of view, it would not be obvious why there is supposed to be a problem about our use of abstraction to form the concept of absolute space.

Anticipating this sort of objection, Du Châtelet argues that "The abstract cannot subsist without anything Concrete, that is to say without a real and determined Being from which we are abstracting." The idea of space is generated by means of abstraction from our ideas of spatially extended bodies, as all parties to this debate agree. We have ideas of extended bodies first, then we mentally operate on them to form the idea of space. In this way, our abstract ideas depend for their existence on our ideas of concrete things. Du Châtelet thinks this same order of dependence must be found in the *objects* of our abstract ideas. Just as our abstract ideas depend on the unabstracted ideas from which they are generated, so too abstract entities themselves must depend on the corresponding "real and determined" entities. By such reasoning, Du Châtelet concludes that empty space—something we can only think about by means of abstraction—could not exist without any spatially extended bodies. So, even if in some sense there is an abstract object, "space," it will not have the substance-like independence that Clarke attributes to it.

To bolster her case, Du Châtelet suggests an analogy between the notion of space and the notion of number. Near the end of the extract, she writes that "numbered things . . . each form a unit with respect to their Number, because we abstract the internal determinations of these things." In order to count a number of items, we set aside the various qualities that make each of them unique and attend only to their bare distinctness from one another. So, for example, if you want to count the number of marbles in a jar, you must abstract away their variations in color, pattern, size, and texture—even though your perceptual experience of each marble is richly adorned with these qualities. To treat each marble as an equivalent unit, Du Châtelet thinks, one must selectively ignore such qualitative differences. But this, she points out, makes our ideas of number purely the product of abstraction. Her principle that the abstract depends on the concrete renders a clear verdict: if there were nothing to be counted, "there would be no real and existing Numbers, but only possible Numbers." The same is true, she thinks, of absolute space.

Even if this line of reasoning seems strong, though, Du Châtelet's discussion does not directly address Clarke's main argument in favor of treating space as absolute rather than merely relative. That argument, recall, was that we can observe the *effects* of absolute motion even when an object is at rest relative to its immediate surroundings. Thus, even if we cannot directly observe absolute space, we can tell that it exists because it explains what we do directly observe—such as, for instance, the water in a spinning bucket receding from its axis of rotation. If absolute space is merely an abstraction, not a real entity (or, as Clarke has it, a real property of God), then it could not explain the real deformation of the water's surface in the bucket experiment. Du Châtelet, it seems, owes some alternative explanation of the series of events we observe in that experiment.

How *could* she explain cases in which there seem to be observable effects of motion in a body that is relatively at rest? One option would be to say that although the body is at rest relative to its immediate surroundings, it is not at rest with respect to some larger system of bodies. The water is at rest with respect to the bucket, yes—but not with respect to, say, the distant stars. However, this is not on its own a decisive reply to the challenge. Clarke and Newton do not think any broader frame of reference is relevant to the interpretation of the bucket experiment. After all, it's not clear how the water's motion relative to distant stars could explain the deformation of its surface without some sort of action at a distance.

Philosophers researching these issues today have suggested a more plausible account of the bucket experiment that Du Châtelet might make. In a recent essay on this topic, scholars Katherine Brading and Qiu Lin point out that the ultimate explanation for the deformation of the water's surface must be due not to motion per se, but to the *forces* in the bodies involved in the experiment. As Brading and Lin put the point:

> The ontological explanation for these motions lies in the forces of bodies, and indeed ultimately in the forces of the simples from which bodies arise. It is not motion that is explanatory of the presence/absence of forces, but the forces of bodies that explain the apparent motions.[8]

The interplay of these forces explains both (i) the relative motion or rest of water and bucket, and (ii) the changes we observe in the surface of the water. Because both (i) and (ii) have a common cause, we often in practice use one (relative motion) to account for the other (observable effects of forces). But even in cases where a body is relatively at rest, the underlying forces in that body may still produce observable effects. When we observe such effects, like the deformation of the water, we can reasonably infer that the body we're examining is subject to some forces that explain those effects. The fact that the body is at relative rest implies only that we are ignorant about the source of the forces at work in it. Yet our ignorance of this certainly doesn't justify the conclusion that there an underlying absolute space.

As a closing note, it is worthwhile to observe that the question we have examined in this chapter remains open today. At the beginning of the twentieth century, Einstein initiated a series of radical revisions to our understanding of space and time. Space and time are not distinct in the way our early modern authors presumed, but merely different aspects of a unified four-dimensional spacetime. And where Newton gave no account of how gravity works, Einstein proposed to explain it in terms of the geometry of spacetime: massive bodies are attracted to one another because their very presence changes the curvature of spacetime, altering the paths of other bodies. However, the guiding question of this chapter can be raised about spacetime just as easily as it was raised about space: Is spacetime like a container that could in principle exist without anything in it? Or is it nothing more than a set of relations (spatiotemporal relations) among massive objects? Philosophers of physics continue to search for reasons to prefer one of these views over the other—and often these reasons have clear analogues in the early modern arguments that have been discussed in this chapter.

> **Key Points**
>
> - Émilie du Châtelet advances a relational view of space, against Clarke and Newton.
> - Du Châtelet endorses the principle of sufficient reason, which (like Leibniz) she takes to be incompatible with the existence of absolute space.
> - The idea we have of empty, absolute space is an *abstract idea*: it is formed by mentally removing all of the concrete features from an idea of an extended field.
> - Du Châtelet therefore takes space to be an abstract object, like numbers: just as numbers could not exist without things to be counted, space could not exist without bodies to stand in spatial relationships.

> **Suggested Further Reading**
>
> Brading, Katherine. "Du Châtelet and the Philosophy of Physics." In *Routledge Handbook of Early Modern European Women Philosophers*, edited by Karen Detlefsen and Lisa Shapiro. New York: Routledge, 2023, pp. 519–532.
>
> Brading, Katherine and Qiu Lin. "Du Châtelet on Absolute and Relative Motion." In *Current Debates in Philosophy of Science: In Honor of Roberto Torretti*, edited by Cristián Soto. New York: Springer, forthcoming.
>
> Hagengruber, Ruth. "Émilie du Châtelet Between Leibniz and Newton: The Transformation of Metaphysics." In *Émilie du Châtelet Between Leibniz and Newton*, edited by Ruth Hagengruber. New York: Springer, 2012, pp. 1–59.
>
> Hutton, Sarah. "Between Newton and Leibniz: Emilie du Châtelet and Samuel Clarke." In *Émilie du Châtelet Between Leibniz and Newton*, edited by Ruth Hagengruber. New York: Springer, 2012, pp. 77–95.
>
> Janiak, Andrew. "Émilie du Châtelet: Physics, Metaphysics, and the Case of Gravity." In *Early Modern Women on Metaphysics*, edited by Emily Thomas. Cambridge: Cambridge University Press, 2018, pp. 49–71.

Questions for Reflection

- We've surveyed several arguments about whether space could exist even if there were no bodies to occupy it. Do you think similar arguments could be made about *time*?
- Many of the arguments in this debate are based on the principle of sufficient reason. Do you think it's true that every fact must have a complete (or "sufficient") explanation?
- Du Châtelet proposed an account of how we acquire the idea of empty, absolute space. Do you agree with her proposal that it is an abstract idea?
- Du Châtelet holds that "The abstract cannot subsist without anything Concrete, that is to say without a real and determined Being from which we are abstracting." Do you agree? Are there other examples where this principle seems to apply?

12

The Nature of Causation
David Hume and Thomas Reid

Chapter Outline

12a. Hume on Our Idea of Causation	304
12b. Reid's Critique of Hume	317
Questions for Reflection	328

As we have seen already, the question of the nature of causation is one that interested many philosophers of the early modern period. In this chapter, we are going to consider one of the most influential accounts of causation of the eighteenth century that continues to have an impact today, namely, David Hume's theory as outlined in his *A Treatise of Human Nature*. We will see that Hume denies that we have either rational insight into, or empirical observation of, causation in the world; rather, our idea of necessary connections between events is derived from a habit of the mind upon observing regular patterns of occurrences in the world. However, this does not necessarily mean that we must reduce our idea of causation to that of mere regularity, as we shall see. In the second part of this chapter, we will consider the critique of Hume's account offered by Thomas Reid, who argues that the kind of "system of ideas" followed by Hume inevitably leads to unacceptable skeptical consequences. Instead, Reid proposes that our causal judgments are grounded in an original principle embedded in the natural constitution of our minds, which, in virtue of this status, is epistemically justified and does not require rational support.

12A. HUME ON OUR IDEA OF CAUSATION

> **David Hume: Brief Chronology**
> - 1711: Born in Edinburgh
> - c. 1722: Begins studies at the University of Edinburgh, initially considering a legal career
> - 1729: Decides to dedicate his life to philosophical and other academic studies
> - 1734: Moves briefly to Bristol to work for a merchant, but soon travels to France to continue his studies
> - 1739: Publication of the first volume of his most significant philosophical work, *A Treatise of Human Nature*
> - 1745: Refused an academic post at the University of Edinburgh due to his suspected atheism
> - 1752: Appointed as librarian of the Advocate's Library in Edinburgh, giving him the resources to write his *History of England*, for which he was best-known in his own lifetime
> - 1763: Returns to Paris as private secretary to the British ambassador, where he forged friendships with many prominent intellectuals, including Jean-Jacques Rousseau (with whom he would famously fall out)
> - 1776: Dies in Edinburgh
> - 1779: An important later work, *Dialogues Concerning Natural Religion*, is published posthumously

Since Hume's philosophical works were published in the mid-eighteenth century, much ink has been spilled over his notorious account of causation. In order to understand this account, it is first vital to consider the nature of his philosophical project, which he discusses in the Introduction to his first major work, *A Treatise of Human Nature*. Having despaired at the speculative nature of much of the philosophical systems of the past, and the apparent lack of progress in answering the perennial questions of philosophy, Hume seeks to find a new path to set the discipline on a more secure basis. His proposal is for a new "science of man," bringing the success found by the natural sciences in their experimental method to a study of human nature. Such an enterprise would spread beyond the narrow confines of epistemology and metaphysics: given that all intellectual pursuits are carried out by a human being, a greater understanding of the being that is undertaking this activity would help us comprehend wider moral and political matters too.

In formulating general principles of human nature, Hume sought a holistic view of how the human mind operates, in terms of how it generates its ideas through the interaction of our reason, sense perception, emotions, desires, and imagination. As an attempt, as Hume states, to "introduce the experimental Method of Reasoning INTO MORAL SUBJECTS," (T: title page)[1] he intends to use observations and experiments (on the model of the natural sciences) to discover general principles of the object of the study, in this case, the nature of human beings. One of Hume's interests, in Book I of the *Treatise*, is to consider how it is that we view events in the world as connected by chains of causal relations, rather than as a series of unconnected, random events, and are able to think about objects beyond our immediate senses and our memories (clearly quite an important facet of human psychology).

One perhaps initially surprising aspect of Hume's account is that he denies that we have any knowledge of events being causally connected: for example, though I might watch a white ball travel across a pool table, then apparently touch a red ball, followed by the red ball travelling across the table, I cannot *know* that the white ball caused the red ball to move. This seems like rather a strange thing to claim, for surely I know that events can cause others to occur (the lighted match causes the hay to set on fire, the push of the button causes the computer to turn on, the vibration of air molecules causes me to hear a sound, etc.).

Indeed, it has seemed to many philosophers that we can know that all occurrences must have a cause that brings it about. However, Hume denies that such a rule, in his words, "that *whatever begins to exist, must have a cause of existence*" (T I.III.III: 78), can be justified, either intuitively or demonstratively. Such a justification, however, would be the only way in which we could have knowledge of such a rule, bearing in mind that Hume uses the term "knowledge" in quite a specific and restricted sense. Hume thinks of knowledge as involving *certainty*, to the extent that we cannot even conceive of the opposite being true: as an example, we know with certainty that a triangle has three sides, and as an implication of that, we cannot conceive of a triangle as having four sides. An intuitive or demonstrative justification of the rule would be the only way in which we could achieve certainty concerning its universal application, so the lack of such a justification would entail a lack of knowledge. The following extract presents his argument for this view:

Extract 12.1. Hume, *A Treatise of Human Nature* (Book I, Part III, Section III "Why a cause is always necessary" — extract)

But here is an argument, which proves at once, that the foregoing proposition [*Whatever has a beginning has also a cause of existence*] is neither intuitively nor demonstratively certain. We can never demonstrate the necessity of a cause to every new existence, or new modification of existence, without showing at the same time the impossibility there is, that any thing can ever begin to exist without some productive principle; and where the latter proposition cannot be proved, we must despair of ever being able to prove the former. Now that the latter proposition is utterly incapable of a demonstrative proof, we may satisfy ourselves by considering, that as all distinct ideas are separable from each other, and as the ideas of cause and effect are evidently distinct, 'twill be easy for us to conceive any object to be non-existent this moment, and existent the next, without conjoining to it the distinct idea of a cause or productive principle. The separation, therefore, of the idea of a cause from that of a beginning of existence, is plainly possible for the imagination; and consequently the actual separation of these objects is so far possible, that it implies no contradiction nor absurdity; and is therefore incapable of being refuted by any reasoning from mere ideas; without which 'tis impossible to demonstrate the necessity of a cause.

[David Hume, *A Treatise of Human Nature* (Oxford: Clarendon Press, 1888). Some language has been modernized.]

Hume assumes that any intuitive or demonstrative justification of the causal rule would offer certainty, which could only be the case if it were inconceivable that something could begin to be without having a cause of its existence. However, Hume argues, such a thing is not inconceivable. Any occurrence can be thought of as taking place as a distinct idea, without any related idea concerning what caused it. Indeed, when we reflect upon events that are apparently causally linked, we can conceive of another state of affairs being the case: I can conceive of objects popping into existence without a cause, I can imagine the lighted match causing the hay to freeze, and the white ball causing the red ball to jump ten feet into the air, rather than travel across the table.

Nevertheless, though we cannot have knowledge *in the strict sense* concerning causal relations, such **matters of fact**[†] can be subject to proofs (see T I.III.XI: 124) on the basis of the patterns of events that we observe in our experience (what we might refer to in Humean terms as the "constant conjunction" of events). Though we cannot know that a matter of fact has taken place with the certainty that attaches to some mathematical proposition, such as "the sum of angles in a triangle add up to two right angles," degrees of evidence are available that can leave us without doubt concerning such matters, and this can perhaps stretch to our beliefs concerning causal relations between objects in the world. To investigate the matter of our trust in the causal rule further, leaving aside the desire to have knowledge of it in the strict sense, Hume states we need to look to our observation and experience.

Such a quest forms part of Hume's new "science of man," which holds that we can clear up some of the obscurity concerning ideas such as causation by considering their possible source in experience. So, where does our idea of causation come from? In attempting to answer this question, Hume relies upon his so-called "copy principle," which treats our simple ideas as copies of simple "impressions" or sensations (see T I.I.I: 4). The main consequence of this principle is that all the content of our ideas can be traced back to experiences. These impressions themselves can be put into two groups: first, impressions of *sensation*, which have their source in some unknown cause exterior to us, and second, impressions of *reflection*, which are those feelings occasioned when we reflect on ideas that we already have. If we have an idea, such as causation, which seems obscure to us, we can try to determine what impressions the idea is derived from and thereby clarify its content for us. When we consider our idea of causation, Hume argues, we see that it involves the idea of necessary connection: given that the cause occurred, the effect then *had* to occur, of necessity. Causally connected events do not just follow each other at random; rather, they produce each other in an ordered, unavoidable way. However, we cannot just stop there when considering causation, as we then have to consider the source of our idea of necessary connection.

In the following extract, we find Hume's account of the source of our idea of "necessary connection," one of the most notorious parts of his philosophy. Most significantly, Hume argues that our idea of necessary connection does not arise in a straightforward way from our observing (apparently) causally connected events in our experience:

Extract 12.2. Hume, *A Treatise of Human Nature* (Book I, Part III, Section XIV "Of the idea of necessary connexion" — extracts)

What is our idea of necessity, when we say that two objects are necessarily connected together. Upon this head I repeat what I have often had occasion to observe, that as we have no idea, that is not derived from an impression, we must find some impression, that gives rise to this idea of necessity, if we assert we have really such an idea. In order to this I consider, in what objects necessity is commonly supposed to lie; and finding that it is always ascribed to causes and effects, I turn my eye to two objects supposed to be placed in that relation; and examine them in all the situations, of which they are susceptible. I immediately perceive, that they are *contiguous* in time and place, and that the object we call cause *precedes* the other we call effect. In no one instance can I go any farther, nor is it possible for me to discover any third relation betwixt these objects. I therefore enlarge my view to comprehend several instances; where I find like objects always existing in like relations of contiguity and succession. At first sight this seems to serve but little to my purpose. The reflection on several instances only repeats the same objects; and therefore can never give rise to a new idea. But upon further enquiry I find, that the repetition is not in every particular the same, but produces a new impression, and by that means the idea, which I at present examine.

For after a frequent repetition, I find, that upon the appearance of one of the objects, the mind is *determined* by custom to consider its usual attendant, and to consider it in a stronger light upon account of its relation to the first object. 'Tis this impression, then, or *determination*, which affords me the idea of necessity.

-

Suppose two objects to be presented to us, of which the one is the cause and the other the effect; 'tis plain, that from the simple consideration of one, or both these objects we shall never perceive the tie, by which they are united, or be able certainly to pronounce, that there is a connexion betwixt them. 'Tis not, therefore, from any one instance, that we arrive at the idea of cause and effect, of a necessary connexion of power, of force, of energy, and of efficacy. Did we never see any but particular conjunctions of objects, entirely different from each other, we should never be able to form any such ideas.

But again; suppose we observe several instances, in which the same objects are always conjoined together, we immediately conceive a connexion betwixt them, and begin to draw an inference from one to another. This multiplicity of resembling instances, therefore, constitutes the very essence of power or connexion, and is the source, from which the idea of it arises. In order, then, to understand the idea of power, we must consider that multiplicity; nor do I ask more to give a solution of that difficulty, which has so long perplexed us. For thus I reason. The repetition of perfectly similar instances can never *alone* give rise to an original idea, different from what is to be found in any particular instance, as has been observed, and as evidently follows from our fundamental principle, *that all ideas are copied from impressions*. Since therefore the idea of power is a new original idea, not to be found in any one instance, and which yet arises from the repetition of several instances, it follows, that the repetition *alone* has not that effect, but must either *discover* or *produce* something new, which is the source of that idea. Did the repetition neither discover nor produce any thing new, our ideas might be multiplied by it, but would not be enlarged above what they are upon the observation of one single instance. Every enlargement, therefore, (such as the idea of power or connexion) which arises from the multiplicity of similar instances, is copied from some effects of the multiplicity, and will be perfectly understood by understanding these effects. Wherever we find any thing new to be discovered or produced by the repetition, there we must place the power, and must never look for it in any other object.

But 'tis evident, in the first place, that the repetition of like objects in like relations of succession and contiguity *discovers* nothing new in any one of them; since we can draw no inference from it, nor make it a subject either of our demonstrative or probable reasonings; as has been already proved[2]. Nay suppose we could draw an inference, it would be of no consequence in the present case; since no kind of reasoning can give rise to a new idea, such as this power is; but wherever we reason, we must antecedently be possessed of clear ideas, which may be the objects of our reasoning. The conception always precedes the understanding; and where the one is obscure, the other is uncertain; where the one fails, the other must fail also.

Secondly, 'Tis certain that this repetition of similar objects in similar situations *produces* nothing new either in these objects, or in any external body. For it will readily be allowed, that the several instances we have of the conjunction of resembling causes and effects are in themselves entirely independent, and that the communication of motion, which I see result at present from the shock of two billiard-balls, is totally distinct from that which I saw result from such an impulse a twelve-month ago. These impulses have no influence on each other. They are entirely divided by time and place; and the one might have existed and communicated motion, though the other never had been in being.

There is, then, nothing new either discovered or produced in any objects by their constant conjunction, and by the uninterrupted resemblance of their relations of succession and contiguity. But it is from this resemblance, that the ideas of necessity, of power, and of efficacy, are derived. These ideas, therefore, represent not any thing, that does or can belong to the objects, which are constantly conjoined. This is an argument, which, in every view we can examine it, will be found perfectly unanswerable. Similar instances are still the first source of our idea of power or necessity; at the same time that they have no influence by their similarity either on each other, or on any external object. We must therefore, turn ourselves to some other quarter to seek the origin of that idea.

Though the several resembling instances, which give rise to the idea of power, have no influence on each other, and can never produce any new quality *in the object*, which can be the model of that idea, yet the *observation* of this resemblance produces a new impression *in the mind*, which is its real model. For after we have observed the resemblance in a sufficient number of instances, we immediately feel a determination of the mind to pass from one object to its usual attendant, and to conceive it in a stronger light upon account of that relation. This determination is the only effect of the resemblance; and therefore must be the same with power or efficacy, whose idea is derived from the resemblance. The several instances of resembling conjunctions leads us into the notion of power and necessity. These instances are in themselves totally distinct from each other, and have no union but in the mind, which observes them, and collects their ideas. Necessity, then, is the effect of this observation, and is nothing but an internal impression of the mind, or a determination to carry our thoughts from one object to another. Without considering it in this view, we can never arrive at the most distant notion of it, or be able to attribute it either to external or internal objects, to spirit or body, to causes or effects.

The necessary connexion betwixt causes and effects is the foundation of our inference from one to the other. The foundation of our inference is the transition arising from the accustomed union. These are, therefore, the same.

The idea of necessity arises from some impression. There is no impression conveyed by our senses, which can give rise to that idea. It must, therefore, be derived from some internal impression, or impression of reflection. There is no internal impression, which has any relation to the present business, but that propensity, which custom produces, to pass from an object to the idea of its usual attendant. This therefore is the essence of necessity. Upon the whole, necessity is something, that exists in the mind, not in objects; nor is it possible for us ever to form the most distant idea of it, considered as a quality in bodies. Either we have no idea of necessity, or necessity is nothing but that determination of the thought to pass from causes to effects and from effects to causes, according to their experienced union.

Thus as the necessity, which makes two times two equal to four, or three angles of a triangle equal to two right ones, lies only in the act of the understanding, by which we consider and compare these ideas; in like manner the necessity or power, which unites causes and effects, lies in the determination of the mind to pass from one to the other. The efficacy or energy of causes is neither placed in the causes themselves, nor in the deity, nor in the concurrence of these two principles; but belongs entirely to the soul, which considers the union of two or more objects in all past instances. 'Tis here that the real power of causes is placed, along with their connexion and necessity.

-

As to what may be said, that the operations of nature are independent of our thought and reasoning, I allow it; and accordingly have observed, that objects bear to each other the relations of contiguity and succession; that like objects may be observed in several instances to have like relations; and that all this is independent of, and antecedent to the operations of the understanding. But if we go any farther, and ascribe a power or necessary connexion to these objects; this is what we can never observe in them, but must draw the idea of it from what we feel internally in contemplating them. And this I carry so far, that I am ready to convert my present reasoning into an instance of it, by a subtility [argument], which it will not be difficult to comprehend.

When any object is presented to us, it immediately conveys to the mind a lively idea of that object, which is usually found to attend it; and this determination of the mind forms the necessary connexion of these objects. But when we change the point of view, from the objects to the perceptions; in that case the impression is to be considered as the cause, and the lively idea as the effect; and their necessary connection is that new determination, which we feel to pass from the idea of the one to that of the other. The uniting principle among our internal perceptions is as unintelligible as that among external objects, and is not known to us any other way than through experience. Now the nature and effects of experience have been already sufficiently examined and explained. It never gives us any insight into the internal structure or operating principle of objects, but only accustoms the mind to pass from one to another.

[David Hume, *A Treatise of Human Nature* (Oxford: Clarendon Press, 1888). Some language has been modernized.]

To begin with, Hume seeks the source of our idea of necessary connection in our experience of events that are apparently causally linked, such as the billiard ball causing the other ball to travel across the table. Though this would seem like the obvious place to look for an impression of causal power, nevertheless Hume denies that this can be found here. When we see two supposedly linked events in our experience, we certainly see that they are "contiguous" (in other words, they are situated next to each other in time and space) and that the cause precedes the effect: indeed, Hume claims, this is what we see in all examples we could draw upon from our impressions of sensation. However, this is not an experience of a causal link, in which one event *necessitates* another. To show this, we can imagine two events that follow each other in the expected manner and yet are not in fact causally connected: suppose, for example, that the two balls on the table are being controlled remotely so that it only appears that one causes the other to move. The reason we cannot discern the difference between the genuine and fake causal scenarios is that we do not observe the necessitating aspect (or the causal power) of a causal relation, which would allow us to see that one event did indeed make the other happen. The epistemic situation is not improved by viewing repeated patterns of events supposedly necessitating each other, as all we ever see is contiguity and precedence.

Nevertheless, Hume argues, our observations of regular patterns of events do lead in an indirect manner to our idea of necessary connection. While we do not observe anything new through such repetition, a change takes place in us as we make these repeated observations, which gives rise to the impressions of reflection from which we gain our idea of necessary connection. After having repeatedly observed the patterns of events in nature, we begin to feel a sense of anticipation or expectation upon viewing events in the world with regard to what may follow them. If I see the white ball running toward the red ball on the table, my mind expects the red ball to be moved. This expectation or "determination," by which the mind immediately jumps from believing in the existence of the cause to expecting or inferring the existence of the effect, gives us the feeling of one event necessitating the other. In addition, it becomes more difficult for us to consider the events as possibly existing apart from each other, again reinforcing the idea of an inextricable connection between events. It is this impression of reflection that gives rise to our idea of necessary connection.

So, where does this leave us with regard to the legitimacy of our talk concerning causal relations in the world? If we do not get our idea of causation from a genuine experience of causal power, does that not entail that the idea is illegitimate or illusory in some sense? Does Hume think that we cannot talk about causal power in the world at all, and instead merely note that events seem to follow each other in regular patterns? Taking this anti-realist implication from Hume's account seems to be encouraged by the author himself, when he discusses two definitions of cause that he thinks we are left with. The first defines cause simply in terms of regular patterns of events: "an object precedent and contiguous to another, and where all the objects resembling the former are placed in like relations of precedency and contiguity to those objects, that resemble the latter" (T I.III.XIV: 170). The second defines cause in terms of the determination of the mind upon viewing regular patterns of events: "an object precedent and contiguous to another, and so united with it, that the idea of the one determines the mind to form the idea of the other, and the impression of the one to form a more lively idea of the other" (ibid.) In defining cause without any mention of a necessary connection between events in the world, Hume seems to have given up on maintaining a realist view regarding causal power.

The two definitions of cause that Hume offers may lead us to think that he denies that we can have any way of legitimately talking about the operation of causal power in the world: indeed, we may be forced to state that causation just is the bare "brute regularity" that we observe. However, things are perhaps not so clear-cut. Hume is clearly dissatisfied with these two definitions of cause, both being "drawn from objects foreign to the cause" (ibid.): in the first, a cause is defined in relation to other sets of events (and not its connection to the effect), and in the second, a cause is defined in terms of mental operations. Hume's point is that we do not have the rational resources to offer a direct definition of what a cause is, though this does not necessarily entail the sort of reductionist view that causation must be reduced to mere regularity. Arguably, Hume provides hints at the intellectual resources *we do have* in order to talk meaningfully about necessary connections between objects.

In a recent paper, the scholar Peter Kail[3] has argued that as far as Hume is concerned, the feeling of anticipation and determination of the mind, following repeated observations of the same patterns of behavior by objects in nature, gives us a "what it would be like" to have a direct grasp of the causal power that objects have. If we were to have such a direct grasp, we would be able to immediately infer the effect of any given event, having observed or anticipated the event taking place. As we have seen, once the habits of the mind are sufficiently ingrained, our mind has an immediate anticipation of the effect given the observation of the cause, which thus mimics to some extent what it would be like to have a genuine grasp of causal power. As Kail has put it, this provides us with a "reference fixer" for power that "tells us that power is *that which* would yield such and such consequences while giving us no conception of *what* that might be . . . Nevertheless, the formal specification of the [reference fixer for power] allows us to form thoughts precisely about that of which we can have no conception."[4] In other words, our feeling of anticipation and immediate inference can give us a sense of a necessary connection between events despite having no direct insight into its metaphysical nature.

Hume argues that, when we suppose that we have such a grasp of causal power, we in effect mistake the feeling of determination in the mind for a direct observation of a necessitated change between two external objects. As Hume puts it, the mind thereby "feels the necessity" (T II.III.I: 406) between objects, rather than observes or rationally infers it. Our attribution of causal power to objects is therefore a projection of the mind on to the world on the basis of the character of its own activity: as Hume states, "the mind has a great propensity to spread itself on external objects, and to conjoin with them any internal impressions, which they occasion, and which always make their appearance at the same time that these objects discover themselves to the senses" (T I.III.XIV: 167). Such a projection is something that the human mind naturally does and turns out to be a great boon insofar as it allows us some sort of indirect way of referring to causal relations in the world despite lacking a direct observation of causal power between objects and thus having no insight into the kind of causal principle that is in fact at work in the world.

So, what are Hume's conclusions regarding causation and our understanding of it? As stated at the beginning of the section, Hume denies that we have any knowledge *in the strict sense* of causal power or relations in the world. At best, we have an idea of necessary connection taken from our own mental operations, a feeling of anticipation based on the patterns of events we observe in nature. Given the indirect process by which we grasp something of causal power, we have no real insight into its nature and relatedly we cannot define it directly. As such, we have a "deficiency in our ideas" that leaves us "ignorant of the ultimate principle, which binds [cause and effect] together" (T I.IV.VII: 267). We may assume that there is some ultimate principle in the world that produces the regularity and patterns we see in the workings of nature, and we naturally do make that assumption, but such a principle is beyond the limits of our understanding. From the perspective of reason in the narrow sense, we are unacquainted with genuine causal power, though this does not mean that we cannot have a thought "of a kind" about it: our mind has a determination on observing patterns in nature that, in effect, mimics what it would be like to have a direct insight into causal power through our experience. As such, we are not entirely epistemically cut off from causal power in the world, though we are by no means as in touch with it as is often supposed by philosophers.

There is, of course, much that could be discussed on this topic, such as the nature of Hume's own self-professed skepticism and how he thinks philosophy should deal with the skeptical conclusions that some of his discussions lead to, but these would necessarily lead into a much broader examination of his philosophy than we can offer here. It is worth noting that the explanation of Hume's approach to causation offered here is just one interpretation among other possibilities that have textual backing. We have proposed in this section a kind of "skeptical realist" interpretation of Hume's account of causality, according to which Hume both assumes the existence of causal power in the world while, at the same time, significantly delimiting our cognitive grasp of it. There are other interpretations of Hume available in the literature: for example, a *reductivist* interpretation, according to which we cannot meaningfully talk about causal power in any way and are thus relegated to a view of nature ordered by brute regularity alone, and a *quasi-realist* interpretation, which construes Hume's talk of necessary connections alone in terms of the habits of the mind, without any attempt to offer a description of what in fact takes place in the world.[5] The situation is complicated by the fact that Hume revisited his account of causation later, in his *An Enquiry Concerning Human Understanding* (1748), and there may be significant differences between this later text and the *Treatise*. The textual evidence is mixed, and so there is no doubt that this account will be discussed by scholars for many years to come.

Key Points

- According to Hume, we do not have any knowledge of events being causally connected, nor do we have any insight into the metaphysical nature of causal power.
- In order to gain a greater understanding of our idea of causation, Hume seeks to trace its content back to immediate sensations or impressions.
- Our idea of events being "necessarily connected" in causal relations is traceable to impressions of reflection that are grounded in our habituated anticipation of the effect given our observation of the cause.
- The implications of Hume's account for the metaphysical nature of causation is unclear, though perhaps the only way we can speak of causation is merely in terms of "brute regularity."

Suggested Further Reading

Beebee, Helen. *Hume on Causation*, ch. 4. London: Routledge, 2006.
Broackes, Justin. "Did Hume Hold a Regularity Theory of Causation?" *British Journal for the History of Philosophy* 1, no. 1 (1993): 99–114.
Garrett, Don. "Hume." In *The Oxford Handbook of Causation*, edited by Helen Beebee, Christopher Hitchcock and Peter Menzies, 87–99. Oxford: Oxford University Press, 2009.
Kail, P. J. E. "How to Understand Hume's Realism." In *The New Hume Debate*, rev. ed., edited by Rupert Read and Kenneth A. Richman, 253–69. London: Routledge, 2007.
Wright, John P. *Hume's A Treatise of Human Nature: An Introduction*, ch. 3. Cambridge: Cambridge University Press, 2009.

12B. REID'S CRITIQUE OF HUME

Thomas Reid: Brief Chronology

- 1710: Born in Strachan, Aberdeenshire
- 1723: Begins studies at Marischal College, Aberdeen
- 1737: Becomes minister in the Church of Scotland, following travels in England
- 1751: Appointed lecturer at King's College, Aberdeen
- 1764: Publishes major philosophical work, *Inquiry into the Human Mind on the Principles of Common Sense*, and takes the Chair of Moral Philosophy at the Old College, Glasgow
- 1780s: Retires from teaching and publishes two books based on his lectures, *Essays on the Intellectual Powers* and *Essays on the Active Powers*
- 1796: Dies in Glasgow

Thomas Reid was exactly one year older than Hume (to the day), but his work can be viewed as formed in some important ways as a response to the philosophy of his younger compatriot, as well as other figures of the early modern period we have considered, such as Descartes, Locke, and Berkeley. Reid sees all these thinkers, despite their philosophical differences, as committing the same fundamental error, which inevitably leads to some form of unacceptable skepticism. This error is the "ideal system," which Reid targets in his first major philosophical work, the *Inquiry*.

One major claim of the ideal system is with regard to the nature of our mental functions: "that every object of thought must be an impression, or an idea, that is, a faint copy of some preceding impression."[6] Thinking takes place, according to this model, by manipulating these ideas in various ways: "They acknowledge that nature has given us various simple ideas . . . They acknowledge likewise a natural power by which ideas are compounded, disjoined, associated, compared . . . From these principles they attempt to explain the phenomena of the human understanding."[7] In short, Reid objects to the view that posits mental acts as involving a mind manipulating an object—an impression or an idea—that it is in direct contact with. For one thing, Reid argues, if we can only think of such impressions or ideas, that means that we are unable to think of a mind itself, a consequence that he was unwilling to accept.

So, what does thinking involve, according to Reid? To begin with, in the case of perception, we directly perceive an external object, not an impression or idea. The mind *senses* (rather than *has a sensation*) and actively grasps that it is perceiving an external object through an act of "conception," which takes place according to certain innate principles embedded naturally in the constitution of our mind, accompanied by a belief in the existence of what is being sensed. In undertaking these acts of conception and belief, the mind responds to "natural signs" in our sensations that we are hardwired to detect and on that basis generates trustworthy knowledge of the external world (and indeed the same model applies to our knowledge of our own mental functions too). Reid argues that we are generally entitled to trust the products of our mental acts and can therefore safely refute the skeptic: "All reasoning must be from first principles; and for first principles no other reason can be given but this, that, by the constitution of our nature, we are under a necessity of assenting to them. Such principles are parts of our constitution, no less than the power of thinking: reason can neither make nor destroy them; nor can it do anything without them."[8] Against the skeptic, Reid states both that we should treat all of our faculties as equally trustworthy (thus, we cannot use our reason to overturn the evidence of our senses, as those who doubt the existence of the external world would do) and that it is unavoidable for us to do anything other than live by these original beliefs in such things as the existence of external objects and of the causal relations that bind them.

This brings us to our main text from Reid, taken from his later work, *Essays on the Intellectual Powers of Man*. Here, Reid is discussing the principle of causation as one of the set of first principles that we naturally follow when we make judgments about what is occurring in the world. Reid describes these first principles in this way: they are "propositions which are no sooner understood than they are believed. The judgment follows the apprehension of them necessarily, and both are equally the work of nature, and the result of our original powers. There is no searching for evidence, no weighing of arguments; the proposition is not deduced or inferred from another; it has the light of truth in itself."[9] By having the "light of truth" in themselves, Reid means that they are self-evident to us. Specifically, in the case of our general belief in causation, we are naturally constituted to believe, and it is self-evident to us, that all events by necessity are causally linked:

Extract 12.3. Reid, *Essays on the Intellectual Powers of Man* (VI.vi: pp. 455–7)

The second metaphysical principle I mention is—*That whatever begins to exist, must have a cause which produced it.*

Philosophy is indebted to Mr. Hume in this respect among others, that, by calling in question many of the first principles of human knowledge, he hath put speculative men upon inquiring more carefully than was done before into the nature of the evidence upon which they rest. Truth can never suffer by a fair inquiry; it can bear to be seen naked and in the fullest light; and the strictest examination will always turn out in the issue to its advantage. I believe Mr. Hume was the first who ever called in question whether things that begin to exist must have a cause.

With regard to this point, we must hold one of these three things, either that it is an opinion for which we have no evidence, and which men have foolishly taken up without ground; or, *secondly*, That it is capable of direct proof by argument; or, *thirdly*, That it is self-evident, and needs no proof, but ought to be received as an axiom, which cannot, by reasonable men, be called in question.

The first of these suppositions would put an end to all philosophy, to all religion, to all reasoning that would carry us beyond the objects of sense, and to all prudence in the conduct of life.

As to the second supposition, that this principle may be proved by direct reasoning. I am afraid we shall find the proof extremely difficult, if not altogether impossible.

I know only of three or four arguments that have been urged by philosophers, in the way of abstract reasoning, to prove that things which begin to exist must have a cause.

One is offered by Mr. Hobbes, another by Dr. Samuel Clarke, another by Mr. Locke. Mr. Hume, in his "Treatise of Human Nature," has examined them all; and, in my opinion, has shewn that they take for granted the thing to be proved; a kind of false reasoning, which men are very apt to fall into when they attempt to prove what is self-evident.

It has been thought, that, although this principle does not admit of proof from abstract reasoning, it may be proved from experience, and may be justly drawn by induction, from instances that fall within our observation.

I conceive this method of proof will leave us in great uncertainty, for these three reasons:

1st, Because the proposition to be proved is not a contingent but a *necessary* proposition. It is not that things which begin to exist commonly have a cause, or even that they always in fact have a cause; but that they must have a cause, and cannot begin to exist without a cause.

Propositions of this kind, from their nature, are incapable of proof by induction. Experience informs us only of what *is* or *has been*, not of what *must be*; and the conclusion must be of the same nature with the premises.

For this reason, no mathematical proposition can be proved by induction. Though it should be found by experience in a thousand cases, that the area of a plane triangle is equal to the rectangle under the altitude and half the base, this would not prove that it must be so in all cases, and cannot be otherwise; which is what the mathematician affirms.

In like manner, though we had the most ample experimental proof that things which have begun to exist had a cause, this would not prove that they must have a cause. Experience may show us what is the established course of nature, but can never show what connections of things are in their nature necessary.

2dly, General maxims, grounded on experience, have only a degree of probability proportioned to the extent of our experience, and ought always to be understood so as to leave room for exceptions, if future experience shall discover any such.

The law of gravitation has as full a proof from experience and induction as any principle can be supposed to have. Yet, if any philosopher should, by clear experiment, show that there is a kind of matter in some bodies which does not gravitate, the law of gravitation ought to be limited by that exception.

Now, it is evident that men have never considered the principle of the necessity of causes, as a truth of this kind which may admit of limitation or exception; and therefore it has not been received upon this kind of evidence.

3dly, I do not see that experience could satisfy us that every change in nature actually has a cause.

In the far greatest part of the changes in nature that fall within our observation, the causes are unknown; and, therefore, from experience, we cannot know whether they have causes or not.

Causation is not an object of sense. The only experience we can have of it, is in the consciousness we have of exerting some power in ordering our thoughts and actions. But this experience is surely too narrow a foundation for a general conclusion, that all things that have had or shall have a beginning, must have a cause.

For these reasons, this principle cannot be drawn from experience, any more than from abstract reasoning.

The *third* supposition is—That it is to be admitted as a first or self-evident principle. Two reasons may be urged for this.

1. The universal consent of mankind, not of philosophers only, but of the rude and unlearned vulgar. Mr. Hume, as far as I know, was the first that ever expressed any doubt of this principle. And when we consider that he has rejected every principle of human knowledge, excepting that of consciousness, and has not even spared the axioms of mathematics, his authority is of small weight.

Indeed, with regard to first principles, there is no reason why the opinion of a philosopher should have more authority than that of another man of common sense, who has been accustomed to judge in such cases. The illiterate vulgar are competent judges; and the philosopher has no prerogative in matters of this kind; but he is more liable than they to be misled by a favourite system, especially if it is his own.

Setting aside the authority of Mr. Hume, what has philosophy been employed in since men first began to philosophise, but in the investigation of the causes of things? This it has always professed, when we trace it to its cradle. It never entered into any man's thought, before the philosopher we have mentioned, to put the previous question, whether things have a cause or not? Had it been thought possible that they might not, it may be presumed that, in the variety of absurd and contradictory causes assigned, some one would have had recourse to this hypothesis.

They could conceive the world to arise from an egg, from a struggle between love and strife, between moisture and drought, between heat and cold; but they never supposed that it had no cause. We know not any atheistic sect that ever had recourse to this topic, though by it, they might have evaded every argument that could be brought against them, and answered all objections to their system.

But rather than adopt such an absurdity, they contrived some imaginary cause—such as chance, a concourse of atoms, or necessity—as the cause of the universe.

The account which philosophers have given of particular phenomena, as well as of the universe in general, proceed upon the same principle. That every phenomenon must have a cause, was always taken for granted. *Nil turpius physico*, says Cicero, *quam fieri sine causa quicquam dicere* [Nothing is more repulsive to science than to say that anything happens without a cause][10]. Though an Academic [skeptic], he was dogmatical in this. And Plato, the father of the Academy, was no less so . . . "it is impossible that anything should have its origin without a cause"[11]— TIMAEUS.

I believe Mr. Hume was the first who ever held the contrary. This, indeed, he avows, and assumes the honour of the discovery. "It is," says he, "a maxim in philosophy, that whatever begins to exist, must have a cause of existence. This is commonly taken from granted in all reasonings, without any proof given or demanded. It is supposed to be founded on intuition, and to be one of those maxims which, though they may be denied with the lips, it is impossible for men in their hearts really to doubt of. But, if we examine this maxim by the idea of knowledge above explained, we shall discover in it no mark of such intuitive certainty"[12]. The meaning of this seems to be, that it did not suit with his theory of intuitive certainty, and, therefore, he excludes it from that privilege.

The vulgar adhere to this maxim as firmly and universally as the philosophers. Their superstitions have the same origin as the systems of philosophers—to wit, a desire to know the causes of things. *Felix qui potuit rerum cognoscere causas* [Happy are those who can learn the causes of things], is the universal sense of men; but to say that anything can happen without a cause, shocks the common sense of a savage.

This universal belief of mankind is easily accounted for, if we allow that the necessity of a cause of every event is obvious to the rational powers of a man. But it is impossible to account for it otherwise. It cannot be ascribed to education, to systems of philosophy, or to priestcraft. One would think that a philosopher who takes it to be a general delusion or prejudice, would endeavour to show from what causes in human nature such a general error may take its rise. But I forget that Mr. Hume might answer upon his own principles, that since things may happen without a cause- this error and delusion of men may be universal without any cause.

2. A second reason why I conceive this to be a first principle, is, That mankind not only assent to it in speculation, but that the practice of life is grounded upon it in the most important matters, even in cases where experience leaves us doubtful; and it is impossible to act with common prudence if we set it aside . . .

Suppose a man's house to be broke open, his money and jewels taken away. Such things have happened times innumerable without any apparent cause; and were he only to reason from experience in such a case, how must he behave? He must put in one scale the instances wherein a cause was found of such an event, and in the other scale the instances where no cause was found, and the preponderant scale must determine whether it be most probable that there was a cause of this event, or that there was none. Would any man of common understanding have recourse to such an expedient to direct his judgement?

Suppose a man to be found dead on the highway, his skull fractured, his body pierced with deadly wounds, his watch and money carried off. The coroner's jury sits upon the body; and the question is put, What was the cause of this man's death?—was it accident, or *felo de se* [suicide], or murder by persons unknown? Let us suppose an adept in Mr. Hume's philosophy to make one of the jury, and that he insists upon the previous question, whether there was any cause of the event, and whether it happened without a cause.

Surely, upon Mr. Hume's principles, a great deal might be said upon this point; and, if the matter is to be determined by past experience, it is dubious on which side the weight of argument might stand. But we may venture to say, that, if Mr. Hume had been of such a jury, he would have laid aside his philosophical principles, and acted according to the dictates of common prudence . . .

The arguments which Mr. Hume offers to prove that this is not a self-evident principle, are three. *First*, That all certainty arises from a comparison of ideas, and a discovery of their unalterable relations, none of which relations imply this proposition, That whatever has a beginning must have a cause of existence. This theory of certainty has been examined before [earlier in the extract, where Reid argues for a kind of natural certainty in causation based on a "universal belief of mankind"].

The *second* argument is, That whatever we can conceive is possible. This likewise has been examined [see below for details concerning Reid's argument (in an earlier part of the text, not extracted here) that we can conceive the impossible, and so the fact that I can conceive of things not following regular causal patterns does not imply that the causal principle cannot be self-evident].

The *third* argument is, That what we call a cause, is only something antecedent to, and always conjoined with, the effect. This is also one of Mr. Hume's peculiar doctrines, which we may have occasion to consider afterwards. It is sufficient here to observe, that we may learn from it that night is the cause of day, and day the cause of night[13]: for no two things have more constantly followed each other since the beginning of the world.

[From *Essays on the Intellectual Powers of Man* (Edinburgh: Machlachlan and Stewart, 1853). Some language has been modernized.]

Before we proceed to consider this passage in detail, it is worth noting to begin with that philosophers often misinterpret each other. Sometimes it is deliberate (if they wish to paint their opponent in an unfairly bad light), but mostly it is unintended. It is important to note when misinterpretation has occurred, for whatever reason, not only so that we are not misled ourselves, but also so we can understand what the philosopher in question thinks they are reacting to when they are proposing their own views. Arguably in this case, Reid has misread Hume, and we will conclude this chapter with some reflections on how the two philosophers might have been closer than either realized. So, we should not take this passage as a particularly convincing example of Hume scholarship (as we saw earlier, Hume is interested in the question of the source of our belief in causation, rather than seeking to "question whether things that begin to exist must have a cause"), but nevertheless it is revealing about what Reid thought he was up against and how he sought to establish his own theory of causation.

One important aim that Reid has in this passage (if we look beyond the barbs directed at Hume) is to show that our idea or conception of causation meets the criteria he suggests for an innate principle of the mind that can *and should be* generally trusted with regard to capturing the truth of things. In his earlier *Inquiry*, Reid states this regarding the origin of our idea of the primary quality of hardness: "Is it self-evident, from comparing the ideas, that such a sensation could not be felt, unless such a quality of bodies existed? No. Can it be proved by probable or certain arguments? No, it cannot. Have we got this belief then by tradition, by education, or by experience? No, it is not got in any of these ways. Shall we then throw off this belief, as having no foundation in reason? Alas! it is not in our power; it triumphs over reason, and laughs at all the arguments of a philosopher."[14] Given that our conception of hardness could not come from these sources (or at least, Reid thinks he has shown this), then the only way of avoiding a skeptical conclusion is to follow his account, that our sensation acts as a natural sign for us of hardness, on the suggestion of which the mind provides a conception of, and belief in, the existence of that hardness (as a result of the original principles of its constitution).

In the previous passage, Reid similarly goes through an argument of elimination, stating that the causal principle cannot come from various possible epistemic sources, and thus must be a self-evident, innate first principle of the operations of our mind. It cannot be mere supposition without any ground, Reid argues, on the basis that it would leave vast swathes of our beliefs, indeed anything regarding that which lies beyond what we currently perceive, as entirely without any epistemic standing. So, can we draw the principle from some kind of reasoning, either on the basis of abstract ideas or our experience? Reid takes Hume to have shown that all attempts to ground the causal principle through deduction ends up in circularity (i.e. assuming the truth of the conclusion in the premises, which does not prove anything). The text implicitly refers to Book I, Part III, Section III of Hume's *Treatise*, where Hume goes through a series of arguments (including by Hobbes, Locke, and Clarke) that attempt to rationally deduce the conclusion that everything that begins to exist must have a cause of existence. All these arguments, Hume states, assume a general **causal principle**[†], and so do not prove anything: for example, Clarke's argument (as Hume has it) states that an object could not come into existence without a cause because otherwise it would have to produce itself, and contradictorily exist before it existed. Hume rightly points out that this assumes that the object would have *caused itself* to come into existence, which is exactly the point at issue, and argues that other attempts to rationally prove the causal principle make similar errors (see T I.III.III: 80f.).

If we cannot prove the causal principle through rational deduction, then, can we show it through our experience? If by our observation all things that begin to exist have a cause of their existence, this could perhaps form the basis of a strong intuitive demonstration of the causal principle. Against this attempt to ground the causal principle empirically, Reid makes some related, Hume-inspired points. First, a finite number of observations (which is all that experience could furnish us with) could never establish a principle that we take to be necessary and without exception. Our experience shows us what is the case, but not what *must* be the case. Second, we do not observe many of the causes of the things we come across in our experience. If I am walking across a field, and I find a mobile phone on the ground, I will assume that someone left it there, but my experience does not in fact tell me that anything caused it to be there (rather than just popping into existence uncaused). Given that we often experience things as occurring without experiencing their cause, perhaps our experience does not in fact furnish that strong an intuitive demonstration of the causal principle.

As a result, Reid concludes, if we are to have an epistemically trustworthy principle of causation, we have to take it to be a first principle of the mind. Reid takes general agreement in the principle of causation across humankind (apart from a few misguided philosophers) as striking evidence for its status as a self-evident, trustworthy first principle. With regard to judging whether a principle does indeed have this standing, Reid states that we have to look at what is generally agreed across different times and places: "The learned and the unlearned, the philosopher and the day-labourer, are upon a level, and will pass the same judgement, when they are not misled by some bias ... [In] matters of common sense, the few must yield to the many."[15] The general assent behind the principle of causation (which cannot be attributed to education or any other sort of social ground) and the manner in which it is a natural belief for us is shown by the way in which it is assumed in everyday life: so, following Reid's example, if we returned to our house and found some of our possessions missing, we would naturally assume that there would be some cause underlying this (such as the objects being taken by a thief), rather than there being no cause for this whatsoever (perhaps the possessions just popped out of existence uncaused).

Our belief in causation is therefore just part of "common sense": it is a belief that perhaps cannot be justified through rational argumentation, but, as Reid states, does not in fact require such an argument for us to be justified in relying upon it in our judgments regarding the world. The philosopher does not have any special epistemic standing with regard to determining the authority of the causal principle for us. The general understanding of those who have not engaged in philosophical reasoning (who Reid refers to as the "vulgar") has sufficient authority in itself, and this quite clearly shows the general trustworthiness of the causal principle.

The previous passage concludes with Reid briefly considering some of Hume's arguments against considering the causal principle as a self-evident, first principle of the mind. Working backward, Reid construes a Humean "constant conjunction" analysis of causation, based on the mere observation of patterns of events in nature, as undermining the status of the causal principle as self-evident. Having to base our understanding of causation on the basis of an accumulation of observations over time would show that it cannot be self-evident to us how causal relations operate in the world. In response to this, Reid argues that a mere "constant conjunction" analysis of causation would be insufficient to capture what we mean when we talk of things being causally connected, as mere observation of patterns of events (such as night following day) clearly does not show that one causes the other in the widely accepted sense. Thus, our understanding of causation cannot be based on a mere accumulation of observations of patterns in nature.

The second Humean argument is that we can conceive of events as not following generally understood causal patterns (e.g., I can imagine the red ball floating into the air after being struck by the white ball, instead of the usual pattern of travelling across the table), and thus we must accept that it is possible that events not follow each other in line with the causal principle. Thus, the causal principle cannot be self-evident. Elsewhere in this text (in Essay IV, Chapter III), Reid had already offered a critique of any reasoning that uses what can be conceived as a test for what we take to be possible. As one of a number of arguments he offers, Reid argues that conceiving a proposition to be necessarily true involves conceiving a contradictory proposition as being necessarily false: "a man who believes that two and three necessarily make five, must believe it to be impossible that two and three should not make five. He conceives both propositions when he believes one. Every proposition carries its contradictory in its bosom, and both are conceived at the same time."[16] Our ability to conceive something does not show that it is possible, and we in fact need to be able to conceive the impossible in order to think of something as necessarily being the case. Thus, Reid argues that, the fact that I can conceive of things not following regular causal patterns does not imply that the causal principle cannot be self-evident. The claim that we can conceive the impossible is perhaps a controversial one and one that may be worth further consideration.

Finally, Reid refers back to his argument regarding the universal assent by the "vulgar" to the causal principle to show that there must be natural certainty in our beliefs regarding causal relations, in contradiction to Hume's claim that our causal beliefs cannot be based on mere consideration of a priori relations of ideas that would be, in principle, open to all. The question of natural beliefs, though, brings us back to the suggestion raised earlier that Reid and Hume might have been rather closer than the former makes out in the passage from the *Essays* earlier. As has been pointed out by scholars such as Copleston[17] and Loeb,[18] both Hume and Reid base their accounts of causation on a natural belief or instinct that is justified in its use apart from any rational argumentation. They both emphasize that we share our customs and habits, including in our causal inferences, not only with the rest of humankind, but even with the more intelligent animals, and given that the latter do not have rational faculties, they must be based on something other than reason. Nevertheless, our beliefs based on custom or instinct should still have significant epistemic standing for us. For his part, Reid seems to have overlooked this more constructive aspect of Hume's philosophy, instead following a more skeptical reading than is generally warranted by the text. As mentioned earlier, it is hardly unusual for philosophers to misread each other, or indeed to focus on what distinguishes them, rather than what is shared. Any potential overlap with Hume should also not obscure the substantial and original contribution that Reid makes to the history of philosophy in his own right, which is still often overlooked relative to other more traditionally canonical figures.

Key Points

- Reid rejects the "system of ideas" followed by Hume and others that posits an impression or ideas as the object of our thinking.
- Thinking is based on the mind being active in various ways, rather than taking place on the basis of the manipulation of ideas.
- Judgments that events are causally connected are based on one of a set of original principles that are natural to the constitution of our mind, by which we both conceive of and believe in the existence of things.
- These natural principles are epistemically justified in and of themselves, without any requirement for rational argumentation or demonstration.

Suggested Further Reading

Greco, John. "Reid's Reply to the Sceptic." In *The Cambridge Companion to Thomas Reid*, edited by Terence Cuneo and Rene van Woudenberg, 134–55. Cambridge: Cambridge University Press, 2004.

Lehrer, Keith. *Thomas Reid*, chs. 2 and 9. London: Routledge, 1989.

Loeb, Louis E. "The Naturalisms of Hume and Reid." *Proceedings and Addresses of the American Philosophical Association* 81, no. 2 (2007): 65–92.

Van Cleve, James. *Problems from Reid*, chs. 11 and 12. New York: Oxford University Press, 2015.

Wolterstorff, Nicholas. *Thomas Reid and the Story of Epistemology*, chs. 2 and 9. Cambridge: Cambridge University Press, 2001.

Questions for Reflection

- How do we acquire the idea of causation?
- Do we directly perceive objects, or do we only directly perceive ideas or mental representations?
- Are there original principles innate to our nature by which we judge the truth of things?
- Can we rely upon "common sense" to solve philosophical problems?

13

A Transcendental Approach
Mary Shepherd and Immanuel Kant

Chapter Outline

13a.	Kant on Appearance and Reality	330
13b.	Shepherd on Reason and Causation	344
	Questions for Reflection	356

As we have seen already in the case of Thomas Reid, Hume's notorious empiricist account of causation provoked numerous reactions from different philosophers in the following decades. In this chapter, we will consider two philosophers who, in addition to Reid, sought to answer Hume and address the possible skeptical effects of his work: Immanuel Kant and Mary Shepherd. As we will see, both Kant and Shepherd sought to provide a rational justification for our causal beliefs, against Hume's account that based them on non-rational custom or habit. However, whether either of them can truly overcome the specter of Hume's skepticism is open for debate.

13A. KANT ON APPEARANCE AND REALITY

> **Immanuel Kant: Brief Chronology**
> - 1724: Born in Königsberg, East Prussia (now part of Russia, called Kaliningrad), to a family of modest means
> - 1740: Becomes a student at the University of Königsberg, where he studies a wide range of subjects, including philosophy and the natural sciences
> - 1755: Begins teaching at the university and publishes his first major work, *Universal Natural History and Theory of the Heavens*
> - 1770: Appointed Professor of Logic and Metaphysics at Königsberg, begins preparatory work on Critical Philosophy
> - 1781: Publishes *Critique of Pure Reason*, inaugurating a series of "Critical" works, including *Groundwork of the Metaphysics of Morals* (1785) and *Critique of the Power of Judgement* (1790), that would revolutionize philosophy in a number of areas
> - 1794: Forbidden to write or speak on the subject of religious matters by the Prussian authorities, due to controversial work *Religion within the Bounds of Mere Reason*
> - 1804: Dies in Königsberg, leaving behind notes that would be later published in the 1930s as *Opus Postumum*

Immanuel Kant was greatly disturbed by the skeptical conclusions of Hume's philosophy. In the introduction to his 1783 work, *Prolegomena to Any Future Metaphysics*, when reflecting on how he had come to formulate the philosophy explored in his later works,[1] he writes that the work of David Hume "was the very thing which many years ago first interrupted my dogmatic slumber and gave my investigations in the field of speculative philosophy a quite new direction."[2] Much ink has been spilled on this comment by Kant, with regard to precisely what it is that he might have abandoned from his earlier work in response to Hume, and how his reaction to Hume went on to shape his later philosophy. Certainly, reading Hume seems to have given Kant a greater determination to find a sound basis for our knowledge of principles that seem fundamental to the way in which the world works, such as the principle that every event has a cause.

In order to understand Kant's strategy regarding the avoidance of these skeptical worries, we need to consider his key notion of synthetic *a priori* judgments. Take the principle "Every bachelor must be male." For Kant, this would be an example of an **analytic**†, rather than a **synthetic**†, judgment.³ The reason for this is that being male is part of the concept of being a bachelor, so it is an example of a judgment that is true in virtue of what is contained within a particular concept. If you analyze or break down the concept of "being a bachelor," you see that it necessarily includes the notion of "being male," without having to consider anything beyond that to grasp the truth of your judgment. While we may need experience to give us concepts such as "being male" or "being a bachelor," our recognition that "Every bachelor must be male" is true does not depend on our experience, but merely upon what is rationally implied by the concepts involved. We can think of the distinction between analytic and synthetic judgments as one centered on semantics: in other words, the distinction is centered on the question of what our concepts or particular terms mean. It is the meaning of "bachelor" and other constituent concepts that makes the principle "Every bachelor must be male" true. On the other hand, the concept "having white hair" is not part of the concept of "cat," so the judgment "This cat has white hair" is a synthetic judgment, one that adds extra content beyond what is already contained in the primary concept we are working with.

Where does the **causal principle**†, "Every event must have a cause," fit into this distinction? At first glance, you might think that this would be an analytic judgment, insofar as it seems that, necessarily, things happen only because they have been caused. As we saw in the previous chapter, this was a claim that Hume rejected: we can conceive of events that confound our expectations regarding causal patterns in nature—including objects popping into existence without a cause—and this would suggest that it is *not* included in the concept of an event that it must have a cause. For his part, Kant argues that the causal principle is synthetic:

> Let us take, for example, the proposition, "everything that happens has a cause." In the concept of something that happens, I indeed think an existence which lies before it in a certain time, and from this I can derive analytic judgements. But the concept of a cause lies quite outside of the concept of something that happens, and indicates something entirely different from it, and is consequently not contained in that concept. (A9/B13)⁴

The causal principle must be a synthetic one, on the grounds that it is not part of the concept of "being an event" that it is an effect of something.

Like Hume, Kant was also interested in the reasons we have for holding our beliefs, including questions regarding what evidence we hold for particular beliefs and where that evidence ultimately derives from. The distinction between analytic and synthetic is about meaning, which does not necessarily tell us anything about the source of our beliefs. To investigate this question of the evidential basis of our beliefs further, Kant develops the epistemic distinction between **a priori**† and **a posteriori**† justification. *A posteriori* knowledge derives its justification from our experience of particular things (so, I am justified in judging that "The cat is sat on the mat," by observing through my vision that that appears to be the case), while *a priori* knowledge does not derive its justification in such a way. As already mentioned, though, our *a priori* knowledge is not necessarily entirely separate from our experience in the way it is generated. Take, for example, the statement that "All bachelors are male." Experience will be required to *understand* what each of the words contained in that statement means, but it can be *justified* apart from my experience: once I know that being a bachelor implies being male, I do not have to go around the world checking whether all bachelors are indeed male. Further, Kant singles out the causal principle as an example of an "impure" proposition known *a priori*, one that is justified apart from our experience, but that is only possible for us to have on the basis of our experience (which originally gives us the concept of "change" or "alteration": see B2). The *a priori*/*a posteriori* distinction is based on the question of *what gives us good reason* to believe what we believe. It is possible for us to have knowledge that ultimately relies on experience for its constituent ideas, but the *justification* for believing the proposition in question does not rest on that basis.

So, what does justify our *a priori* knowledge? You might assume that the analytic/synthetic and *a priori*/*a posteriori* distinctions map onto each other neatly, namely, that all analytic judgments are known *a priori* and all synthetic judgments known *a posteriori*. If we were to make that assumption, then the question of how *a priori* knowledge is justified would seem to be straightforward: through a process of internal reflection, we discover that the concepts we have conceptually contain other ideas, and we can make true judgments on that basis (e.g., "Every bachelor must be male"). Our reason for such a belief does not rest on our experience but on the basis of this process of analysis, and as such does not count as *a posteriori* knowledge. However, this clearly cannot be the whole story for

Kant. As we have seen already, Kant believes that the causal principle is both synthetic and yet known *a priori*. Indeed, the postulation of synthetic *a priori* judgments is often taken as one of Kant's great philosophical innovations. That leaves us with the question, though, of how we could have such knowledge: in other words, how are synthetic *a priori* judgments possible?

For Kant, there is a body of knowledge that is justified apart from our experience, and yet can tell us something substantive about the world that we experience (e.g., "everything that happens has a cause"). What epistemically grounds these judgments? Kant's argument is that through an investigation or "critique" of reason, we can discover that the foundations of these principles lie within ourselves, or more specifically, in our "mode of cognition of objects" (A11/B25). The way in which we experience the world is filtered through our own cognitive processes and the manner in which we thereby shape the way in which the world appears to us is expressible in judgments that are both synthetic (going beyond mere concepts by telling us something about the fundamental nature of the world, albeit only in the way it appears to us) and *a priori* (by being grounded in the way our reason processes sensory data prior to our experience of it). While we do get raw sensory data through what Kant calls our "sensibility" regarding the world as it is apart from us, we are unable to make sense of it without imposing our own structure upon it, through our *intuition* (according to Kant, the faculty through which we are able to directly apprehend objects) and *understanding* (the faculty by which we unify our representations into the coherent, understandable world that we experience). Another way of putting this is that our mind constructs the world of our experience, on the basis of the information provided by the senses and an underlying architecture that has been imposed by us on that picture of the world. As a result, our knowledge of the world is shaped by the mental filter that our experience necessarily flows through, in order to make sense of things: Kant states that we "know nothing more than our mode of perceiving [objects], which is peculiar to us, and which, though not of necessity pertaining to every animated being, is to the whole human race" (A42/B59). By reflecting upon this structure that we impose on our experience of the world, though, we can come to discover a body of knowledge that is *a priori* (justified apart from our experience) and yet synthetic, in that it tells us something substantive about the way *the world must be*, in order for it to be experienceable at all, beyond what we can discover through mere analysis of concepts.

This *a priori* structure that we impose on the world, Kant argues, goes down to the very basic constituents of how the world appears to us. Indeed, space and time are both part of this structure through which we intuit and understand the world (Kant labels them the "pure forms" of our intuition, which "appertain absolutely and necessarily to our sensibility" (A42/B60)). The same goes for causation too, which is one of the rules or categories (the "conditions of thinking in a possible experience" (A111)) by which we construct an experienceable world for us (in the case of causal relations, a world that follows patterns over time that we can make sense of). In this way, causation becomes the rule of "the succession of the manifold" of our experience (A144/B183). Indeed, in an interesting parallel with Hume, Kant grants an important role to the imagination in bringing us to see events in the world as structured by causal relations. Kant argues that we have a faculty of "productive imagination," which plays a constant underlying function in producing our experience. Crucially, it is through the productive imagination that we are able to posit objects that are not currently present to us in our experience.[5] This allows us to think of those objects that *are* currently appearing to us as part of a unified manifold that extends across both time and space. For this reason, Kant states that "the synthesis of representations rests on the imagination," (A155/B194) which is to say that the way in which our experience is built—by which we are able to know anything at all—relies upon the imagination's role in imaginatively connecting objects together causally across time and space.

This role granted to imagination goes far beyond that posited by Hume. Hume granted a significant role to the imagination in generating beliefs in (among other things) causal relations, personal identity and the existence of external objects, but even this falls short of Kantian claims regarding the imagination's role in constructing our very experience of the world. Even more significantly, the role that human cognition as a whole has to play in constructing our experience forms part of Kant's anti-skeptical strategy, which seeks to avoid what he saw as the damaging skeptical consequences of Humean empiricism. In short, Kant's response to skepticism regarding the basic principles of the world (e.g., that there are objects external to us that exist in space and time, which interact with each other through regular causal patterns) is to argue that these are principles that we can know *must be the case* in order for there to be a world for us to experience. From the very fact that we experience the world, we know they must hold without exception, for they are principles that must structure our world in order for us to have any experience at all (in other words, they are *the conditions of the possibility of experience*). This should avoid the kind of skepticism regarding causation that haunted Hume: the causal principle is part of the necessary structure that we impose on our sensibility in order to construct an intelligible experience of the world for us, and thus it is something that we know will hold of necessity of all events we experience. In other words, Hume was wrong to infer from the fact that we lack an experience of causal power that we also lack a rational guarantee that regular causal relations will continue to hold. On Kant's view, such relations are a necessary and universal feature of any experience that we could have.

The following extract forms part of Kant's argument in the *Critique of Pure Reason* for the claim that the causal principle is justified as a necessary feature of our experience of the world, due to the indispensable role it plays in allowing us to represent objects as persisting over time and forming part of a successive series of temporal events. Kant poses the question of how it is that we are able to experience a world of objects, and events involving those objects, that have definite, objective positions in time. In the extract, we find the argument that such an experience is only possible if there is an objective sequence of events which owes its objectivity to a pre-given rule of causality that determines the very form of our experience of external objects.

For the purposes of Kant's argument that is provided here, it is important to grasp the distinction between a mere change in our representations and an objective change in events in the world. As we shall see, Kant contrasts two examples of a succession of appearances. In the first, we can imagine looking at different parts of a house in succession (so I might look at the roof first, then a first-floor window, then a door on the ground floor, etc.). Such a series of appearances certainly involves change in what appears to us over a period of time, but we do not think of this series as revealing an objectively determined series of events (I could have looked at the first-floor window and then the roof, rather than the other way around). In the second example, Kant has us imagine watching a ship float down a river: let's say it first goes past a tree and then past a rock. I naturally understand this to be an objectively determined series of events, insofar as the flowing water causes the ship to first float past the tree, which is higher up the river, and then past the rock. However, what is it that allows us to tell that our experiences of the ship are of a causally determined series of events, as opposed to a mere subjective change in our apprehension that does not correlate to a change in the object of our perception (as in the case where we are viewing different parts of the house in succession)? By exploring this question, in relation to these two examples, Kant argues that he can show that the causal principle must be necessarily true of all events in our experience, as it is required for any experience involving an object of the senses that has a successive existence over a period of time.

Extract 13.1—Kant, *Critique of Pure Reason* ("Second Analogy: Principle of the Succession of Time according to the Law of Causality. All Changes Take Place according to the Law of the Connection of Cause and Effect"—Selection)

I perceive that phenomena succeed one another, that is to say, a state of things exists at one time, the opposite of which existed in a former state. In that case, then, I really connect together two perceptions in time. Now connection is not an operation of mere sense and intuition, but is the product of a synthetic faculty of imagination, which determines our inner sense in respect of a relation of time. But imagination can connect these two states in two ways, so that either one or the other may antecede in time; for time in itself cannot be an object of perception, and what in an object precedes and what follows cannot be empirically determined in relation to it. I am only conscious, then, that my imagination places one state before and the other after; not that the state antecedes the other in the object. In other words, the objective relation of the successive phenomena remains quite undetermined by means of mere perception. Now in order that this relation may be cognized as determined, the relation between the two states must be so thought that it is thereby determined as necessary, which of them must be placed and which after, and not conversely. But the concept which carries with it a necessity of synthetic unity can be none other than a pure conception of the understanding which does not lie in mere perception; and in this case it is the concept of "the relation of cause and effect," the former of which determines the latter in time, as its necessary consequence, and not as something which might possibly antecede it in the imagination (or which might in some cases not be perceived to follow). It follows that it is only because we subject the sequence of phenomena, and consequently all change, to the law of causality, that experience itself, that is, empirical cognition of phenomena, becomes possible; and consequently, that phenomena themselves, as objects of experience, are possible only in accordance with this law . . .

That something happens, that is to say, that something or some state exists which before was not, cannot be empirically perceived, unless a phenomenon precedes, which does not contain this state in itself. For a reality which should follow upon an empty time, in other words, a beginning, which no state of things precedes, can just as little be apprehended as the empty time itself. Every apprehension of an event is therefore a perception which follows upon other perception. But as this is the case with all synthesis of apprehension, as I have shown above in the example of a house, my apprehension of an event is not yet sufficiently distinguished from other apprehensions. But I remark also that if in a phenomenon which contains an occurrence, I call the antecedent state of my perception, A, and the following state, B, the perception B can only follow A in apprehension, and the perception A cannot follow B, but only precede it. For example, I see a ship float down the stream of a river. My perception of its place lower down follows upon my perception of its place higher up in the course of the river, and it is impossible that, in the apprehension of this phenomenon, the vessel should be perceived first below and afterwards higher up the stream. Here, therefore, the order in the sequence of perceptions in apprehension is determined; and by this order apprehension is regulated. In the [other] example, my perceptions in the apprehension of a house might begin at the roof and end at the foundation or vice versa; or I might apprehend the manifold in this empirical intuition, by going from left to right, and from right to left. Accordingly, in the series of these perceptions, there was no determined order, which necessitated my beginning at a certain point, in order empirically to connect the manifold. But this rule is always to be found in the perception of that which happens, and it makes the order of the successive perceptions in the apprehension of such a phenomenon necessary.

I must, therefore, in the present case, deduce the subjective sequence of apprehension from the objective sequence of phenomena, for otherwise the former is quite undetermined, and one phenomenon is not distinguishable from another. The former alone proves nothing as to the connection of the manifold in an object, for it is completely arbitrary. The connection must therefore consist in the order of the manifold in a phenomenon, according to which order the apprehension of one thing (that which happens) follows that of another thing (which precedes), in conformity with a rule. In this way alone can I be authorized to say of the phenomenon itself, and not merely of my own apprehension, that a certain order or sequence is to be found therein. That is, in other words, I cannot arrange my apprehension otherwise than in this order.

In conformity with this rule, then, it is necessary that in that which antecedes an event there be found the condition of a rule, according to which this event follows always and necessarily; but I cannot reverse this and go back from the event, and determine (by apprehension) that which antecedes it. For no phenomenon goes back from the following point of time to the preceding point, although it does certainly relate to a preceding point of time; from a given time, on the other hand, there is always a necessary progression to the determined following time. Therefore, because there certainly is something that follows, I must of necessity connect it with something else in general which antecedes it, and upon which it follows in conformity with a rule, that is necessarily, so that the event, as conditioned, affords a secure indication of a condition, and this condition determines the event.

Let us suppose that nothing precedes an event, upon which this event must follow in conformity with a rule. All sequence of perception would then exist only in apprehension, that is to say, would be merely subjective, and it could not thereby be objectively determined what thing ought to precede, and what ought to follow in perception. In such a case, we should have nothing but a play of representations, which would not relate to any object. That is to say, it would not be possible through perception to distinguish one phenomenon from another, as regards relations of time; because the succession in the act of apprehension is always of the same sort, and therefore there would be nothing in the phenomenon to determine the succession, and to render a certain sequence objectively necessary. And, in this case, I cannot say that two states in a phenomenon follow one upon the other, but only that one apprehension follows upon another, which would be merely subjective, and determining no object, and consequently cannot be held to be cognition of an object—not even in the phenomenal world.

Accordingly, when we know in experience that something happens, we always presuppose that something else precedes it, whereupon it follows in conformity with a rule. For otherwise I could not say of the object that it follows; because the mere succession in my apprehension, if it be not determined by a rule in relation to something preceding, does not authorize succession in the object. Only, therefore, in reference to a rule, according to which phenomena are determined in their sequence, that is, as they happen, by the preceding state, can I make my subjective synthesis (of apprehension) objective, and it is only under this presupposition that even the experience of an event is possible.

No doubt it appears as if this were in thorough contradiction to all the notions which people have hitherto entertained in regard to the procedure of the human understanding. According to these opinions, it is only by means of the perception and comparison of similar consequences following upon certain antecedent phenomena that the understanding is led to the discovery of a rule, according to which certain events always follow certain phenomena, and it is only by this process that we attain to the concept of cause. Upon such a basis, it is clear that this concept must be merely empirical, and the rule which it furnishes us with—"Everything that happens must have a cause"—would be just as contingent as experience itself. The universality and necessity of the rule or law would be perfectly spurious attributes of it. Indeed, it could not possess universal validity, inasmuch as it would not in this case be a priori, but founded on induction. But the same is the case with this law as with other pure a priori representations (e.g. space and time), which we can draw in perfect clearness and completeness from experience, only because we had already placed them therein, and by that means, and by that alone, had rendered experience possible. Indeed, the logical clearness of this representation of a rule, determining the series of events, is possible only when we have made use of it in experience. Nevertheless, the recognition of this rule, as a condition of the synthetic unity of phenomena in time, was the ground of experience itself and consequently preceded it a priori.

It is now our duty to show by an example that we never, even in experience, attribute to an object the notion of succession or effect (of an event—that is, the happening of something that did not exist before), and distinguish it from the subjective succession of apprehension, unless when a rule lies at the foundation, which compels us to observe this order of perception in preference to any other, and that, indeed, it is this necessity which first renders possible the representation of a succession in the object.

We have representations within us, of which also we can be conscious. But, however widely extended, however accurate and thoroughgoing this consciousness may be, these representations are still nothing more than representations, that is, internal determinations of the mind in this or that relation of time. Now how does it happen that to these representations we should posit an object, or that, in addition to their subjective reality, as modifications, we should still further attribute to them a certain unknown objective reality? It is clear that objective significance cannot consist in a relation to another representation (of that which we desire to term object), for in that case the question again arises: "How does this other representation go beyond itself, and obtain objective significance over and above the subjective, which is proper to it, as a determination of a state of mind?" If we try to discover what sort of new property the relation to an object gives to our subjective representations, and what new dignity they thereby receive, we shall find that this relation has no other effect than that of rendering necessary the connection of our representations in a certain manner, and of subjecting them to a rule; and that conversely, it is only because a certain order is necessary in the relations of time of our representations, that objective significance is ascribed to them.

In the synthesis of phenomena, the manifold of our representations is always successive. Now by these means alone no object at all is represented, for through this succession, which is common to all apprehension, no one thing is distinguished from another. But as soon as I perceive or assume that in this succession there is a relation to an antecedent state, from which the representations follow in accordance with a rule, so soon do I represent something as an event, or as a thing that happens; in other words, I cognize an object to which I must assign a certain determinate position in time, which cannot be altered, because of the preceding state in the object. When, therefore, I perceive that something happens, there is contained in this representation, in the first place, the fact that something antecedes; because it is only in relation to this that the phenomenon obtains its proper relation of time, in other words, exists after an antecedent time, in which it did not exist. But it can receive its determined place in time only by the presupposition that something existed in the foregoing state, upon which it follows inevitably and always, that is, in conformity with a rule. From all this it is evident that, in the first place, I cannot reverse the order of succession, and make that which happens precede that upon which it follows; and that, in the second place, if the antecedent state can be posited, a certain determinate event inevitably and necessarily follows. Hence it follows that there exists a certain order in our representations, whereby the present gives a sure indication of some previously existing state as a correlate, though still undetermined, of the existing event which is given—a correlate which itself relates to the event as its consequence, conditions it, and connects it necessarily with itself in the series of time.

If then it be admitted as a necessary law of sensibility, and consequently a formal condition of all perception, that the preceding necessarily determines the succeeding time (inasmuch as I cannot arrive at the succeeding except through the preceding), it must likewise be an indispensable law of empirical representation of the series of time that the phenomena of the past determine all phenomena in the following time, and that the latter, as events, cannot take place except in so far as the former determine their existence in time, that is to say, establish it according to a rule. For it is of course only in phenomena that we can empirically cognize this continuity in the connection of times.

[Immanuel Kant, *Critique of Pure Reason*, translated by J. M. D. Meiklejohn (London: Henry G. Bohn, 1855). Translation amended.]

In the extract provided here, Kant begins by summarizing his position, namely, that all experience must be subject to the causal principle in order for us to have any successive experience of enduring changing objects at all. Kant echoes Hume's point that we cannot, from our perception alone, determine that two events are causally connected, and neither can imagination alone achieve this: given that the imagination could as easily place effect before cause as cause before effect, this shows that the kind of idea of necessary determination that we understand to be part of a causal connection could not come from this faculty. Neither do we perceive time as a separate thing by which we can compare events and determine their succession.[6] We clearly do have a sense of an objective order of events, which is what allows us to distinguish between the example of the ship floating down-river (which reflects a change in the object itself) and the example of looking at different parts of a house (which does not reflect a change in the object, but merely a change in the perceiver). So, where does this sense of an objective order of events come from? It must be from a law, Kant argues, that our mind imposes on our experience, in order to have experience of a comprehensible world, as opposed to a mere play of representations.

Kant's key claim here is that, in our experience, what makes an event an objective happening, something that signals a genuine change in an object, with a determinate position in time, is that this event is conceived of as being connected by a causal rule or principle to a state that came before it (even though we may not know what did actually cause the event in question). If we did not conceive of an event in such a way, it would rather just be a part of a jumbled play of representations that did not come together to make up an experienceable world with a clear structure in space and time. As far as Kant is concerned, Hume's mistake was to overlook the possibility of *a priori* synthetic principles. Though it is indeed the case that causal power is not to be found (*a posteriori*) in our experience, the guarantee of necessary connections between events in our experience can be found (*a priori*) in our own cognitive structure, insofar as this is required for us to experience the world in the way we do. The causal principle also explains the irreversibility that we see in cases of genuine alterations in objects: the irreversibility of our experience of observing the ship float down-river is grounded in the objectively necessary determination of events in our experience by this pre-given structure.

Kant's position clearly has skeptical implications. On the one hand, Kant does seem to provide us with a guarantee that the causal principle holds for all events in the world, on the basis that we could not experience such a world without there being such a universal rule. Despite this potentially being an effective anti-skeptical strategy, though, we may nevertheless conclude in the end that it comes with other costs too great to be acceptable. Note that, according to Kant, the world that we experience is, in terms of its fundamental constitution, one that we have constructed ourselves through our mental faculties. We can perhaps safely assume that there is a world out there, external to ourselves. Yet all we can really know of that world is how it *appears* to us, rather than how it is in itself. It is guaranteed for us that the world will conform to certain basic principles (indeed, we can know *a priori* that this is the case), but this guarantee is strictly limited to the world as it appears to us. It has appeared to some critics that this approach concedes too much to the skeptic by ultimately denying that we can have knowledge of reality beyond our own individual mental activity.

How we view Kant's anti-skeptical achievement may depend upon how we view the nature of the mental apparatus we rely upon to generate an intelligible experience of the world for us: does it act as a barrier between us and the world? Or does it act rather as an instrument to facilitate our access to the world, in an analogous way to how glasses help some with visual impairments to see the world more clearly? We do not necessarily have to see the mind's mental processes as standing between us and the world, though we can perhaps never know for sure what the nature of the world is like apart from our experience of it. How skeptical this position is, and whether it is an acceptable one to take, may ultimately be a matter of taste as much as rational argumentation.

> ## Key Points
>
> - Kant wishes to challenge the skeptical view that we lack knowledge of the fundamental features of the world we experience.
> - Kant's anti-skeptical strategy revolves around the notion of synthetic *a priori* knowledge, which is justified apart from our experience, but nevertheless is able to tell us something substantive about the nature of the world.
> - The possibility of synthetic *a priori* knowledge rests on the fact that the way in which we experience the world is necessarily constituted by certain principles that we impose on things, including the causal principle.
> - We are justified in claiming knowledge that events are linked with each other by necessary causal relations, on the basis that it is one of the conditions of us being able to experience anything at all.

Suggested Further Reading

Buroker, Jill Vance. *Kant's Critique of Pure Reason: An Introduction*, chs. 1–3. Cambridge: Cambridge University Press, 2006.

Guyer, Paul. *Knowledge, Reason, and Taste: Kant's Response to Hume*, ch. 2. Princeton: Princeton University Press, 2008.

Hall, Bryan. *The Arguments of Kant's Critique of Pure Reason*, ch. 11. Lanham: Lexington, 2011.

Rosenberg, Jay F. *Accessing Kant: A Relaxed Introduction to the Critique of Pure Reason*, ch. 10. New York: Oxford University Press, 2005.

Shabel, Lisa. "The Transcendental Aesthetic." In *The Cambridge Companion to Kant's Critique of Pure Reason*, edited by Paul Guyer, 93–117. Cambridge: Cambridge University Press, 2010.

13B. SHEPHERD ON REASON AND CAUSATION

> **Mary Shepherd: Brief Chronology**
> - 1777: Born at Barnbougle Castle, near Edinburgh
> - 1808: Moves to London, following marriage to Henry Shepherd, a barrister. There she joins an intellectual circle that includes Charles Babbage (often credited as the inventor of the first computer) and the Cambridge academic, William Whewell (who would later use some of Shepherd's work in his teaching at the university)
> - 1824: Publishes first major work, *Essay upon the Relation of Cause and Effect*
> - 1827: Publishes *Essay on the Perception of an External Universe*. Apart from a few later short essays, this would be her last published work
> - 1847: Dies on January 7 in London

We come to the end of our survey of early modern philosophy with a consideration of the work of Mary Shepherd. Though her works, published in the 1820s, admittedly lie at the very fringe of (and some would say beyond) the limits of the early modern period, nevertheless her ideas stand as both an interesting response to Hume and a counterpoint to Kant. Very little is known of her life, but we do know that one early impetus for her philosophical studies was her rejection of a Humean account of causation, proposed by Thomas Brown (1778–1820),[7] that sought to reduce causality to mere regularity or patterns of events. In Shepherd's view, the productive power of causes is something that we can infer from our experience of the occurrence of events. Shepherd also wished to show that such a causal inference is based on reason, rather than a mental mechanism of (non-rational) custom or habit.

One aspect of Hume's account of causation is his claim (discussed in the previous chapter) that judgments of causal relations could not be a matter of rational deduction, on the basis that we can conceive of a cause and effect as separable: we can conceive of the cause having brought about something different, and we can conceive of the effect having come into existence without the cause. In response to this argument, Shepherd makes two key claims: (1) cause and effect can only be separable in such a way if we think of cause as antecedent to its effect, whereas in fact cause and effect are *synchronous* (they occur at the same time), and (2) given the rational nature of our understanding of causation, and the deterministic nature of the world, it is a necessary truth (which we can know) that the effect could not come into existence without its cause.

Let's begin with the claim that cause and effect are in fact synchronous with each other. In her *Essay upon the Relation of Cause and Effect*, Shepherd encourages us to think of causal relations not as a chronological matter (in other words, not as effect following cause), but rather along the model of a mathematical equation, in which the sum instantly follows from the combination of addends: "[the cause] is really *included* in the mixture *of* A *and* B, although to our senses, we are forced to *note down* (as it were) the sum arising from their union, *after the observance of their coalescence*."[8] Such a model of causation might be plausible in the case of something like chemical bonding, in which the bonding of atomic components synchronously gives rise to a molecule that has distinctive qualities (which are explained by the qualities of the atoms and their bonds with one another). We will see more on this synchronous model of causation in the following extract, but for now, it is worth reviewing the ontology of objects that underlies this model of causation.

Shepherd understands objects as collections or bundles of qualities. An object is a *particular* bundle of qualities, such that, strictly speaking, if you have a new collection of qualities (that is, if any of an object's qualities change), you have a new object. While this might seem like a strange view of what makes an object the individual object it is, Shepherd is by no means the only philosopher to have made such a claim (for example, such a view is similar to that of the contemporary theory of "mereological essentialism," according to which an object has its parts necessarily, such that if it loses or gains a part, that object no longer exists and another object takes its place[9]). One important implication of this view for our understanding of causation is that you do not have the traditional model that Hume was critiquing of one object in some sense passing on a quality or property to another object. Rather, you in effect have the instantaneous creation of a new nature at the point in which the qualities of two pre-existing natures are mixed in some way. There is no process of transference going on here, which could take a certain period of time, as there is an instantaneous creation of a new thing.

In addition, Shepherd argues, not only does Hume's analysis of causation fail on the basis that it assumes an incorrect chronological model, but it also overlooks a possible rational proof of the key causal principle that every event that occurs must have a cause of its occurrence. Shepherd states that, when we observe a change in the world, we are seeing a change in the quality of an object. Specifically, when we identify something as an effect, we attribute to it the quality of coming-into-existence. However, this change in quality is one that presupposes an already-existing object. Shepherd has us suppose an event

> to be *no effect*; there shall be no [preceding] circumstances whatever that affect it, nor any existence in the universe: let it be so; let there be nought but a blank; and a mass of whatsoever can be supposed not to require a cause START FORTH into existence, and make the first breach on the wide nonentity around;—now, what is this starting forth, beginning, coming into existence, but an action, which is a quality of an object not yet in being, and so not possible to have its qualities determined, nevertheless exhibiting its qualities?[10]

Someone who thinks that an object could exist uncaused, Shepherd argues, has to suppose the notion of a quality or action of coming-into-existence existing without an object, but the idea of an activity without an object undertaking that activity is incoherent. Thus, the only rationally coherent supposition is that all coming-into-existences are preceded by an object (in other words, that every object that comes about must have a cause of its occurrence).

In this way, Shepherd gives a robust role to reason in the identification of causal relations between events that we observe. When we experience a single potential case of some quality beginning to exist that was not there before, our reason naturally assumes a cause, on the basis of two key causal *a priori* principles: that every event that occurs must have a cause, and that like causes bring about like effects. As the scholar Martha Brandt Bolton has put it, according to Shepherd,

> A human mind is naturally disposed to execute "latent," largely non-conscious, operations which give a certain relational structure to the intentional objects of sense perception. A mind with no disposition to perform such operations would be deficient in rationality.[11]

Our rationality gives a comprehensible, causal structure to our experience of the world, which can be justified on the basis of rational argumentation latent in our reasoning that can be brought out by philosophical reflection. Despite admittedly being a fallible rational procedure, we can justify such a supposition, and indeed explain the universality of agreement regarding the fundamental role of causation with regard to structuring events in the world, on the basis that reason allows us to grasp that there is indeed an underlying causal structure to those things that we observe (though we may not have the kind of metaphysical insight into the real nature of causation that Hume also denies us).

Underlying this argument is also Shepherd's understanding of the synchronous nature of causation. As mentioned earlier, Shepherd argues that an effect is a new nature that results from the simultaneous mixture of two pre-existing natures. Clearly, if you understand an effect in this way, it is easy to see why you might suppose that an effect must require a preexisting cause. In the following extract, we will see Shepherd expanding further on her synchronous model of causation, as part of her critique of Hume's account, as well as seeking to offer a rational proof of another core metaphysical principle that Hume has sought to undermine, namely, the claim that causation acts in a regular manner.

Extract 13.2—Shepherd, *Essay upon the Relation of Cause and Effect* (Chapter II, Section II)

> We will now proceed to the second part of the original inquiry; that is, Why we conclude that such particular causes must necessarily have such particular effects; and what is the nature of that inference we draw from one to the other, and of the belief we repose in it? The question, however, ought to stand thus, why like causes must necessarily have like effects? Because what is really enquired into, is the *general notion of necessary connexion*, between *all like* Cause and Effect; and by thus putting the question respecting *particulars only*, although they might be included in an universal answer, yet no answer applicable to them merely, could authorize an *universal axiom* . . .

> [According to Hume], *necessary connexion* of cause and effect is only a custom of the mind! *Power* is only a custom of the mind! Expectations, and experience, are only customs of the mind! The consequence of which doctrine is, that as a *custom of the mind* is entirely a different circumstance from the *operation of nature*, we may "conceive" at least the contrary of what we have been accustomed to may take place—we may conceive the "course of nature to change."

> Now it is my intention to show, in contradiction to these ideas of Mr. Hume, that it is *Reason*, and not *Custom*, which guides our minds in forming the notions of necessary connexion, of belief and of expectation.

In order to this let us bear in mind the reasoning already adduced in the foregoing chapter [i.e. Shepherd's proof of the causal principle], and it then immediately follows, that objects which we know by our senses do begin their existences, and by our reason know they cannot begin it of themselves, must begin it by the operation of some *other beings* in existence, producing these new qualities in nature, and introducing them to our observation. The very meaning of the word Cause, is *Producer* or *Creator*; of Effect, the *Produced* or *Created*—and the idea is gained by such an observance of nature, as we think is efficient in any given case, to an *experimentum crucis* [crucial experiment].

Long observation of the invariableness of antecedency, and subsequency, is not wanted; many trials are not wanted, to generate the notion of *producing power*.

One trial is enough, in such circumstances, as will bring the mind to the following reasoning.

Here is a new quality, which appears to my senses:

But it could not arise of itself; nor could any surrounding objects, but one (or more) affect it; therefore that one, (or more) have occasioned it, for there is nothing else to make a difference; and a *difference* could not "*begin of itself.*"

This is an argument, which all persons, however illiterate, feel the force of. It is the only foundation for the demonstrations of the laboratory of the chemist; which all life resembles, and so closely, in many instances, that the philosopher, and the vulgar, are equally sure of what cause is absolutely necessary to the production of certain effects; for instance, each knows that in certain given circumstances, *the closing of the Eye* will eclipse the prospect of nature; and the slight motion of reopening it, will restore all the objects to view. Therefore, the Eye (in these circumstances,) is the *Cause* or *Producer of vision*. One trial would be enough, under certain *known* circumstances. [Footnote by author: When more trials are needed than one, it is in order to *detect* the circumstances, not to lay a *foundation for the general principle*, that a like Cause repeated, a like Effect will take place.] Why? Not from "custom," because there has been *one trial only*; but from *Reason*, because vision not being able *to produce itself, nor any of the surrounding objects by the supposition*; it is the *Eye* which must necessarily perform the operation; for there is nothing else to make a difference; and a different quality could not "*begin its own existence.*" It is this sort of reasoning upon experiment, which takes place in every man's mind, concerning every affair in life, which generates the notion of Power, and necessary Connexion; and gives birth to that maxim, "*a like Cause must produce a like Effect."* The circumstances being supposed the same on a second occasion as on a former one, and carefully observed to be so; the Eye when opened would be expected to let in light, and all her objects. "I observe (says the mind) in this or any other case, all the *prevening* [preceding] circumstances the same as before; for there is nothing to make a difference; and a difference cannot arise without something to occasion it; else there would be a *beginning of existence* by itself, which is impossible."

It is this compound idea, therefore, *the result of the experience of what does take place upon any given trial*, mixed with the *reasoning that nothing else could ensue*, unless on the one hand, *efficient causes were allowed for the alteration*; or, on the other, that things could *"alter their existences* for themselves"; which generates the notion of *power or "producing principle,"* and for which we have formed the word.

It is in vain to say that a habit of association of ideas from observing *"contiguity in time, and place,"* between objects is all we know of *power*; a habit of the mind will not *begin existence*, will not *introduce a quality*. The really philosophical method of viewing the subject is this: that objects in relation to us, are nothing but masses of certain qualities, affecting certain of our senses; and which, when independent of our senses, are *unknown* powers or qualities in nature. These masses change their qualities by their mixture with any other mass, and then the corresponding qualities determined to the senses must of course also change. These changed qualities, are termed *effects*; or *consequents*; but are really no more than new qualities arising from *new objects*, which have been formed by the *junctions of other objects* (previously formed) or might be considered as the *unobserved qualities of existing objects;* which *shall be observed when properly exhibited.*

If then an existence now in being, *conjoined with any other*, forms thereby *a new nature*, capable of exhibiting *new qualities*, these new qualities must enter into the definition of the objects; they become a part of their nature; and when by careful experiment, or judicious observation, no new prevening circumstances are supposed to make an alteration in the conjunction of the same bodies, the *new qualities*, that are named *effects*, are expected without a doubt to arise upon every such conjunction; because, they as much belong to this *newly combined nature*, as the original qualities did to each separate nature, before their conjunction. So little is custom the principle of cause and effect, that if upon the *first* and original trial of the element of fire, all surrounding circumstances were put away from having any influence over it, saving the body it destroyed; that power of *discerptibility* [*divisibility*] would be ever after considered as one of its qualities; as much as its colour or its light, or its warmth, without the presence of which, it would not be fire.

This conjunction with a grosser material than itself, is the new circumstance, on which it exhibits its essential and permanent quality of discerptibility to the senses; now if the trial be complete, when upon a second occasion an object having the same sensible qualities as fire has, known also to have been elicited from the same prevening circumstances, meets with the same gross body as heretofore, it must of *necessity* consume it. There is nothing to make a *difference*. A *difference* is an *Effect*, a *change of being*, an *altered existence*, an existence which *cannot "begin* of itself" any more than any other in Nature; could the fire be supposed not to consume the gross body, there would be a *difference* of qualities, that is, new qualities, which by the data there is no cause for. The original circumstances, of which fire is the compound Effect, from which it results as a *formed object*, are supposed to be ordered the same as on a former occasion; these are necessarily compelled to be attended with the same effect or combined qualities; otherwise there would be the *"beginnings of existence"* by themselves, which has before been shown to be impossible. But the *combined qualities*, are the whole qualities that fire in every circumstance, is capable of producing. Meeting, therefore, with a gross body, which on any one occasion, in certain circumstances, it once consumed; under the same circumstances, it must necessarily again consume it. That differences of existence cannot begin of themselves; is therefore the second conclusion supposed to be established.

"*Antecedency* and *subsequency*," are therefore immaterial to the proper definition of Cause and Effect; on the contrary, although an object, in order to act as a Cause, must be in Being antecedently to such action; yet when it *acts as a Cause*, its *Effects* are *synchronous with that action*, and are *included in it*; which a close inspection into the nature of cause will prove. For effects are not more than the new qualities, of newly formed objects. Each conjunction of bodies, (now separately in existence, and of certain defined qualities), produces upon their union those new natures, whose qualities must necessarily *be in*, and *with them*, *in the very moment of their formation*.

Thus *the union of two distinct natures*, is the *cause, producer* or *creator* of another; which must instantly, and immediately, have all its peculiar qualities; but the cause has not acted, is not completed, till the *union* has taken place, and the new nature is formed with all its qualities, *in*, and *about it*. *Cause producing Effect*, therefore, under the strict eye of philosophical scrutiny, is a *new object* exhibiting *new qualities*; or shortly, the formation of a new *mass of qualities*. A *chain of conjunctions of bodies*, of course, *occupies time*; and is the reason why the careless observation of philosophers, enabling them to take notice only of some one distinct effect, (after perhaps innumerable successive conjunctions of bodies,) occasions the mistake, by which they consider *subsequency of effect*, as a part of the *essential definition* of that term; and *priority*, as *essential* to the nature of Cause.

As a short illustration of the doctrine unfolded, let us take the idea of nourishment, considered as the effect, subsequent to the taking of food, its cause. Here the *nature* of nourishment, is *a process* which begins to act immediately that food is in conjunction with the stomach. "That we are nourished"; is only the last result of a continuous chain of causes and effects, in formation from the first moment the food enters the stomach, to that, in which every particle is absorbed and deposited in the proper place in the body. Here, the capacity of food to exhibit certain qualities, when in conjunction with the body, is shown; the nature of the human body, to exhibit certain other qualities, in consequence of that conjunction is also shown; but the *effect of nourishment*, being *subsequent* to, and at such a distance of time from, the original Cause, is only so, on account of its being the effect of a vast number of causes, or unions of objects in succession, of which the union of the stomach and the food was first in order.

Our deficient observation, is apt to prevent our taking notice of the second, third, or indefinite number of effects; which arise in consequence of as many conjunctions of objects.

But the first, and other *effects* successively, are as much and entirely synchronous with their *causes*, as any other quality of any single object, which is always exhibited along with it.

[Mary Shepherd, Essay upon the Relation of Cause and Effect (London: T. Hookham, 1824)].

In this extract, Shepherd argues for a rational justification of a **causal likeness principle**[†], according to which like causes necessarily lead to like effects. This is an important aspect of our common understanding of causation in nature, as it guarantees the uniformity of patterns of natural events: not only does everything that occurs have a cause, but it follows from that cause in a regular, reliable manner. Given the nature of a particular cause, we can make a reasonable prediction as to what will follow, given our experience of how things tend to work in the natural course of things. Given that Hume had argued that our idea of causation is based on custom, rather than reason, this is a clear challenge to his account. Shepherd goes further, though, in rejecting Hume's custom-based account by arguing that repeated observation of patterns of events is not required to gain an idea of causal power. Rather, the mind can reason to such an idea from a single instance of observing causation in action.

The reasoning is as follows: any causal interaction involves a difference, a change in quality, that is an activity that could only come about through the "difference-making" of another object. We only need to close our eyes once, Shepherd argues, to reason that it was the eye causing our vision all along: for the only difference that has occurred when our vision ceases is that the eye has been hindered from seeing. The causal likeness principle also naturally follows from such reasoning. We now know that the opening of the eye is sufficient cause (all other things being equal) for our vision to occur, and from this we can rationally infer a necessary power within the eye that can bring about the change in activity required for our vision. The existence of such a necessary power guarantees that the same effect will follow from similar circumstances: in all comparable instances in which my eye is opened, vision will result. If there were a different result, this would have to be from a relevant change in the preceding circumstances (such as being in a pitch-black room), rather than from the causal power of the eye not bringing about vision, for otherwise we would have to suppose an original action by the brain or mind to hinder the causal impact of the eye (which is the kind of self-initiated activity that Shepherd has already ruled out). The causal principle thus rules out the possibility that the same preceding circumstances could lead to a different result. On the basis of the causal principle therefore, Shepherd argues, the causal likeness principle can also be rationally proved.

As the scholar Cristina Paoletti has noted,[12] Shepherd here seems to assume that the course of nature is deterministic, insofar as objects have necessary productive powers that will always operate in a predictable fashion unless there is a relevant difference in preceding circumstances. If an object acts in a way that is contrary to our expectations, that is because there is something we misunderstood about the preceding conditions that brought about this object. An object could not act differently than it normally would because, as we saw earlier, it is constituted of a bundle of qualities that determines how it will act: if it would act differently, it would not be that very object but some other. This might, at first glance, appear to beg the question against Hume. Nevertheless, Shepherd believes that she can offer a strong rational and empirical basis for our trust in our judgments regarding causal relations between objects that offers a more powerful explanation than Hume is able to of the basis of our beliefs in causation.

Shepherd's assumption regarding the deterministic course of nature is tied to her underlying mathematical model of causation. In the same way that two and two together can only ever make four, the circumstances that apply in any causal interaction can only ever lead to a particular effect. Going back to the previous extract, Shepherd argues that we can learn about the types of things that are in the world (such as fire and wood) and part of this is discovering the kind of qualities that they usually have. On the basis of such knowledge, we can rationally infer a causal principle such as "iron plus heat equals glow," without relying on the kind of analogical inference of the continuation of the laws of nature that can be challenged by the Humean argument that the course of nature could change. Shepherd argues that we can justifiably use the same kind of reasoning that we use in mathematics to infer a necessary connection between cause and effect:

> *when objects are formed the same upon one occasion as another, their qualities, properties, and effects, will be similar.* It is this proposition on which mathematical demonstration, and physical induction equally, and only, rest for their truth. There is no difference; objects are what their formations render them, whether in the shape of mathematical diagrams, or other aggregates in nature.[13]

In the same way that we grasp the qualities of numbers or shapes in order to construct mathematical proofs, we can grasp the qualities of kinds of things in the world and on that basis rationally infer the patterns of events that ground the causal likeness principle. Though there is undoubtedly more uncertainty with regard to causal claims, this is due to our often-limited knowledge regarding the circumstances of any given situation, rather than any skepticism connected with the causally determined course of nature.

In the second half of the previous extract, Shepherd moves to her account of the synchronous nature of causation, and why we are so readily tricked into thinking of cause as antecedent to effect. In order to illustrate this, we are given the example of someone eating food which then goes on to nourish the body. In such circumstances, it is natural to think of the causal effect in this way: the eating of the food at time t1 causes the nourishment of the body at time t2. However, Shepherd argues, the reality of the causal process is more complicated than this. The process that begins with the food entering the body and finishes with the body being nourished is in fact a chain of synchronous unions of objects that bring about a change in qualities. It is this individual synchronous union of objects that is rightly called a causal interaction, rather than picking out two temporally discrete events in the digestive process and calling one "cause" and the other "effect." We are inclined to do so mistakenly, though, due to the limits of our observation: we are unable to see the succession of unions of objects that make up the digestive process and so we suppose that the events that we do observe (the eating of the food and, perhaps, the feeling of satisfaction from being nourished), one of which is antecedent to the other, are the only constituent parts of the causal interactions that take place. Thus, we mistake a chain of synchronous causal interactions for a causal process that takes place over a particular period of time. As mentioned earlier, this is significant for Shepherd's critique of Hume's account of causation, insofar as it seeks to prove that an effect cannot occur without a cause. Once we rightly understand what it is we are in fact observing, we see that cause and effect are inextricably bound together in a single moment of time, and thus it is impossible that one occurs without the other.

There are a couple of quick objections we can consider here to Shepherd's account. First, Shepherd assumes that all causal interactions are accurately captured in a λ-type intersection (two processes go in, one process comes out), for example when a malnourished body and a slice of bread interact (through a series of synchronous unions of natures) to produce a nourished body. However, it is not at all clear that all causal interactions can be understood in this way: for example, two balls colliding with each other would seem to instead make an X-type intersection (two processes go in, two processes go out), while the action of a hen laying an egg would be a Y-type intersection (one process goes in, two processes go out: in this case with the egg and a lighter hen the result).[14] In response to this objection, Shepherd may claim that apparent X and Y-type causal interactions are just an artifact of our limited powers of observation, and that all genuine causal interactions are of λ-type, though this might not be a wholly plausible response. Further, it is not clear that our epistemic reliance upon the regularity of nature is secured by Shepherd's argument that a given object cannot exhibit any other causal powers than it in fact does. As the scholar Walter Ott argues, we cannot justify our beliefs regarding the regularity of nature by simply stipulating that particular objects must act according to a certain pattern:

> Suppose that the white stuff falling from the sky in winter were to behave exactly as snow does except it burned human flesh. In such a case, Shepherd "contends that it is not snow." This preserves our inductions at the price of vacuity. If one builds into the concept *snow* all its characteristic powers as we now understand them, one can of course insulate oneself from any possible falsification just by declaring that any putative counterexample is, by definition, not snow.[15]

If we follow Hume's reasoning, there seems to be no reason why snow could not simply take on different causal powers at a particular moment in time, whether it is right to then call snow "snow" or not. Thus, Humean worries regarding our justification in believing in the regularity of nature persist.

We can conclude with some thoughts regarding the relation between Shepherd's and Kant's respective responses to Hume's account of causation. As Bolton writes, we can read Shepherd's approach as having

> a Kantian flavour: human nature, equipped with faculties of reason and sense, is affected by "things as they are in themselves," with the result that we have experience of a causally determined, spatial-temporally ordered world; yet the concepts of cause-effect, space and time, which apply to all possible objects of experience, are strictly inapplicable to reality as it is apart from its appearance.[16]

However, Bolton also notes, there is an important difference with Kant regarding the nature of the divide between our experience and reality: the underlying structure of objects in the world *directly determines* what qualities of objects appear to us in our experience. Shepherd argues that there is a sense in which the relations between the qualities of objects that we perceive map onto relations between the natures and powers of those objects independently of our experience, whereas Kant would deny any such guarantee of a link between our experience and reality transcendent to it.

Key Points

- Shepherd argues that rational proofs can be given both for the causal principle, "everything that occurs must have a cause," and the causal likeness principle, "like causes bring about like effects."
- Objects are bundles of qualities that give rise to their own distinct nature.
- Causal interactions are in fact synchronous combinations of two distinct natures.
- Our observation of a causal interaction in the world and our rational grasp of causal principles are sufficient to justifiably ground our knowledge-claims regarding causation.

Suggested Further Reading

Atherton, Margaret. "Reading Lady Mary Shepherd." *Harvard Philosophy Review* 13, no. 2 (2005): 73–85.

Bolton, Martha Brandt. "Causality and Causal Induction: The Necessitarian Theory of Lady Mary Shepherd." In *Causation and Modern Philosophy*, edited by Keith Allen and Tom Stoneham, 242–61. New York: Routledge, 2011.

Fantl, Jeremy. "Mary Shepherd on Causal Necessity." *Metaphysica* 17, no. 1 (2016): 87–108.

LoLordo, Antonia. "Mary Shepherd on Causation, Induction, and Natural Kinds." *Philosophers' Imprint* 19, no. 52 (2019): 1–14.

Paoletti, Christina. "Restoring Necessary Connections: Lady Mary Shepherd on Hume and the Early Nineteenth-Century Debate on Causality." *I Castelli di Yale* 11 (2011): 47–59.

Questions for Reflection

- Is reason required to identify events as causally connected?
- Does imagination play a role in the construction of our experience in the world?
- Can we know anything about the world apart from the way we experience it?
- Can we be sure that all events in the world are causally connected?

Conclusion

There are many ways to tell the story of early modern philosophy as it developed in Europe. For example: early modern philosophy was a series of responses to the mechanistic picture of the world advanced by Galileo and other early scientists, an attempt to carve out a place for human beings in that world. In this version of the story, the central philosophical problem is how to make sense of phenomena such as human consciousness and free will—phenomena that are difficult to reconcile with the picture of the entire world as a vast, interlocking, infinitely complex machine.

Alternatively: early modern philosophy was an attempt to explain and understand human relationships and social practices, without taking existing hierarchies and institutions for granted. On this version of the story, early modern philosophy was animated by the notion that many of our received beliefs about how it is *normal* or *natural* for human beings to live could be mistaken. For instance, we are raised with specific expectations about what makes for a virtuous life, about who (or what) it is appropriate to love or to sympathize with, about who ought to receive an education and what the content of that education should be, and about whether institutions such as chattel slavery are inevitable or necessary parts of human society. Early modern philosophers called the received expectations about these topics into question, laying the groundwork for subsequent social reforms and debates which continue today.

Alternatively: early modern philosophers aimed to establish metaphysical foundations for the rapidly developing physical sciences of the seventeenth and eighteenth centuries. This version of the story places the emphasis on the problem of understanding the ultimate building blocks of reality—bodies, space, time, causation, and natural laws. Early modern philosophers hoped to clarify these concepts and so to place our scientific knowledge of the world on firmer footing.

In fact, as the selected texts in the various parts of this textbook demonstrate, each of these stories has some truth to it. Each of these topics was the subject of intense philosophical investigation during the period. Indeed, each version of the story is to some degree interconnected with the others. The attempt to understand how the human mind fits into the natural world suggests that we should reexamine which aspects of human social life are merely the product of convention and tradition. It also suggests that we need to interrogate the concepts that are treated as primitive or fundamental in the scientific picture of the natural world.

Nevertheless, as we have now seen, these big-picture concerns moved people to take up an amazing range of more specific philosophical questions. The texts presented in this book address questions as far ranging as whether the human mind could exist without a body, whether morality depends on reason or only on emotion, who ought to receive an education, and whether we are able to perceive causal relationships. We have also seen that, even when philosophers in this period share very similar social and educational backgrounds, their respective answers to the questions raised in these texts are shockingly diverse. Rather than dwell on a single overarching story in discussing the debates of the period, then, our aim in this textbook has been to introduce students to a broader cross-section of the topics that were taken up by these philosophers.

Different versions of the story give leading roles to different characters. Here too we find a more diverse cast than has traditionally figured in introductory surveys of the period. In particular, almost every section of the textbook showcases texts written by women. Taken together, these texts demonstrate that women philosophers were active participants in practically every philosophical debate that took place in early modern Europe. Moreover, their contributions did not tend to go unrecognized in the early modern period itself. Many of the women who penned these works became famous, publicly celebrated intellectuals in their own time, as a number of the preceding chapters in this book attest. It is true that sexism and misogyny were more widespread and powerful in early modern Europe than they are today. Yet it would be a mistake to assume on that basis that women did not participate in these intellectual debates at the highest level, or that their contributions to these debates went unrecognized by their peers. Almost every chapter of this textbook contains evidence to the contrary.

It is harder to find people of color participating in these philosophical debates in the early modern period. This is not a historical accident, but a byproduct of the rise in this period of racist ideas about the moral and intellectual significance of skin color. Many of the nations of Western Europe during this period had a direct hand in the transatlantic slave trade, which reached its peak in the late eighteenth century. Historians believe that the widespread acceptance of the slave trade led people to treat skin color as a marker of moral status to a far greater extent than before: in this way, differences in skin color were used to make conceivable "within the framework of European thought, the placing of blacks, and blacks only, in permanent slavery."[1] Even during a time when there was growing acceptance that there are universal human rights, then, it was extremely uncommon for people of color to attend university during this period. Anton Wilhelm Amo, discussed in Chapter 1, was the first African to attend a European university, receiving his doctorate at the University of Wittenberg in 1734. But cases like Amo's remained extremely rare in early modern Europe. The first Black person to graduate from Oxford, for example, was Christian Cole in 1876—almost a century and a half after Amo's graduation.[2] And in most other, earlier cases, the official records are murky. The Black mathematician and poet Francis Williams (1692–1762) is said to have attended the University of Cambridge early in the eighteenth century, but the institution has no official record of his matriculation or graduation.[3] The fact that people of color were generally not permitted to pursue advanced studies in the humanities or sciences served as a barrier to their participation in the major philosophical debates going on in Europe at the time. Even so, we have seen that there were important exceptions to this general trend. As the chapter on the philosophical debate about slavery attests, a number of freed slaves from Africa and the West Indies wrote books about the morality and legality of chattel slavery. Even though there were many fewer philosophers of color during this period than there are today, they made influential contributions to this extraordinarily important philosophical debate.

What, finally, are the lessons that we can draw from the present survey of early modern philosophy? Three observations tentatively suggest themselves.

First, almost all of the most influential works of the period were written by authors outside the academy. Although all of the authors in the volume received some form of education (official or unofficial) in philosophy, few of them actually worked at universities. It is easier to list the few philosophers who had some official academic post than to list the ones who did not. Of the twenty-five authors discussed in this textbook, only six taught at a university (Anton Wilhelm Amo, George Berkeley, Immanuel Kant, John Locke, Henry More, and John Norris). The fact that the many women philosophers discussed in this volume did not have academic posts has an obvious explanation: they were barred from such posts because they were women. Yet a further puzzle remains. Academics obviously continued to write books and essays during the seventeenth and eighteenth centuries. But for some reason their work has not in general exerted the same long-term influence as philosophical writing that came from outside the academy. This is a surprising outcome. Not only did many of these authors end up working as philosophers outside of academia, but when compared to their peers in the academy, their philosophical writings have had an outsized impact on the history of philosophy.

Why is this? A full explanation of this phenomenon would require a volume all its own. However, one possible explanation has to do with the scientific revolution. The scientific innovations of the turn of the fifteenth century, especially the heliocentric model of the solar system and the mechanical model of physics (discussed in Chapter 2), led to much social and intellectual tumult. In such a time of upheaval, early modern academic institutions may have played an intellectually conservative role. Early modern academics had little incentive to update their courses to keep pace with the changing philosophical landscape. Their jobs didn't depend on it, and since some early modern philosophical ideas were particularly controversial, an academic's job might have been threatened had they embraced novelty. (David Hume *tried* to get an academic post, but university officials declined to appoint him because his philosophical claims seemed to conflict with certain received religious beliefs.) By contrast, philosophers outside of the academy would have had little incentive to hold on to pre-modern ideas when they no longer seemed viable in light of the new science. Indeed, these outsiders had every motivation to take up new and exciting ideas as they presented themselves. This, at least, is one possible explanation for the enduring impact of philosophical work done outside of the academy during this period: the outsiders were more often able to engage with new philosophical possibilities than were the insiders. If this explanation is correct, one lesson we might draw from our survey of early modern philosophy is that educational institutions don't always promote the advancement of knowledge. In certain conditions—as in the context of the social, scientific, and technological developments of early modern Europe—deeply significant contributions to philosophical thought are more likely to come from outside of official academic institutions.

A second lesson that is suggested by the present survey is that philosophical theorizing in the early modern period was not insulated from scientific inquiry or social commentary. Marx's famous criticism of his predecessors—"Philosophers have hitherto only interpreted the world . . .; the point is to change it"[4]—might lead one to expect that early modern philosophers were solely concerned with abstract puzzles, or with uncritically describing reality. We have seen, however, that this is not the case. Many philosophers in the period engaged with the practical problem of figuring out how we ought to live, both individually and collectively, as the second part of this volume attests. Sometimes their proposals involved radical revisions to the status quo—recall, for instance, Cugoano's call to treat slave-owners just the same as we treat robbers. Similarly, many early modern philosophers turned a critical eye to the foundations of the new sciences. Here too we find that the early moderns were concerned not merely to accept the new status quo, but to challenge what they saw as unjustified metaphysical or epistemological assumptions that early modern scientists were making.

A final lesson we can draw is that, despite the vast distance in time and cultural context that divides us from the early moderns, our philosophical concerns and interests still overlap to a striking degree with theirs. This is a point worth special emphasis. The philosophers we have studied lived in a world practically alien to us. This is clear enough when we canvass the technological possibilities that are open to us but were not open to them. They did not have electric lights, flushing toilets, cars, phones, digital computers, or the internet; they lacked antibiotics, heart transplants, chemotherapy, and even knowledge of the importance of washing one's hands. Nearly all of these technologies came well after the early modern period. Given how much our daily lives are shaped by such technologies, it can be hard to see the early moderns as our peers. How could the writings of people who led lives so alien to us give us any insights about our own situation?

Yet when we turn to the *philosophical* problems that obsessed the early moderns, we find ourselves in familiar territory. They want to know what explains human consciousness and whether death is its end; and so do we. They want to know whether their convictions about morality and justice have objective, mind-independent grounds or are merely artificial conventions; and so do we. They want to identify the limits of human knowledge of reality as well as of the self; and so do we. In so many cases, it seems, the problems of early modern philosophy are just the problems of philosophy—problems we still grapple with today.

Notes

Chapter 2

1. For a slightly different formulation of the paradox, see Jonathan Westphal, *The Mind-Body Problem* (Cambridge, MA: MIT Press, 2016), 1–4.
2. The details of the letters' rediscovery are drawn from T. Verbeek, E.-J. Bos, and J. M. M. van de Ven (eds.), *The Correspondence of René Descartes 1643* (Utrecht: Zeno Institute, 2003), xxxiv.
3. René Descartes, *The Philosophical Writings of Descartes, Vol. I*, eds. John Cottingham, Robert Stoothoff, and Dugald Murdoch (Cambridge: Cambridge University Press, 1984), 288.
4. Descartes, *Philosophical Writings, Vol. I*, 329–30.
5. Pierre Gassendi, "Fifth Set of Objections," in *The Philosophical Writings of Descartes, Vol. II*, ed. and trans. John Cottingham, Robert Stoothoff, and Dugald Murdoch (Cambridge: Cambridge University Press, 1984), 239.
6. Descartes, *Philosophical Writings, Vol. II*, 266.
7. See, e.g., Richard A. Watson, *The Breakdown of Cartesian Metaphysics* (Indianapolis: Hackett, 1987); and Eileen O'Neill, "Mind-Body Interaction and Metaphysical Consistency: A Defense of Descartes," *Journal of the History of Philosophy* 25, no. 2 (1987): 227–45.
8. Simon Foucher, "Critique [of Nicolas Malebranche's] *Of the Search for the Truth*," in *Malebranche's First and Last Critics: Simon Foucher and Dortous de Mairan*, ed. and trans. R. A. Watson and M. Grene (Carbondale: Southern Illinois University Press, 1995), 29.
9. In his *Principles of Philosophy*, Descartes provides his own purely mechanical explanation of the phenomenon of gravity, though it, too, turns out to be incorrect. See Descartes, *Philosophical Writings, Vol. I*, 268–9.
10. See Lisa Shapiro, "Volume Editor's Introduction," in *The Correspondence between Princess Elisabeth of Bohemia and René Descartes*, ed. L. Shapiro (Chicago: University of Chicago Press, 2007), 1–51. For an opposing reading, see Frederique Janssen-Lauret, "Elisabeth of Bohemia as a Naturalistic Dualist," in *Early Modern Women on Metaphysics*, ed. E. Thomas (Cambridge: Cambridge University Press, 2018), 171–87.

Chapter 3

1. Anne Conway, *The Principles of the Most Ancient and Modern Philosophy etc.* (London: np., 1692), 2.4; 11. Translation modified. References are to section and page number.
2. Augustine, *The Confessions of St. Augustine, Bishop of Hippo*, trans. Pilkington (Edinburgh: T & T Clark, 1876), 7.12.18; 159f. Translation modified.
3. Conway, *Principles*, 3.1; 15. Translation modified.
4. Conway, *Principles*, 8.5; 141.
5. Gottfried Leibniz, *Die Philosophischen Schriften von G.W. Leibniz: Band 3*, ed. Gerhardt (Berlin: Weidmannsche Buchhandlung, 1875), 217.
6. For more on Leibniz's arguments regarding the indistinct nature of size, figure, and motion, see Gonzalo Rodriguez-Pereyra, *Leibniz: Discourse on Metaphysics* (Oxford: Oxford University Press, 2020), 95f.
7. The account of causation offered here is arguably similar to the influential counterfactual analysis offered in recent literature. According to the simplest such analysis, event c is a cause of event e iff: (1) c and e occurred, (2) if c had not occurred, then e would not have occurred. For an in-depth discussion of the counterfactual analysis of causation, see Douglas Kutach, *Causation* (Cambridge: Polity, 2014), 62–83.
8. It is worth noting, though, that at the very least Leibniz, at this point, has to reject Descartes's conceivability argument for substance dualism, on the basis of his claim that we cannot form a clear and distinct idea of the body as extended and unthinking.
9. John Shand has examined this possible objection to Leibniz's account in more detail: see John Shand, *Philosophy and Philosophers: An Introduction to Western Philosophy* (Chesham: Acumen, 2002), 103f.

Chapter 4

1. Thomas Hobbes, *Leviathan, or The Matter, Forme, & Power of a Common-Wealth Ecclesiasticall and Civill* (London: Andrew Crooke, 1651), 4.20, 17. References to this text are by chapter and paragraph, followed by page number.
2. Hobbes, *Leviathan*, 46.14, 371.
3. Thomas Hobbes, *The English Works of Thomas Hobbes of Malmesbury: Vol. I – Elements of Philosophy. The First Section, Concerning Body*, ed. Molesworth (London: John Bohn, 1839), 2.4, 16.

4   See Stewart Duncan, "Hobbes, Signification, and Insignificant Names," *Hobbes Studies* 24, no. 2 (2011): 158–78.
5   Hobbes, *Leviathan*, 34.2, 207.
6   Hobbes, *Leviathan*, 34.2, 207.
7   Hobbes, *Leviathan*, 4.23, 17.
8   Hobbes, *Leviathan*, 11.25, 51.
9   Hobbes, *Concerning Body*, 1.8, 10.
10 See Thomas Hobbes, *The English Works of Thomas Hobbes of Malmesbury: Vol. IV*, ed. Molesworth (London: John Bohn, 1840), 306.
11 Margaret Cavendish, *The Philosophical and Physical Opinions* (London: J. Martin & J. Allestrye, 1655), "An Epilogue to my Philosophical Opinions," unnumbered.
12 Margaret Cavendish, *Philosophical Letters* (London: np., 1664), 3.23, 330.
13 Cavendish, *Philosophical Letters*, 3.23, 329f.
14 Cavendish, *Philosophical Letters*, 3.23, 331.
15 Margaret Cavendish, *Observations upon Experimental Philosophy* (London: A. Maxwell, 1666), "Further Observations upon Experimental Philosophy," 46f.
16 See, for example, Descartes's identification of the pineal gland as the "principal seat of the soul," and as the physical locus for the mind's interaction with the body, in his *The Passions of the Soul*: Rene Descartes, *The Philosophical Writings of Descartes: Vol. 1* (Cambridge: Cambridge University Press, 1985), 340f.
17 Cavendish, *Observations*, "Further Observations," 51.

Chapter 5

1   See John Norris, *The Theory and Regulation of Love: A Moral Essay* (Oxford: H. Clements, 1688), 6f.
2   Astell & Norris, *Letters Concerning the Love of God* (London: Manship and Wilkin, 1695), Preface A5. Some language has been modernized in this quote and subsequent ones throughout the chapter.
3   Norris, *The Theory and Regulation of Love*, 3f.
4   This is actually the fourth part of this section, so the '5' is clearly a misprint.
5   Norris, *The Theory and Regulation of Love*, 11.
6   See Norris, *The Theory and Regulation of Love*, 51f.
7   Norris, *The Theory and Regulation of Love*, 54.
8   See Plato, *The Republic*, ed. Ferrari; trans. Griffith (Cambridge: Cambridge University Press, 2000), 220–4.

9   Catherine Pickstock, "Christian Love and Platonic Friendship," in *Christian Platonism: A History*, eds. Hampton & Kenney (Cambridge: Cambridge University Press, 2021), 460.
10 Mander also explores the manner in which Norris draws upon Aristotle's discussion of the nature of true friendship in the *Nicomachean Ethics*: see W. J. Mander, *The Philosophy of John Norris* (Oxford: Oxford University Press, 2008), 133.
11 John Norris, *Practical Discourses upon Several Divine Subjects: Vol. 3* (London: S. Manship, 1693), 28.
12 Norris, *Practical Discourses*, 34.
13 Norris, *Practical Discourses*, 54.
14 This is a reference to Luke 12:5, a warning given by Jesus to his disciples and followers.
15 Damaris Masham, *A Discourse Concerning the Love of God* (London: Awnsham and John Churchill, 1696), 7.
16 Masham also rejects the view from Malebranche that this sin of love for other creatures is essentially the fault of the mother, who transmits their love for things other than God to their child in the womb—see Masham, *Discourse*, 74–9.
17 Masham, *Discourse*, 119.
18 Masham, *Discourse*, 83.
19 Masham, *Discourse*, 7.
20 In fact, Masham claims that our love of God can intensify our love of other creatures, as we come to love them as creations of a beloved creator—see Masham, *Discourse*, 89.
21 Masham, *Discourse*, 62.
22 See Masham, *Discourse*, 14f.
23 Masham seems to assume that 1 John was written by John the Apostle (one of Jesus's disciples), which is now disputed.
24 See Masham, *Discourse*, 66.
25 Masham, *Discourse*, 18.
26 Masham, *Discourse*, 44.
27 Masham, *Discourse*, 99.
28 Masham ends the *Discourse* with an argument for balance in both philosophical thought and our way of life, avoiding the kind of extreme position proposed by Norris: "our natures are so suited to a mediocrity in all things, that we can scare exceed in any kind with safety: to be always busy in the affairs of the world, or always shut up from them, cannot be borne: always company, or always solitude, are dangerous: and so with any other extremes" (Masham, *Discourse*, 126).
29 Masham, *Discourse*, 110.

30 Masham, *Discourse*, 110.
31 Masham, *Discourse*, 31f.

Chapter 6

1 John Locke, *An Essay Concerning Human Understanding*, 4th ed. (London: Awnsham and J. Churchill, 1700), Bk. II, Ch. XXI, S. 42.
2 For more on how the questions of moral motivation and obligation are linked in Locke's account, see Ruth Boeker, "Locke's Moral Psychology," in *The Lockean Mind,* eds. Jessica Gordon-Roth and Shelley Weinberg (Abingdon: Routledge, 2022), 362–5.
3 Locke, *Essay*, Bk. II, Ch. XXII, S. 2.
4 Nathan Guy provides a useful overview of Locke's place within the Christian natural law tradition: see Nathan Guy, *Finding Locke's God: The Theological Basis of John Locke's Political Thought* (London: Bloomsbury, 2020), 106–12.
5 John Locke, *Questions Concerning the Law of Nature*, eds. Robert Horwitz, Diskin Clay, and Jenny Strauss Clay (Ithaca: Cornell University Press, 1990), 99–101.
6 Locke, *Questions*, 155.
7 Patricia Sheridan, "Pirates, Kings and Reasons to Act: Moral Motivation and the Role of Sanctions in Locke's Moral Theory," *Canadian Journal of Philosophy* 37, no. 1 (2007): 43–5.
8 John Locke, *Political Essays*, ed. Mark Goldie (Cambridge: Cambridge University Press, 1997), 319.
9 Myles Burnyeat examines the key role of pleasure within Aristotle's account of moral education: see Myles Burnyeat, "Aristotle on Learning to be Good," in *Essays on Aristotle's Ethics*, ed. Rorty (Berkeley: University of California Press, 1980), 69–92.
10 Locke, *Political Essays*, 319.
11 The *Remarks* have traditionally been attributed to Thomas Burnet (*c.* 1635–1715), a theologian who had formerly been Master of Charterhouse School in Surrey. However, a recent paper has challenged this view, arguing instead for the authorship of Richard Willis, a prominent Bishop in the Church of England (*c.* 1663–1734): see J. C. Walmsley, H. Craig, and J. Burrows, "The Authorship of the Remarks upon an Essay Concerning Humane Understanding," *Eighteenth-Century Thought* 6 (2016): 205–43.
12 George Watson, ed., *Remarks on John Locke by Thomas Burnet, with Locke's Replies* (Doncaster: The Brynmill Press, 1989), 49.

13 Elizabeth Sund suggests that Cockburn may be picking up on a latent Aristotelianism in Locke's ethics: see Elizabeth Sund, "Catherine Trotter Cockburn's Moral Philosophy" (PhD diss., Monash University, 2013), 26f.
14 Locke argues for a conceptual link between the notions of property and injustice in the *Essay*: see Locke, *Essay*, Book IV, Ch. III, S. 18.
15 Catherine Cockburn, *The Works of Mrs. Catherine Cockburn: Volume 1* (London: J & P Knapton, 1751), 57f.
16 Watson, *Remarks*, 90.
17 Locke, *Essay*, Bk. I, Ch. III, S. 12.
18 Watson, *Remarks*, pg. 51.
19 Catherine Wilson, "The Moral Epistemology of Locke's *Essay*," in *The Cambridge Companion to Locke's "Essay Concerning Human Understanding*," ed. Lex Newman (Cambridge: Cambridge University Press, 2007), 399.
20 See Victor Nuovo, *Christianity, Antiquity and Enlightenment: Interpretations of Locke* (Dordrecht: Springer, 2011), 259.

Chapter 7

1 Dirk van Miert, "Education," in *Cambridge Companion to the Dutch Golden Age*, eds. Helmer J. Helmers and Geert H. Janssen (Cambridge: Cambridge University Press, 2018), 333–49.
2 Most of the following information is drawn from Carol Pal, *Republic of Women: Rethinking the Republic of Letters in the Seventeenth Century* (New York: Cambridge University Press, 2012), 52–77.
3 National Center for Education Statistics, "Condition of Education," U.S. Department of Education, https://nces.ed.gov/programs/coe/indicator/cta (accessed April 10, 2023).
4 While there are no reliable official records of the rate of unmarried women in England during this period, historians draw this inference from changes in the ratio of the *dowry*, or the amount paid by a woman's family to the husband when she is married, and the *jointure*, the amount of money that a husband promised to his wife in the event of his death; see Bridget Hill, "A Refuge from Men: The Idea of a Protestant Nunnery," *Past & Present* 117 (1985): 115. The ratio of dowry to jointure was 5 to 1 in the middle of the sixteenth century, but it rose to as high as 10 to 1 in the seventeenth century (ibid.) The implication is that—to put the thought bluntly—the supply of marriageable women rose more quickly than the demand for them did.

Chapter 8

1. Adam Smith, *The Theory of Moral Sentiments*, ed. D. D. Raphael and A. L. Macfie (Indianapolis: Liberty Fund, 1976), 10.
2. Smith, *Theory of Moral Sentiments*, 319.
3. Smith, *Theory of Moral Sentiments*, 9.

Chapter 9

1. James Tobin, *Cursory Remarks upon the Reverend Mr. Ramsay's Essay on the Treatment and Conversion of African Slaves in the Sugar Colonies* (London: G. and T. Wilkie, 1785), 6.
2. Quoted in Chike Jeffers, "Rights, Race, and the Beginnings of Modern Africana Philosophy," in *The Routledge Companion to the Philosophy of Race*, eds. Paul Taylor, Linda Alcoff, and Luvell Anderson (New York: Routledge, 2017), 136.
3. For further details on Capitein's life and historical context, see Grant Parker, "An Introduction to the Life and Work of Capitein," in Jacobus Elisa Johannes Capitein, *The Agony of Asar: A Thesis on Slavery by the Former Slave, Jacobus Elisa Johannes Capitein 1717-1747*, ed. and trans. Grant Parker (Princeton: Markus Wiener, 2001).
4. Aristotle, *Aristotle's Politics*, translated with commentaries and glossary by Hippocrates G. Apostle and Lloyd P. Gerson (Grinnell: Peripatetic Press, 1986), 22 [1254b19-20].
5. Thomas Hobbes, *Leviathan, with Selected Variants from the Latin Edition of 1668*, ed. Edwin Curley (Indianapolis: Hackett, 1994), 74–5 [I.XIII.1-2].
6. Notably, Hobbes did *not* oppose the institution of slavery; like Capitein, he merely rejects one traditional defense of its validity. See Iziah C. Topete, "Hobbes and Leibniz on the Nature and Grounds of Slavery," *Hobbes Studies* 36 no. 1 (2023): 51–73.
7. Jean-Jacques Rousseau, *The Social Contract and The First and Second Discourses*, ed. Susan Dunn (New Haven: Yale University Press, 2002), 158, emphasis added.
8. Voltaire, *Political Writings*, ed. David Williams (Cambridge: Cambridge University Press, 1994), 135.
9. Jacobus Elisa Johannes Capitein, *The Agony of Asar: A Thesis on Slavery by the Former Slave, Jacobus Elisa Johannes Capitein 1717-1747*, ed. and trans. Grant Parker (Princeton: Markus Wiener, 2001), 97.

10 Capitein, *Agony of Asar*, 97.
11 Lester B. Scherer, *Slavery and the Churches in Early America 1619-1819* (Grand Rapids: Wm. B. Eerdmans Publishing, 1975), 15.
12 In fact, in the chapter Capitein cites, More identifies yet a *third* kind of freedom at issue in the New Covenant: the freedom to live justly. Capitein likely elides this third kind of freedom because More suggests it simply follows from the other two. More writes, "Indeed, after someone has been freed from the burden of useless ceremonies, from the indoctrination of . . . superstitious beliefs, and finally from the body of sin, what can now, I beseech you, prevent that divine principle of regeneration from active, free, and delightful activity? For every hill is already lowered, and every valley raised up, and the lowlands made level and equal before him, so that he may walk with pleasure, peace, and joy in the paths of that eternal justice that Christ introduced into the world" (translation by John Grey). See Henry More, *Opera Theologica* (London: Macock, Martyn, and Kettilby, 1675), 394 [Bk. IX, Ch. VII, par. 10].
13 John Calvin, *The Institutes of the Christian Religion*, trans. and ed. John Allen (New York: S. Huestis, 1819), 370 [Bk. III, Ch. XIX, sec. IX].
14 Philemon 1:15-18.
15 This section makes it difficult to accept an interpretation of Capitein that has recently been proposed by Smith: "understood correctly Capitein is arguing neither for nor against slavery; he is, rather, arguing conditionally that, given the existence of slavery, there is no good argument for withholding baptism from slaves"; see Justin E. H. Smith, "The Life of Anton Wilhelm Amo," in *Anton Wilhelm Amo's Philosophical Dissertations on Mind and Body*, ed. and trans. Stephen Menn and Justin E. H. Smith (New York: Oxford University Press, 2020), 12.
16 Parker, "An Introduction to the Life and Work of Capitein," 69.
17 Tobin, *Cursory Remarks*, 13-14.
18 Tobin, *Cursory Remarks*, 59-60.
19 Tobin, *Cursory Remarks*, 89-90.
20 Tobin, *Cursory Remarks*, 119.
21 For a detailed discussion of the historical debate, see Justin Smith, *Nature, Human Nature, and Human Difference* (Princeton: Princeton University Press, 2015). For a helpful compilation of primary sources from the period, see Hannah Franziska Augstein (ed.), *Race: The Origins of an Idea, 1760-1850* (Bristol: Thoemmes Press, 1996).

Chapter 10

1 Isaiah 64:8.
2 Descartes, *Philosophical Writings, Vol. I*, 210.

3. For discussion of Berkeley's attempt to start a university overseas, see Nancy Kendrick, "Berkeley's Bermuda Project in Context," in *The Bloomsbury Companion to Berkeley*, ed. Richard Brook and Bertil Belfrage, 21–48 (London: Bloomsbury Academic, 2017).
4. George Berkeley, *A Proposal For the Better Supplying of Churches in Our Foreign Plantations, and for Converting the Savage Americans to Christianity, By a College to be Erected in the Summer Islands, Otherwise Called the Isles of Bermuda* (London: H. Woodfall, 1725).
5. Scholars are divided about how exactly to understand Berkeley's likeness principle. The interpretation presented here follows that advanced by Kenneth Winkler in his *Berkeley: An Interpretation*. A recent article by Peter West provides helpful overview and criticism of this interpretation; references to Winkler and West are given in the Suggested Readings herein.
6. For a more nuanced and historically complete interpretation than we present here, see Keota Fields, *Berkeley: Ideas, Immaterialism, and Objective Presence* (Plymouth: Lexington Books, 2010), Chapter 7 ("Immaterialism"). Fields suggests that the master argument is an extension of Berkeley's earlier attacks on the possibility of attributing "independent existence and active power" to matter (263).
7. The bracketed sentence was added by Berkeley in the second edition of the *Principles*.

Chapter 11

1. Isaac Newton, *The* Principia: *Mathematical Principles of Natural Philosophy*, trans. I. Bernard Cohen and Anne Whitman (Berkeley and Los Angeles: University of California Press, 1999 [1687]), 408–9.
2. Newton, *The* Principia, 410–11.
3. Though it is not at issue in these letters, similar reasoning is involved in another famous philosophical view that Leibniz defended: the belief that there must be a best of all possible worlds. God is bound by his wisdom to create only the best, on Leibniz's view, and so if there were two possible worlds that were (i) equally as good as one another, but (ii) better than all the other possible worlds, then God would have no reason to choose to create one of those worlds rather than the other. As we'll see, Clarke simply denies that this would pose a problem: God could arbitrarily select any of the best-possible-worlds to create.
4. Newton, *The* Principia, 412.
5. Newton, *The* Principia, 412–13.

6. See Ruth Hagengruber, "Emilie du Châtelet Between Leibniz and Newton: The Transformation of Metaphysics," in *Emilie du Châtelet Between Leibniz and Newton*, ed. Ruth Hagengruber (New York: Springer, 2012).
7. Newton, *The* Principia, 411.
8. Katherine Brading and Qiu Lin, "Du Châtelet on Absolute and Relative Motion," in *Current Debates in Philosophy of Science: In Honor of Roberto Torretti*, ed. Cristián Soto (New York: Springer, forthcoming).

Chapter 12

1. References to Hume's *Treatise* in this chapter are by Book number, Part number, Section number, then page number from the Selby-Bigge / Nidditch edition published by OUP in 1978.
2. Hume directs the reader here, in a footnote, back to Book I, Part III, Section VI of the *Treatise*, "Of the inference from the impression to the idea," where he discusses the impossibility of a rational inference of effect from cause.
3. P. J. E. Kail, "How to Understand Hume's Realism," in *The New Hume Debate*, rev. ed., eds. Rupert Read and Kenneth A. Richman (London: Routledge, 2007), 253–69.
4. Kail, "How to Understand Hume's Realism," 256.
5. You can find some of these competing interpretations discussed in the suggested further reading listed below, though Helen Beebee's book *Hume on Causation* is particularly good at explaining the differing interpretive options and the evidence in their favor.
6. Thomas Reid, *An Inquiry into the Human Mind, On the Principles of Common Sense* (Edinburgh: A. Kincaid & J. Bell, 1764), 59.
7. Reid, *Inquiry*, 524f.
8. Reid, *Inquiry*, 156.
9. Thomas Reid, *Essays on the Intellectual Powers of Man* (Edinburgh: Maclachlan & Stewart, 1853), 434.
10. This is taken from Cicero's dialogue *De finibus*, Book I.
11. Reid is probably referring to Timaeus' speech at *Timaeus* 28a.
12. Reid is quoting here from Book I, Part III, Section III of Hume's *Treatise* (page 78f. in the Selby-Bigge / Nidditch edition).
13. Reid takes this to be an absurd implication of Hume's supposed analysis of causation based on mere regularity.
14. Reid, *Inquiry*, 121.
15. Reid, *Essays*, 438.

16 Reid, *Essays*, 378.
17 See Frederick Copleston, *A History of Philosophy: Volume 5, Part II* (New York: Image Books, 1964), 172f.
18 Louis E. Loeb, "The Naturalisms of Hume and Reid," *Proceedings and Addresses of the American Philosophical Association* 81, no. 2 (2007): 65–92.

Chapter 13

1 Kant's works are often split by scholars into two periods—"pre-Critical" and "Critical"—the latter beginning with the publication of his groundbreaking *Critique of Pure Reason* in 1781. The "Critical" works of this later period have historically been much more influential and have received far more attention from scholars.
2 Immanuel Kant, *Prolegomena to any Future Metaphysics*, 2nd ed., trans. Paul Carus and James W. Ellington (Indianapolis: Hackett, 2001), 5.
3 Kant discusses the distinction between analytic and synthetic judgments in the Introduction to his *Critique of Pure Reason*: see A6/B10ff. The references to this text are in the "A/B" format that is generally followed by scholars and often provided in the margins of modern editions of the *Critique* (they refer to the relevant page numbers in the original first and second German-language editions).
4 Quotations from Kant's *Critique of Pure Reason* are taken from the widely available translation by J. M. D. Meiklejohn, first published in 1855, with some modifications.
5 See B151 for Kant's characterization of the nature of the productive imagination.
6 Kant states further on that "absolute time is not an object of perception by means of which phenomena can be connected with each other" (A215/B262); rather, we just experience objects *in time*.
7 Brown taught philosophy at the University of Edinburgh from 1808 until his death. He is best known for his *Inquiry into the Relation of Cause and Effect*, published in 1818.
8 Mary Shepherd, *An Essay upon the Relation of Cause and Effect* (London: T. Hookham, 1824), 141f.
9 For a useful discussion of this view, see Roderick Chisholm, "Parts as Essential to Their Wholes," *Review of Metaphysics* 26 (1973): 581–603.
10 Shepherd, *Cause and Effect*, 35.
11 Martha Brandt Bolton, "Lady Mary Shepherd and David Hume on Cause and Effect," in *Feminist History of Philosophy: The Recovery and Evaluation*

of Women's Philosophical Thought, eds. Eileen O'Neill and Marcy Lascano (Cham: Springer, 2019), 133.
12 Cristina Paoletti, "Restoring Necessary Connections: Lady Mary Shepherd on Hume and the Early Nineteenth-Century Debate on Causality," *I Castelli di Yale* 11 (2011): 51.
13 Mary Shepherd, *Essays on the Perception of an External Universe* (London: Hatchard, 1827), 279.
14 Terminology and examples are taken from Wesley C. Salmon, "Causation," in *The Blackwell Guide to Metaphysics*, ed. Richard M. Gale (Oxford: Blackwell Publishers, 2002), 32.
15 Walter Ott, "Review of *Causation and Modern Philosophy*, Keith Allen and Tom Stoneham (eds.)," *Notre Dame Philosophical Reviews*, 2011, ndpr.nd.edu/reviews/causation-and-modern-philosophy/ (accessed September 5, 2022).
16 Bolton, "Lady Mary Shepherd and David Hume," 140.

Conclusion

1 James A. Rawley and Stephen D. Behrendt, *The Transatlantic Slave Trade: A History*, revised edn. (Lincoln: University of Nebraska Press, 2005), 364.
2 Marcus Liddell, "Christian Cole: Oxford University's First Black Student," *BBC News*, October 18, 2017, https://www.bbc.com/news/uk-england-oxfordshire-40429917 (accessed August 21, 2023).
3 Williams's biography is recounted briefly in Henri Grégoire, *On the Cultural Achievements of Negroes*, ed. and trans. Thomas Cassirer and Jean-François Brière (Amherst: University of Massachusetts Press, 1996), 98–9. According to the records of the University of Cambridge, the first Black student to receive a degree there was William Crummell, over a century after Williams would have attended; see, e.g., "The Remarkable Story of Alexander Crummell," University of Cambridge, October 20, 2011, https://www.cam.ac.uk/research/news/the-remarkable-story-of-alexander-crummell (accessed January 26, 2024).
4 Karl Marx, "Eleven Theses on Feuerbach," trans. W. Lough, https://www.marxists.org/archive/marx/works/1845/theses/theses.htm (accessed August 22, 2023).

Glossary

Analytic judgment A claim that is true in virtue of the meaning of the concepts involved.

***A posteriori* justification** A good reason for a belief that derives from our experience of particular things.

***A priori* justification** A good reason for a belief that is in some way independent of experience.

Artificial virtue A characteristic that is only regarded as a virtue because of social conventions that a community has adopted. Artificial virtues tend to the benefit of the whole community, but do not necessarily benefit each individual on any given occasion (e.g., the rules of justice are good for the whole community, but may be bad for you when a just court rules against you).

Causal Likeness Principle The principle that similar causes must produce similar effects.

Causal Principle The principle that every object or event has some cause of its existence or occurrence.

Circular argument An argument that commits the logical fallacy of assuming the truth of the conclusion (either explicitly or implicitly) somewhere within the premises.

Clear and distinct ideas (in Descartes) An idea is clear when it is present or accessible to the mind. An idea is distinct when both it and all its parts are clear. (E.g., a pain is clear, since it is accessible to your mind when you feel it; but it is not distinct, since some elements of the pain, such as its precise source in your body, are not clear.)

Complete concept (in Leibniz) An idea of an individual that contains all of the predicates that apply to that individual.

Conceptual-containment theory of truth The claim that propositions are true if the predicate involved is contained within the concept of the subject.

Dead matter (in Conway) Matter construed as entirely lacking any mental or spiritual qualities.

Direct realism The claim that our perception of real objects does not rely on an intermediate mental representation.

Discerpibility/divisibility A property of a thing whose parts can be actually divided from each other.

Divine attributes The properties of God.

Empiricism The theory that all the basic building-blocks of our ideas come from our experience.

Free will defense An argument that God's existence is compatible with the existence of evil on the basis of the misuse of free will by creatures.

Immutability The property of being entirely unchanging.

Indirect realism The theory that our perception of real objects relies at least partly on an intermediate mental representation.

Inductive inference Reasoning from observed cases to unobserved cases.

Innate knowledge Knowledge that you are born with, in some sense.

Intellectualism (or, Moral Intellectualism) The view that morality is grounded in God's immutable nature or understanding and is not merely dependent on his will.

Materialist monism (or, Materialism) An ontological theory that says the only (created) substance is matter.

Matters of fact (in Hume) Contingent truths that are learned through experience. (E.g., the fact that it is raining out right now, or the fact that the table in this room is dark brown.)

Metaphysical idealism An ontological theory that posits thinking, perceiving things as the only type of fundamental thing.

Mind-Body Problem (or the Problem of Interaction) The problem of explaining how it is possible for the human mind or spirit to influence, and be influenced by, the states of the human body.

Mode A property or a way that a thing can be. Typically, modes are construed as dependent upon substances, in which they inhere. (E.g., for Descartes, the *shape* of a tree is a mode of that tree.)

Monad Created things that are perfect, indivisible, and shapeless unities.

Monogenism A theory about the origins of humanity according to which all human beings are descended from a common ancestor. Opposed to polygenism.

Natural law tradition A tradition in moral philosophy that takes moral principles to be laws erected by God, such that they are naturally discoverable by human beings (e.g., through the examination of human nature).

Natural Virtues (in Hume) A characteristic that is regarded as a virtue, not merely due to the social conventions of the community, but because its good effects (either on the virtuous person, or on those with whom she interacts) are immediately apparent.

Non-reductive materialism The view that material objects can have mental properties, but that these mental properties are not reducible or identical to any physical properties.

Occasionalism An account of the relationship between cause and effect as mediated or indirect (such that the cause merely provides an "occasion" for the effect to be brought about). Typically (but not always) occasionalist views take cause and effect to be mediated by the direct intervention of God.

Omnipotence The property of being able to do anything that is logically possible (usually ascribed to God).

Omniscience The property of knowing all truths (usually ascribed to God).

Ontological argument for the existence of God An attempt at rationally proving the existence of God based on a definition or mere concept of God.

Ontology A branch of philosophy concerning the nature of being or existence, including the kinds of things that exist.

Passion A state that is brought about in one thing (the "patient") by the action of another (the "agent"). Often, the term is taken to encompass not only emotions, but also sense perceptions, since these are the result of the body's sense organs being acted upon by external objects.

Penetrability A property of a thing through which other things can move without resistance.

Pietism A movement in the Lutheran church that attempted to return the church to its original focus on the importance of the study of the Bible and the religious experience of individuals.

Platonism A very broad collection of philosophical views loosely derived from the ideas of Plato. Typically, they emphasize the degraded, corrupted, and constantly changing nature of the material world, in contrast to a higher, incorruptible, spiritual level of reality, which is the source of all being.

Plenum (spatial) The idea that space is entirely full of material substance, so that there are no vacuums or regions of genuinely empty space.

Polygenism A theory about the origins of humanity according to which different groups of human beings (typically, different racial or ethnic groups) originated independently of one another rather than descending from a common ancestor. Opposed to monogenism.

Pre-established harmony A theory of causation in which the appearance of (only apparent) causal relations between things is explained on the basis of God's "pre-programming" of their behavior.

Principle of the identity of indiscernibles The claim that if two things share all their properties, then they must be identical (that is, the same object "under two different names," as Leibniz puts it).

Principle of plenitude The claim that God creates as much as he is able to.

Principle of sufficient reason The claim that everything that exists must have an explanation of its existence, and everything that does not exist must have an explanation for its nonexistence.

Problem of evil An argument for the incompatibility of God's existence with the existence of evil in the world.

Problem of moral motivation The problem of explaining why humans are inclined to act morally, even when doing so appears contrary to their self-interest.

Prudential account (of moral motivation) The view that our motivation for obeying moral rules is that we anticipate future rewards for doing so, or punishments for failing to do so (i.e., that we act morally out of "prudent" self-interest).

Rationalism The view that we can use pure reason, independent of experience, to obtain knowledge of at least some facts about reality (e.g., that a mind-independent physical world exists).

Relationalism The view that space is nothing more than the spatial properties of, and relations among, bodies.

Relations of ideas (in Hume) Necessary truths that we can learn simply by analysis of our own concepts. (E.g., the fact that squares have four sides, or that blue is a color.)

Skepticism The claim that at least some of your ordinary beliefs about yourself and about the world, while seeming to you to be true, turn out to be false.

Substance Typically, the term refers to something that could exist independently of any other thing (besides, perhaps, God). Sometimes, it refers to something that is the subject of predication, or that in which properties inhere.

Substance Dualism The theory that the human body and the human mind are distinct substances.

Substance monism An ontology that is committed to the existence of a single, universal substance.

Substantivalism The view that space exists as a distinct thing, in addition to the objects within it.

Synthetic judgment A claim that adds extra content beyond what is already contained in the primary concept we are working with.

Theism A commitment to the existence of a God.

Type monism The view that there is only one fundamental type of thing in the universe.

Volition A particular act of will (e.g., willing your right arm to move right now).

Voluntarism (or Moral Voluntarism) The view that morality depends on the arbitrary will of God.

Index

abstraction   76–7, 102–4, 107, 276–7, 292–4, 296–8
Amo, Anton Wilhelm   31–41, 218
animate matter/bodies   64, 69–70, 106–10
Astell, Mary   121–8, 167–8, 180–9

Babbage, Charles   344
Barclay, Robert   45–6
Berkeley, George   260–71, 317

Capitein, Jacobus Elisa Johannes   219–30, 232
causation   82–5, 94–5, 107, 303–28, 344–7, 351–5, 364 n.3, 372 n.13
   causal principle, the   325–7, 332–5, 341–2, 352–3
   causes as synchronous with effects   345–7, 352–5
   mechanical view of   49–50
   and primitive notions   53–6
Cavendish, Margaret   100–11
Chanut, Pierre   46
Châtelet, Émilie du   273–4, 289–300
clarity and distinctness. *See* ideas, clear and distinct
Clarke, Samuel   273–88, 291–2, 294–9, 319, 324
Cockburn, Catherine Trotter   139–40, 152–66
complete concepts   81
consciousness   97–8
Conway, Anne Finch   63–74, 87, 95, 109–10
Cooper, Anthony Ashley   141
Cudworth, Ralph   127

Cugoano, Ottobah   230–41
custom   187–8, 327, 351

dead matter   69–70, 72–3
death   27–8, 108–9
Descartes, René   11–26, 34–7, 43–62, 80, 102–6, 108, 249–50, 255, 260, 317
dualism
   Cartesian   108
   substance   10–11, 18–20, 364 n.8

education
   in early modern Europe   168
   moral   184–8, 196
   purpose of   172–7, 182–4
Elisabeth of Bohemia   11, 43–62, 169
empiricism   130–1, 135–6, 139–40, 149, 152–3, 158, 161, 164–5

Foucher, Simon   52–3
freedom
   Christian liberty   225–8
   from slavery   233–4, 237–8
   of the will   33, 71–2, 85, 357

Galilei, Galileo   50, 273
Gassendi, Pierre   52–3, 141, 291
God   65, 69–73
   and creation   69–72, 245–6, 251
   idealist conceptions   267–71
   identical with nature   250–1
   love of   116–21, 124–5, 128–31, 133–6
   materialist conceptions   98
   and morality   148–9, 153–4, 159–64
Grouchy, Sophie de   191–202, 204, 211, 213

habit/habituation 313, 327
hedonism 150, 161
Helmont, Francis Mercury van 64, 75
Hobbes, Thomas 88–100, 220–1, 319, 324–5
Hume, David 191–2, 203–16, 303–27, 332–6, 341–2, 345–7, 351
Huygens, Constantijn 46

idealism. *See* monism, idealist
ideas 31–6, 52–6, 187
   clear and distinct 14–15, 18–19, 55–6
imagination 267–8, 334–5, 341
infants/infancy 195–6

judgments
   analytic 331–4
   synthetic 331–5, 341–3
justice 125, 163
   as artificial virtue 211

Kant, Immanuel 192, 329–44, 355
knowledge
   of morality (*see* moral knowledge)
   a priori/a posteriori knowledge 332–4

Labadie, Jean de 169–70
Le Clerc, Jean 127
Leibniz, Gottfried 75–87, 127, 247, 254–6, 275–88, 290–6
life 23–4, 69–70, 82, 95, 108–9
   mechanical view of 50–1
Locke, John 36, 75, 116, 125, 127, 136, 139–66
love 115–35, 161, 366 nn.16, 20

Malebranche, Nicolas 46, 75, 120, 129–30
Masham, Damaris Cudworth 127–37, 141, 163–5
materialism. *See* monism, materialist

matters of fact 209, 306
mechanical properties/relations 49–50
memory 95, 97
Mersenne, Marin 11, 52, 100
mind 9–11, 14–15, 17–19, 25–7, 33–7, 43–4, 48–9, 54, 97–8
mind-body problem 25, 43–4, 47–9, 84, 100–2, 107, 120
   early versions 52–4
modes 144–5, 249, 251
monads 64, 76, 82–5
monism
   idealist 63–85, 260
   materialist 87–110
   nonreductive materialism 61
   substance 63, 250–8
moral
   education (*see* education, moral)
   intellectualism 153, 164
   knowledge 139–40, 144–6, 153–4, 158–61
   motivation 145, 148–50, 191–2, 196–201, 204–5, 208–15
   obligation 128, 160–3
   psychology 191–2, 194–6
   voluntarism 153–4, 163–4
More, Henry 21–9, 64, 95, 106–8, 223, 225–6

Norris, John 115–37

occasionalism 107, 120–1, 134–6

parents/parenthood 10, 45, 100, 101, 121, 171, 195, 196
passions 32–3, 36–7
Penn, William 45–6
perception 36–40, 69, 81, 82, 305, 318, 336–41, 346–7
   direct realism 266
   indirect realism 264–5
perfection 72, 83–4
Platonism 119–20

pre-established harmony 83
pregnancy 100–1
prejudice 187–8
principle of identity of indiscernibles 283–4
principle of sufficient reason 256–8, 277–84, 294–5
problem of evil 70–2
problem of interaction. *See* mind-body problem

race. *See* slavery and race
rationalism 165
reason 318, 346–7, 351–3
   and motivation 208–10
Reid, Thomas 303, 317–29
relations of ideas 209, 327
right(s) 198–201, 220–1
Rousseau, Jean-Jacques 203, 220–1, 304

Schurman, Anna Maria van 167–80, 182–3
self-interest 150, 160–1, 163
sensation 12, 15, 36–40, 89–90, 94–5, 267–70, 305, 307, 318, 333–4
sentiment 194–201, 206–8
Shepherd, Mary 329, 344–56
slavery
   and Christianity 220–8, 230–1
   and colonization 217–18, 232, 261–2
   natural slavery doctrine 219–20, 232
   and race 232–6, 238–40, 358–9
Smith, Adam 193–4, 204
soul 17, 23, 25–8, 100–1, 118

space 273–4, 334
   as an abstraction from body 292–4, 296–8
   arguments for relational view of space 277–9, 291–2, 294–6
   arguments for substantival view of space 285–7, 298–9
   and spacetime 299–300
Spinoza, Baruch/Benedictus 247–59, 281
spirit 64–9, 71–3, 90, 109–10, 120
   as active/intentional substance (in Amo) 31–3, 35–46
   as penetrable/indiscerpible substance (in More) 22–3, 25
   as thinking/unextended substance (in Descartes) 13–15, 17–20, 28
substance 80–3, 249, 251
   extended substance 14–15, 19
   immaterial substance 88, 95–7
   material substance 262–7
   thinking substance 14–15, 19
sympathy 191–201, 206–8
   particular *vs.* general 201
   and virtue 211–13

theism 245
time 299–300, 334, 373 n.6

vice 184–8, 226
virtue 128, 150, 161, 184–8
   artificial virtues 211
   natural virtues 211–12
volition 44, 85, 210

will 44, 49–50, 55, 187
   free will (*see* freedom of the will)